10—

AQUARIUM
FISH
of the World

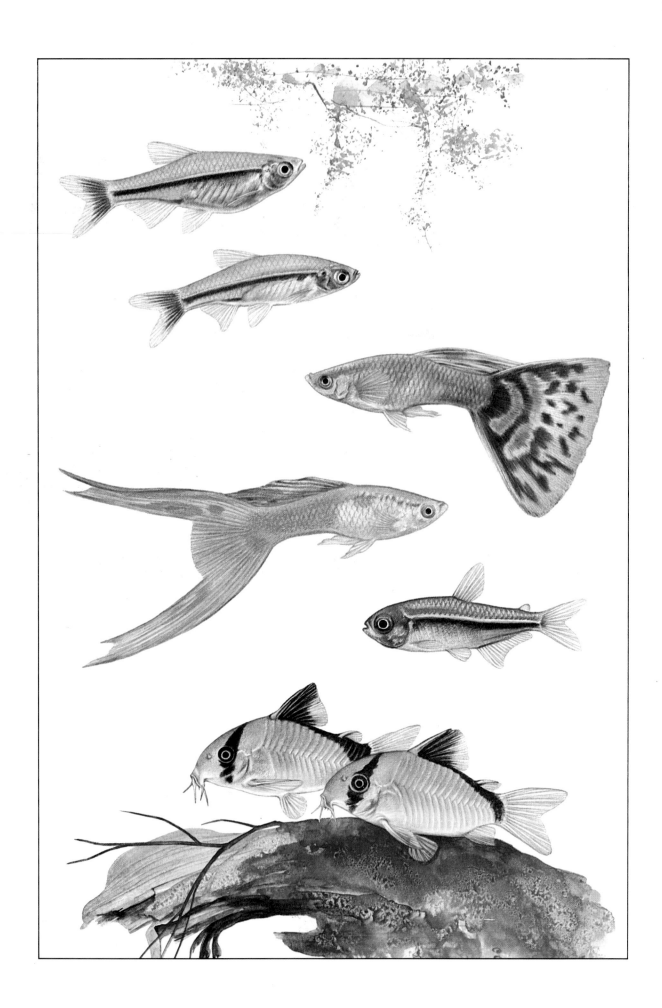

AQUARIUM
FISH
of the World

Ivan Petrovický

Illustrated by Libuše and Jaromír Knotek

Arch Cape Press
New York

Text by Ivan Petrovický
Illustrations by Libuše and Jaromír Knotek
Cooperation with the artists Vladimír Jaroch
Graphic design by Jaromír Knotek
Translated by Olga Kuthanová and Ivan Kuthan

First published by The Hamlyn Publishing Group Limited,
a Division of the Octopus Publishing Group,
Michelin House, 81 Fulham Road,
London SW3 6RB, England

This 1990 edition published by Arch Cape Press,
a division of dilithium Press Ltd.
Distributed by Crown Publishers, Inc.,
225 Park Avenue South,
New York, New York 10003

Printed and bound in Czechoslovakia

ISBN 0-517-67903-5

h g f e d c b

3/19/03/51-03

Contents

Acknowledgements

In writing this book I was aided immensely by my collection of specialized literature which has expanded over the years to sizeable proportions, thanks in great part to the contributions of a number of people to whom I should like to express my gratitude. I thank my friend Dr. Herbert R. Axelrod of the USA for sending me the Tropical Fish Hobbyist *magazine for 24 years and for making me an honorary member of the magazine. My thanks to Mrs. Gisele Böhme and her colleagues at the Kosmos publishing house, FRG, for supplying me with literature and for sending me the* Aquarien Magazin *for many years, to Mr. Dieter Vogt, Editor-in-Chief of the* Datz *magazine, FRG, and to Mr. Jean Schnugg, founder of the* Aquarama *magazine, France, and Dr. David G. Senn, Editor-in-Chief of the* Aquaria *magazine, Switzerland, for sending me their magazines for many years. I should also like to express my appreciation to the staff of the Tetra Co. and to Mr. H. A. Beansch, owner of the Mergus publishing house, FRG, for supplying me with literature. I am also indebted to Dr. Karel Lohniský and Dr. Karel Pecl, who reviewed my book, for their valued suggestions, as well as to Dr. Stanislav Frank and the Czech aquarists Ladislav Volf and Jaroslav Cintl, specialists in breeding and raising killie fish. And last of all my profoundest thanks to my father Dr. Karel Petrovický for his invaluable aid in coping with foreign language literature and to my wife Jiřina for her understanding and sympathetic tolerance of the limited time I was able to devote to the family.*

I. Petrovický

Introduction

Economists and dealers estimate that the world turnover in the aquarium fish trade already exceeds 4,000 million US dollars annually and it is expected to go even higher. Sixty per cent of the aquarium fish sold throughout the world is produced by Asia, 30 per cent by South America, and the remaining 10 per cent by the other continents. Asia supplies mostly fish raised on fish farms in Singapore, Hong Kong, Thailand and the Philippines, but those supplied by South America are largely collected in the wild. Freshwater species are in far greater demand on the world market (90 per cent) than sea animals, which continue to be of marginal importance despite the greater interest in their breeding.

Biologists believe that collecting in the wild has reached capacity limits in many places and will gradually have to stop. They are finding that numerous localities are either exhausted by excessive collecting or destroyed by other human activities. For that reason collecting in the wild is being increasingly limited and the collecting of some species is prohibited altogether.

In the near future this will naturally place greater demands on the breeders of exotic fish, not only in terms of work but also in terms of their professionalism and skill. The demand for ornamental fish will have to be increasingly met by artificial breeding. In terms of prices breeding centres in countries with a temperate climate will be able to compete with those of tropical countries (particularly in view of the continually diminishing supply of energy and hence increasing costs) only if they produce fish of top quality and in the widest possible assortment. This will also require sufficient highly specialized literature. Nowadays a great many authoritative works have been written on the subject of tropical fish but these appear randomly in various journals or as separate papers to which aquarists often do not have access. That is why the main purpose of this book is to sum up the author's own existing knowledge as well as that of others on the principles of breeding fish in the aquarium. Nevertheless much in the book remains unresolved and much may have been discarded or changed between the time of the book's writing and its publication. There are still a great many species of fish that have not yet been bred in the aquarium. However, the barriers presented by our lack of knowledge are being overcome step by step and from year to year and today's great success may be tomorrow's commonplace or may even have become obsolete. New knowledge, however, continually raises new questions that need to be answered, and so the work of the aquarist-breeder never really ends.

If we stop to consider whether the result is worth all the effort, whether the exertion and money entailed in breeding and raising ornamental fish are not expended needlessly, the answer is simple. Yes, it's worth the effort, because only by the detailed observation of natural phenomena can we better understand nature and find ways to protect it from Man for Man. If we do not succeed in doing so then all mankind's further efforts will be useless for nature's demise will be accompanied by the extinction of the species *Homo sapiens* as well. That is why the endeavour to preserve nature must be the main credo not only of biological institutions, but of all people throughout the world.

Early History of Fish

The years since the days of Charles Darwin (1809–1882), English naturalist and founder of the theory of evolution, have witnessed the development of the science of palaeontology, which deals with life of past geological periods as known from fossil remains. It is thanks to palaeontological research that we are also able to reconstruct the life and history of fish of bygone ages.

The first remains and impressions of fish-like primitive vertebrates are found in the Silurian Period (about 425 million years ago). But because these remains already show evidence of a certain evolutionary development many scientists believe that the beginnings of these primitive vertebrates date from the early Paleozoic Era, from the Cambrian Period (about 600 million years ago). These hypothetical predecessors were probably very simple creatures and their soft body parts left no traces. The fossil remains of fish-like primitive vertebrates from the Silurian, however, are well preserved and reveal the typical characteristics of those creatures: a thick armour composed of bony plates serving to protect the body, an unpaired nasal opening, paired eyes plus an additional eye on top of the head, the absence of a lower jaw and the absence of paired fins. The dorsal cord (*chorda dorsalis*) formed the supporting axis of the body. All known Silurian forms are collectively called Ostracodermi.

The marked development of the predecessors of fish begins in the Devonian Period (about 405 million years ago), hence also called the 'Age of Fish'. In addition to the jawless vertebrates the Devonian witnessed the appearance of the first jawed vertebrates, the first shark-like fish, ray-finned fish (Actinopterygians), tassel-finned fish (Crossopterygians), and lungfish (Dipnoans). The primitive shark-like fish are of evolutionary importance in that they are the first animals possessing paired limbs (fins). The Dipnoans represent an ancient group of fish exhibiting practically no evolutionary changes since the Devonian. Because they possess developed gills and lungs the Dipnoans were long considered to be the precursors of the amphibians. According to present-day opinion, however, they are merely an evolutionary branch that did not develop any further. The direct precursors of the primitive amphibious Stegocephalians are the Crossopterygians, whose fins are rounded into a lobe with a scaly central axis and a fringed border. The primitive Crossopterygians reached their maximum development in the Devonian, Carboniferous and Permian periods, with more developed types not appearing until the Cretaceous Period. In all probability it is these fish or similar forms that gave rise to the first terrestrial vertebrates. The primitive groups of Actinopterygians evolved further into the cartilaginous fish (Chondrostei) and the bony fish (Teleostei), which can be traced back to the Triassic Period (about 230 million years ago). The bony fish (which include all the species of aquarium fish in this book) are at present the only group that is continuing to develop.

Morphology and Anatomy of Fish

The body shape of most fish is aerodynamic or spindle-shaped, but there exist many deviations from this basic contour.

The body of a fish consists of a head, trunk and tail. In describing fish, their size, that is the full length from the tip of the snout to the tip of the tail fin, is given in centimetres.

The fins of the fish are the organs of locomotion. Most fins have hard front rays and behind these a greater number of soft branched rays. The number of fin rays is characteristic of and important for the identification of fish species. The fins are of two kinds: paired and unpaired. The paired fins are the pectoral or breast fins (*pinna pectoralis*) and the ventral or pelvic fins (*pina ventralis*). These fins correspond to the limbs of the higher vertebrates. The unpaired fins are the dorsal or back fin (*p. dorsalis*), caudal or tail fin (*p. caudalis*) and the anal fin (*p. analis*). These serve to keep the body balanced and to steer it in the desired direction. Some types of fish have another small fatty or adipose fin (*p. adiposa*) on the back. The fins differ in shape and size in the various species and may also be an important means of differentiating the sexes. The dorsal fin may consist of two completely separated or else joined parts, its rays sometimes form spines, and it may be drawn-out lengthwise or vertically. The ventral fins are sometimes thread-like and furnished with tactile

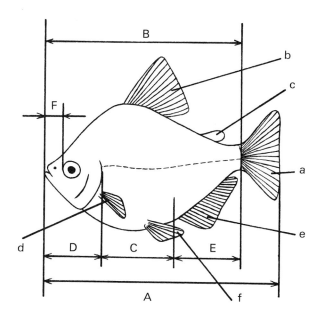

Body of a fish A — full length B — body length C — length of trunk D — length of head E — length of caudal section F — length of snout a — unpaired caudal fin b — unpaired dorsal fin c — adipose fin d — paired pectoral fins e — unpaired anal fin f — paired pelvic fins

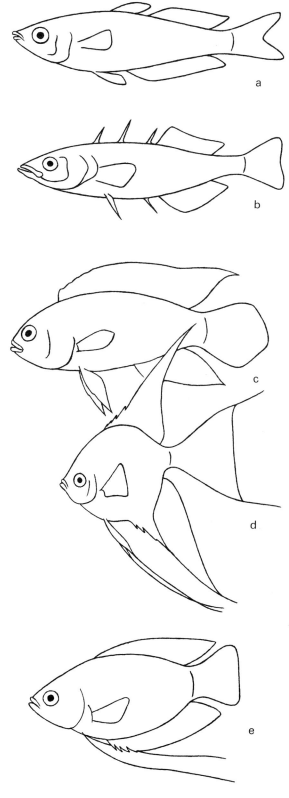

cells; in some species they are absent. The caudal fin is usually symmetrical (homocercal) and its shape varies: it may be indented, straight edged or rounded, or asymmetrical (heterocercal).

The body of a fish is covered with skin composed of several layers. The outer layer is called the epidermis and is covered by a fine membrane or cuticle. Beneath this membrane is a great number of mucus cells producing a secretion that keeps the body surface smooth and slippery. The layer of skin tissue beneath the epidermis is called the corium or dermis and contains the blood vessels that nourish the skin, nerves, and pigment-bearing cells (chromatophores). The grains of pigment in these cells

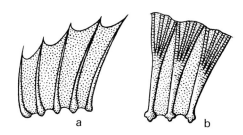

Fin rays a — spiny b — soft

Various types of fin
a — double dorsal fin b — the spiny rays of the dorsal fin are not joined c — dorsal fin drawn out lengthwise d — dorsal fin extended vertically in the shape of a sail e — thread-like pelvic fins

9

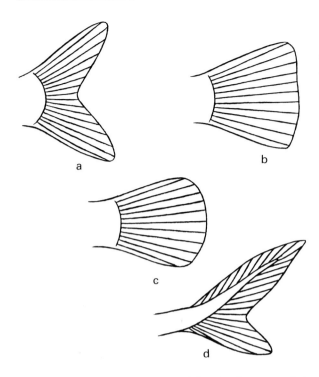

Caudal fin a — indented b — straight-edged c — rounded
d — asymmetrical, heterocercal

body in double rows located on both sides of the body axis — two on the upper, dorsal side and two on the lower, ventral side. The head contains the jaw and gill muscles, which are greatly developed particularly in predatory fish. The muscles that move the limbs are attached to bony supports and to the fin rays, moving the fins by erecting and dropping them.

The digestive system is composed of the oral cavity, the oesophagus, the stomach and the intestine. The oral cavity is enclosed by the jaws with which it forms the mouth. The mouth opening may be directed forward (terminal mouth), upward (supraterminal mouth), or downward (subterminal mouth). If it is terminal then it is located at the tip of the snout. Theoretically fish with such a mouth generally hunt for food in the middle strata of water. A subterminal mouth is formed by the prolongation of the upper jaw. It is found in fish that generally hunt for food in the immediate vicinity of the bottom. A supraterminal mouth is formed by the prolongation of the lower jaw and facilitates taking food from the surface. In many fish the oral cavity is equipped with teeth. The teeth do not have roots and are firmly attached to the bone or embedded in the mucus membrane. The teeth are renewed throughout the life of the fish, with the old ones being pushed out by the new. The teeth are used for gripping, crushing, cutting or rasping off food, but not for masticating. They may be located not only on the jaws but also on the tongue bone, the palate, and at the opening into the oesophagus, particularly in predatory fish. Predatory fish have a large mouth that can be opened very wide. Not only can such a well-toothed mouth keep a firm grip on the squirming, slippery prey, but with the aid of its strong muscles it can swallow even large pieces. In some, chiefly Cyprinid fish, the teeth are augmented or supplanted by permanent tooth-like bony plates usually located on the palate. These are capable of crushing and grinding. Instead of a movable tongue there is a tongue bone covered with soft muscle tissue on the bottom of the oral cavity.

Swallowed food is digested in the stomach and the intestine. The small intestine passes smoothly into the large intestine which terminates in the rectum and anus. The intestine of predatory fish is short, that of omnivorous and, above all, herbivorous, or vegetarian fish is very

are capable of contracting or expanding when stimulated by a nerve impulse and this manifests itself externally by a change in the colour of the fish. The dermis is also the layer in which the scales are formed. The scales of most fish are fully developed and form a protective outer coat. They are arranged in regular rows, the number of which is an important character of identification. Some species of fish have only occasional scales and in others they are completely lacking or replaced by bony plates.

The scales together with the outer bones of the skull form the external skeleton or so-called dermal skeleton. The internal skeleton is composed of the axial skeleton or dorsal spine, consisting of a series of vertebrae, the ribs, and the so-called spines or ossified walls which separate the layers of muscles, the inner skull (jaw arches, gill arches and tongue bone) and the bones supporting the individual fins.

Fish have two types of muscle: smooth muscles that govern the internal organs and striated muscles that respond to external stimuli. The striated muscles are divided into the muscles of the head, the muscles of the trunk, and the muscles that move the limbs. Very strong bands of muscles stretch the length of the

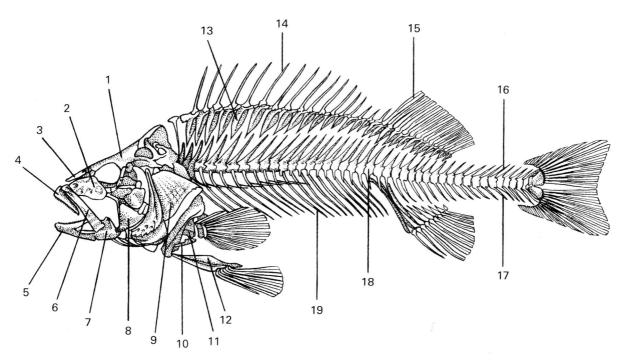

Skeleton of a perch *(Perca fluviatilis)*
1 – premaxilla 2 – dental bone 3 – nasal bone 4 – maxilla
5 – preorbital bone 6 – parasphenoid bone 7 – frontal bone
8 – metapterygoid bone 9 – hyomandibular bone
10 – supraoccipital bone 11 – operculum 12 – preoperculum
13 – quadrate bone 14 – angular bone 15 – articular bone
16 – coracoid bone 17 – procoracoid bone 18 – scapula
19 – pterygiophores

Anatomy of a fish
1 – operculum 2 – heart 3 – liver 4 – gall bladder 5 – spleen
6 – pancreas 7 – intestine 8 anus 9 – sexual opening
10 – sex glands 11 – brain 12 – oesophagus 13 – kidneys
14 – stomach 15 – gas bladder 16 – muscles

long. Adjoining the windings of the intestine are the liver and gall bladder. Pancreatic tissue is found in the whole of the digestive tract and the spleen is located on the stomach or at the beginning of the intestine.

The excretory system consists of paired kidneys located close to the spinal column, from which they are separated by the lining of the ventral cavity. The wastes eliminated by them from the body pass through the urinary ducts on the underside of the kidneys into a joint outlet and are discharged either through the urogenital

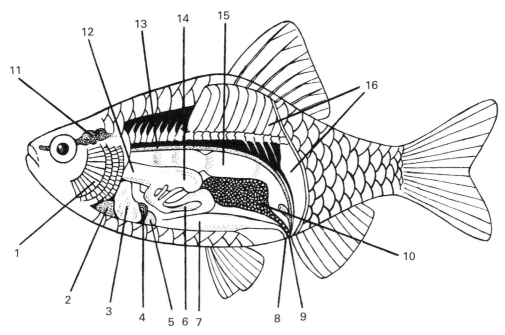

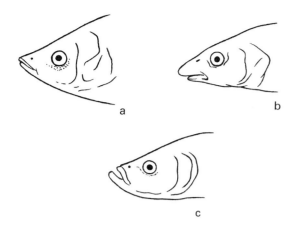

Position of the mouth a — terminal b — subterminal or inferior c — supraterminal or superior

papilla or a separate papilla behind the sexual opening. The urogenital papilla is generally cylindrical or tubular in females and narrowed into a point at the end in males. The sex glands (gonads) are generally paired and located on either side of the alimentary canal.

To conform its specific weight (the pressure of the gas within the body) to the pressure of the surrounding water, which fluctuates according to the various depths at which the fish is swimming, the fish is equipped with a hydrostatic organ called the gas, air or swim-bladder. The pressure of the gas inside the bladder also changes in accordance with the atmospheric pressure (that is why fish react to changes in atmospheric pressure by changes in their activity, e.g. by spawning). In some species the swim-bladder may be totally lacking or atrophied. Such fish dwell on the bottom where they move by making long leaps from one spot to another.

The circulatory system is governed by the action of the heart, which consists of the chamber, antechamber and sinus or channel for venous blood. It is located on the underside of the body behind the head, under the gills. The gills consist of gill lamellae attached to and supported by cartilaginous/bony gill arches. On the inner side the gill arches carry projections called gill rakers. The gills are rich in blood capillaries where oxygen is absorbed by the blood. Besides breathing by means of gills, some fish are also able to breathe accessorily through the skin, by means of the intestine, the

gas or swim-bladder, the mouth cavity, or by a special cavity called the respiratory labyrinth.

The nervous system of fish is composed of the central nervous system (the brain and spinal medulla) and the peripheral nervous system made up of nerves and ganglia. The sensory organs of fish warn them of danger, serve to locate food, and are important in reproduction. The lateral line, which runs along the sides of the fish, is a typical sensory organ. It consists of rows of sensory buds along a certain line which is located in a narrow channel beneath the skin and the scales and filled with mucus and which may be observed where the scales are pierced to enable a connection with the external environment. It serves as a tactile organ sensitive to stimuli from the surrounding world, informing the fish of the strength and direction of currents, of the undulation of the water, the pressure of the water, and the like. It also serves as a means of orientation when fish are migrating, helps keep schools of fish together in the darkness of night and in cloudy water, enables the fish to locate food in murky water, and warns the fish of danger. The olfactory organs of fish consist of paired nasal pits which are located on the snout between the mouth and the eyes. The organs of taste are located on the barbels (the number, length and shape of which are an important character of identification), on the lips, on the palate, and at the opening into the oesophagus. Those parts of the body that are most frequently in contact with the environment are also the seat

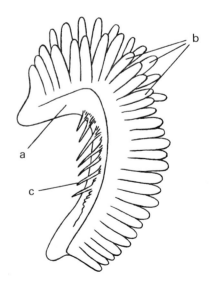

Gills a — gill arch b — gill leaf, lamella, filament c — gill rakers

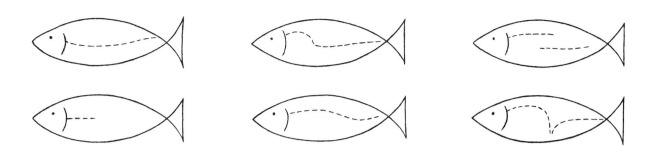

Various shapes of the lateral line in fish

of the tactile sense. These are first and foremost the lower jaw, barbels and lips, and then the dorsal fin, the first ray of the pelvic fin, and the end of the caudal fin.

The organ of hearing is connected with the organ of equilibrium and consists of the labyrinth of the inner ear (there is no outer ear). The labyrinth is composed of a constricted membranous sac and three semicircular canals. This is filled with a special liquid and enclosed in a bony cover, an auditory capsule. The sac contains little ear stones or otoliths that rest on sensory hairs, on which they exert pressure in case of a change of position. In some fish, e.g. Cyprinids, the labyrinth is connected with the swim-bladder by means of a chain of small bonelets, transformed from the forward vertebrae and called the Weberian Apparatus. Most fish produce and perceive low-frequency sounds, inaudible to the human ear, that spread like waves in the water.

The eyes of fish are well adapted to seeing in water. In substance they are no different from the eyes of higher vertebrates but have no lachrymal (tear) glands and no eyelids. They are covered with skin. A peculiarity of the fish's eye is the so-called Haller's Bell — a special muscle attached to the lens from below at an angle which brings the lens and retina nearer to each other to accommodate the eye to greater distances (the eye does not flatten). The eyes located on either side of the head enable the fish to see to the rear and to the sides and, within a small angle, also towards the front. In some species the eyes are reduced, and in adult cave-dwelling fish they are (further) covered in fatty tissue.

In conclusion note must be taken of the morphological and anatomical changes that occur in populations of fish raised and bred in captivity. Identifying species, subspecies and colour forms of fish raised for generations in aquariums is sometimes extremely difficult, if not impossible. A great many fish can be identified with certainty only in the case of imported specimens collected in the wild but not in the case of fish raised in breeding centres where they are kept in changed conditions. A different temperature and concentration of salt during embryonic development, both in the aquarium and outdoors in the open, result in changes in the number of vertebrae, scales, fin rays, etc. in the very first generation. That means that a species of fish imported from breeding centres and imports of the same species of fish collected in the wild can differ in many morphological and anatomical characteristics.

Occurrence of Fish in Various Waters

The present forms of bony fish are so numerous that the number of existing species represents 50 per cent of all living species of vertebrates. According to an estimate published in 1970 by the American ichthyologist D. M. Cohenon the earth's population currently numbers about 50 species of jawless fish (Agnatha), 515 to 555 species of cartilaginous fish (Chondrostei) and

19,135 to 20,980 species of true fish (Osteichthyes). This estimate is the result of years of work, for the systematic classification of fish is made very difficult by the great number of synonyms. In determining the actual number of existing species (not the number of described species) it was, therefore, necessary to eliminate synonyms, a task that required great effort on the part of ichthyologists.

Fish are divided according to their habitat into the following three basic groups: freshwater fish, diadromous fish, and sea fish.

Freshwater fish — 8,275 species (41.2 per cent) are divided into primary freshwater fish and secondary freshwater fish. Primary freshwater fish are ones that live only in fresh waters. They include, for example, fish of the Cyprinidae, Characidae and Siluridae families, and number 6,650 species (33.1 per cent). Secondary freshwater fish inhabit fresh waters but are able to live in waters of a wide range of salinity — they are said to be euryhaline — and of making their way into brackish and even salt waters. Examples are members of the Cichlidae, Cyprinodontidae, and Poeciliidae families. They number 1,625 species (8.1 per cent).

Diadromous fish — 115 species (0.6 per cent) are ones that migrate from fresh to salt waters and vice versa. They include, for example, the eel, salmon, and of aquarium species *Monodactylus sebae, M. argenteus, Scatophagus argus,* etc.

Sea fish — 11,675 species (58.2 per cent) dwell in the coastal zone to depths of 200 metres (littoral fish), in the open sea to depths of 200 metres (epipelagic fish), by continental slopes at depths of more than 200 metres (bathybenthic fish), or in the open sea at depths of more than 200 metres (bathypelagic fish). Littoral fish include the greatest number of species — 9,130 (45.5 per cent). Of these, 8,000 species dwell in warm waters and 1,130 species in cold waters. Epipelagic sea fish — 255 species (1.3 per cent) are excellent swimmers with a torpedo-shaped body. When migrating they cover vast distances and are often cosmopolitan. Examples are the tunnies, mackerels, various species of flying fish, etc. Bathybenthic fish — 1,280 species (6.4 per cent) are characterized by an elongated body. Bathypelagic fish — 1,500 species (5 per cent) have unusual luminescent organs. As a group they inhabit the greatest space. Considering the vast space they occupy the last two groups include relatively few species, but authorities believe there are as yet many unknown species hidden in the depths. According to Cohenon and other ichthyologists this environment is characterized by physico-chemical and thermal uniformity (living conditions are constant).

Ichthyologists and Aquaristics

Ichthyology is the scientific study of fish (from the Greek words *ichthys* meaning fish and *logos* meaning science). Present-day ichthyology is a broad and greatly branched scientific discipline that is becoming increasingly important, particularly because new sources of food must be found to meet the needs of the growing world population.

An attempt at the systematic classification of fish was made by C. Linné in his work 'Systema Naturae' and it must be stated that the classification of fish is the least successful section of the treatise. This, however, does not alter that fact that the year 1758, which saw the tenth edition of this work, marks a milestone for modern systematic zoology, and hence also for ichthyology. That year is considered as the year of the official introduction of binominal nomenclature — a system of scientific nomenclature in which each species receives a name consisting of two terms — the first identifying the genus to which it belongs (this begins with a capital letter) and the second the species itself (this begins with a small letter). For lower taxonomic units, e.g. subspecies, a third name is added to the first two; this likewise begins with a small letter. The name of the species is followed by the name of the author who first described the fish and, separated by a comma, by the year in which the paper with the description was published. For example: *Betta splendens* Regan, 1909. If following the first description there is a change in opinion as to the classification of the fish and it is transferred to another genus, the name of the author and the date of the original description are put in parentheses, e.g. *Trichopsis pumilus* (Arnold, 1936).

During the more than 200 years since Linné's day there have been many prominent ichthyologists of various nationalities each of whom has expanded the horizon of man's knowledge a bit further. In the second half of the 20th century, however, new discoveries in science are less and less a matter of the individual and more and more a matter of team work. The system of classification used in this book is the work of L. S. Berg and is taken from his book 'The System of Recent and Fossil Fish'. Some British aquarists prefer the classification of Greenwood *et al* (1966).

Aquaristics, which by the detailed and exact study of fish has made it possible to supply information that would be difficult to obtain in the wild, in places that are often inaccessible, is of importance to ichthyology as an auxiliary discipline.

In Asia the raising and breeding of fish has a long-standing tradition of more than a thousand years. In Europe and the USA, however, the development of modern aquaristics did not begin until the mid-19th century.

Fishkeeping

Fishkeeping means providing such conditions in the aquarium that the fish will live and remain in good condition for several months or years, depending on the life-span of the given species.

The primary principles of successful fishkeeping are proper water conditions — composition, temperature, amount of oxygen and carbon dioxide (so-called respiratory gases) in the water — and correct feeding. Other important factors are lighting, planting and shelter in the aquarium, composition of the bottom substrate, and suitable selection of fish. Fishkeeping nowadays is greatly facilitated by modern technology.

An aquarium that is provided with suitable equipment and flourishing plants and that is above all not overcrowded with a chaotic assortment of fish should prosper practically by itself. This alone, however, is not enough. The aquarist must have at least a basic knowledge of fish and their environment, particularly those species he or she intends to keep. Even the less demanding species of fish require a certain amount of care and have their specific food and environmental requirements. A basic rule is never to keep big and small fish, predatory and peaceful fish, etc. together in a single (mixed) aquarium. Do not skimp on space and always choose a larger rather than a smaller aquarium. The bigger the aquarium the less work there is and the greater the success of the aquarist. The aquarium should be located permanently in a spot where it fits in with the layout and furnishings of the room.

In nature fish live in salt, brackish and fresh waters. Those in this book are from freshwater and brackish habitats. Each such habitat in nature has its ecosystem, i.e. an independently functioning system made up of a community of animals, plants and the physical and chemical environment. The living organisms and non-living environment affect one another. The ecosystem is composed of individual biotopes, which are the smallest natural areas with a uniform environment occupied by a unified community of organisms. Such a biotope is a well-equipped aquarium. If we can provide the fish with water conditions (composition and temperature) that are as much like those of the given species' natural habitat then perhaps we will succeed in having fish that are not only healthy but that will also spawn. Providing exactly the same conditions as in nature is impossible and experience has shown that strict observance of chemical composition and temperature according to data from nature need not always lead to the desired end. These may serve only as a guide and it is up to the aquarist to find the ways and means to success as it is impossible to provide unequivocal instructions. The aquarist's success in raising fish in captivity is due in great part to the fact that most freshwater and brackish species are adaptable as to their environmental requirements. This makes it possible to raise and breed a wide assortment of fish species in the aquarium. This adaptability is generally absent in sea fish and that is why keeping them in an aquarium is far more difficult.

Another decisive factor in raising fish is food. Foraging for food is one of their main activities. In nature fish are a link in a certain food chain, i.e. phytoplankton − zooplankton − small fish − predatory fish − man. It is impossible to provide the whole chain in the aquarium but we must know which parts of such a chain the fish in our aquarium need. According to the type of food they eat fish are divided into the following groups: carnivorous, piscivorous or predatory fish that feed only on animal food, herbivorous or vegetarian fish that feed only on plant food, and omnivorous fish that feed on both animal and vegetable substances. Carnivorous fish are fed planktonic crustaceans (*Daphnia, Cyclops*), tubifex worms, white worms, chopped earthworms, mosquito and midge larvae, adult insects (fruit flies − *Drosophila melanogaster,* mayflies), scrapped beef, chicken or fish meat, small fish, and occasionally also certain good-quality artificial granulated fish foods. However, it is necessary to know that not all carnivores can be fed all the above foods alternately. It is necessary to know their other requirements (the size of the individual pieces of food, which depends on the size of the fish's mouth, whether the fish collect food on the bottom or from the surface, or whether they catch live plankton in the middle strata of the water, etc.). In the pictorial section of the book carnivorous fish are marked with ◁.

Aquarium fish that eat only plant food are few in number, but for many vegetable food is a necessary part of the diet if they are to remain in good condition. Such fish are given blanched lettuce or strained spinach and dried vegetable foods. Herbivorous fish rasp algae off the glass sides of the aquarium and off plants, some species (often to our annoyance) nibble finely-leaved aquatic plants. In the pictorial section of the book fish that must be given plant food are marked with ◻.

Feeding omnivorous fish, marked with ○ gives aquarists the least trouble. These fish are often content with a wide variety of artificial foods which have the added advantage that they contain vitamins and other supplementary substances. However, remnants of such food rapidly decompose and spoil in water. With omnivorous as with other fish it is likewise necessary to alter the diet within possible limits and keep it varied.

The correct functioning of the fish's metabolism depends on the amount of food it eats. Only over and above a certain quantity are the absorbed nutrients utilized, new muscle tissue is formed, fats and glycogen are stored, and the skeleton increases in size, which is evidenced by the growth of the fish. Fish that are fed well and regularly continue to grow even after they attain sexual maturity, practically until the end of their lives, though at a slower rate than young fish. The amount of food the fish eat depends directly on the amount of oxygen in the water, the (favourable) chemical composition of the water, and the water's temperature. It also depends on the species, age, and condition of the fish.

Sexual Dimorphism and Reproduction

Sexual differentiation is characterized by the fact that the male and female reproductive glands, or primary (direct) characteristics of sex, occur separately, in separate individuals. Male reproductive glands are present only in the male and female reproductive glands only in the female. Natural hermaphroditism (having both male and female reproductive organs) is not known to occur in freshwater tropical fish. The male reproductive glands − testes − produce sperm (milt), the female reproductive glands – ovaries – contain eggs (roe). The reproductive glands also produce hormones – androgens in males and oestrogens and gestagens in females. These sex hormones stimulate the development of the secondary sex characteristics. Secondary sex characteristics are of two kinds – microscopic and macroscopic. The microscopic ones include the sex chromosomes. Macroscopic characteristics are body structure, coloration, length and shape of the fins, various protuberances, pads of fat on the head, etc. In many species of fish the external differences between the male and female are minute or practically non-existent; such fish are said to be monomorphic. In some species, however, the secondary sex characteristics are very pronounced and in such a case we speak of sexual dimorphism. Sexual dimorphism is generally evidenced in the brighter coloration of the males (very occasionally of the females). If the coloration is entirely different we speak of sexual dichromatism but only if the body parameters are similar. The females of many species of fish are larger than males of the same age (in other species it is the males that are larger). In the genus *Xiphophorus* the female sex characteristics are sometimes transformed into male sex characteristics. Females capable of reproduction gradually change into males which in some instances may even be fertile. Transformation from male to female, however, is not known.

During the spawning period certain sexual differences become more pronounced, particularly the coloration, which is called the spawning or nuptial dress. In some Cyprinid fish, chiefly catfish, one characteristic of the nuptial dress is the so-called spawning rash. As a rule, when spawning the female releases the eggs in the water and the male simultaneously releases milt close to the eggs. The eggs are thus fertilized outside the body of the female; this is called external fertilization. Internal fertilization, common in higher vertebrates, is a more developed form from the viewpoint of evolution and is less frequent in fish. In connection with internal fertilization we find the development of ovoviviparity in some groups of fish, where the fertilized eggs develop within the maternal body until hatching and are extruded as living young. Ovoviviparity differs from viviparity in that the embryo is not nourished by the mother.

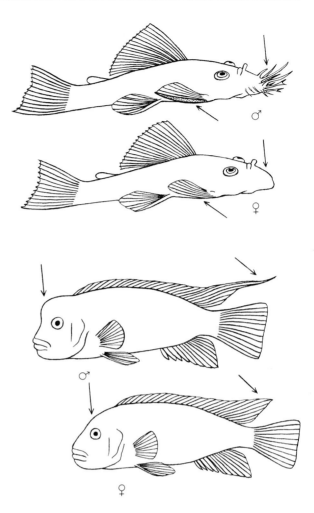

Examples of sexual dimorphism

The male germinal cell, or sperm, consists of a head, a small midsection, and a whiplike tail used for locomotion. The ability to penetrate and fertilize the egg is determined by the sperm's motility. The life of a sperm is a matter of seconds and depends on the species of fish. If the sperm does not succeed in penetrating the egg within this time it dies. In some species of fish the motility of the sperm is stimulated by a saline solution. As the male fish grows older the quality of the sperm (milt) gradually deteriorates and its ability to fertilize the egg decreases.

The female germinal cell, or egg, is enclosed within a firm elastic membrane with a great number of fine pores. When the egg comes in contact with water the water enters the egg which then swells up. In some species the surface is coated with a sticky secretion enabling

17

Examples of sexual dimorphism

following fertilization, and the food yolk, from which the embryo obtains nourishment.

Healthy eggs may be glassily transparent, yellow, orange, carmine-red, green, etc. depending on the species of fish. A dead egg is white with curdy content (curdled proteins) that causes it to become cloudy. This coloration, however, must not be mistaken for the natural white colour of the eggs of some species of fish. Dead eggs are a rich growing medium for rapidly spreading fungi (particularly in warm, alkaline water), whose mycelia are capable of penetrating sound eggs and destroying them. The spread of fungi may be combated by means of certain remedies based on methylene blue and Trypaflavin (Acriflavine).

The shape of the egg is typical for each species of fish and may be round, oval, barrel-shaped, tear-shaped, etc. The size of the eggs and the amount laid depends not only on the species of fish but also on the age and size of the female. A smaller number of minute eggs may be expected during the first spawnings of young females. As they grow older and bigger — up to a certain age (depending on the species) — they produce eggs of better quality and in greater numbers.

If the fish cannot spawn the females either release the eggs without their being fertilized (e.g. labyrinth fish) or else do not expel them at all. Such unexpelled eggs are sometimes absorbed by the organism but more often remain inside the body of the female in a mummified state (e.g. in Cyprinid fish). When eggs are retained in the body and become mummified the result is the infertility or death of the female. Such incomplete spawning endangers the health of the female. Also overfeeding, which results in the excessive storing of fat, causes the degeneration of the reproductive glands and permanent infertility.

the egg to adhere to a firm object. In the membrane there is a minute opening (micropyle) through which the sperm enters the egg during fecundation. Beneath the outer membrane is another fine membrane enclosing the germinal disc, which develops into the embryo

Development of Fish Eggs

The life of a fish, from egg fertilization to death, can be divided into five main periods: embryonic, larval, juvenile, adult, and senescent. From the aquarist's viewpoint the first two — the embryonic and larval periods, which mark the early phase of a fish's development — are the most important.

The embryonic period starts with the fertiliz-

18

ation of the egg and lasts until the fry becomes free-swimming. It is characterized by endogenous nutrition, i.e. internal nutrition from the yolk stored in the yolk sac. The embryo takes its nourishment from the yolk while inside the egg and also for a brief period after hatching. The period from fertilization until hatching is called the incubation period. The length of this period depends on the species of fish. It is also influenced by the temperature of the water, less so by the atmospheric pressure and intensity of the light. The higher the temperature of the water (up to a certain limit determined by the given species) the shorter the incubation period. Shortly before hatching the activity of the embryo becomes more intense; this is accompanied by the formation of an enzyme that disrupts the egg membrane thereby enabling the emergence of the embryo. On emerging from the eggs the embryos either fall freely to the bottom or hang by means of thin threads from surrounding objects (plants).

As soon as the embryos consume the yolk they begin to swim freely and take fine food scattered in the water. This marks the beginning of the larval period. When they thus start actively hunting for food the fry are said to have switched over to exogenous nutrition or to have become free-swimming. In the majority of fish a number of temporary specific organs develop during the larval period that serve to fill the function of the as yet undeveloped definite organs. This is a critical period in the raising of tropical fish which the aquarist tries to master in as short a time as possible. Lack of suitable food plays the most important role in the survival of the larvae, for if it does not obtain suitable food in time the larva dies within a very few days after consuming the yolk.

If the amount of food it obtains exceeds the amount of energy expended in looking for it then the larva survives, grows, and develops into a young fish. The larval period ends with the ossification of the axial skeleton and complete absorption of the fin border, which in young fish is replaced by the fins.

Fish Breeding and Various Methods of Protecting Eggs and Fry

Fish breeding means the selection of paired breeding (parent) fish, reproduction (spawning), and successful rearing of the fry until they reach the juvenile stage. Both external and internal factors play a role in the breeding of fish. Most important of the external factors is the temperature of the water and changes in temperature. The ideal values vary and are specific for each species of fish. Other important factors are the physical and chemical properties of the water (concentration of oxygen, pH values, hardness), changes in these properties, atmospheric pressure and changes in atmospheric pressure, height of the water column (water level), and the behaviour of male and female fish (or of shoals of fish in the case of fish that spawn in groups), as well as a supply of suitable food for the brood fish as well as for the future fry. Also important is the state of motion of the water, its turbidity, lighting, and suitable spawning substrate.

The process of reproduction is governed by hormones formed in the brain (hypothalamus), hypophysis, and gonads (ovaries and testes). The release of hormones is stimulated by seasonal changes in the environment. In the case of fish living in natural conditions this depends primarily on the climate. In the case of fish kept in artificial conditions, where it is possible to regulate the temperature of the water, the spawning period may be shifted — retarded by cooling or hastened by warming the water.

The aim of breeding is to obtain by means of the intensive breeding of fish the greatest number of young specimens of the original, wild form as well as of new colour and structural mutations or hybrids. The improvement of breeding techniques and the publishing of new information is of immense importance for the future, for soon it may no longer be possible to obtain fish from natural habitats. The existence

1 – fish with low rate of metabolism (e.g. Characidae, Lebiasinidae). Tank without plants, with a single efficient mechanical filter, water 23–26 °C, dGH 6.0° or more. Presumed maintenance: replacement of 50 per cent of the water every 7 days + cleaning of the filter.

2 – fish with moderate rate of metabolism (e.g. Callichthyidae, Cyprinidae, Cyprinodontidae). Tank, filter and water same as for (1), presumed maintenance: replacement of 90 per cent of the water every 7 days + cleaning of the filter.

3 – fish with high rate of metabolism (e.g. Poeciliidae, Belontiidae, Cichlidae). Tank, filter, water and maintenance same as for (2).

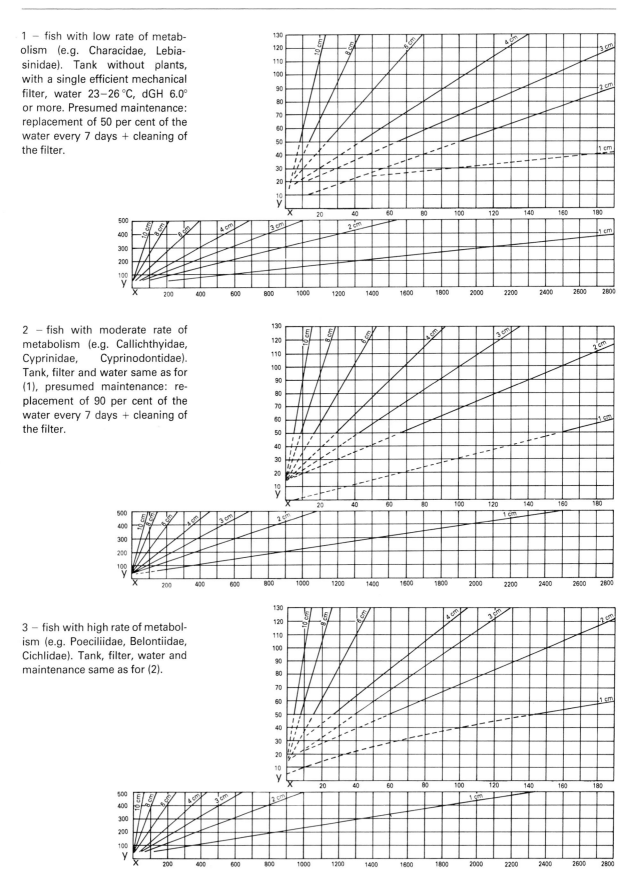

Limits of population density for various sizes of fish (in centimetres) in relation to tank size (in litres)
The axis x indicates the number of fish (population density). The axis y indicates the water content of the tank in litres.

of many species of fish will be dependent on artificial or semi-artificial breeding governed by man, a condition that already exists nowadays in the case of many species of vertebrates.

Artificial breeding enables detailed observation of the characteristic behaviour patterns of fish (ethology). In the case of those species where attempts at breeding have met without success it will apparently be necessary to concentrate on the study of ecological factors such as food chains, population density, effect of the natural environment on local populations, etc. In this way it will be possible to determine the reasons why so many species still refuse to spawn in captivity, even under relatively ideal conditions. In present-day aquaristic practice use is made of numerous tried-and-tested basic techniques with an eye to the requirements and habits of the respective fish. This knowledge makes possible the profitable and permanent breeding of a great number of species.

One of the basic factors determining the rapid and healthy growth of populations of young fish as well as their condition and ability to reproduce is the number of fish in the aquarium (population density). Graphs showing the maximum population density limits in relation to the capacity of the aquarium in litres serve as a means of quick orientation.

In free nature fish are dispersed throughout a relatively large space and usually a great number of fish spawn. Even so, a negligible percentage of the eggs develop and hatch and even fewer grow into sexually mature fish. And in the aquarium, where spawning is a matter of a single pair or only a small group of fish in a small space, practically no eggs would have a chance of surviving unless provided with protection. With the proper care, however, a large percentage of young and later adult fish can be raised in the aquarium from the eggs that are laid. Besides composition of the water, temperature, and clean environment, breeders must seek the best methods of providing suitable conditions for spawning and afterwards for protecting the eggs from being eaten by the parent fish. The basic principle for success is for spawning to take place in a monospecies keeping tank which contains adult and sexually mature fish of both sexes. Other fish not only disturb the breeding pairs during spawning but often eat both the eggs and the fry, and,

therefore, their presence is undesirable. On the basis of numerous ethological observations by aquarists various techniques have been worked out for equipping breeding tanks. Many species of fish spawn in a like manner, but there exist special requirements that must be respected if breeding is to be successful.

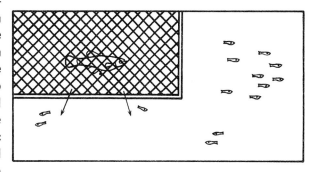

The best means of protecting the fry of live-bearing fish has proved to be the so-called breeding trap. This is a framework of plastic covered with 3 × 3 to 5 × 5 mm mesh nylon netting or similar. The top of the cage is covered with a removable lid to prevent the fish from jumping out. The cages are hung on the sides of the tank. The fry escape through the openings in the netting out of reach of the female. Large frameworks covered with netting and furnished with polystyrene floats may be successfully used for sorting and raising young fish outdoors in pools or in gently flowing water in milder climates.

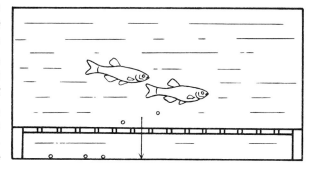

For species that lay non-sticky eggs which fall freely to the bottom (e.g. the Characidae family) use is made of protective spawning grids. The dimensions of the grid correspond to the inner dimensions of the tank with just enough clearance to enable it to be placed on the bottom and removed without difficulty, but to prevent a breeding fish from squeezing through between the sides of the tank and the frame. The grid consists of a plastic frame with 3 × 3 to 5 × 5 mm mesh netting attached (glued) to the upper side. On the underside it is provided with supports so that it rests about 10 mm above the bottom. This makes it possible to check on the eggs underneath the grid.

The eggs of many species of fish (so-called phytophilic fish) are sticky as soon as they are fertilized and become anchored to plants (e.g. fish of the Cyprinidae family). In this case protecting the eggs from being eaten by the

These are mostly members of the Cichlidae family, which provide the eggs and fry with intensive care. Their number includes also species that take up the eggs into their mouth (mouth-brooders), where they develop further. In the case of fish with a tendency towards cannibalism either the eggs are transferred to another tank along with the object on which they have been laid or else the parent fish are removed. (Cannibalism in fish that otherwise provide good brood care may be caused by a number of factors: young and inexperienced breeding pairs, frequent disturbance of the fish, insufficient room, unsuitable conditions).

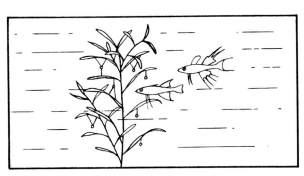

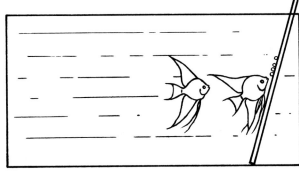

parents is relatively difficult but for species that produce a large number of eggs a spawning grid will also serve the purpose to some degree. Choose netting with the largest possible mesh so the eggs can fall through more readily. Even those eggs that stick to the underside of the netting are protected for the breeding fish are able to collect them there only with difficulty. Compact, impenetrable thickets of finely-leaved plants are also suitable protection for such eggs.

Many fish deposit their eggs on flat stones or branches near the bottom (lithophilic fish).

The manner of breeding fish that spawn on vertical rock walls or the stems and leaves of large bog plants is similar. In the aquarium they spawn on the sides of the tank, on filters, heating elements, etc., but it is much more practical to provide them with pieces of slate, drainage pipes, flowerpots, or large-leaved plants, e.g. of the genus *Echinodorus,* placed on the bottom of the tank. The eggs may then be transferred to a separate tank along with the object on which they have been deposited. Where this is not possible the eggs may be scraped off with a fine brush into a net held underneath the object.

Members of the genus *Pterophyllum* and *Symphysodon* are examples of fish that spawn in this manner.

Certain other species of the Cichlidae family spawn in cavities, crevices, and caves. Serving as substitutes for these are flowerpots with knocked-out bottoms, drainage pipes, plastic pipes, hollow bricks, and the like. Such an arrangement makes it possible to handle the eggs on the given object. The spawning site is cared for by both partners or else by one of them.

Shallow pits are dug in the gravel as nests by the North American perch-like fish of the Centrarchidae family. In suitable places there may be whole colonies but each nest is guarded by only a single male. Some species dig not just one but several pits to which they later transfer the eggs or the fry (Cichlidae family). In such cases care of the fry is generally left to the parent fish until the fry become free-swimming.

Fish from periodically dry waters (Cyprinodontidae family) lay their eggs in the soft substrate of the bottom which protects them from drying up. In places where the water dries up completely the adult fish die and the eggs survive in the damp bottom. As soon as the depressions fill with water again the eggs complete their development and the fry hatch. Here growth and sexual maturation must be very rapid. This kind of breeding places special demands on the breeder: there must be a sufficiently thick layer of peat in the breeding tank and the peat with the eggs must be stored under specific conditions (temperature, humidity, period of storage).

Labyrinth fish generally deposit their eggs in bubble nests on the surface. These are built by the males and are composed of air bubbles cemented together by a secretion. They are generally anchored in a thicket of aquatic plants.

Some species use bits of plants in making the nests. Some catfish (e.g. of the Callichthyidae family) build the nest under the broad floating leaves of water-lilies, under fallen roots, etc. The secretion cementing the air bubbles together contains bacteriostatic substances which protect the eggs. That is why eggs stripped of this foam often die. The eggs and embryos are cared for by the male labyrinth fish until the self-sufficient fry abandon the nest. In the case of catfish this care may continue beyond the point when the fry become free-swimming. Bubble nests may be built not only on the surface but also immediate-

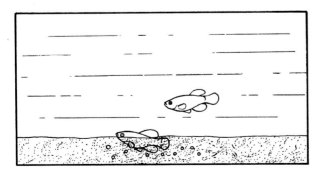 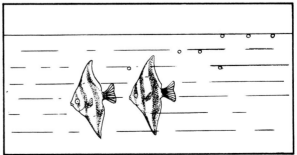

ly beneath the surface, in the middle strata of water, or under rock overhangs.

During the act of spawning in the case of fish that spawn in open water (pelagophilic fish) thousands or even more eggs are released within a few seconds. The light eggs, containing a drop of oil, scatter over a wide area and rise to the surface. Such eggs are called pelagic and are typical of fish that inhabit large expanses of deep water. Aquarium fish that spawn in this way, for instance, are those of the genus *Monodactylus*. Only the largest aquariums with sufficiently large water surface are suitable for these fish.

The spawning of the Splash Tetra (*Copella arnoldi*), which takes place out of water, is unique in the realm of fish, as is the spawning of the Three-Spined Stickleback (*Gasterosteus aculeatus*), which lays eggs in nests constructed of plant pieces cemented together with a kidney secretion, or that of the Bitterling (*Rhodeus sericeus*), which deposits eggs between the gills of a mussel. A more detailed description of these unusual methods of spawning will be found in the text pertaining to the respective species; they do not occur elsewhere.

Native Waters of Freshwater Aquarium Fish

Fresh waters are aquatic habitats of great diversity and may be divided into the following two groups: standing or still waters (lakes, pools, swamps, wetlands) and flowing waters (springs, streams, rivers). Flowing waters are furthermore divided into white waters (rapids) and calm waters. Though freshwater habitats are found in all climatic zones of the earth the overwhelming majority of fish kept in aquariums are from the tropics and subtropics, from five main regions: 1. the Amazon region with water poor in mineral substances and adjoining regions to the south (Paraná – Paraguay) and to the north (Central America), 2. the water system of the large Congo River Basin (now the Zaire River), 3. the lakes of the East African Great Rift Valley, 4. the waters of tropical South and Southeast Asia including the islands of Indonesia, New Guinea and the Philippines, and 5. the waters of coastal regions that cannot be described as brackish, even though they have a high concentration of dissolved salts.

Brackish water, which is also the dwelling place of many aquarium fish, must be viewed as an entirely separate biotope. Brackish waters are formed by the merging of sea and fresh water in bays in the mouths of rivers, in tidal wetlands with stands of mangrove, and in expanses of water separated from the sea by sand spits. Brackish waters are intermediate zones between

fresh waters and sea water. Their salinity may change during the course of the day, month or year, and requires a broad tolerance to the salinity of the environment on the part of the organisms dwelling there (euryhaline species).

Amazon River Region

The Amazon River – greatest reservoir of fresh water on the earth – flows across practically the whole width of the South American continent. It is fed by mighty rivers such as the Negro, Madeira, Japurá, Tapajós, and Nepo, and countless smaller rivers and streams. The waters of this largest river system differ not only in appearance but also in chemical composition. The water of the Amazon, so-called white water, is muddy-whitish, cloudy. The cloudiness is caused by the particles of matter washed out by the river on its lengthy journey. The whitish coloration is caused by anorganic infiltrations from the Andes. The pH values are 6.2–7.2, dCH 0.2–0.4°, dGH 0.6–1.2°, conductivity μS 30/28 °C, μS 70/20 °C. (The conductivity of water is determined by the content of all conductive compounds in the water, chiefly acids, alkalis and salts. It is measured in microseimenses – μS). The so-called clean water of the Tapajós River is yellow to olive green and clear. It has a low content of dissolved organic and inorganic substances or none whatsoever, a pH of 4.5−7.8, dCH 0.0−0.3°, dGH 0.3−0.8°, and a temperature of 30/20 °C. This water flows into larger rivers mainly from small streams with a sandy or stony bottom where it is naturally filtered. The black water of the Negro River is olive green to coffee-brown and clear, the strong brown colour being caused by dissolved humic acids from the surrounding forest soil. This water is found in country that is inundated for long periods of time and its characteristics are pH 3.8−4.7, dCH 0.0−0.1°, dGH max. 0.1°, and conductivity µS 8/28 °C, µS 15/20 °C.

Ichthyologists estimate that there are 2,500 species of fish in the Amazon region. Aquarium fish are found chiefly in small streams, lagoons, blind river arms and pools. In the main rivers most fish dwell in the calm waters by the shore richly overgrown with vegetation. The narrower the water courses the more shaded the shoreline vegetation and that is why many species from these localities like subdued lighting.

Waters of the Large Zaire (Congo) River Basin

Next to the South American jungles the tropical rain forests of Africa form the greatest continuous expanse of forest in the world, extending from the coast of Guinea almost 5,000 kilometres west to east and about 1,600 kilometres north to south to the basin of the Congo River (Zaire River). Because of the jungle-like character of the territory and lack of mineral salts the waters here are soft and slightly to strongly acidic due to the humic acids from the fallen vegetation, like the waters of the Amazon basin. The tropical rain forests are criss-crossed by small brooks and streams, with the occasional small shallow lake and pool, that flow into the Zaire River. The rivers rise at mountain sources, rushing as rapids through narrow canyons with countless waterfalls to the lowlands where they change into broad, more slowly-flowing courses. Tropical downpours during the rainy season raise the level of the rivers but floods are not a frequent phenomenon. Numerous species of aquarium fish from this region like morning sunlight.

Lakes of Africa's Great Rift Valley

The volcanic mountain range running north to south down the middle of the African continent forms a natural water divide separating the Zaire River basin from the Great Rift Valley in East Africa. The lakes in this region are of great interest from the viewpoint of the aquarist, particularly Mobutu Sese Seko (formerly Lake Albert), Lake Dward, Lake Victoria, Lake Kiwu, Lake Malawi (formerly Nyasa), and Lake Tanganyika. The water in all these lakes is alkaline with pH value between 7.0 and 10.0. The hardness is not as great as one would expect at such pH values, about 10° dGH (an exception are the sodium lakes Natron and Magadi between Kenya and Tanzania that have extremely high dGH values and temperatures). The lakes of East Africa contain an amazing wealth of endemic species and forms (ones that do not occur elsewhere) of cichlids, particularly mouthbrooders. The most interesting new ones are from Lakes Tanganyika and Malawi, which, according to ichthyologists, are currently the scene of tempestuous development of the Cichlidae family. The kind of fish (species) found in various localities in these lakes is determined by the character of the shoreline waters, i.e. rocky and sandy bottoms, of the pelagic, deep waters.

Waters of Tropical Monsoon Asia

The region where the native waters of aquarium fish are found extends from southern India and Sri Lanka through Indonesia and the Philippines to New Guinea. The climate is determined chiefly by the monsoon winds accompanied by tropical rains that strongly affect nature in these parts.

Sri Lanka has an average temperature of 27 °C and annual rainfall of 2,000 mm, with humidity in the tropical rain forests between 90 and 100 per cent. The average temperature of the waters is 20 to 27 °C (depending on the altitude above sea level). At higher elevations the temperature of the water may drop to 5 °C, and in mountain valleys it may fall as low as 2 to 3 °C. The water in mountain streams rising from crystalline rocks is soft and acidic with a pH value of 5.5−6.8. The waters of south Indian rivers in the Decca plateau are likewise soft and acidic with a large concentration of humic substances leached from the fallen vegetation. Fish from mountain regions usually require water that is rich in oxygen.

Pictorial Scheme of Fish Families

(the illustrated representative of each family bears its characteristic features;
according to G. U. Lindberg)

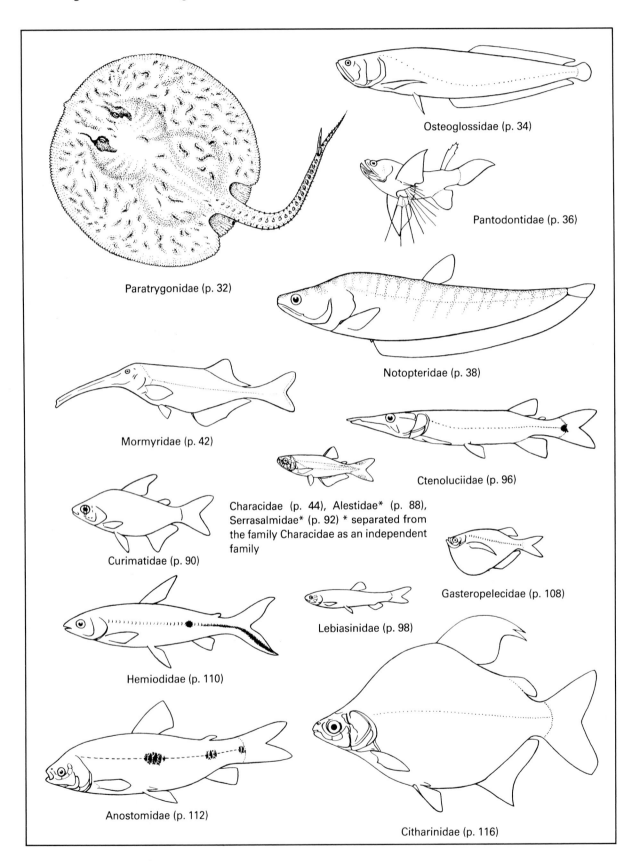

Osteoglossidae (p. 34)

Pantodontidae (p. 36)

Paratrygonidae (p. 32)

Notopteridae (p. 38)

Mormyridae (p. 42)

Ctenoluciidae (p. 96)

Characidae (p. 44), Alestidae* (p. 88),
Serrasalmidae* (p. 92) * separated from
the family Characidae as an independent
family

Curimatidae (p. 90)

Gasteropelecidae (p. 108)

Lebiasinidae (p. 98)

Hemiodidae (p. 110)

Anostomidae (p. 112)

Citharinidae (p. 116)

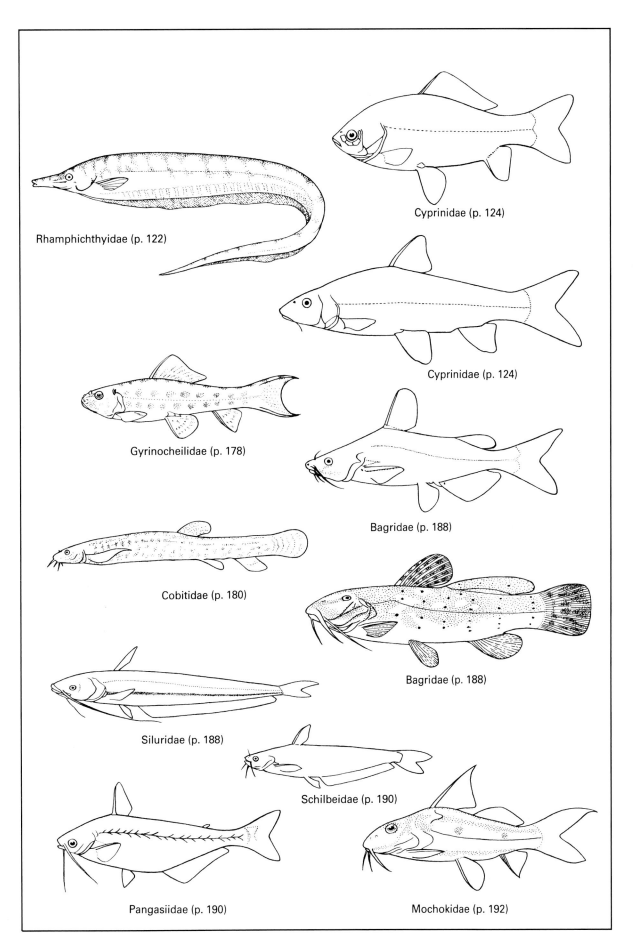

Rhamphichthyidae (p. 122)

Cyprinidae (p. 124)

Cyprinidae (p. 124)

Gyrinocheilidae (p. 178)

Bagridae (p. 188)

Cobitidae (p. 180)

Bagridae (p. 188)

Siluridae (p. 188)

Schilbeidae (p. 190)

Pangasiidae (p. 190)

Mochokidae (p. 192)

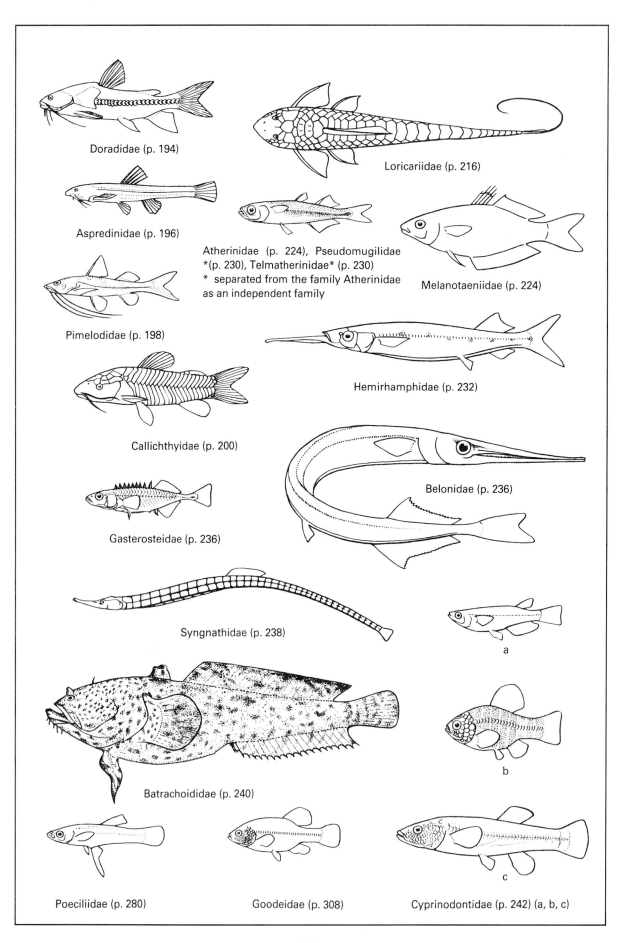

Doradidae (p. 194)

Loricariidae (p. 216)

Aspredinidae (p. 196)

Atherinidae (p. 224), Pseudomugilidae
(p. 230), Telmatherinidae (p. 230)
* separated from the family Atherinidae
as an independent family

Melanotaeniidae (p. 224)

Pimelodidae (p. 198)

Hemirhamphidae (p. 232)

Callichthyidae (p. 200)

Belonidae (p. 236)

Gasterosteidae (p. 236)

Syngnathidae (p. 238)

a

Batrachoididae (p. 240)

b

c

Poeciliidae (p. 280)

Goodeidae (p. 308)

Cyprinodontidae (p. 242) (a, b, c)

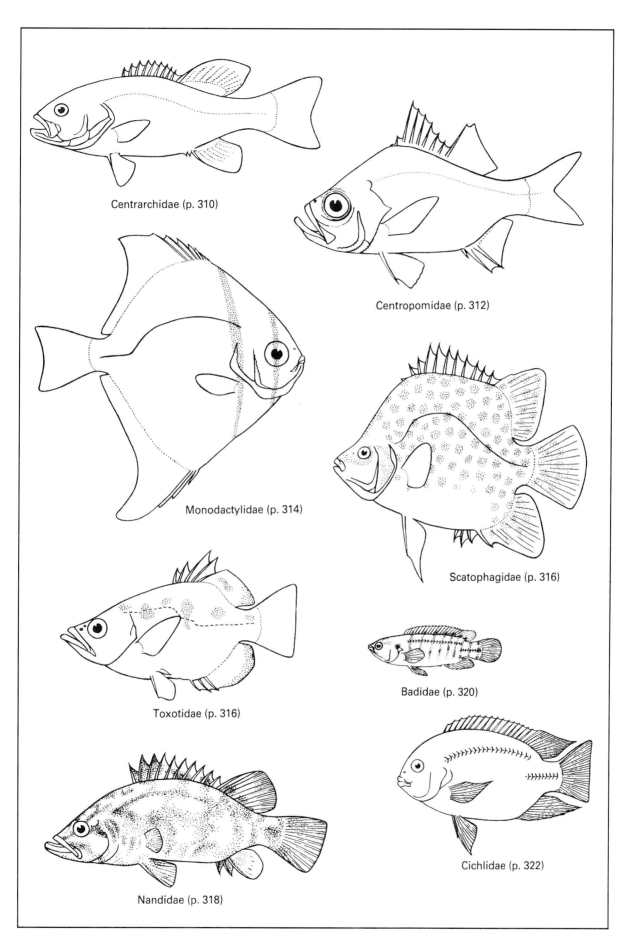

Centrarchidae (p. 310)

Centropomidae (p. 312)

Monodactylidae (p. 314)

Scatophagidae (p. 316)

Toxotidae (p. 316)

Badidae (p. 320)

Nandidae (p. 318)

Cichlidae (p. 322)

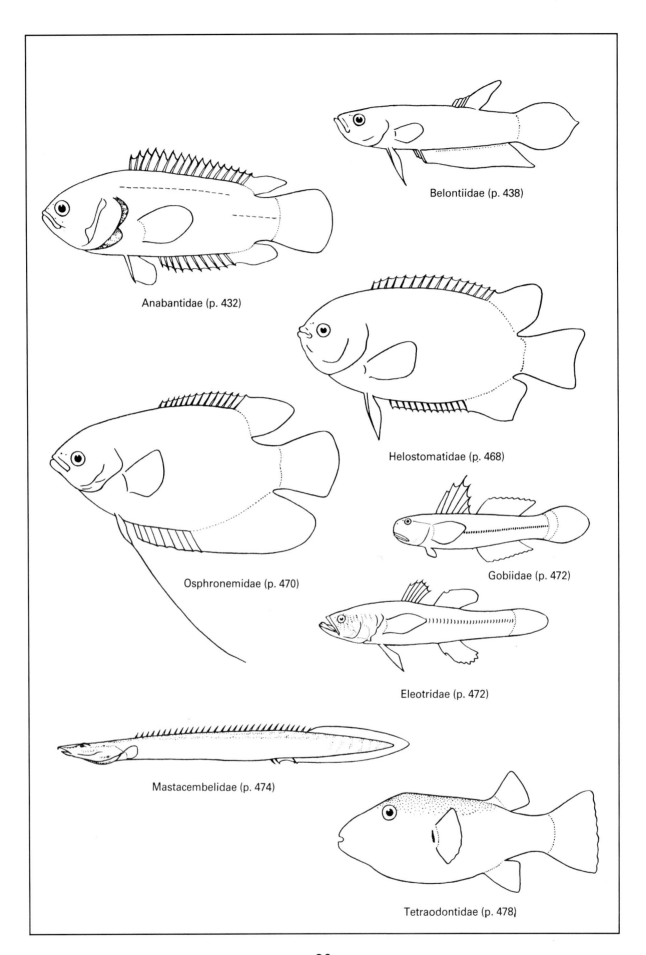

Belontiidae (p. 438)

Anabantidae (p. 432)

Helostomatidae (p. 468)

Osphronemidae (p. 470)

Gobiidae (p. 472)

Eleotridae (p. 472)

Mastacembelidae (p. 474)

Tetraodontidae (p. 478)

30

Pictorial Section

Explanatory notes:

○   omnivorous fish

◁   carnivorous or predatory fish

▭   fish also requiring vegetable food

◑   fish kept in community tanks

●   fish kept in monospecies tanks

☐   oviparous fish

■   viviparous fish

Family Paratrygonidae

This family includes freshwater aquarium fish belonging to the order of rays and skates (Rajiformes). The body is flattened dorsoventrally and the paired fins are moved to the sides and joined to form a continuous fin border round the entire body. The internal skeleton is cartilaginous. The outer protective coat consists of placoid scales and strong teeth in the jaws; the placoid scales and teeth may be secondarily reduced. The mouth has the shape of a transverse slit. The gill filaments are attached along their entire length to the gill arches. Fertilization is internal; the males have a paired copulatory organ (pterygopodium), which is a modified part of the ventral fins. The eggs are large, many species are live-bearers, there is no larval stage. All rays and skates have a paired spiraculum on top of the head behind the eyes and five gill slits on the underside of the body. Some species have a spine with a poisonous gland at the base either on the back at the base of the tail or directly on the whip-like tail.

1 Stingray
Potamotrygon laticeps GARMAN, ?
Syn. *Disceus laticeps, Paratrygon laticeps*
(Rare in aquariums)   Paratrygonidae

◁ Distribution: large region of South America from the Orinoco and Magdalena basin in the north to ● Argentina in the south. Full length: male − 54 cm, including the tail which is 18 cm long; width 33 cm; female − 68 cm, including 25 cm long tail; width 41 cm. Diet: worms, crayfish, flesh of shell-fish, flesh of salt water and freshwater fish, live fish, pieces of beef and heart, tabletted foods. Monospecies keeping tank with capacity of 1,000 litres or more, a 10 to 20 cm layer of fine sand on the bottom, floating plants. Breeding tank: same as keeping tank. Sexual dimorphism: the male has a paired pterigopodium and one poisonous spine on the tail; the female has two poisonous spines. Sex ratio: 1:1, or there may be a slight preponderance of females. Breeding water: 25 °C; pH 7.0−7.5; fresh. Live-bearing species, interval between births: 3−4 months. Feeding of fry: chopped earthworms, minced fish meat, snails (it may be several weeks before the young begin to take food. This may be determined according to the presence of excrement).

Typical benthophagous fish (they feed on the bottom) that are active at night. When hunting they press the live victim to the bottom with their body. Their coloration is variable.

When courting the male bites the female. The wounds caused by copulatory biting heal quickly and leave disc-shaped scars. Two to three months after copulation bulges appear on the backs of pregnant females and simultaneously movements of the embryos inside become noticeable. The newly-born young are relatively large − 9 to 13 cm long; they begin swimming freely right away and are exact miniature copies of the adult fish. The greatest number of young produced by one female in a Detroit aquarium was four. The young fish were transferred to 80-litre aquariums with a layer of fine sand on the bottom to facilitate a better check on their metabolism. When young fish have eaten their fill two bumps appear at the base of the whip-like tail; these gradually disappear as the food is digested. The growth of young fish is slow but without problems.

Paratrygonidae

Family Osteoglossidae

The members of this family are large fish that live near the surface of standing waters in shallow, blind arms of rivers and lakes. The fish often congregate in large shoals. They are distributed in Australia, the islands of the Indian Ocean, Africa and South America. The South American members of this family are endangered species and according to some reports catching them is prohibited. The Osteoglossidae are distinguished by certain evolutionary peculiarities: they have very big scales and the fourth gill arch carries an accessory respiratory organ. In some species the swimbladder is used for breathing, e.g. in *Arapaima gigas,* which is one of the largest freshwater fish with its length of up to 3 metres and weight of up to 160 kilograms.

1 Arowana
Osteoglossum bicirrhosum VANDELLI, 1829
Syn. *Ischnosoma bicirrhosum, Osteoglossum vandelli*

Osteoglossidae

◁
●
Distribution: northern South America, Guyana and the Amazon basin — standing and slow-flowing waters, blind arms of rivers, swamps. Full length: 120 cm. Diet: live food of all kinds, chiefly fish (also pieces of beef and fish meat). Monospecies keeping tank, capacity depending on the size of the fish. Tanks must be covered so the fish cannot leap out and must have a sufficiently high water column. The bottom should be planted with scattered groups of robust plants. The tank used for breeding is of the same type as the monospecies keeping tank but breeding in this species is most unlikely. Sexual dimorphism: the male's anal fin is elongate and longer than the female's. The lower jaw is conspicuously extended and overlaps the upper jaw. Sex ratio: 1:1. The keeping pool may contain a number of fish if it is sufficiently large (at least 1,000 litres of water per pair). Breeding water: 25 °C; pH 6.5; dCH < 1°; dGH 8°, filtered through peat. Eggs: ∅ 16 mm, incubation period in the female's mouth 50 to 60 days. Feeding of fry: zooplankton, then mosquito larvae, later small fish.

Prior to spawning the fish engage in simple courtship games. The female gathers the laid eggs in her mouth where they continue to develop. The fry leave the shelter of the female's mouth when they are 8 to 10 cm long. Young fish are yellow-green, adult fish silvery. The mouth opening is deeply cleft and directed upwards. A characteristic feature are the two barbels on the lower jaw in which the olfactory organs are located. The fish have an accessory respiratory organ (swim-bladder) with which they are able to breathe atmospheric air. This helps them survive in oxygen-poor swampy waters. In captivity the fish can be tamed so they will take food from the hand, otherwise they are wary. In a small space they become aggressive and bite one another. Currently a protected species that cannot be imported.

1 juv.

Family Pantodontidae

A monotypic family with only one species, *Pantodon buchholzi.* A surface fish with deeply cleft mouth opening directed upwards.

1 Butterfly Fish
Pantodon buchholzi PETERS, 1876

Distribution: West Africa, Nigeria, Cameroons, Zaire. Full length: 10–15 cm (male 10, female 15). Diet: live foods (prefers large pieces, pays no attention to small ones), e.g. spiders, insect larvae, moths, cockroaches, crickets, small fish. When these are not available will also feed on bits of fish, beef or chicken meat. Monospecies keeping tank. Breeding tank: 100-litre capacity, water column 20 cm high. Large water surface with floating plants. Sexual dimorphism: the hind edge of the male's anal fin is deeply indented, the central fin rays form a tube; the hind edge of the female's anal fin is straight. Sex ratio: 1:1. Breeding water: 25–28 °C; pH 6.5; dCH <2°, filtered through peat. Eggs: incubation period 36 hrs./25 °C. Feeding of fry: brine shrimp nauplii, later fruit flies, spring-tails, aphids.

Breeding fish should be put in spacious tanks with at least 100 litres of water per pair. They jump so the aquarium must be covered with glass. Lengthy mating games precede the actual spawning, which may last several days. During this time the female may lay more than 200 eggs. The relatively large, transparent (later dark brown) eggs with large oil content float at the surface. They are gathered with a catching pipe and transferred to the nursery tank with water column 5–10 cm high. The eleutherembryos sink to the bottom. After consuming the yolk sac the fry return to the surface. They do not actively forage for food but wait for it to be brought to them by the water. *P. buchholzi* is an aggressive, nocturnal fish.

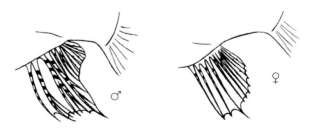

anal fin of male and female

1 ♂

1 ♀

Family Notopteridae

The Afro-Asiatic 'knife fish' resemble the New World 'knife fish' (family Rhamehichthyidae) but the only feature they have in common is the shape of the body; taxonomically each is a separate group. The anal fin is very long, like a fin border, and by its undulating motions enables the fish to swim backwards as well as forward. The anal opening is situated far to the front. The dorsal fin is absent or small and pennant-like. The ventral fins are very small, or absent. The caudal fin is grown together with the anal fin. The scales are small. The fish have an accessory respiratory organ, a specially developed lung-like swim-bladder. They are crepuscular fish.

1 African Knife Fish
Papyrocranus afer GÜNTHER, 1868
Syn. *Notopterus afer*   Notopteridae

Distribution: Tropical west Africa, Gambia River, slow-flowing or standing, densely-planted waters. Full length: 60 cm. Diet: live foods (fish, insect larvae and adult insects, snails, worms, etc.). Keeping tank: monospecies with capacity of at least 500 litres. Breeding tank: with capacity of 500 litres or more, stony bottom and hiding places. Sexual dimorphism: monomorphic fish. Sex ratio: 1:1. This species has apparently not been bred in captivity to date. Water: 26–29 °C; pH 6.5–7.0; dCH < 2°; dGH < 10°.

A special characteristic of the genus *Papyrocranus,* with the one species *P. afer,* is the absence of ventral fins; the dorsal fin is small. In the wild *P. afer* spawns during the rainy season. The eggs, $\varnothing$ 4 mm, are ovoid and larger than those of the other members of this family.

2 Clown Knife fish
Notopterus chitala (HAMILTON-BUCHANAN, 1822)   Notopteridae

Distribution: India, Thailand, Cambodia, Burma, Greater Sunda Islands. Full length: 80 cm. Diet: live foods (fish and beef, large earthworms, coarse zooplankton). Monospecies keeping tank. Breeding tank: with capacity of 1,000 litres or more, or pools with stony bottom and hiding places. Sexual dimorphism: monomorphic fish. Sex ratio: 1:1. Breeding water: 26–29 °C; pH 6.0–7.0; dCH < 2°; dGH < 10°. Eggs: small in relation to the size of the fish, incubation period not known. Feeding of fry: brine shrimp nauplii. Rarely imported fish.

The fish were propagated by the American breeder T. Berardo: in 1973 one pair of fish spawned in a 1,400-litre tank. The fish were 58 cm long. The more active of the two was the female, which lured the male to the spawning ground. The female laid up to 15 eggs at one time on the hard rock substrate and these were immediately fertilized by the male. The temperature of the water was raised from 20 °C to 29 °C and the pH was 6.2. In both fish the genital papilla protruded during spawning. The eggs fell prey to another species of fish and thus it was impossible to observe their development. In the wild the spawning period is from May till July. The female lays up to 500 eggs in a single layer and the larvae hatch within two weeks. Before spawning the breeding fish clean the area of the spawning ground within a radius of 60 cm and here the free-swimming fry move about for a time. The cleared area of the spawning ground also serves as a point of orientation for the returning parents. The duties of caring for the spawning ground are shared by both fish, both also fanning the eggs with their anal and caudal fins. Fish of the genus *Notopterus* have developed ventral as well as dorsal fins.

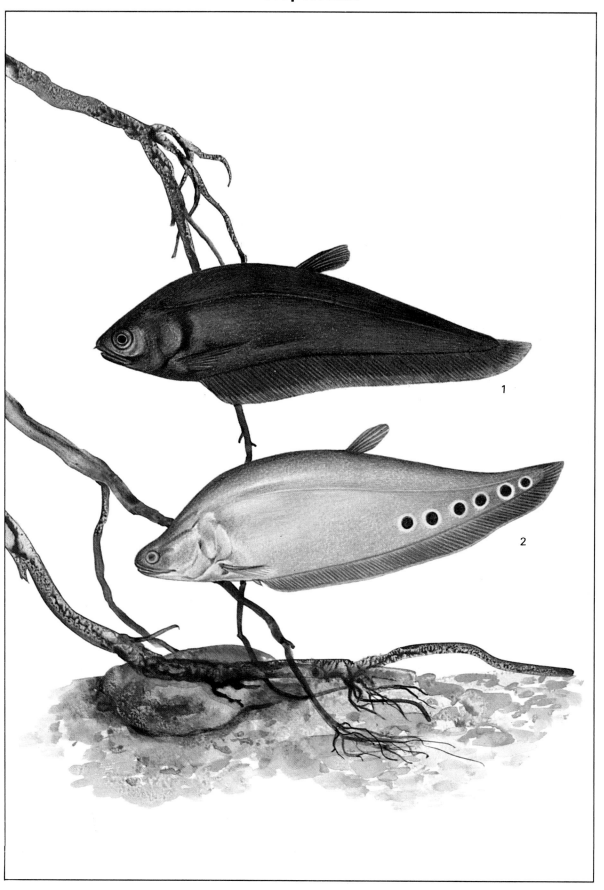

◁
●
Distribution: India, Burma, Cambodia, Thailand, Jawa and Sumatra. Full length: 40 cm (very occasionally 58 cm). Diet: live foods (purportedly also the roots of aquatic vegetation). Keeping tank: monospecies. Breeding tank: with capacity of at least 300 litres. Sexual dimorphism: monomorphic fish; the female may be distinguished only during the spawning period and is usually larger. Sex ratio: 1:1. Breeding water: 26–29 °C; pH 6.5–7.0; dCH < 2°; dGH < 10°. Eggs: ∅ 3–4 mm, incubation period 5–11 days. (According to the observations of the Japanese breeder K. Yasuschi the development of the eggs is not uniform). Feeding of fry: brine shrimp nauplii.

The fish attain sexual maturity when they reach a length of 30 cm. A number of specimens are kept in the tank so pairs can mate according to preference. Prior to spawning the abdomen of both the male and female becomes enlarged. The female lays the eggs on a solid substrate hidden by surrounding stones. The actual spawning takes place at night. Within 30 hours some embryos are already moving about inside the eggs. Both the male and female carefully watch over the eggs and supply them with fresh water with the aid of their gills. Both fish often take the eggs up in their mouths, seemingly not only to clean them but also to help the embryo break through the egg case. The egg is 'chewed' for a few seconds and often leaves the mouth as an eleutherembryo. The embryos hatch successively over a period of one week and are about 7 mm long. Endogenous nutrition from the large yolk sacs lasts about a week. During the daytime the young fry keep out of sight, emerging to forage for food only at night, and it is therefore difficult to determine the presence of fry. During the spawning period the breeding pair mates at very brief intervals, often when the larvae from the first mating are hatching. The presence of the parent fish is essential, otherwise the fry die.

2 African Knife Fish
Xenomystus nigri (GÜNTHER, 1868)
Syn. *Notopterus nigri*   Notopteridae

◁
●
Distribution: Sudan, Zaire, Gabon, Nigeria, Liberia. Full length: 30 cm. Diet: coarser live foods, (worms, insects and insect larvae, snails and small fish; when these are not available pieces of beef and heart). Monospecies keeping tank with capacity of 300 litres or more. Breeding tank: of at least 300-litre capacity with stony bottom and hiding places. Sexual dimorphism: monomorphic fish. Sex ratio: 1:1. Apparently has not been bred in captivity. Water: 24–28 °C; pH 6.5–7.0; dCH < 2°; dGH < 10°.

Unlike members of the genus *Papyrocranus* and *Notopterus,* fish of the genus *Xenomystus* have ventral fins but no dorsal fin. *X. nigri* is the only species in this genus. In the wild the females lay 150 to 200 eggs approximately ∅ 2 mm. The fish make barking sounds. This sound is produced by the flow of air in the tube, called *ductus pneumaticus,* linking the gut with the swimbladder.

Family Mormyridae

The members of this family are African twilight fish, mostly of peculiar appearance, that inhabit muddy, slow-flowing waters. Their colouring corresponds to their environment. Some species have the snout extended like a trunk or have appendages hanging from the snout. The brain is remarkably large. Some members of the family possess an electric organ on the tail which functions like a radar, enabling the fish to find their way in murky water, to locate food and to mark their territories. They are typical benthophagous fish.

1 Peter's Elephant-nose
Gnathonemus petersi (GÜNTHER, 1862)
Syn. *Mormyrus petersi, Gnathonemus pictus*   Mormyridae

Distribution: water systems of the Congo and Zaire Rivers. Full length: 25 cm. Diet: live foods, chiefly tubifex worms and larvae of midges. Monospecies keeping tank with capacity of 500 litres or more. Put blunt, rather coarse gravel on the bottom and provide the fish with sufficient hiding possibilities (mineralized wood from moors, flowerpots with the bottom knocked out, etc.). The lighting should be diffused, there should be floating plants on the surface and the tank must be well covered with glass. Breeding tank: same as keeping tank. Sexual dimorphism: not known. Sex ratio: Put a small group of fish of the same size in the tank; smaller fish are the victims of aggression on the part of larger specimens. Water: 22–28 °C; pH 6.5; dCH < 2°; dGH < 10°; not too fresh (that has been allowed to stand for a time). Details of breeding are not known.

During the day the fish are timid, particularly in a new environment. Typical is the trunk-like prolongation of the lower jaw, which with the electric organ and other sensory organs facilitates finding food in the muddy bottom. Electrical impulses are also used by the fish to mark their territories; in a small space they constantly disturb one another.

Unlike *Gnathonemus petersi*, *G. elephas*, *G. gibis* and other species have a real trunk with a mouth at the end of the trunk. *G. moori*, on the other hand, has no trunk whatsoever and *G. schilthuisiae* has only an indication of a trunk.

2 Black-spot Mormyrid
Petrocephalus bovei (CUVIER and VALENCIENNES, 1846)   Mormyridae

Distribution: from the lower Nile through north central Africa to west Africa — Nigeria, Gambia. Full length: 12–14 cm (up to 45 cm according to some authorities). Diet: live foods, chiefly tubifex worms, larvae of midges, as well as artificial foods. Monospecies keeping tank, spacious, with capacity of about 500 litres, sufficient plants and hiding possibilities, diffused lighting. Breeding tank: same as keeping tank. Sexual dimorphism: not known. Sex ratio: The fish should be kept in the tank in a small shoal. Water: 24–28 °C; pH 6.5–7.0; dCH max. 2°; dGH max. 10°; aged. There are no reports of the species having been bred in captivity.

The fish have a greatly compressed body which enables them to swim through narrow crevices. They are aggressive to others of the same species and must be provided with sufficient space so that individual specimens may establish separate territories. Putting the fish into newly set up aquariums is not recommended.

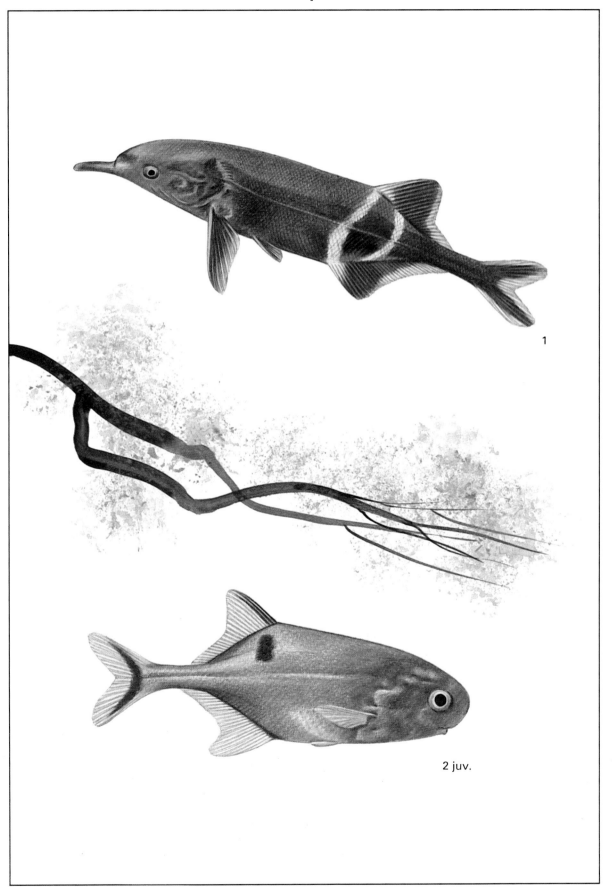

1

2 juv.

Family Characidae

This family includes many small, variegated fish that live mostly in shoals. For that reason they should never be kept singly but in a larger group. They are distributed throughout Central and South America. A characteristic feature of most members of this family is the small adipose fin. The jaws are toothed, the teeth often very sharp and strong. The shape and number of teeth is an important means of identifying the various species. Some species are predatory, others herbivorous. Soft, slightly acidic water is suitable for most species. The water temperature given in the description of the individual species may be 3 to 4 °C lower outside the spawning period.

1 Blind Cave Fish or Mexican Tetra
Astyanax fasciatus mexicanus (CUVIER, 1819)
Syn. *Anoptichthys jordani, A. hubbsi, A. antrobius*   Characidae

Distribution: cave systems of the province of San Luis Potosí, Mexico. Full length: male 12 cm, female 9 cm. Diet: live as well as artificial foods. Monospecies keeping tank, sandy-stony, without plants. Breeding tank: of 50- to 100-litre capacity with spawning grid. Sexual dimorphism: male slimmer, smaller. Sex ratio: 1:1. Breeding water: 24–27 °C; pH 6.7–7.0; dCH max. 15°; dGH 15–20° (in soft water the larvae suffer constitutional noninfectious dropsy and die). Eggs: incubation period 18–24 hrs. Feeding of fry: nauplii of brine shrimp or *Cyclops* nauplii, likewise small water fleas (*Bosmina longirostris*), which other fry do not eat.

A special adaptation to its cave habitat is the reduction of the eyes and the loss of sight. The sense of sight is compensated for by the tactile sense and sense of smell. The lateral line is well developed and serves as a means of orientation. Populations kept for a long time under light in aquariums are not the usual meat-red colour of imported fish but silvery. The female lays more than 1,000 eggs during spawning. The larvae switch to exogenous nutrition after two days. They have small eyes, 0.2 mm in diameter, which gradually become completely covered with fatty tissue.

2 Sword-tailed Characin
Corynopoma riisei GILL, 1858
Syn. *Corynopoma albipinne, C. aliata, C. searlesi, C. veedoni, Nematopoma searlesi, Stevardia aliata, S. albipinnis, S. riisei*   Characidae

Distribution: Trinidad, Colombia (Meta River). Full length: 7 cm. Diet: live as well as artificial foods. Community tank. Breeding tank: of 50-litre capacity with fine-leaved plants. Sexual dimorphism: male has larger fins, particularly the dorsal and anal ones, lengthened fin rays on the lower lobe of the caudal fin, and a long extension of the gill covers sometimes reaching as far as the dorsal fin. Sex ratio: 1 male: 3–4 females. Breeding water: 24 °C; pH 6.5–7.0; DCH < 2°. Eggs: sticky; incubation period 20–36 hrs. Feeding of fry: nauplii of brine shrimp or *Cyclops* nauplii.

During spawning the male deposits the sperm enclosed in spermatophores next to the genital opening of the female. After the eggs have matured in the ovaries the female deposits the fertilized eggs amidst the plants. She is capable of spawning several times in succession without the presence of a male. Whenever eggs are laid some of the sperm are released from the supply in the spermatophore. Bundles of plants with eggs should be regularly transferred from the breeding to the nursery tank.

Characidae

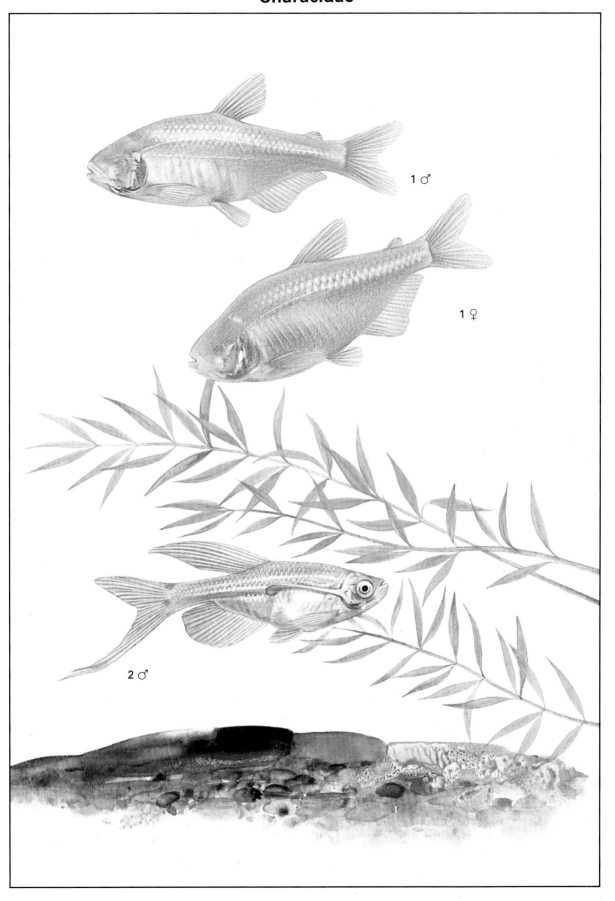

1 Glass Redfin or Translucent Bloodfin

Prionobrama filigera (COPE, 1870)

Syn. *Aphyocharax filigerus, A. analis, A. analialbis, Bleptonema amazoni,
Paragoniates muelleri, Prionobrama madeirae*

Distribution: Amazon River and its numerous tributaries in southeast Brazil. Full length: 6 cm. Diet: live as well as artificial foods. Community tank. Breeding tank: of at least 20-litre capacity with spawning grid. Sexual dimorphism: female larger with deeper body and characteristic gold spot (the ovaries shining through) above the abdominal cavity. Sex ratio: 1:1, or with a slightly greater preponderance of males in the group. Breeding water: 24–27 °C; pH 7.0; dCH 1°. Eggs: glassily translucent, $\emptyset$ 0.9 mm, incubation period 14–15 hrs/27 °C. Feeding of fry: nauplii of brine shrimp or *Cyclops* nauplii.

The fish are sensitive to water that is too acidic – in such a case the edges of the fins become mouldy. The aquarium must be covered with glass for the slightest impulse may frighten the fish into jumping considerable distances. Spawning usually takes place in the morning in sun-flooded aquariums. The female lays about 300 eggs. The glassy eleutherembryos attach themselves by the sticky secretion exuded by the glands on the top of the head to the sides of the tank, to surrounding objects, or in clusters to the water-surface membrane. Common amongst breeders is the mistaken belief that the eggs develop in harder water; at a carbonate hardness of 2° or more, however, the eggs die. Decisive for the development of the eggs, therefore, is a dCH of less than 2°.

2 Bloodfin

Aphyocharax anisitsi EIGENMANN and KENNEDY, 1903

Syn. *Tetragonopterus rubropictus, Aphyocharax affinis, A. rubripinnis*

Distribution: Paraná River, Argentina. Full length: 5 cm. Diet: live as well as artificial foods. Community tank. Breeding tank: of at least 20-litre capacity with spawning grid, well covered with glass and placed in a light or sunlit spot. Sexual dimorphism: the male is more slender with small hooks on the anal fin. Sex ratio: 1:1, or with a slight preponderance of males, in pairs or in a rather larger shoal. Breeding water: 24 °C; pH 6.0–7.0; dCH < 2°. Eggs: incubation period 24 hrs. Feeding of fry: nauplii of brine shrimp or *Cyclops* nauplii.

Good swimmers associating in schools. The female lays 300 to 500 eggs during the spawning period. The fry are extremely wary, seeking the slightest shelter and thus easily overlooked. Because these fish are very adept at leaping the aquarium must be kept covered with glass. The young fish grow very quickly if provided with sufficient natural food and fresh, oxygen-rich water. They are fond of flowing water, which may be provided by forced-circulation filters.

Characidae

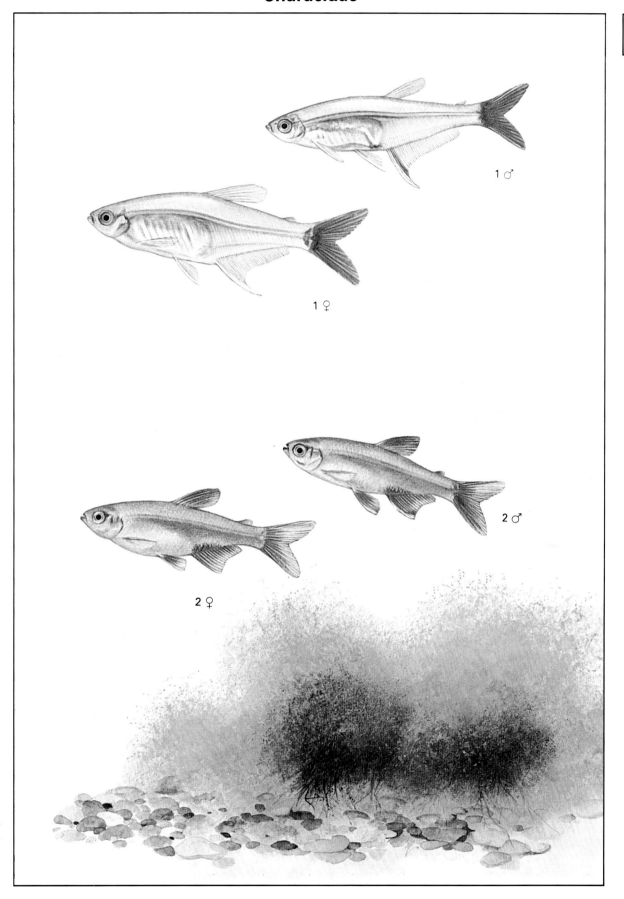

1 ♂

1 ♀

2 ♂

2 ♀

1 Rathbun's Bloodfin
Aphyocharax rathbuni EIGENMANN, 1907
Commercial name: *'Hyphessobrycon federalis'*

Distribution: Paraguay. Full length: 4.5 cm. Diet: live as well as artificial foods. Community tank, dark bottom. Breeding tank: of 10-litre capacity with spawning grid and finely-leaved plants. Sexual dimorphism: the male's dorsal and anal fins have a sharper point and the caudal fin is indented more deeply than the female's. The female is less colourful and plumper. Sex ratio: 1:1. Breeding water: 27 °C; pH 7.0−7.6; dCH < 2°. Eggs: glassy, clear, ∅ 0.86 mm, incubation period 16−18 hrs. Feeding of fry: brine shrimp nauplii.

The fish prefer to spawn on plants. When they are 85 hours old the larvae become free-swimming. Then − for two to three months − the young fish 'crawl' on their backs and make peculiar twisting movements. Only after this period do they assume a normal position and swim in open water like adult fish. Sexual maturity is attained at six to seven months. According to Dr. S. Frank the young fish are often infested with parasitic fungi which cause great losses.

2 Head-and-tail-light Tetra or Beaconfish
Hemigrammus ocellifer ocellifer (STEINDACHNER, 1882)
Syn. *Tetragonopterus ocellifer, Holopristis ocellifer*

Distribution: French Guiana, Brazil − Amazon basin, Venezuela − Orinoco basin, Bolivia. Full length: 4.5 cm. Diet: live as well as artificial foods. Community tank. Breeding tank: of 6- to 10-litre capacity with spawning grid. Sexual dimorphism: the male has a pointed swim-bladder, the female is slightly bigger and fuller in the belly section and has a rounded swim-bladder. Sex ratio: 1:1. Breeding water: 24 °C; pH 6.5; dCH 2°. Eggs: incubation period 24 hrs. Feeding of fry: nauplii of brine shrimp or *Cyclops* nauplii.

Peaceful school fish. Before spawning the males should be separated from the females for about 14 days and the breeding fish should be amply fed. The females are very prolific, laying several hundred eggs. The tank should be shaded during the incubation period. The fry should be reared in flat tanks with water column 10 cm high, water being gradually added as the young fish grow.

3 False Head-and-tail-light Tetra
Hemigrammus ocellifer falsus (MEINKEN, 1958)
H. ocellifer falsus is considered by Géry to be a synonym for *Hemigrammus mattei* Eigenmann, 1910

Distribution: Amazon basin (Brazil) and Orinoco basin (Venezuela), according to other sources also Argentina.

Unlike *H. ocellifer ocellifer* the fish do not have the dark spot at the upper edge of the gill covers. The other morphological characters, diet, keeping, and rearing of the fry are the same as for *H. o. ocellifer.*

1 ♀

1 ♂

2 ♀

2 ♂

3 ♂

1 Glow-light Tetra

Hemigrammus erythrozonus Durbin, 1909
Syn. *Hyphessobrycon gracilis*

Distribution: Guyana. Full length: 4.5 cm. Diet: live as well as artificial foods. Community tank. Breeding tank: of 3- to 6-litre capacity with spawning grid. Sexual dimorphism: the male is more slender, the female has a markedly convex belly section. Sex ratio: 1:1. Breeding water: 24 °C; pH 6.5–7.0; dCH 1°; dGH 8–10°. Eggs: $\varnothing$ 0.9 mm, incubation period 19 hrs. Feeding of fry: nauplii of brine shrimp or *Cyclops* nauplii.

For many years this fish was confused with the similar smaller species *Hyphessobrycon gracilis.* Spawning takes place in dim light. After spawning the parent fish should be taken out.

The tank should be kept absolutely clean and fresh water should be added in ample amounts during the growing period; the young fish are very sensitive to the concentration of nitrites in the water. The fry should also be gradually conditioned to carbonate hardness; when they are five days old start adding ordinary tapwater, first in small doses, later in larger amounts. Though the eggs will hatch in very soft and acidic water the eleutherembryos suffer from constitutional dropsy, are unable to fill the swim-bladder with air, jump about on the bottom, and after a few days die.

2 Green Neon

Hemigrammus hyanuary Durbin, 1918

Distribution: Lake Hyanuary near Manaus, Amazon River from Iquitos to São Paulo. Full length: 4 cm. Diet: live as well as artificial foods. Community tank. Breeding tank: with capacity of 3–6 litres per pair and with spawning grid. Sexual dimorphism: the male's anal fin is furnished with a hook that often catches in the net, the female is fuller and larger. Sex ratio: 1:1. Breeding water: 24–26 °C; pH 6.0; dCH max. 1°; fresh water with addition of peat extract or filtered through peat. Eggs: yellowish, incubation period 24 hrs./26 °C. Feeding of fry: the first two days *Paramecium caudatum* or the finest *Cyclops* nauplii, or else newly-hatched small type of brine shrimp.

Species of fish that spawns at dusk. In aquariums spawning takes place in the afternoon or evening with artificial illumination. The female deposits 100 to 200 eggs. Incubation takes place in dim light. Endogenous nutrition ends on the sixth day. At the beginning the fry should be kept in shallow water and the water level should be increased gradually. During the growth period of the young fish the water should be filtered through peat and every 14 days or so about 50 per cent of the water should be replaced by fresh water. Singapore fish farms propagate and export this South American species in large numbers.

3 Feather Fin

Hemigrammus unilineatus (Gill, 1858)
Syn. *Poecilurichthyis hemigrammus unilineatus, Tetragonopterus unilineatus*

Distribution: Paraguay, Brazil, Guyana, Trinidad. Full length: 5 cm. Diet: live as well as artificial foods. Community tank. Breeding tank: of 6- to 10-litre capacity, light, with spawning grid, finely-leaved plants. Sexual dimorphism: the male is slimmer and his swim-bladder is more pointed than that of the female. Sex ratio: 1:1 or 2 males: 1 female. Breeding water: 24–26 °C; pH 6.0–6.5; dCH max. 1°; dGH < 10°. Eggs: incubation period five days. Feeding of fry: *Paramecium caudatum,* rotatoria, *Cyclops* nauplii or the finest brine shrimp nauplii.

Peaceful school fish. They like sunlit tanks with dense vegetation. The female deposits up to 500 eggs amidst plants. The larvae begin exogenous nutrition four days after hatching.

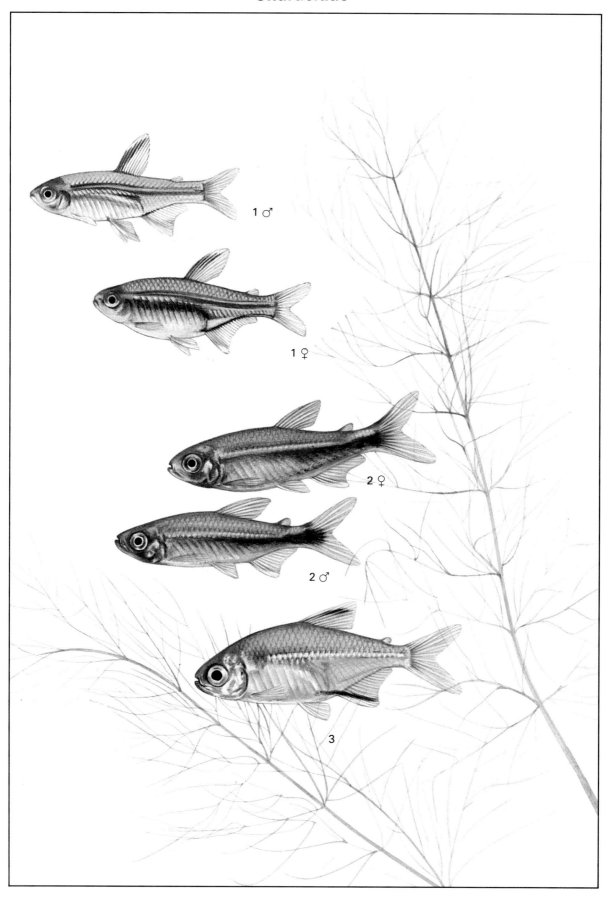

1 ♂

1 ♀

2 ♀

2 ♂

3

1 Buenos Aires Tetra
Hemigrammus caudovittatus AHL, 1923
Syn. *Hyphessobrycon anisitsi*

Distribution: the La Plata region, Argentina. Full length: 10 cm. Diet: live, artificial and plant foods. Community tank. Breeding tank: with capacity of at least 50 litres and spawning grid. Sexual dimorphism: the male is slimmer in the body. Sex ratio: c. 1:1; may be set up to spawn in individual pairs as well as in a shoal. Breeding water: 20–24 °C; pH 6.5–7.0; dCH max. 2°. Eggs: incubation period 24 hrs. Feeding of fry: nauplii of brine shrimp or *Cyclops* nauplii, artificial fry foods.

The fish nibble at most aquatic plants. Therefore tanks with these fish should be provided only with tough, solid plants, ones to which the fish pay no heed – to include Java moss and the ferns *Microsorium pteropus* and *Bolbitis heudeloti.*

H. caudovittatus is a very prolific species; a mature female may deposit several thousand eggs during the spawning period. The greatest number of fertilized eggs are obtained from young, regularly spawning females. In fish that are two years old or more and that do not spawn regularly (when males and females are separated for a long time) the percentage of fertilized eggs and number of viable larvae drops to the minimum. This is caused primarily by degeneration and fattiness of the ovaries.

As soon as spawning is over the parent fish should be removed. Then take out the spawning grid and tap it lightly against the water's surface to loosen any eggs that may be caught in it. Treat the eggs with methylene blue. Transfer the rapidly-growing fry to roomy nursery tanks in time. Spacious aquariums, regular changing of the water, sufficient amounts of the right kind of foods and appropriate stock density (number of fish in the tank) are factors that are necessary for the regular and rapid growth of the fish.

2 *Hemigrammus caudovittatus* – albinotic form

The albinotic form measuring 7 cm in length was selectively bred and genetically fixed in captivity. Like the wild form, it, too, is very prolific.

1 ♂

1 ♀

2 ♀

2 ♂

1 **Pretty Tetra** or **Garnet Tetra**
Hemigrammus pulcher pulcher LADIGES, 1938

○
◑

Distribution: Peru, Brazil – Amazon River and its tributaries. Full length: 4.5 cm. Diet: live as well as artificial foods. Community tank. Breeding tank: with capacity of 6 litres per pair, spawning grid, dim light. Sexual dimorphism: the male's swim-bladder is pointed at the lower end, the female is larger, fuller, with swim-bladder rounded at the lower end. Sex ratio: 1:1. Breeding water: 26–28 °C; pH 6.5; dCH < 1°. Eggs: incubation period 24 hrs. Feeding of fry: nauplii of brine shrimp or *Cyclops* nauplii.

A prerequisite for successful breeding is the selection of suitable pairs. Many breeders advise keeping reliable pairs together, for not every male will spawn with every female. In 1961 Géry described the subspecies *Hemigrammus pulcher haraldi;* this, however, is apparently not kept in aquariums at all.

2 **German Flag Tetra**
Hemigrammus ulreyi (BOULENGER, 1895)
Syn. *Tetragonopterus ulreyi*

○
◑

Distribution: Paraguay River in South America. Full length: 5 cm. Diet: live as well as artificial foods. Community tank. Breeding tank: of 10-litre capacity with spawning grid, finely-leaved plants. Sexual dimorphism: the female is larger and fuller in the body. Sex ratio: 1:1. Breeding water: 24–26 °C; pH 6.0–6.5; dCH < 1° (or 0°); dGH < 10°. Eggs: incubation period?. Feeding of fry: brine shrimp nauplii (these figures are purely hypothetical inasmuch as to all appearances this species has not been propagated so far).

Peaceful school fish. It is recommended that they be kept in a light to sun-flooded, moderately planted, roomy tank with slight streaming of water. The fish should be kept in a large shoal. This species is imported only rarely, because the region of its occurrence is outside the usual hunting grounds. It is often confused with the species *Hyphessobrycon heterorhabdus* (Ulrey, 1895).

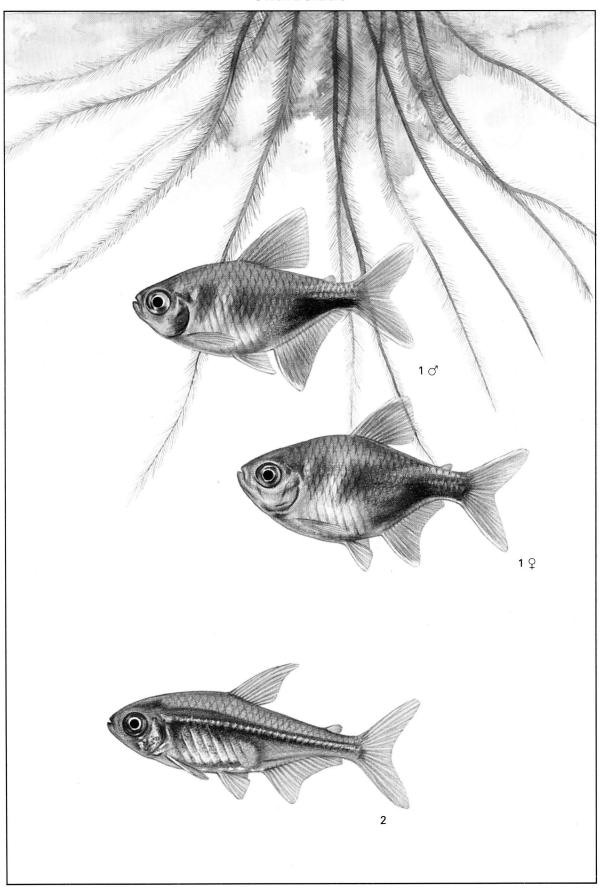

1 ♂

1 ♀

2

1 Red Tetra or Rummy-nosed Tetra
Hemigrammus rhodostomus AHL 1924

Distribution: Amazon delta. Full length: 4.5 cm. Diet: live as well as artificial foods. Community tank. Breeding tank: of 50- to 100-litre capacity with spawning grid; put the plant *Microsorium pteropus* inside. Sexual dimorphism: the male is smaller, more slender, with smaller ventral fins. Sex ratio: 1:1; set up several pairs together. Breeding water: 26 °C; pH 6.5; dCH < 0.5°. Eggs: ∅ 0.98 mm, incubation period 15 hrs. Feeding of fry: first eight days on infusoria (*Paramecium caudatum*) monoculture or rotatoria, then the finest nauplii of brine shrimp or *Cyclops* nauplii.

Long confused with the similar *Petitella georgiae,* which, however, was not described as a separate species until 1964. The visible differences are primarily in the shape of the body, the red colouring on the head (sometimes on the flanks), the markings at the base of the caudal fin, on the caudal fin itself, and on the anal fin. Compared with *P. georgiae, H. rhodostomus* is smaller, more slender, more shy, and little inclined to spawn. The fish spawn in the early morning while it is still dark. Spawning is triggered by a high daytime temperature (30 °C) followed by gradual cooling of the water during the night to approximately 26 °C. During spawning the female lays up to 200 eggs. The eleutherembryos are 2.7 mm long and adhere to firm objects by means of a sticky secretion produced by glands on top of the head. After four days they switch to exogenous nutrition. Harder water should be gradually added as the young fish grow and as soon as black-and-white markings appear on the caudal fin they should be moved to a larger tank. Young fish are shy and sensitive to increased concentrations of nitrates and nitrites. Growth is relatively rapid and sexual maturity is reached at the age of six months.

2 Red-headed Tetra
Petitella georgiae GÉRY et BOUTIERE, 1964

Distribution: Peru — Huallaga River, upper Amazon River above Leticia, Marañón River. Full length: male 5 cm, female 6 cm. Diet: live as well as artificial foods. Community tank. Breeding tank: of 20- to 50-litre capacity with spawning grid; put a young plant of *Microsorium pteropus* inside. Sexual dimorphism: the male is smaller, more slender. Sex ratio: 1:1, set up several pairs. Breeding water: 26 °C; pH 6.5; dCH < 0.5°. Eggs: incubation period 24 hrs. Feeding of fry: first eight days on infusoria (*Paramecium caudatum*) monoculture or rotatoria, later the finest nauplii of brine shrimp or *Cyclops* nauplii.

Often confused with *Hemigrammus rhodostomus. P. georgiae* is more robust and the red colour on the head extends only to the gill covers (in *H. rhodostomus* the red colour extends from the head along the lateral line practically half the length of the body). There is a black mark above at the base of the caudal fin whereas in *H. rhodostomus* there are two such marks at the base of the caudal fin — one above and one below. There is also a difference in the length of the incubation period. Unlike *H. rhodostomus, P. georgiae* spawns in full daylight, during the morning hours. Further care is the same as for *H. rhodostomus.*

1

2 ♂

2 ♀

1 Silver-tipped Tetra
Hasemania nana (LÜTKEN, 1874)
Syn. *Hasemania marginata, Hemigrammus nanus*

Distribution: São Francisco basin in east Brazil, north of the city of Bahia, and in the Purus River in west Brazil, in small to smallest streams with white or black water. Full length: 5 cm. Diet: live as well as artificial foods. Community tank. Breeding tank: of 3- to 6-litre capacity with spawning grid, finely-leaved plants, dim light. Sexual dimorphism: the male is more slender, smaller, a deep copper colour and with anal fin tipped silvery-white; the female is yellowish to olive green. Sex ratio: 1:1. Breeding water: 24 °C; pH 6.5; dCH max. 1°. Eggs: small, sticky, with glassy case and yolk coloured brownish to black; incubation period 24–36 hrs. Feeding of fry: on infusoria (*Paramecium caudatum*) mono-culture, rotatoria, finest *Cyclops* nauplii, after five days freshly hatched brine shrimp nauplii.

A species not firmly established systematically as yet. Unlike the genera *Hemigrammus* and *Hyphessobrycon*, fish of the genus *Hasemania* do not have an adipose fin (though the literature states that the adipose fin is present in some populations). Apart from the spawning period the fish are kept in the tank in a large shoal. The larvae become free-swimming five or six days after hatching. They are glassily translucent and hence readily escape notice after the yolk sac has been consumed. Their growth is rapid.

2 Silver Tetra
Ctenobrycon spilurus spilurus (CUVIER and VALENCIENNES, 1848)
Syn. *Tetragonopterus spilurus*

Distribution: northern South America from Surinam to Venezuela. Full length: 8 cm. Diet: live, artificial and plant foods. Community tank. Breeding tank: with capacity of 50 litres per pair, spawning grid and clumps of aquatic plants. Sexual dimorphism: the male is more colourful, the female is fuller in the body. Sex ratio: 1:1. Breeding water: 24–26 °C; pH 6.5–7.0; dCH up to 2°. Eggs: incubation period 24 hrs./26 °C. Feeding of fry: nauplii of brine shrimp or *Cyclops* nauplii, after 14 days provide plant food.

The equally large subspecies *Ctenobrycon spilurus hauxwellianus* (Cuvier, 1870), found in the Amazon River, has the same requirements. These are hardy and prolific fish. Following vigorous mating games the fish spawn amidst the plant thickets. During spawning the female deposits up to 2,000 eggs. The young fish grow rapidly and must therefore be moved to roomy nursery tanks in time.

1 ♂

1 ♀

2

1 Black Neon Tetra
Hyphessobrycon herbertaxelrodi GÉRY, 1961 Characidae

Distribution: Brazil, Tacuarí River (tributary of the Paraná River) in Mato Grosso state. Length: 4 cm. Diet: live as well as artificial foods. Community tank. Breeding tank: of 10-litre capacity with spawning grid, lighting markedly dim, finely-leaved plants. Sexual dimorphism: the male is more slender and smaller. Sex ratio: 1:1. Breeding water: 26 °C; pH 6.5; dCH 0°. Eggs: small, glassy, incubation period 18 hrs. Feeding of fry: first three days on infusoria (*Paramecium caudatum*) monoculture or the finest, freshly hatched brine shrimp nauplii.

The fish reach sexual maturity at the age of eight months; before spawning the males and females should be separated for 14 days. The temperature of the water should be kept at 20–22 °C. Ripe females are not strikingly plump. Breeding pairs ere very shy and reluctant to spawn in the new environment; spawning takes place after three to seven days. The fifth day after hatching the fry switch to normal nutrition. Their growth is rapid.

2 Flag Tetra
Hyphessobrycon heterorhabdus (ULREY, 1895)
Syn. *Tetragonopterus heterorhabdus, T. ulrey* (not Boulenger), *Hemigrammus heterorhabdus* Characidae

Distribution: Brazil, Tocantins River in Amazonas state. Full length: 5 cm. Diet: live as well as artificial foods. Community tank. Breeding tank: of 10-litre capacity with spawning grid. Sexual dimorphism: the female is larger and fuller in the body. Sex ratio: 1:1. Breeding water: 24–26 °C; pH 6.0–6.5; dCH < 1°; filter water through peat or add peat extract. Eggs: incubation period 24 hrs. Feeding of fry: nauplii of brine shrimp or *Cyclops* nauplii.

A peaceful shoal fish. Colouring closely resembles that of *Hemigrammus ulreyi*, which, however, is deeper in the body. Before spawning the males should be separated from the females for about 14 days. The fish are not very prolific. In larger tanks the fish may be put to spawn in a smaller or larger group. Rearing is simple and the procedure is the same as for a great many small tetras.

3 Blue Neon Tetra
Hyphessobrycon simulans GÉRY, 1963 Characidae

Distribution: Lufaris River and Negro River basin in Brazil. Full length: 2–3 cm. Diet: live as well as artificial foods. Community tank (with other small tetras). Breeding tank: of 20- to 50-litre capacity with spawning grid, lighting dim. Sexual dimorphism: the female is larger and fuller. Sex ratio: 1:1. Put a large shoal of fish in the tank for spawning. Breeding water: 24–26 °C; pH 5.5–6.0; dCH 0°; dGH < 10°; filter water through peat or add peat extract (the fish are very sensitive to the concentration of nitrates in the water). Eggs: incubation period 24 hrs. Feeding of fry: first three to four days on infusoria (*Paramecium caudatum*) monoculture, *Cyclops* nauplii or the finest brine shrimp nauplii.

The fish greatly resembles *Paracheirodon innesi* but is distinguished by a neon stripe along the sides extending from the upper jaw across the eye to the base of the caudal fin; the red colour below the stripe is paler.

Characidae

1

2 ♂

2 ♀

3

61

1 Lemon Tetra
Hyphessobrycon pulchripinnis AHL, 1937 Characidae

Distribution: Central Brazil – tributaries of the Tocantins River, in small streams with dense vegetation. Full length: 4.5 cm. Diet: live as well as artificial foods. Community tank. Breeding tank: of 6-litre capacity with spawning grid, finely-leaved plants. Sexual dimorphism: the male is slimmer, his dorsal and anal fin are a brilliant yellow edged with black. Sex ratio: 1:1. Breeding water: 26 °C; pH 6.5; dCH < 1°. Eggs: incubation period 24 hrs. Feeding of fry: nauplii of brine shrimp or *Cyclops* nauplii.

The frequent reluctance of the fish to spawn is caused by the slow attaining of sexual maturity by the females. This causes some difficulties in breeding. Before spawning the males and females should be separated for about 14 days and generously fed varied food, mainly mosquito and midge larvae, coarser *Cyclops*, etc. The pairs of fish should spawn within five days at the latest. Rising barometric pressure increases the chances of success. After spawning remove the parent fish and protect the eggs from strong light. As the fry grow condition them by slowly adding water used in the keeping tank and in due course transfer them to roomy tanks with a lowered water level. Raise the water level gradually as the fish grow. Adult fish are always kept in a small or large shoal.

2 *Hyphessobrycon pulchripinnis,* albino form Characidae

Albinism in fish is distinguished by a general loss of pigment cells not only in the skin but in the body organs as well; the eyes are red. The red colour of some parts of the body may be due to the dense underlying network of blood capillaries shining through the unpigmented skin.

3 Black-lined Tetra
Hyphessobrycon scholzei AHL, 1936 Characidae

Distribution: East Brazil and Paraguay. Full length: 5 cm. Diet: live as well as artificial foods, plant food as a supplement. Community tank (the fish damage finely-leaved plants). Breeding tank: of 10-litre capacity with spawning grid. Sexual dimorphism: the male is smaller, slimmer and has the caudal fin more deeply indented than the female. Sex ratio: 1:1 (may spawn in a shoal). Breeding water: 24–26 °C; pH 6.5–7.0; dCH 2°. Eggs: incubation period 24 hrs. Feeding of fry: nauplii of brine shrimp or *Cyclops* nauplii, good quality artificial food for fry.

A peaceful shoal fish, partly herbivorous. Rearing is simple and the procedure is the same as for *Hyphessobrycon flammeus.* The females are very prolific, each laying 800 to 1600 eggs during the spawning period. A roomy tank, lesser stock density, fresh water and ample food promote rapid growth of the young.

Characidae

1 ♂

1 ♀

2

3 ♂

3 ♀

1 Jewel Tetra

Hyphessobrycon callistus (BOULENGER, 1900)

Syn. *Tetragonopterus callistus, Hyphessobrycon melanopterus, Hemigrammus melanopterus*   Characidae

Distribution: lowland Amazon region, water systems of the Paraguay River. Full length: 4 cm. Diet: live as well as artificial foods. Community tank. Breeding tank: of 6- to 10-litre capacity with spawning grid, dim light, finely-leaved plants. Sexual dimorphism: the male is slimmer and coloured a vivid red. Sex ratio: 1:1. Breeding water: 24 °C; pH 6.5–7.0; dCH max. 2°. Eggs: minute, greyish, incubation period 24 hrs. Feeding of fry: nauplii of brine shrimp or *Cyclops* nauplii.

Prolific school fish. Young fish sometimes attack one another and tear each other's fins. The lengthy, unplanned hybridization of the so-called *'Callistus group'* produced whole generations of very similar and fertile hybrids. Today it cannot be said with certainty what is a pure-blood *H. callistus!* The matter is further complicated by the fact that the fish populations on the market are either from Asian breeding centres or home-bred specimens. That is why the present classification of these fish is so complicated. In 1954 Hoedeman proposed a great number of subspecies but as early as 1961 Géry considered this division into subspecies inadmissible because these species are similar only in external appearance and proposed establishing the so-called *'Callistus* group' embracing fish that are mutually related and similar. These include *H. callistus, H. serpae, H. minor, H. hasemani* and *H. haraldschultzi,* which readily interbreed in captivity as well as with *H. georgettae* and *H. takasei.* There are, however, misgivings as to the validity of the name *H. hasemani (nomen nudum)* and *H. minor* and *H. takasei* are species that are practically unknown.

2 Tetra Perez or Bleeding Heart Tetra

Hyphessobrycon erythrostigma (FOWLER, 1943)

Syn. *Hyphessobrycon callistus rubrostigma, H. rubrostigma*   Characidae

Distribution: Amazon basin, Colombia. Full length: 12 cm. Diet: live as well as artificial foods. Community tank. Breeding tank: of 50- to 100-litre capacity with spawning grid, clumps of plants, dim light. Sexual dimorphism: the male is bigger, his dorsal and anal fin are greatly extended and pointed. Sex ratio: 1:1. Breeding water: 26 °C; pH 6.5; dCH < 1°, filtered through peat. Eggs: incubation period 48 hrs. Feeding of fry: brine shrimp nauplii.

For a long time this fish was confused with the more frequently imported *H. socolofi,* described by the American ichthyologist S. H. Weitzman in 1977. Reports of its successful breeding are few. According to M. Reed brood fish feed on brine shrimp and the fry of *Poecilia reticulata.* They should be put in a large tank with thick clumps of plants in the corners. Spawning takes place in these clumps. The female deposits 20 to 30 eggs during each act of mating. The fry hatch in three days and switch over to exogenous nutrition on the fourth day. The first month their growth is rapid but then it slows.

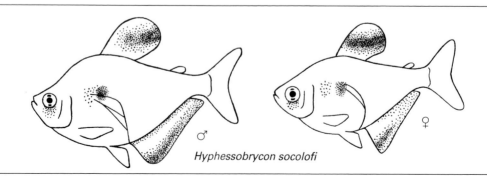

Hyphessobrycon socolofi

1 ♀

1 ♂

2 ♂

2 ♀

1 Pink Jewel Tetra or Unspotted Jewel Tetra
Hyphessobrycon bentosi bentosi DURBIN, 1908

Syn. *Hyphessobrycon ornatus, H. callistus bentosi*

Distribution: Guyana, Brazil – lower reaches of the Amazon. Full length: 6 cm. Diet: live as well as artificial foods. Community tank. Breeding tank: with capacity of 6 litres per pair, spawning grid, finely-leaved plants (Java moss). Sexual dimorphism: the male is larger, his dorsal and anal fins are longer and extended into a point. Sex ratio: 1:1. Breeding water: 26 °C; pH 6.8; dCH < 1°. Eggs: ∅ 0.8 mm, the colour of tea, incubation period 24 hrs. Feeding of fry: nauplii of brine shrimp or *Cyclops* nauplii.

The parent fish often refuse to spawn even though the females are ripe to spawn and filled with so many eggs that the belly is enormously distended. The fish are very sensitive to atmospheric pressure and generally begin spawning when a lengthy period of high pressure is followed by a slow, gradual drop in pressure. A count taken at the complete end of spawning showed that one female produced 1,200 eggs. The little-developed eleutherembryos attach themselves by a fine filament to a firm object or rest on the bottom. The young fish grow very rapidly if provided regularly with ample food, and in three months it is already possible to distinguish the first males.

2 Georgetta's Tetra
Hyphessobrycon georgettae GÉRY, 1961

Distribution: Surinam, near the Brazilian border, in small, densely overgrown waters; it is never found in open waters. Full length: imported fish – 4 cm, aquarium fish – male 2 cm, female 2.5–3 cm. Diet: live as well as artificial foods. Community tank (only together with small species of fish). Breeding tank: of 6-litre capacity with spawning grid, finely-leaved plants. Sexual dimorphism: the male is smaller with anal fin conspicuously edged with white, the female is fuller in the body. Sex ratio: 1:1. Breeding water: 25 °C; pH 6.5; dCH < 1°. Eggs: large in proportion to the size of the fish, incubation period 18–24 hrs. Feeding of fry: nauplii of brine shrimp or *Cyclops* nauplii.

Adult fish may be kept together with other fish in a mixed aquarium but do best if kept in a small shoal with others of the same species, which makes their full colours show to advantage. The fish are shy. If the brood fish are ripe they usually spawn within two days after being placed in the breeding tank. The female deposits more than 100 eggs. The fry become free-swimming five days after hatching and if fed regularly their growth is uniform and rapid. At the age of three weeks the young acquire the same body colours as the adults and sexual maturity is attained at the age of three months. The fish are susceptible to some diseases and are relatively short-lived.

Characidae

1 ♀

1 ♂

2

1 Flame Tetra, Red Tetra or Tetra from Rio
Hyphessobrycon flammeus MYERS, 1924
Syn. *Hyphessobrycon bifasciatus* (not Ellis, 1911)

○ Distribution: eastern Brazil in the vicinity of Rio
◑ de Janeiro. Full length: 4 cm. Diet: live as well as artificial foods. Community tank. Breeding tank: with capacity of 6 litres per pair, spawning grid, finely-leaved plants, dim light. Sexual dimorphism: the male is slimmer, his ventral and anal fins are blood-red, the anal fin edged with black. Sex ratio: 1:1. Breeding water: 24 °C; pH 6.5—7.0; dCH max. 2°. Eggs: small, adhesive, incubation period 24 hrs. Feeding of fry: nauplii of brine shrimp or *Cyclops* nauplii.

The males and females should be separated for about one week before spawning. Spawning takes place in the afternoon till evening. Healthy, mature fish are nearly always willing to spawn. The free-swimming fry are timid and prefer to remain hidden. The water level should be lower while they are growing. The fish should always be kept in a large shoal.

2 Red Gold Dot Tetra or Griem's Tetra
Hyphessobrycon griemi HOEDEMAN, 1957

○ Distribution: in the vicinity of the city of Goiás,
◑ west of Brasilia. Full length: 3—5.5 cm. Diet: live as well as artificial foods. Community tank. Breeding tank: of 3- to 6-litre capacity with spawning grid. Sexual dimorphism: the male's anal fin is blood-red edged with white, the female's is paler. Sex ratio: 1:1. Breeding water: 24—26 °C; pH 6.5—7.0; dCH 2°. Eggs: incubation period 24 hrs? Feeding of fry: the first three days

Paramecium caudatum or the finest *Cyclops* nauplii, then brine shrimp.

The males and females should be separated for about 14 days before spawning. One female deposits 200 or more eggs during spawning. Rearing is the same as for the very similar species *H. flammeus.*

3 Yellow Tetra
Hyphessobrycon bifasciatus ELLIS, 1911

○ Distribution: coastal region of southeastern
◑ Brazil. Full length: 5 cm. Diet: live as well as artificial foods. Community tank. Breeding tank: of 10-litre capacity with spawning grid, finely-leaved plants. Sexual dimorphism: the ventral and anal fins of the male are yellowish with a narrow dark border. The male's anal fin is longer and straight the entire length, the female's is transparent and indented, concave. Sex ratio: 1:1. Breeding water: 24 °C; pH 6.5—7.5; dCH max. 3°. Eggs: non-adhesive, small, glassy, incubation period 26—30 hrs. Feeding of fry: nauplii of brine shrimp or *Cyclops* nauplii.

Hardy school fish, bellicose towards others of the same species. The free-swimming larvae are shy and keep hidden. At the age of ten weeks the young fish acquire the juvenile coloration with reddish dorsal, anal and caudal fins. At three months this red colouring disappears. Many specimens collected in their native waters are an attractive silvery colour. In the first generation of aquarium offspring, however, this colouring is absent.

Characidae

1 ♂

1 ♀

2

3

1 Coffee Bean Tetra
Hyphessobrycon takasei GÉRY, 1964

Distribution: Amazon delta, northwest of the town of Macapá. Full length: 4 cm. Diet: live as well as artificial foods. Community tank. Breeding tank: of 6- to 10-litre capacity with spawning grid, dim light. Sexual dimorphism: secondary characteristics are not known. Sex ratio: 1:1. Breeding water: 24–26 °C; pH 6.0–6.5; dCH < 1°; dGH < 10°; peat filter. There is no record of these fish having been bred in captivity and therefore these values must be viewed as hypothetical.

In contour this fish resembles *H. callistus* but the body is more elongated. Typical of this species is the large, dark, coffee-bean-shaped spot on the sides. *H. takasei* is little kept by aquarists.

2 Callistus Tetra
Hyphessobrycon copelandi DURBIN, 1909
Syn. *Hyphessobrycon callistus copelandi*

Distribution: upper and middle reaches of the Amazon (vicinity of Tabatinga). Full length: 5 cm. Diet: live as well as artificial foods. Community tank. Breeding tank: of 10- to 20-litre capacity with spawning grid, finely-leaved plants. Sexual dimorphism: the male's dorsal fin is longer, the female is fuller in the body. Sex ratio: 1:1. Breeding water: 24–26 °C; pH 6.5–7.0; dCH < 2°; dGH max. 10°. Eggs: small, yellowish, incubation period 24 hrs./26 °C. Feeding of fry: nauplii of brine shrimp or *Cyclops* nauplii.

The parent fish spawn amidst finely-leaved plants near the bottom, generally in the evening. The female deposits several hundred eggs. The fry become free-swimming five days after hatching. They are 3 mm long, very shy, and readily escape notice. Their growth is rapid. At the age of three weeks the young fish are 1 cm long and resemble the adult fish both in shape and coloration.

3 Peruvian Tetra
Hyphessobrycon peruvianus LADIGES, 1938

Distribution: water system in the vicinity of the city of Iquitos in northeastern Peru. Full length: 4 cm. Diet: live as well as artificial foods. Community tank, only together with peaceful, small species of fish. Breeding tank: of 5- to 10-litre capacity with spawning grid, finely-leaved plants, dim light. Sexual dimorphism: the male is more slender. Sexual ratio: 1:1. Breeding water: 24–26 °C; pH 6.0–6.5; dCH max. 0.5°; dGH < 10°; filtered through peat (these values must be viewed as hypothetical for there are no records of breeding this fish in captivity).

A peaceful, shy, school fish. In 1961 Géry differentiated the following two species: *Hyphessobrycon peruvianus* and *H. metae* Eigenmann and Henn, 1914. The two had been sold under the single commercial name 'Hemigrammus niger'. Both resemble *Hyphessobrycon loretoensis* Ladiges, 1938.

Characidae

1 *Hyphessobrycon metae* EIGENMANN and HENN, 1914

Distribution: region of the Meta River in eastern Colombia. Full length: 4.5 cm. Diet: live as well as artificial foods. Community tank. Breeding tank: of 6- to 10-litre capacity with spawning grid, finely-leaved plants, dim lighting. Sexual dimorphism: the male is slimmer, the female fuller in the body. Sex ratio: 1:1. Breeding water: 24–26 °C; pH 6.0–6.5; dCH < 1° (0°); dGH < 10°; filtered through peat? Eggs: incubation period? Feeding of fry: *Paramecium caudatum*, later brine shrimp nauplii? (data with ? must be viewed as hypothetical because there is no record that this species has been bred in captivity and it is quite possible that this fish, unknown to most breeders, has never even been propagated).

In the past this species was often confused with *H. loretoensis*. According to Géry there are differences between the two species but these are not explained in the available literature. All we know is that *H. metae* has a more greatly compressed body than *H. loretoensis* and different markings on the gill covers (see *H. loretoensis*).

2 **Tetra Loreto**
Hyphessobrycon loretoensis LADIGES, 1938

Distribution: Meta River in Colombia and the Loreto region in the Peruvian section of the Amazon region. Full length: 4 cm. Diet: live as well as artificial foods. Community tank. Breeding tank: of 6- to 10-litre capacity with spawning grid, finely-leaved plants, dim lighting. Sexual dimorphism: the female fuller in the body. Sex ratio: 1:1. Breeding water: 24–26 °C; pH 6.0–6.5; dCH < 1° (0°); dGH < 10°; filtered through peat (hypothetical data). Eggs: incubation period? Feeding of fry: *Paramecium caudatum* – brine shrimp nauplii? (hypothetical data).

School fish readily confused with *H. peruvianus* and *H. metae* from which they differ by having a bright orange-red caudal fin and different markings on the gill covers. The gill covers of *H. peruvianus* are practically without pigmentation, *H. loretoensis* has a dark spot on the gill covers, those of *H. metae* are almost dark (continuation of the blackish longitudinal band). According to Géry *Hyphessobrycon peruvianus* belongs rather in the genus *Hemigrammus*. Géry further points out the close kinship of *Hyphessobrycon loretoensis* to *H. metae* and *H. herbertaxelrodi*.

H. loretoensis is a delicate species.

Characidae

1 Black Phantom Tetra
Megalamphodus megalopterus Eigenmann, 1915

Characidae

Distribution: Southwest Brazil – Gauporé River (Madeira River system), Iten River in central Brazil. Full length: 4.5 cm. Diet: live as well as artificial foods. Community tank. Breeding tank: of 6-litre capacity with spawning grid, greatly shaded. Sexual dimorphism: the male is a smoky grey with larger dorsal and anal fin; in the female the ventral fins, anal fin and adipose fin are coloured red. Sex ratio: 1:1. Breeding water: 26 °C; pH 6.0; dCH 1°; filtered through peat. Eggs: brownish-red, incubation period 24 hrs. Feeding of fry: finest nauplii of brine shrimp or *Cyclops.*

The female lays approximately 200 eggs. They rest on the bottom at first and later hang suspended close to the water's surface. On the sixth day the fry become free-swimming, generally keeping out of sight amongst the plants. Slowly add harder water and after 14 days move the young fish to a larger tank. The fry grow very slowly and should be given dust food for at least five weeks.

2 Red Phantom Tetra
Megalamphodus sweglesi Géry, 1961

Characidae

Distribution: Upper Orinoco basin, Muco and Meta rivers – Colombia, Venezuela. Full length: 4 cm. Diet: live as well as artificial foods. Community tank. Breeding tank: of 6-litre capacity with spawning grid, dim light. Sexual dimorphism: the male has a prolonged, red dorsal fin, the female has a shorter dorsal fin coloured red, black and white. Sex ratio: 1:1. Breeding water: 24 °C; pH 6.0; dCH < 1° + peat extract (till water is the colour of amber). Eggs: brownish-red, incubation period 24 hrs. Feeding of fry: nauplii of brine shrimp or *Cyclops* nauplii.

Breeding is difficult. The brood fish often refuse to spawn, the eggs become overly ripe and incapable of being fertilized. Even pairs that spawn normally suddenly cease to do so or have a very long interval. The female lays more than 300 eggs. The fry grow rapidly at first but later growth becomes slower.

3 Rainbow Tetra
Nematobrycon lacortei Weitzman and Fink, 1971
Syn. *Nematobrycon amphiloxus*

Characidae

Distribution: Atrato River in west Colombia. Full length: 6 cm. Diet: live as well as artificial foods. Community tank. Breeding tank: of 10- to 50-litre capacity with spawning grid; put a tuft of Java moss inside. Sexual dimorphism: the male has a longer dorsal fin. Sex ratio: 1:1. Breeding water: 24–26 °C; pH 7.0–7.5; dCH < 2°; dGH < 10°. Eggs: incubation period 24 hrs. Feeding of fry: brine shrimp nauplii.

The breeding of *N. lacortei,* though not on record, can be presumed to be the same as for *N. palmeri.* The two species are quite similar. Both do not have an adipose fin. According to Géry they differ in the number of fin rays, teeth, and coloration. *N. lacortei* and *N. palmeri* interbreed but it is not known whether the offspring are fertile. The two do not occur together in the wild.

1 Emperor Tetra
Nematobrycon palmeri EIGENMANN, 1911

Distribution: West Colombia, San Juan River system. Full length: 5.5 cm. Diet: live as well as artificial foods. Community tank. Breeding tank: 10 litres per pair (for several pairs 50 or more litres), with spawning grid, dim light, clumps of aquatic plants. Sexual dimorphism: the male has a longer, pointed dorsal fin, larger ventral fin, anal fin of greater area with straight lower edge, and caudal fin with the rays on the margin of the upper and lower lobe and in the centre, giving it a trident-like appearance; the female is smaller, fuller in the body. Sex ratio: 1:1, preferably a greater number of fish with slight preponderance of females. Breeding water: 24–26 °C; pH 7.0–7.5; dCH 2°. Eggs: incubation period 24 hrs. Feeding of fry: brine shrimp nauplii.

The females of *N. palmeri* have a low reproductive capacity. Successful breeding depends on the selection of suitable males. Before spawning the males should be separated from the females for about 14 days. Water taken from the normal keeping tank has proved favourable for the development of eggs. In excessively acidic and soft water a large percentage of the larvae suffer constitutional dropsy and die. If the tank is roomy and well planted several generations of young fish may develop there in the company of the parent fish. Based on the studies of Dr. Weitzman and Dr. Fink a new subspecies *Nematobrycon palmeri amphiloxus* was established in 1971.

Picture 1a shows the natural colour variety of *N. palmeri.*

2 Blue Emperor
Inpaichthys kerri GÉRY and JUNK, 1977

Distribution: Brazil – Aripuaná River in northern Mato Grosso. Full length: 5 cm. Diet: live as well as artificial foods. Community tank. Breeding tank: of 3- to 6-litre capacity, with spawning grid, dim lighting, finely-leaved plants. Sexual dimorphism: the male is azure blue, his adipose fin a lustrous pale blue, the ventral fins larger, the anal fin elongated with rounded tips; the female is smaller, yellow-brown with a broad brown band running the length of the body on the sides, the adipose fin is orange to red, the anal fin has sharp tips. Sex ratio: 1:1. Breeding water: 23–27 °C; pH 6.5; dCH < 1°; dGH 10°; add peat extract. Eggs: ∅ 0.95 mm, incubation period 30–36 hrs/23–24 °C, 18 hrs/26–27 °C. Feeding of fry: freshly hatched brine shrimp nauplii. In naming the fish Dr. J. Géry and Dr. W. J. Junk

used a new generic as well as a new specific name. The generic name was derived from the abbreviation for the 'Instituto Nacional para Amazonas' (INPA) and the specific name is in honour of Dr. Kerr, Director of the Institute.

When the females reach a length of 2 cm the eggs are already ripe; 50 or so are deposited at first, but larger and older females may lay as many as 350. The eleutherembryos are very small, measuring only 1.7 mm. In four to five days they reach a length of 3.2 mm, become free-swimming and begin to feed on minute dust food. The fry are wary, staying close to the bottom and readily escaping notice. Growth is very slow even when they are well fed.

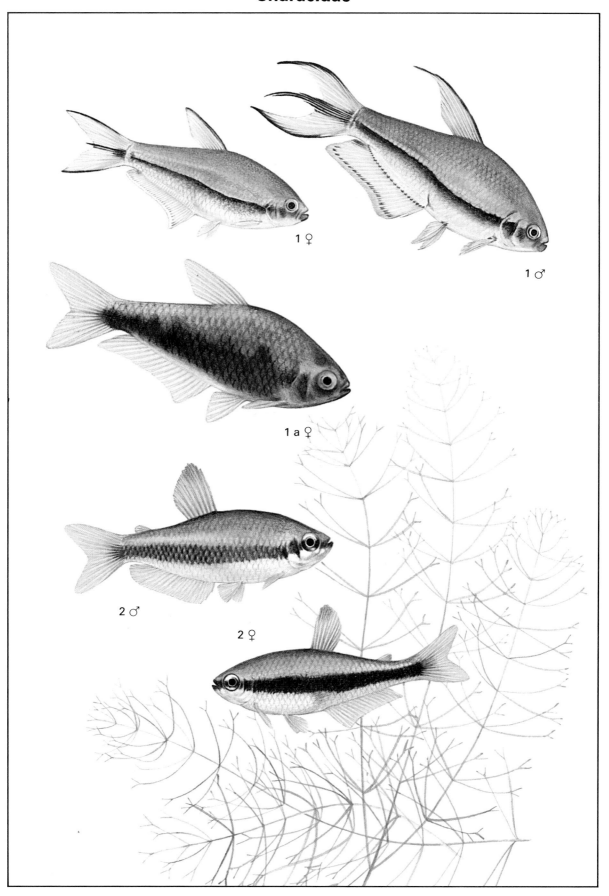

1 ♀

1 ♂

1 a ♀

2 ♂

2 ♀

1 Black Tetra or Blackamoor
Gymnocorymbus ternetzi (BOULENGER, 1895)
Syn. Tetragonopterus ternetzi, Moenkhausia ternetzi

Distribution: Colombia, Brazil — Paraguay and Gauporé rivers. Full length: female 5 cm, the male is smaller. Diet: live as well as artificial foods. Community tank. Breeding tank: of 50-litre capacity with spawning grid. Sexual dimorphism: the male is smaller and black, the female is silvery with a smoky tinge. Sex ratio: 1:1; in individual pairs or in a group. Breeding water: 24 °C; pH 6.5—7.0; dCH < 2°. Eggs: incubation period 20—24 hrs. Feeding of fry: nauplii of brine shrimp or Cyclops.

In the wild these fish inhabit white water clouded green with unicellular algae and exposed to dispersed light. In captivity the fish are set up to spawn in a few pairs or as many as several dozens of pairs in 50- to 200-litre tanks. Regular spawning of the fish makes the females more prolific. After spawning remove the parent fish and lower the water column to 10 cm. In this manner it is possible to rear many thousands of young fish providing the fry are given sufficient amounts of live dust food, chiefly brine shrimp. The juvenile coloration of the young is a deep black; their growth is rapid.

2 Gymnocorymbus ternetzi — veil-finned form

The veil-finned form is a cultivated form bred and genetically fixed in captivity.

3 Bucktoothed Tetra
Exodon paradoxus (MÜLLER and TROSCHEL, 1845)
Syn. Epicyrtus exodon, E. paradoxus, Hystricodon paradoxus

Distribution: Brazil, Guyana — Madeira, Marmelo, Branco and Rupunni Rivers. Full length: 15 cm. Diet: live foods (fish, coarse zooplankton, insect larvae, small snails, tubifex); will eat also granulated and flaked foods. Monospecies keeping tank with capacity of 200 litres or more, well covered. Breeding tank: with capacity of 200 litres or more and thickets of finely-leaved plants. Sexual dimorphism: the female fuller in the belly region. Sex ratio: 1:1 (a single pair or group). Breeding water: 24—28 °C; pH 5.5—6.5; dGH max. 1°; dCH max. 10°; filtered through peat. Eggs: incubation period 25—30 hrs/26—28 °C. Feeding of fry: nauplii of brine shrimp or Cyclops, later sieved zooplankton and

chopped tubifex. Hungry fry become cannibalistic.

Aggressive fish that bite both fish of their own kind as well as other species. They are capable of biting out the victim's scales as well as muscular tissue. In view of their mutual aggression young fish are hard to rear and therefore the stock density in the tank must be low. The fish are rapid swimmers and excellent jumpers. The young are more colourful than the adults. For the fish to attain sexual maturity they require ample space, fresh, clean water and ample food. This species is closely related to members of the genus Roeboides.

1 ♀

1 ♂

2 ♀

3

1 Diamond Tetra
Moenkhausia pittieri EIGENMANN, 1920

○
◑

Distribution: Venezuela – Lake Valencia and nearby rivers (Bue, Tiquirito). Full length: 6 cm. Diet: live as well as artificial foods. Community tank. Breeding tank: of 6- to 10-litre capacity with spawning grid, dim light. Sexual dimorphism: the male has much larger fins, the dorsal fin is elongated, sickle-shaped. Sex ratio: 1:1. Breeding water: 26 °C; pH 6.5–7.0; dCH max 2°. Eggs: yellowish, incubation period 30 hrs. Feeding of fry: nauplii of brine shrimp and *Cyclops.*

A shoal fish that loses its shyness if kept with other Tetras. Following vigorous mating games the fish spawn amidst plants as well as in open water. At each mating the female releases approximately 300 eggs. Four days after hatching the larvae become free-swimming and begin to take dust food. They are very shy and their growth is slow.

2 Red-eyed Moenkhausia
Moenkhausia sanctaefilomenae (STEINDACHNER, 1907)
Syn. *Tetragonopterus sanctaefilomenae, Poecilurichthys agassizi, Moenkhausia agassizi, M. australis, M. filomenae*

○
◑

Distribution: Brazil, Paraguay, Argentina – Paraguay, Paranaíba, Paraná rivers. Full length: 7 cm. Diet: live as well as artificial foods. Community tank. Breeding tank: of 6- to 10-litre capacity with spawning grid, finely-leaved plants. Sexual dimorphism: the female is fuller in the body. Sex ratio: 1:1. Breeding water: 24 °C; pH 6.0–7.0; dCH < 1°. Eggs: incubation period 24 hrs. Feeding of fry: on infusoria (*Paramecium caudatum*) monoculture, after four to five days finest brine shrimp or *Cyclops.*

The name *Moenkhausia* was given the genus in 1903 by Eigenmann in honour of Professor William J. Moenkhaus of the Paulista Museum in São Paulo, Brazil.

Before spawning the males and females are separated for about 14 days and generously fed. The fish are very prolific. The fry are very small and the young fish grow slowly even when fed painstakingly.

1 ♂

1 ♀

2 ♂

2 ♀

1 Neon Tetra
Paracheirodon innesi (MYERS, 1936)
Syn. *Hyphessobrycon innesi*

Distribution: Brazil, Colombia, Peru — rivers: Putumayo, Purus, upper Amazon, Igarapé, Préto (black waters). Full length: 4 cm. Diet: live as well as artificial foods. Community tank. Breeding tank: of 6-litre capacity with spawning grid, finely-leaved plants, dim light. Sexual dimorphism: the female is fuller in the belly region. Sex ratio: 1:1. Breeding water: 23—24 °C; pH 6.2—6.5; dCH 0°; with added peat extract. Eggs: incubation period 24 hrs. Feeding of fry: nauplii of brine shrimp or *Cyclops* nauplii.

Singapore is currently the greatest supplier of these fish to the market, with 95 per cent of the world production. Before putting brood fish to spawn keep the males and females separate for 14 days in cooler water (19 to 21 °C). A fully mature female may lay about 300 eggs during spawning. The tank should be well darkened for the development of the eggs. The eleutherembryos are sensitive to light (photophobic). The young fish are acclimatized to water of different chemical composition by gradually and regularly adding water from the normal keeping tank. During the long time they have been reared in captivity the fish have become fully acclimatized and their breeding poses no difficulties; they may have also become resistant to the previously devastating disease caused by the parasite *Plistophora*.

2 Scarlet Characin or Cardinal Tetra
Cheirodon axelrodi SCHULTZ, 1956
Syn. *Hyphessobrycon cardinalis, Lamprocheirodon axelrodi*

Distribution: Upper reaches of the Negro River (Brazil) and some tributaries of the Orinoco (Venezuela), in greatly shaded and hard to reach places. Full length: 5 cm. Diet: live as well as artificial foods. Community tank with dark bottom, dim light. Breeding tank: of 10-litre capacity with spawning grid. Sexual dimorphism: the male is slimmer, smaller, the female more robust with markedly convex belly region. Sex ratio: 1:1. Breeding water: 24—28 °C; pH 5.0—5.5; dCH 0°; dGH < 5°; with addition of peat extract. Eggs: $\emptyset$ circa 0.8 mm, incubation period 18—20 hrs/27—28 °C. Feeding of fry: nauplii of freshly hatched brine shrimp for about six weeks, after which they are fed finely chopped tubifex.

During the long summer days the fish spawn only rarely. The main spawning period is October to April. The set-up pairs generally do not spawn until several days after being placed in the breeding tank, usually before daybreak, often in the evening hours. Spawning is triggered by a gradual rise in atmospheric pressure. The female may lay as many as 500 eggs. The eggs develop in very dim light (tanks should be well shaded). The eleutherembryos are sensitive to light. The free-swimming fry remain near the bottom, are shy and readily escape notice. As the young fish grow water from the tank in which adult fish are kept should be gradually added to condition them for the different environment to which they will later be transferred. When they are 1 cm long the young fish are fed chopped tubifex after which they grow rapidly. Most fish supplied to the market were freshly caught in Brazil. In recent years, however, catching them in the wild has been greatly restricted.

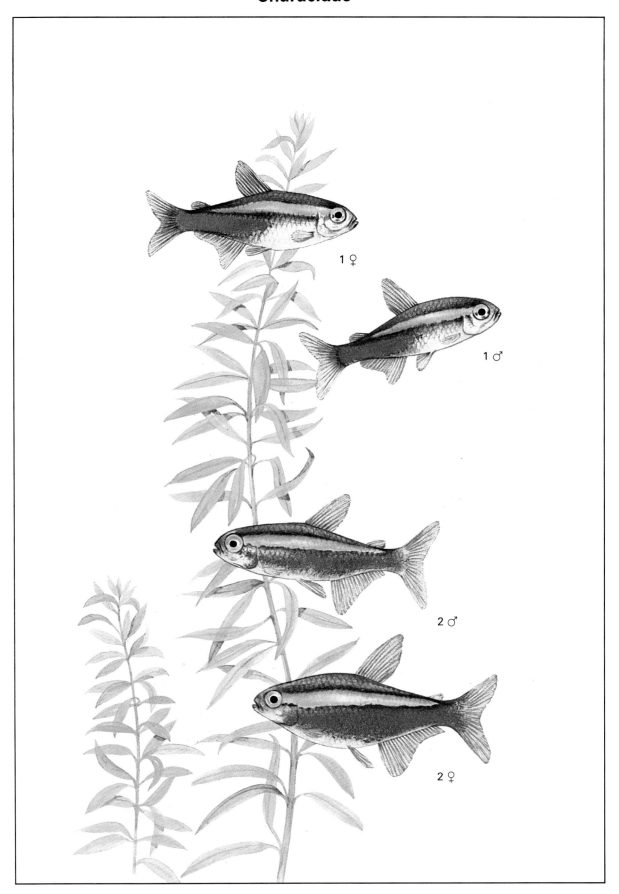

1 ♀

1 ♂

2 ♂

2 ♀

1 *Roeboides caucae* EIGENMANN, 1922

◁
●
Distribution: Cauca River, Colombia. Full length: 6 cm. Diet: live foods including small fish. Mono-species keeping tank. Breeding tank: of 20-litre capacity with spawning grid, finely-leaved plants. Sexual dimorphism: the male is more elongated, slimmer, the female more robust with higher dorsal contour. Sex ratio: 1:1. Breeding water: 24–26 °C; pH 6.5–7.0; dCH < 2°; dGH < 10°. Eggs: incubation period 24–48 hrs. Feeding of fry: brine shrimp nauplii, later sieved plankton. The fry must be continually well fed (satiated) otherwise they become cannibalistic.

A predatory, rapacious fish. Attacks other species of fish, even in transportation bags; it eats pieces of fin and scales.

2 *Roeboides microlepis* (REINHARDT, 1849)
Syn. *Epicyrtus microlepis, Anacyrtus microlepis, Cynopotamus microlepis*

◁
●
Distribution: Venezuela, Paraguay. Full length: 10 cm. Diet: live foods including small fish. Monospecies keeping tank, elongate, not too densely planted. Breeding tank: 50 litres per pair, with spawning grid, finely-leaved plants. Sexual dimorphism: the male is more slender with broader anal fin and throat coloured orange-red during the spawning period; the female has a higher dorsal contour. Sex ratio: 1:1. Breeding water: 24–26 °C; pH 6.5–7.0; dCH < 2°; dGH < 10°; filtered through peat. Eggs: clear, small, incubation period 18–24 hrs. Feeding of fry: brine shrimp nauplii.

Typical of these fish is their manner of swimming with head slightly tilted downward. Pairs spawn with the onset of dusk. The females lay several hundred eggs. Endogenous nutrition ends after five days.

3 Penguin Fish
Thayeria obliqua EIGENMANN, 1908
According to Géry the synonym is probably the species *Thayeria santamarie* Ladiges, 1951, found in the Brazilian state Goyaz.

○
◑
Distribution: Brazil – Guaporé (Mamoré) Madeira river system, Araguaia River. Full length: 8 cm. Diet: live as well as artificial foods. Community tank. Sexual dimorphism: the male is larger and fuller.

T. obliqua is distinguished from *T. boehlkei* by the length of the dark band. In *T. obliqua* it runs from the lower tip of the forked caudal fin and disappears at the level of the adipose fin, whereas in *T. boehlkei* it extends to the gill covers.

4 Hockey-stick Tesas or Blackline Thayeria
Thayeria boehlkei WEITZMAN, 1957
Up to 1958 confused with *Thayeria obliqua*.

○
◑
Distribution: Brazil, Peru. Full length: 6 cm. Diet: live as well as artificial foods. Community tank. Breeding tank: at least of 10-litre capacity with spawning grid. The male is smaller, slimmer, the female fuller in the body. Apart from the spawning period there is practically no difference between the sexes. Sex ratio: 1 male: 3 females. Breeding water: fresh, 26 °C; pH 7.0–7.5; dCH < 1°; dGH < 10°. Eggs: small, brown, incubation period 12 hrs. Feeding of fry: first five days *Paramecium caudatum,* then brine shrimp nauplii.

Shoal fish sensitive to increased concentration of nitrates and nitrites. It is recommended that brood fish are kept in well-planted tanks. The fish swim in a slanted position tilted 30° upwards from the horizontal. The female lays more than 1,000 eggs during the spawning period. After spawning the water should be replaced by fresh water of the same composition and temperature. The fry begin exogenous nutrition in four days; the first five days also one feeding at night in dim light. Young fish grow rapidly.

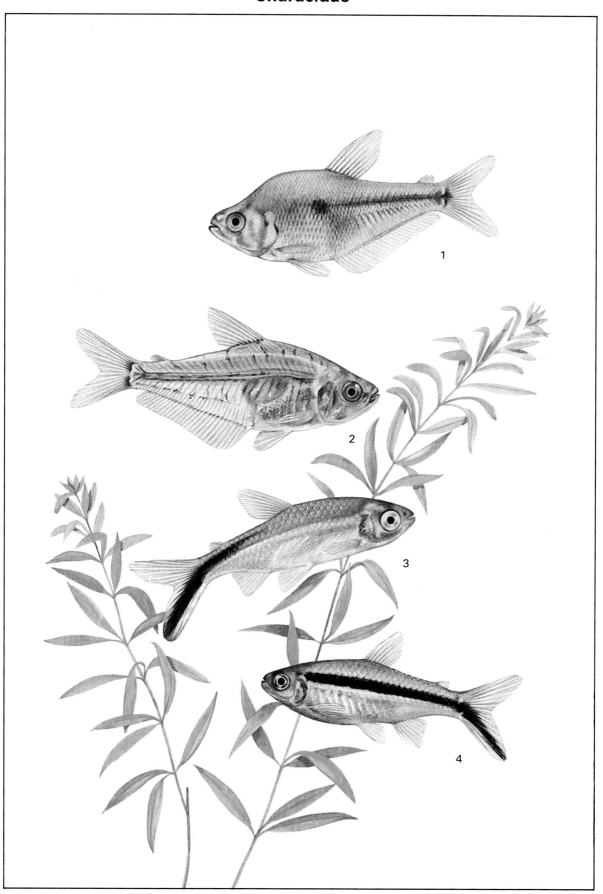

1 Riddle's Pristella

Pristella maxillaris (ULREY, 1894)
Syn. *Holopristes riddlei, Pristella riddlei*

○
◑ Distribution: Venezuela, Guyana, lower Amazon to Brazil; the fish are found also in brackish water. Full length: male − 3.5 cm, female − 4.5 cm. Diet: live as well as artificial foods. Community tank. Breeding tank: with capacity of 6 litres per pair, spawning grid, finely-leaved plants. Sexual dimorphism: the male is smaller, slimmer, more contrastingly coloured. Sex ratio: 1:1. Breeding water: 25 °C; pH 7.0; dCH 2°; dGH 10° (some breeders recommend adding half a teaspoonful NaCl or sea salt for every 10 litres of water). Eggs: incubation period 24 hrs. Feeding of fry: nauplii of brine shrimp or *Cyclops*.

School fish. Before spawning separate the males and females for about 14 days. Spawning takes place amidst finely-leaved plants, usually in the morning and at short intervals for a period of one and a half to two hours. The female deposits about 500 eggs. Remove the parent fish after spawning. The eleutherembryos hang on the walls of the tank and on plants. Endogenous nutrition lasts four days. Well-fed fry grow quickly and in one week reach a length of 7 mm; at four weeks they measure 15 mm and resemble the adult fish in both shape and coloration. They attain sexual maturity at seven months. In recent years an albinotic form was bred and genetically fixed in captivity.

2 Dragon-fin Tetra

Pseudocorynopoma doriae PERUGIA, 1891
Syn. *Bergia altipinnis, Chalcinopelecus argentinus*

○
◑ Distribution: southern Brazil, water system of the Paraguay and Paraná Rivers. Full length: 8 cm. Diet: live as well as artificial foods. Community tank, spacious. Breeding tank: of 50-litre capacity, with spawning grid, finely-leaved plants. The tanks should be low (with large surface expanse of water), well covered with glass (the fish jump), light to sun-flooded. Sexual dimorphism: the male's dorsal and anal fins are strongly extended. Sex ratio: 1:1. Breeding water: 20−24 °C; pH 6.5−7.0; dCH max. 2°; dGH max. 10°; well aerated. Eggs: incubation period 12−48 hrs, depending on the temperature of the water. Feeding of fry: *Paramecium caudatum,* later *Cyclops* and brine shrimp nauplii.

After a lengthy and attractive display by the male, during which he postures and circles round the female, the two fish mate. Spawning takes place in open water among plants. The female is very prolific, depositing approximately 1,000 eggs during spawning. The parent fish should be removed when their spawning activities are over. Endogenous nutrition of the embryos lasts three days. Rearing the fry is not difficult.

Another, less well known species is *P. heterandria* Eigenmann, 1914, from central Brazil, whose full length is 9 cm. This fish is related to *Corynopoma riisei,* but differs in the shape of the body, by having an adipose fin, and by the manner of fertilization − its eggs are fertilized during the act of spawning in open water, not inside the body of the female as in *C. riisei.*

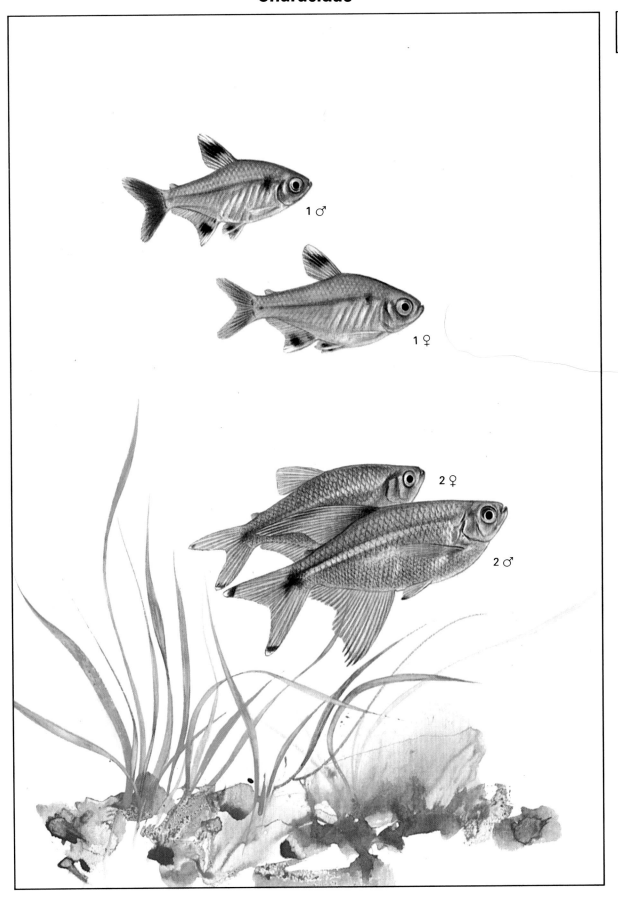

1 ♂

1 ♀

2 ♀

2 ♂

Family Alestidae

This family comprises a group of Tetras native to tropical Africa. It is not universally acknowledged as yet and the African Tetras are generally classed together with the closely related South American Tetras in the family Characidae. African Tetras often measure more than 10 cm in length.

1 Long-finned Characin
Brycinus longipinnis (GÜNTHER, 1864)
Syn. *Alestes longipinnis, Bryconalestes longipinnis*

Distribution: tropical west Africa from Sierra Leone to the Zaire. Full length: 13 cm. Diet: live, artificial, and plant foods. Community tank. Breeding tank: of 100-litre capacity with spawning grid. Sexual dimorphism: the male has a longer dorsal fin and his anal fin is whitish; the female is smaller. Sex ratio: 1:1 (the fish may also be bred in a shoal). Breeding water: 26–28 °C; pH 6.5; dCH < 1°. Eggs: non-adhesive, rigid, glassily transparent, Ø 2.5 mm. Incubation period six to seven days. Feeding of fry: nauplii of brine shrimp or *Cyclops*.

The fish spawn between December and May. Spawning is vigorous and takes place in open water, mostly in the afternoon. The fish spawn on plants as well as in open water close to the walls of the tank. The parent fish should be removed after spawning. The incubation period is longer than that of South American Tetras and therefore the embryos are more fully developed. They have only a small yolk sac, swim upwards at an oblique angle immediately after hatching, and after six to eight hours begin exogenous nutrition. The fry grow rapidly.

2 Big-scaled African Characin or Arnold's Red-eyed Characin
Arnoldichthys spilopterus (BOULENGER, 1909)
Syn. *Petersius spilopterus*

Distribution: tropical waters of west Africa from Lagos to the mouth of the Niger, in biotopes with diverse composition of the water. Full length: 8 cm. Diet: live as well as artificial foods. Community tank: Breeding tank: with capacity of 50–100 litres per pair, well-covered, and with finely-leaved plants and spawning grid. Sexual dimorphism: the anal fin of the male is convex, that of the female is straight to concave with a black patch. Sex ratio: 1:1 (the fish may be bred in a shoal). Breeding water: 24–28 °C; pH 6.0–6.5; dGH < 10°. Eggs: Ø 1.2 mm, adhesive, incubation period 30–36 hrs/25 °C. Feeding of fry: on infusoria (*Paramecium caudatum*) monoculture, rotatoria, *Cyclops* nauplii, after six days brine shrimp nauplii.

A characteristic of the genus *Arnoldichthys* is the possession of two kinds of scales: big scales on the upper part of the body and small ones on the underside. The fish thrive in fresh water filtered through peat. It is recommended to put them in a tank with a large expanse of water and low water column (circa 25–30 cm), flowing water, and low stock density. The females are very prolific, a single female laying about 1,000 eggs during the spawning period. On the fifth day the embryos cluster at the water surface membrane and on the seventh day they become free-swimming. Young fish are easily alarmed and easily injure themselves. They are likewise very sensitive to processed tapwater, particularly to the chlorine it contains. They grow quickly and at the age of three days measure 2.5 to 3 cm.

Alestidae

1 Congo Tetra
Phenacogrammus interruptus (BOULENGER, 1899)
Syn. *Micralestes interruptus, Alestopetersius interruptus, Hemigrammalestes interruptus, Petersius codalus*

Distribution: Zaire. Full length: male 8 cm, female smaller. Diet: live as well as artificial foods. Community tank. Breeding tank: of 100-litre capacity with spawning grid. Sexual dimorphism: the male is larger, more colourful, with longer dorsal, ventral, anal and caudal fins. Sex ratio: 1:1, or a slight preponderance of males. Breeding water: 26 °C; pH 6.5; dCH < 1°. Eggs: non-adhesive, round, glassy, Ø 1.8 mm with pronounced germinal disc, incubation period six days. Feeding of fry: nauplii of brine shrimps or *Cyclops*. The West German aquarist Meder succeeded in breeding this fish without any great acclimatization in 1951 in Neustadt.

Large aquariums and an abundance of soft water are prerequisites for successful breeding.

If the fish are put to spawn in a shoal then the tank must be of at least 200-litre capacity. If soft water is not available in sufficient quantity to fill the tank then the eggs must be taken out immediately after spawning and put in a smaller tank containing water of the given values. The fish are very lively, chasing one another so quickly that the act of spawning is practically unnoticeable. The females are prolific and 400 developed young fish from a single female are not unusual. Shortly after the embryo emerges from the egg case it becomes free-swimming and immediately takes food. Though the eggs are relatively large the fry are not particularly big and in the first few days have difficulty in coping with larger brine shrimp nauplii.

Family Curimatidae

Some authorities are of the opinion that the members of this family are undergoing a reverse evolution; the fish have no teeth in advanced age (the teeth are not renewed) and feed mostly on algae and detritus in the mud on the bottom; some fish have the mouth adapted for rasping benthic organisms and algae off the substrate. The fish swim in a tilted position head downward.

2 Spotted Head-stander
Chilodus punctatus MÜLLER and TROSCHEL, 1844
Syn. *Chaenotropus punctatus, Citharinus chilodus*

Distribution: Guyana, Surinam, Peru. Full length: female 12 cm, male slightly smaller. Diet: live, artificial, and plant foods. Community tank: roomy, covered, with dark bottom and dim light. Breeding tank: of 30- to 50-litre capacity with spawning grid, dim light. Sexual dimorphism: imperceptible, the female is somewhat fuller in the body. Sex ratio: 1:1 (the fish may be bred in a small shoal). Breeding water: 24–28 °C; pH 6.5; dCH 0° (carbonates in the water prevent healthy development of the embryos); dGH < 10°; filter water through peat or add peat extract. Eggs: Ø 2 mm, glassy to faintly yellowish, incubation period three days. Shortly after spawning (within one to two hours) the eggs may double their size. Feeding of fry: rotatoria, *Cyclops* and brine shrimp nauplii, dust plant food (algae).

The fish are quarrelsome, assemble in small shoals. They generally spawn on plants in a single spot. For rearing of the fry the water column should be 10 cm high.

1 ♂

1 ♀

2

Family Serrasalmidae

Fish of high body build, practically disc-shaped, attaining a very large size. They inhabit the waters of South America. The family includes herbivorous species of the genera *Metynnis, Myleus, Mylossoma* and *Colossoma* as well as carnivorous species of the genus *Serrasalmus*. Carnivorous species have strong jaws equipped with extremely sharp saw-like teeth. Some species are gregarious school fish, others solitary fish e.g. *Serrasalmus hollandi, S. rhombeus, S. striolatus*. Little known are members of the genus *Cotoprion* that feed on various foods, purportedly also fish scales.

1 Black-tailed Piranha, Natterer's Piranha
Serrasalmus nattereri (KNER, 1859)
Syn. *Pygocentrus nattereri, P. altus, P. stigmaterythraeus, Rooseveltiella nattereri, Serrasalmo piranha*

Distribution: from Guyana to La Plata. Full length: 30 cm. Diet: live foods, chiefly fish, even freshly killed fish. Monospecies keeping tank. Breeding tank: with capacity of 500 litres per pair, coarse gravel on the bottom, dim light, peaceful environment. Sexual dimorphism: imperceptible; the male is generally somewhat smaller, the keel of the belly viewed from the front is V-shaped, that of the female is U-shaped. Sex ratio: 1:1 (apart from the spawning period the fish are kept in a small shoal). Breeding water: 24−26 °C; pH 6.5; dCH < 2°. Eggs: yellowish, transparent, $\varnothing$ 1.5 mm, incubation period 36 hrs. Feeding of fry: first of all brine shrimp nauplii, later sieved zooplankton, chopped tubifex and shredded fish and beef meat; the fry must be continually well-fed.

Even adult fish must be continually well-fed. When hungry they become aggressive and attack and kill one another. Piranhas are not skilful hunters and generally pay no attention to small, fast fish. They are easily alarmed and shy. The fish must be handled with care, even when taken out of the water, for their bite may cause serious injury. Nets of wire mesh are used to catch the fish, for other material is bitten through easily. The courting dress of the fish is bluish-black. The male makes spawning pits in the bottom where 300 to 400 eggs are later deposited by the female. Spawning is stimulated by ample space, a peaceful environment, fresh water and ample food. The spawning site is guarded by the male. The eleutherembryos stay by the edge of the pit. These should be sucked up with a hose and transferred to a separate tank. The fry become free-swimming after seven days and their growth is rapid. On reaching a length of 1.5 to 2 cm the young fish begin to attack one another. This can be partly avoided by sorting them according to size.

The numerous accounts of the bloodthirstiness of Piranhas are greatly exaggerated or untrue but swarms of fish confined within a certain circumscribed area during the dry season can be dangerous. In the case of swarms that are accustomed to attacking larger prey the Piranhas may attack an injured animal or human being. With their sharp teeth it is no problem for the fish to strip their victim to the bone within a short while. Piranhas are also the bane of fishermen because they devour fish caught in their nets.

Serrasalmidae

1 Spotted Piranha
Serrasalmus rhombeus (LINNAEUS, 1766)
Syn. *Serrasalmus paraense, S. niger, S. gibbus, S. gracilior, Salmo rhombeus, S. albus, S. caribi, S. humeralis, S. immaculatus, S. iridopsis*

Serrasalmidae

◁
●

Distribution: Guyana and the Amazon basin. Full length: 40 cm. Diet: live foods (fish meat, whole fish, earthworms, pieces of beef flesh and heart). Monospecies keeping tank with capacity of 500 litres or more, layer of gravel on the bottom, sufficient hiding possibilities, diffused lighting, floating plants. Breeding tank: same as keeping tank. Sexual dimorphism: the male's anal fin is extended into a point, the female's is straight. Sex ratio: 1:1. Breeding water: assumption: 24–26 °C; pH 6.5; dCH < 2°; dGH max. 10°; well filtered. So far there is no record that the species has been bred in captivity.

A school fish in youth but solitary in adulthood. In cramped quarters the fish may fatally injure one another. The behaviour of the prey (fish) is the signal for attack by the Piranhas; those that are generally attacked are diseased or weakened fish.

2 *Metynnis hypsauchen* (MÜLLER and TROSCHEL, 1844)
Syn. *Myletes hypsauchen, Metynnis callichromus, M. erhardti, M. fasciatus, M. schreitmülleri, M. orinocensis*

Serrasalmidae

▢
●

Distribution: all of tropical South America, standing and densely overgrown waters. Full length: 15 cm. Diet: live, granulated foods, regularly augmented by plant foods. Monospecies keeping tank without plants. Breeding tank: with capacity of 200 litres, spawning grid, dim lighting. Sexual dimorphism: imperceptible. Sex ratio: 1:1. Breeding water: 26–28 °C; pH 6.5–7.0; dCH < 1°; dGH 5°; filtered through peat.

Eggs: clear, faintly yellowish, round, Ø 2 mm, incubation period 70 hrs/28 °C. Feeding of fry: nauplii of brine shrimp or *Cyclops*.

Peaceful school fish. Sexual maturity is not reached for three years. Spawning takes place in open water. The female deposits as many as 2,000 eggs.

3 *Myleus rubripinnis* (MÜLLER and TROSCHEL, 1844)
Syn. *Myloplus rubripinnis, M. asterias, M. ellipticus, M. ternetzi*

Serrasalmidae

▢
●

Distribution: Guyana, Amazon basin. Full length: 25 cm. Diet: live, granulated and plant foods. Monospecies keeping tank. Breeding tank: elongate, well-covered, with capacity of 300–500 litres per pair, spawning grid. Sexual dimorphism: the anal fin of a fully mature male has the central rays prolonged. The reddish colour of the sides is more intense and the head is coloured reddish-black to the gill covers. Sex ratio: 1:1. Breeding water: 25–27 °C; pH 6.5–7.0; dCH < 1°; dGH 5°; strongly aerated and filtered through peat. Eggs: clear, pale yellow, Ø 1.8–2.2 mm, incubation period 50–60 hrs. Feeding of fry: brine shrimp nauplii.

Peaceful, rather delicate school fish. Single specimens kept by themselves are shy. The spawn-ripe female should be put in the tank 24 hours before the male. Spawning takes place within 14 days at the latest.

4 *Myleus gurupyensis* STEINDACHNER, 1911
Syn. *Myloplus arnoldi (Myleus maculatus?)*

Serrasalmidae

▢
●

Distribution: Amazon basin. Full length: 20 cm. Otherwise the same as for *M. rubripinnis.* So far it is not known if this species has been bred.

Serrasalmidae

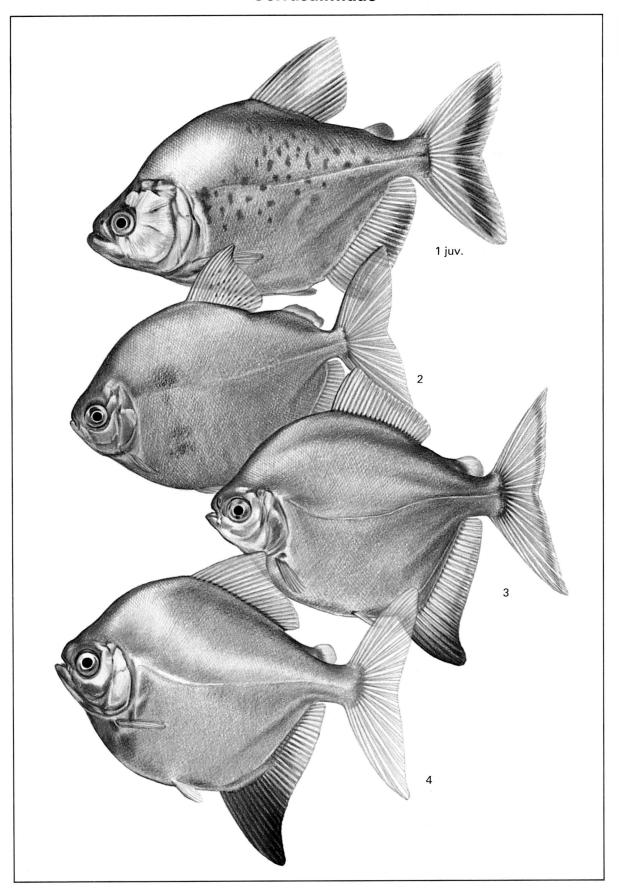

1 juv.

2

3

4

Family Ctenoluciidae

Fish with elongate, pike-shaped body, dorsal and anal fins inserted towards the rear, pointed head, deeply-cleft mouth equipped with teeth. Their full length is from 20 to 100 cm depending on the species.

1 Blunt-nosed Gar, Hujeta

Ctenolucius hujeta (VALENCIENNES, 1849)

Syn. *Luciocharax insculptus*   Ctenoluciidae

Distribution: Central and South America. Full length: 20 cm (Note: Arnold and Ahl, later Géry and Sterba gave it as 70 cm. According to the Peruvian ichthyologist Patrick de Rhama even fish caught in the wild do not exceed 20 cm in length and those bred in captivity are even smaller. Apparently that referred to in the earlier works of Arnold and Ahl is another species, or else a subspecies that has not been described as yet.) Diet: bigger pieces of live food, including small fish. Monospecies keeping tank. Breeding tank: with capacity of 100 litres or more, dense plant thickets. Sexual dimorphism: the anal fin of the male is broad and rounded; that of the female is smaller and pointed and the belly section is fuller. Sex ratio: 2 males : 1 female. Breeding water: 26 °C; pH 7.0; dCH < 2°. Eggs: small, $\varnothing$ 1 mm, glassy, with tufts of fibres by means of which they adhere to a solid substrate, chiefly plants; incubation period 22−24 hrs. Feeding of fry: nauplii of brine shrimp or *Cyclops*, later sieved zooplankton.

Very prolific fish, the female laying as many as 3,000 eggs during the spawning period. After reaching a length of more than 10 cm the fish become sexually mature. They spawn in open water close to the surface. The tank must be covered with glass so the fish cannot jump out. During the act of mating the fish break through the water's surface and thus some of the eggs are sprayed about in the vicinity along with the water. Many stick to the glass cover of the tank and these must be washed off back into water. The eleutherembryos measure 6 mm. They hang suspended in clusters on the water surface membrane. After three days the fry are fully coloured and actively forage for small live foods. They grow rapidly and within four weeks reach a length of 5 cm. Young fish must be continually well-fed (satiated); during the growth period it is necessary to increase the size of the live foods as well as their amount, otherwise the fish exhibit cannibalistic tendencies. Sorting the fish according to size during this period is essential; all larger specimens (clearly cannibalistic) should be transferred to a separate tank. If nothing else is available the young fish can be trained to feed on tubifex, which they gather even on the bottom. In shape and behaviour they resemble the pike *Esox lucius.*

1 ♀

1 ♂

Family Lebiasinidae

The members of this family are distributed throughout a large part of South America. They dwell chiefly in the upper strata of the waters they inhabit. They are elongated, spindle-shaped and a little compressed laterally (almost circular in cross-section). Because of this, they are often called 'pencil-fish'. The head is flattened, the mouth is terminal or slightly supraterminal.

The fish of this family should be kept in rather large tanks densely planted with large-leaved plants, with water slightly acid and soft, the water temperature 25–29 °C. The tanks should be well covered with glass as the fish jump.

1 Red-spotted Copeina
Copeina guttata (STEINDACHNER, 1875)
Syn. *Pyrrhulina guttata, Copeina argirops*

Lebiasinidae

Distribution: secondary waters of the Amazon River. Full length: 15 cm. Diet: live as well as artificial foods. Community tank. Breeding tank: with capacity of 50 litres per pair, bottom covered with a thin layer of sand. Sexual dimorphism: the dark spot on the male's dorsal fin is less pronounced than in the female, the upper lobe of the male's caudal fin is larger. The female is less intensely coloured, in adulthood her body is fuller. Sex ratio: 1:1. Breeding water: 25 °C; pH 6.5–7.0; dCH max. 2°. Eggs: incubation period 30–36 hrs. Feeding of fry: *Paramecium caudatum* or the finest *Cyclops* nauplii, later nauplii of brine shrimp.

After violent chasing the fish spawn in pits in the sand. At short intervals a fully mature female deposits as many as 2,500 eggs. The female should be taken out after spawning; the male guards the spawning pit. The following day the male is taken out as well. The eleutherembryos are dark and hang from the walls of the aquarium. Endogenous nutrition lasts five days; the free-swimming fry keep close to the surface. Because of their great number and voraciousness the fry must be provided with food two to three times daily and the first week likewise once during the night, in dim light.

2 Splash Tetra
Copella arnoldi (REGAN, 1912)
Syn. *Copeina arnoldi, C. callolepis, C. carsevennensis, C. eigenmanni, Pyrrhulina filamentosa, P. rachoviana*

Lebiasinidae

Distribution: northeastern Brazil – Para River, lower Amazon, in flood pools, streams and rivers. Full length: male – 8 cm, female – 6 cm. Diet: live as well as artificial foods. Community tank, well covered with glass. Breeding tank: of 50- to 100-litre capacity, filled so that there is at least 20 cm between the water's surface and the upper edge of the tank or 8–10 cm of free space between the surface and the cover glass. Sexual dimorphism: the male is larger and has larger fins. Sex ratio: breed the fish in a shoal with slight preponderance of females. Breeding water: 26 °C; pH 6.0–7.0; dCH max. 2°. Eggs: incubation period 26 hrs. Feeding of fry: the first 10 days *Paramecium caudatum,* then nauplii of brine shrimp or *Cyclops.*

The fish spawn out of the water. During the act of spawning both partners jump onto the side pane of the tank or onto the cover glass where the female releases the eggs which are immediately fertilized by the male. This is repeated until the female is depleted. The eggs remain out of the water throughout the whole incubation period and the male continually splashes water up at them. On hatching the eleutherembryos fall into the water and the male's care ends. If the parent fish are in a community aquarium the deposited eggs should be scraped off the glass with a goose quill or fine brush into small tanks with water column 1 cm high. The water, from the tank of the parent fish, should be slightly aerated. When the fry become free-swimming raise the height of the water column to 5 cm.

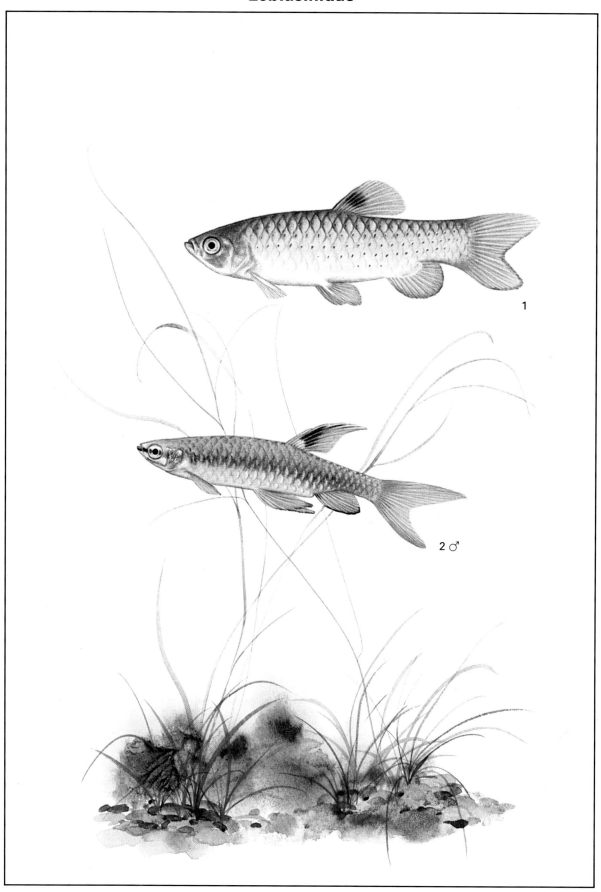

1

2 ♂

1 Rainbow Copella
Copella vilmae GÉRY, 1963

Lebiasinidae

Distribution: water system of the upper Amazon, mostly close to the Brazilian border town of Tabatinga. Full length: 6 cm. Diet: live as well as artificial foods. Community tank (only together with small, peaceful species of fish). Breeding tank: with a capacity of 30−50 litres per pair. Put a large-leaved plant inside, best of all *Echinodorus,* cover the surface with floating plants and cover the tank with glass. Sexual dimorphism: the upper lobe of the male's caudal fin is strongly extended, the female is smaller and the longitudinal band on her body is more vivid. Sex ratio: 1:1. Breeding water: 26−28 °C; pH 6.5−7.0; dCH max. 1°; dGH max. 10°; filtered through peat or with an addition of peat extract. Eggs: very small, incubation period 24 hrs. Feeding of fry: *Cyclops* nauplii or the finest, newly hatched species of brine shrimp.

The female deposits the eggs on the upper side of a leaf that has first been cleaned. After spawning either take out the parent fish or snip off the leaf with the eggs and put it in a separate tank. The parent fish do not care for the eggs. At the beginning the water for the fry should be kept at a low level, about 5 cm high.

2 Meta Copeina
Copella metae (EIGENMANN, 1914)
Syn. *Copeina metae*

Lebiasinidae

Distribution: Amazon River in Peru and the Meta River in Colombia − overgrown blind river arms and inlets. Full length: 6 cm. Diet: live as well as artificial foods. Community tank, only together with small, peaceful species of fish. Breeding tank: of 50- to 100-litre capacity, in a quiet location, with light diffused through floating plants. Put a large-leaved plant inside, e.g. *Echinodorus.* Sexual dimorphism: the male is larger, his dorsal fin is extended into a point, the upper lobe of his caudal fin is distinctly prolonged. Sex ratio: 1:1. Breeding water: 25 °C; pH 6.5−7.0; dCH < 2°; dGH < 10°; filtered through peat or with the addition of peat extract. Eggs: incubation period 30 hrs. Feeding of fry: at first *Paramecium caudatum,* then *Cyclops* nauplii, later brine shrimp nauplii.

The fish spawn on the upper side of the large leaves of aquatic plants, which have first been cleaned by the male. The female deposits 200 to 300 eggs, and should be taken out of the tank after spawning. The male looks after the eggs until they hatch. Forty-eight hours after hatching the fry scatter and attach themselves to a firm object or plant in the tank. At this time the male should be taken out of the tank. Endogenous nutrition lasts five days. Before giving the larvae their first food the water level should be lowered to 5 to 10 cm. In contour the fish resemble *Copella arnoldi.* Typical of this species is the zig-zag longitudinal band extending from the mouth to the base of the tail.

1 ♂

2

1 Tube-mouthed Pencilfish

Nannobrycon eques (STEINDACHNER, 1876)

Syn. *Nannostomus eques, Poecilobrycon eques, P. auratus*

Lebiasinidae

Distribution: Brazil – Amazon and Negro rivers. Full length: 5 cm. Diet: small live as well as artificial foods. Community tank (only with peaceable fish). Breeding tank: of 6- to 10-litre capacity with spawning grid, a large-leaved plant. Sexual dimorphism: inconspicuous; the anal fin of the male is edged with white, the ventral fins have white tips, the female is fuller in the body. Sex ratio: 1:1. Breeding water: 26–28 °C; pH 6.0–6.5; dCH 0°. Eggs: incubation period 24 hrs. Feeding of fry: brine shrimp nauplii.

N. eques occurs in morphologically different forms. The difference is clearly evident in the development of the adipose fin. Whereas in many populations it is well developed, in some it is entirely lacking. An interesting characteristic of this species is the different day and night colouring. The fish swim in a typical slanted position head upwards. They spawn on the undersurface of broadleaved plants. It is important that a protective spawning grid be put in the tank because a great many eggs fall to the bottom. In the initial phase of spawning the male is above the female and their mouths are practically touching so that their bodies form a sharp angle. Spawning may last as long as 10 hours. After spawning the parent fish should be removed and the tank darkened so the eggs are shaded. The number of eggs is extremely variable – from several dozen to as many as 300. At the end of endogenous nutrition the larvae are three times longer than at the moment of hatching. They resemble plant fragments and their growth is rapid.

2 One-lined Pencilfish

Nannobrycon unifasciatus (STEINDACHNER, 1876)

Syn. *Nannostomus unifasciatus, N. eques* (not Steindachner), *Poecilobrycon unifasciatus, P. ocellatus, P. unifasciatus ocellatus, Nannobrycon ocellatus*

Lebiasinidae

Distribution: Brazil – middle reaches of the Amazon and its tributaries, Venezuela – upper reaches of the Orinoco, Guyana. Full length: 6.5 cm. Diet: live foods, may be supplemented with artificial foods. Community tank. Breeding tank: with capacity of 6–10 litres and protective grid for one pair, broadleaved plants. Sexual dimorphism: the anal fin of the male is black-red-white, the female's is black. Sex ratio: 1:1. Breeding water: 26–28 °C; pH 6.0–6.5; dCH 0°; with addition of peat extract. Eggs: incubation period 24 hrs. Feeding of fry: freshly-hatched nauplii of brine shrimp or *Cyclops*.

These fish are slimmer than *N. eques*. They are peaceable and always kept in a shoal. Some specimens from the waters of Guyana and from the Madeira River in Brazil are larger and more intensely coloured due to the greater proportion of red. It was this that prompted Eigenmann to describe this fish in 1909 as a separate species – *N. ocellatus*. Géry, on the other hand, considers it to be merely a local form of *N. unifasciatus*.

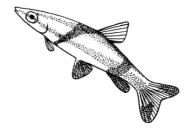

Nannobrycon eques – nocturnal coloration

Lebiasinidae

1 Beckford's Pencilfish
Nannostomus beckfordi (GÜNTHER, 1872)
Syn. *Nannostomus anomalus, N. aripirangensis, N. simplex,
N. beckfordi aripirangensis, N. beckfordi anomalus*

○ ◑ Distribution: Guyana, Brazil — lower reaches of the Negro River, middle and lower Amazon basin. Full length: 6.5 cm. Diet: small live as well as artificial foods. Community tank. Breeding tank: of 6-litre capacity with spawning grid, finely-leaved plants, diffused light. Sexual dimorphism: the male is slimmer, larger, more colourful, with white-tipped ventral fins. Sex ratio: 1:1. Breeding water: 24−26 °C; pH 6.5−6.8; dCH < 1°; dGH < 10°. Eggs: incubation period 30 hrs. Feeding of fry: nauplii of brine shrimp or *Cyclops*.

The fish have a different night colouring. At each mating the female deposits one to three eggs on plants; about 150 eggs in all. Spawning lasts five to six hours and may be repeated at six- to eight-day intervals. The eleutherembryo is very small; after three days it begins exogenous nutrition.

2 Espe's Pencilfish or Barred Pencilfish
Nannostomus espei (MEINKEN, 1956)
Syn. *Poecilobrycon espei*

○ ● Distribution: Guyana. Full length: 3.5 cm. Diet: small live foods (zooplankton and terrestrial insects − aphids, the fruit fly *Drosophila melanogaster,* springtails) as well as artificial foods. Monospecies keeping tank. Breeding tank: of 6- to 10-litre capacity, with clump of large-leaved plants. Sexual dimorphism: the golden stripe in the male is glossier and his anal fin larger, dark and fan-shaped. Sex ratio: 1:1. Breeding water: 26 °C; pH 6.5; dCH < 1°. Eggs: incubation period 48 hrs. Feeding of fry: for three to five days *Paramecium caudatum,* then the finest brine shrimp nauplii.

School fish that swim close to the surface. Always keep at least 10 specimens together. During the act of spawning the female deposits 40 to 50 eggs on the underside of plant leaves. When the fish are set up to spawn in a shoal remove the plants with the eggs and transfer them to a nursery tank. In the case of a single pair of breeders remove the fish as soon as spawning is over. The larvae begin exogenous nutrition four days after hatching.

3 Dwarf Pencilfish or One-lined Pencilfish
Nannostomus marginatus EIGENMANN, 1909

○ ◑ Distribution: Surinam, Guyana, lower reaches of the Amazon, Brazil. Full length: 3.5 cm. Diet: small live as well as artificial foods. Community tank. Breeding tank: of 6-litre capacity with spawning grid, diffused light, Java moss. Sexual dimorphism: the male is more slender, the anal fin is prominently edged with black, the ventral fins are deep black. Sex ratio: 1:1. Breeding water: 26−28 °C; pH 6.0−6.5; dCH 0°. Eggs: incubation period 24 hrs. Feeding of fry: brine shrimp nauplii.

The males and females are separated for about 14 days before spawning. The female lays a maximum of 100 eggs. The eggs are small, glassy and have a large yolk sac. The inactive larvae are equipped with outgrowths and resemble fragments of dead plants, thereby blending perfectly with the bottom environment. At the age of five weeks their colouring resembles that of adult fish.

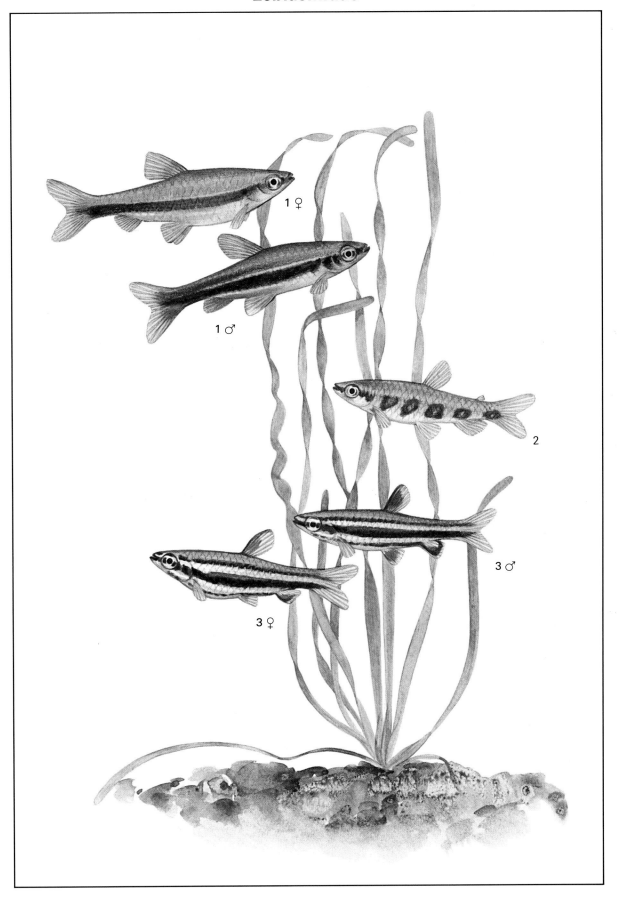

1 Three-lined Pencilfish
Nannostomus trifasciatus STEINDACHNER, 1876

Syn. *Cyprinodon amazona, Poecylobrycon erythrurus, P. vittatus, P. auratus, P. trifasciatus, Nannostomus trilineatus*

Lebiasinidae

Distribution: Brazil — the rivers Tocantins, Madeira, tributaries of the lower Amazon and waters of the Mato Grosso plateau region. Full length: 5.5 cm. Diet: live as well as artificial foods. Community tank — only together with small, peaceful fish. Breeding tank: of 10-litre capacity with spawning grid, Java moss. Sexual dimorphism: the female is rounder in the body and less vividly coloured. Sex ratio: 1:1. Breeding water: 27–28 °C; pH 6.6–6.8; dCH 0.5°; dGH max. 10°. Eggs: ∅ 1.75 mm, incubation period 25 hrs. Feeding of fry: newly-hatched brine shrimp nauplii.

The fish generally spawn in the afternoon and evening. The female deposits up to 200 eggs. In the initial stage of spawning the male is above the female with their mouths nearly touching, the same as *N. eques.* Only ripe females should be set up for spawning, in other words ones in which the eggs are visible as an amber-coloured ring in front of the anal opening. According to S. Frank the fish may be spawned in fresh tapwater that has been allowed to stand a short while — they spawn better in such water than in prepared water. However, it is necessary to transfer the fertilized eggs to breeding water immediately after spawning (this applies to a great many other species of fish). On hatching the fry average 3.1 mm in length and when they become free-swimming they are 5.2 mm long. Add ordinary water to the tank gradually as they grow. The young fish grow quickly.

2 Dotted-scale Pyrrhulina
Pyrrhulina brevis brevis STEINDACHNER, 1875

Lebiasinidae

Distribution: lower reaches of the Negro River round Manaus. Full length: 9 cm. Diet: live foods. Community tank. Breeding tank: with capacity of 50 litres per pair, broadleaved plants of the genus *Echinodorus,* diffused lighting, well covered with glass. Sexual dimorphism: the male is bigger with larger fins. Sex ratio: 1:1. Breeding water: 26 °C; pH 6.5; dCH < 1°; dGH max. 10°. Eggs: incubation period 30 hrs. Feeding of fry: first of all *Paramecium caudatum,* then *Cyclops* nauplii, later brine shrimp nauplii.

The fish require roomy tanks with free expanse of surface water. They keep near the surface. The female deposits the eggs on the leaves of broadleaved plants. After spawning she should be removed. The male watches over the eggs. When the fry hatch remove the male and lower the water level to about 5 cm. The fry grow slowly. The subspecies *P. brevis australe* (Eigenmann and Kennedy, 1903) is distributed farther south, from the region of the Paraguay River across the Paraná River to La Plata.

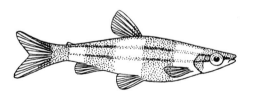

Nannostomus trifasciatus — nocturnal coloration

Lebiasinidae

1 ♀

1 ♂

2 ♀

2 ♂

Family Gasteropelecidae

The members of this family inhabit a large territory from the border of Central America to the mouth of the Paraná River. The deep, laterally compressed body has the shape of a hatchet. The back is straight and the breast and belly section are narrowed into a keel. Attached to the robust shoulder section are the powerful muscles of the pectoral fins. With quick beats of these fins the fish can lift themselves half out of the water and glide along the surface as much as several metres. They are school fish and typical surface-dwellers with upturned (supraterminal) mouths.

1 Pygmy Hatchet Fish
Carnegiella marthae marthae MYERS, 1929   Gasteropelecidae

Distribution: from Venezuela to upper Amazon in Peru and Brazil. Full length: 3 cm. Diet: live foods, small zooplankton, fruit flies (*Drosophila melanogaster*), aphids. Tank: as for *C. strigata*. Sexual dimorphism: monomorphous fish. Sex ratio: put a larger shoal in the tank. Breeding water: 24–26 °C; pH 6.5; dCH 0°; dGH cca 5°; filtered through peat. Breeding unknown.

2 Marbled Hatchet Fish or Striped Hatchet Fish
Carnegiella strigata (GÜNTHER, 1864)
Syn. *Gasteropelecus strigatus, Carnegiella vesca*   Gasteropelecidae

Distribution: Guyana, Colombia, Brazil (Amazon River). Full length: 4 cm. Diet: live foods (augmented with dry terrestrial insects). Community tank: elongate. Breeding tank: of 100-litre capacity, well-covered, with islets of plants at the surface, forced-circulation filter, dim lighting. Sexual dimorphism: monomorphous fish. Sex ratio: spawn in a shoal. Breeding water: 25 °C; pH 5.5–6.5; dCH 0°; filtered through peat. Eggs: incubation period 30 hrs. Feeding of fry: *Paramecium caudatum* or rotatoria, later *Cyclops* nauplii or brine shrimp nauplii.

3 Silver Hatchet Fish
Gasteropelecus levis (EIGENMANN, 1909)   Gasteropelecidae

Distribution: lower Amazon. Full length: 6 cm. Diet: live foods, particularly small zooplankton, fruit flies, etc. Tank: same as for *C. strigata*. Sexual dimorphism: monomorphous fish. Sex ratio: set up the fish in a shoal. Breeding water: 26 °C (a slight drop in temperature is recommended at night); pH 5.5–6.5; dCH 0°; dGH < 10°; filtered through peat. Eggs:?

4 Common Hatchet Fish or Silver Hatchet Fish
Gasteropelecus sternicla (LINNAEUS, 1758)
Syn. *Clupea sternicla, Gasteropelecus coronatus, Salmo gasteropelecus*   Gasteropelecidae

Distribution: Trinidad, Peru, Brazil; also ditches and swamps. Full length: 6.5 cm. Diet: live foods, small zooplankton, small terrestrial insects, mosquito larvae. Tank: as for *C. strigata*. Sexual dimorphism: monomorphous fish. Sex ratio: 1:1 (set up fish in a large shoal). Breeding water: pH 6.5–7.0; dCH 0°; dGH < 10°; filtered through peat; provide slight streaming of water using a filter. Eggs: incubation period 30 to 36 hrs. Feeding of fry: *Paramecium caudatum,* later brine shrimp or *Cyclops* nauplii, springtails.

Gasteropelecidae

1

2

3

4

Family Hemiodidae

Most species of this family have an elongated body and a large, deeply forked caudal fin. Ecologically they are divided into three groups: a) species living in open water, b) species living at or near a sandy bottom, c) species living at or near a stony bottom. All members of the family swim in a horizontal position. They differ from the fish of the Characidae family chiefly by the teeth. The lower jaw is usually without teeth: hence the name 'Half-teeth', as they are called.

1 Barred Hemiodus
Hemiodopsis quadrimaculatus (PELLEGRIN, 1908)
Syn. *Hemiodus quadrimaculatus*   Hemiodidae

☐ Distribution: French Guiana – *H. q. quadrimaculatus;* Surinam, Guyana and the upper Amazon round Leticia – *H. q. vorderwinkleri.* Full length: 12 cm. Diet: live as well as artificial foods, augmented with plant foods. Community tank – together with bottom-dwelling fish, e. g. genus *Corydoras.* Capacity *c.* 500 litres, sufficient open space, islets of tougher plants, well covered with glass, light to sun-flooded. Breeding tank: same as community tank. Sexual dimorphism: not known. Water: 24–26 °C; pH 7.0–7.5; dCH max. 2°; dGH max. 10°; well aerated, streaming of water provided by forced circulation filters. These fish have not been bred in captivity as yet.

Shy and peaceable fish, good swimmers. They should always be kept in a shoal. They must be handled with care, for they are easily damaged; when left out of the water they soon die. *H. quadrimaculatus* is divided into two subspecies: *H. q. quadrimaculatus* and *H. q. vorderwinkleri.* There is no visible difference between them; they differ in morphological-anatomical characteristics. Thriving fish have an ochre-beige band on the lower half of the body. The adipose fin is often reddish. They are easily confused with *H. gracilis* (Günther, 1864), *H. sterni* Géry, 1964, and *H. huarulti* Géry, 1964, which have similar transverse stripes.

2 Half-banded Characin
Hemiodopsis semitaeniatus (KNER, 1859)
                                                                   Hemiodidae

☐ Distribution: water systems of the Orinoco, also the southern tributaries of the Amazon. Full length: 20 cm. Tank without plants – plants are nibbled by the fish. Tank, care and diet the same as for *H. quadrimaculatus.*

Peaceful, slender fish, rapid and active swim-

mers. Behind the middle of the body there is a round black dot from which a narrow, dark, longitudinal band comes out, extending along the middle of the lower lobe of the caudal fin to its end. This band appears and disappears according to the fish's mood. There is no red coloration in the caudal fin of these fish.

3 Stern's Hemiodopsis
Hemiodopsis sterni GÉRY, 1964
                                                                   Hemiodidae

☐ Distribution: region of one of the sources of the river Tapajóz – Río Juruena in Mato Grosso. Full length: 12 cm. Tank, care and breeding the same as for *H. quadrimaculatus.*

Hemiodidae

3 juv.

Family Anostomidae

The members of this family are distributed in South and Central America, including the West Indies. The body is torpedo-shaped with the exception of the high-backed species of the genus *Abramites.* In many species the narrow mouth, functionally adapted in widely diverse ways, points directly upward (is supraterminal); both jaws are provided with teeth. Many species swim in a tilted position, head downward. In their home waters the fish are generally found among rocks and fallen trees, in an environment that corresponds to their coloration. Relatively little is known about the ecology and ethology of these fish.

1 Red-mouth Head-stander
Anostomus ternetzi FERNANDEZ–YEPEZ, 1949

☐ Distribution: Venezuela – Orinoco, territory of Guyana, also Brazil – Xingu and Araguaia Rivers ◑ – southern tributaries of the Amazon delta. Full length: 16 cm. Diet: live, artificial and plant foods. Community tank – see *A. anostomus.* Breeding tank: of at least 500-litre capacity with sufficient hiding possibilities. Sexual dimorphism: monomorphous fish; the adult male is probably more slender and smaller. Sex ratio: the optimum ratio is not known; keep the fish in a smaller shoal. Breeding water: same as for *A. anostomus.* The species has not yet been bred.

Compared with *A. anostomus* this species is smaller, less coloured and hardier. The two are easily confused.

2 Striped Head-stander
Anostomus anostomus (LINNAEUS, 1758)
Syn. *Salmo anostomus, Leporinus anostomus, Anostomus gronovii, A. salmoneus, Pithecocharax anostomus*

☐ Distribution: upper Amazon to Manaus, water systems of the Orinoco in Venezuela, Guyana, ◑ Colombia – shallow biotopes with flowing water. Full length: 18 cm. Diet: live, artificial and plant foods – chiefly algae. Community tank (brood fish, however, should be kept with specimens of their own species). Fish that are inactive and ones that compete with this species in rasping off algae are not suitable companions in the community tank. Breeding tank: with capacity of 500 litres or more, sufficient hiding possibilities, chiefly roots from moors. Sexual dimorphism: extremely slight; the male is slimmer, smaller (applies only to fully developed fish; young fish are monomorphous). Sex ratio: 1:1. Breeding water: 24–28 °C; pH 6.0–6.5; dCH max. 1°; dGH max. 10°; filtered through peat. Otherwise the fish are content with ordinarily used water. First propagated in 1984 by M. I. Likhachev in Moscow (USSR) following the application of human gonadotrophine by injection.

A. anostomus is aggressive and territorial towards others of the same species. It is often confused with the similar but less colourful *A. ternetzi.* Besides the coloration, another means of identification, according to Géry, are the middle and lower longitudinal stripes, which in *A. anostomus* are jagged on the forward edges and in *A. ternetzi* smooth.

Anostomidae

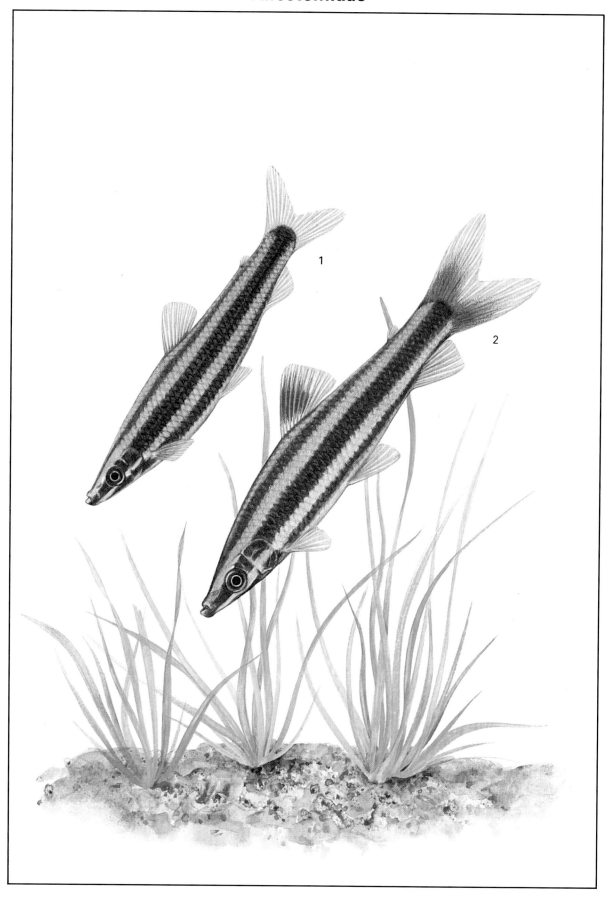

1 Marbled Head-stander, Norman's Head-stander
Abramites hypselonotus (GÜNTHER, 1868)
Syn. *Leporinus hypselonotus, Abramites microcephalus*   Anostomidae

Distribution: Venezuela – Orinoco basin, Brazil – northern tributaries of the Amazon. Full length: 14 cm. Diet: live and plant foods. Community tank of at least 500-litre capacity, well filtered (only together with species of similar characteristics and size). Sexual dimorphism: not known. Water: 24–28 °C; dCH max. 1°; dGH < 10°. The species has not yet been successfully bred in captivity.

Solitary fish, quarrelsome towards others of its own kind. The markings and coloration are variable. The region of the Paraguay River is the home of the slightly different subspecies *A. hypselonotus ternetzi* (Norman, 1926), (the dorsal fin inserts farther to the front, the base of the caudal fin is broader) with a total length of 14 cm, known also under the synonyms *Leporinus solarii* and *L. nigripinnis*. A related species – *Abramites eques* (Steindachner, 1878) – was discovered in the Magdalena River in Colombia.

2 Striped Leporinus
Leporinus striatus KNER, 1859
Syn. *Salmo tiririca*   Anostomidae

Distribution: Venezuela, Colombia, Ecuador, Brazil – Mato Grosso, Bolivia, Paraguay, flowing waters; the fish are often found under waterfalls. Full length: 25 cm. Diet: plant foods (fruit, lettuce, duckweed, algae and other aquatic plants). Monospecies keeping tank of at least 500-litre capacity, vigorously filtered with the aid of forced-circulation filters, simulation of strongly flowing water. Sexual dimorphism: not known. Water: 24–26 °C; pH 6.5–7.0; dCH max. 1°; dGH max. 10°. The species has not been bred in captivity.

Quarrelsome fish. They are not known to attain sexual maturity in captivity. The taxonomy of the genus *Leporinus* is unclear. Only one species – *L. maculatus* Müller and Troschel, 1845 – has been bred in captivity.

3 Banded Leporinus
Leporinus fasciatus fasciatus (BLOCH, 1794)
Syn. *Salmo fasciatus, S. timbure, Chalceus fasciatus, Leporinus novemfasciatus*   Anostomidae

Distribution: Venezuela – region of the Orinoco River, Guyana, Brazil – Amazon basin, Paraguay, Argentina – Paraná. Full length: 30 cm. Diet: chiefly plant foods (spinach leaves, lettuce leaves, duckweed, algae, etc.), augmented with live as well as artificial foods. Monospecies keeping tank with capacity of 500 litres or more, without plants, with sufficient hiding possibilities (mineralized wood from moors, rocks), well covered with glass. Sexual dimorphism: very slight; the male is slimmer, some males have a reddish throat. Sex ratio: 1:1 (the fish should be kept in a small shoal). Water: 25 °C; pH 6.0–7.5; dCH max. 2° (max. 1° in the case of the possible development of eggs); dGH 10°; fresh; streaming of water provided by forced-circulation filters. The species has not been bred in captivity as yet.

Fish kept singly are aggressive. A great number of subspecies and species are not clear in terms of nomenclature.

Family Citharinidae

Typical characteristics of the fish of this family are the straight lateral line and elongated snout. They are closely related to the Characidae family and are found only in Africa. The family is divided into three subfamilies: Citharininae, Distichodinae, and Ichthyoborinae. There are marked differences between the members of the three families.

1 African Tetra or One-striped African Tetra
Nannaethiops unitaeniatus GÜNTHER, 1871

Citharinidae

◁
●
Distribution: from Nigeria to the White Nile, southward to Zaire. Full length: 6.5 cm. Diet: live foods. Monospecies keeping tank. Breeding tank: of 10-litre capacity with spawning grid. Sexual dimorphism: the male is slimmer, more intensely coloured. During the spawning period part of the dorsal fin and part of the caudal fin are coloured red. Sex ratio: 1:1. Breeding water: 26 °C; pH 6.0−6.5; dCH < 1°; dGH < 10°; filtered through peat. Eggs: incubation period 30 hrs. Feeding of fry: nauplii of brine shrimp or *Cyclops*.

Peaceful school fish. They like a sunlit tank containing a small number of fish. Spawning takes place in open water. There are a great many eggs and these are scattered all over the bottom of the tank. After five days of endogenous nutrition the fry become free-swimming and grow quickly. At first keep the height of the water column at 10 cm, later raising it by adding fresh tapwater.

2 *Nannocharax ansorgei* BOULENGER, 1911
Syn. *Nannocharax parvus?*

Citharinidae

□
●
Distribution: border region between Zaire and the Central African Republic. Full length: 5 cm. Diet: live and artificial foods augmented by plant foods (algae). Monospecies keeping tank. The manner of reproduction and sexual dimorphism are not known. Water: 24 °C; pH 6.5−7.0; dCH max. 1°; dGH 10°.

N. ansorgei differs markedly from the other species of *Nannocharax* by its behaviour. The others are bottom-dwelling fish that use the paired fins as a support, whereas *N. ansorgei* lives in open water and its fins are differently shaped. It is a shy fish that seeks out retreats in which to hide. Sudden changes in the composition of the water cause the fish to go into a state of shock which may even end in death. That is why it is necessary to transfer imported fish to the tank with great care and to be equally careful when changing the water in the tank.

3 Ansorge's Neolebias
Neolebias ansorgei BOULENGER, 1912
Syn. *Neolebias landgrafi, Micraethiops ansorgei*

Citharinidae

○
●
Distribution: Angola, Cameroon, Central African Republic − swampy localities. Full length: 3.5 cm. Diet: live as well as artificial foods. Monospecies keeping tank: elongate. Breeding tank: of 6- to 10-litre capacity with spawning grid, finely leaved plants (Java moss). Sexual dimorphism: the male is slimmer. Sex ratio: 1:1.

Breeding water: 24 °C; pH 6.5−7.0; dCH < 1°; dGH < 10°; fresh. Eggs: incubation period 40 hrs. Feeding of fry: *Paramecium caudatum,* later *Cyclops* nauplii, brine shrimp nauplii.

School fish. They spawn in open water near plants. The female deposits up to 300 eggs.

Citharinidae

1 Three-striped African Tetra

Neolebias trilineatus BOULENGER, 1899

Syn. *Rhabdaethiops trilineatus*
(in aquaristic circles known under the name of *Nannaethiops tritaeniatus*)

Citharinidae

Distribution: Zaire basin (Congo). Full length: 4 cm. Diet: live as well as artificial foods. Mono-species keeping tank. Breeding tank: of 6- to 10-litre capacity with spawning grid and Java moss. Sexual dimorphism: the male is smaller, slimmer; during the spawning period his fins are coloured red and there is a blood-red longitudinal band above the middle black stripe. Sex ratio: 1:1. Breeding water: 28–30 °C; pH 6.5–7.5; dCH < 1°, add peat extract or filter the water through peat. Eggs: minute, glassy, incubation period 34 hrs/30 °C. Feeding of fry: the first week on infusoria (*Paramecium caudatum*) culture or rotatoria, then brine shrimp nauplii or *Cyclops* nauplii.

Peaceable school fish. During the spawning period the female deposits about 300 eggs. Spawning takes place in the morning. After spawning remove the parent fish and shade the tank. Endogenous nutrition lasts five days. The fry are very small and have conspicuously pigmented eyes. Their growth is rapid and in two weeks they reach a total length of 10 mm. Sexual maturity is attained at the age of eight months.

2 Nobol Distichodus

Distichodus noboli BOULENGER, 1899

Citharinidae

Distribution: Zaire basin (Congo). Full length: 8–10 cm. Diet: live, artificial and plant foods. Tank: spacious. Because this is a rarely imported species it is recommended to keep it with others of its own kind. It may be kept in a mixed aquarium with certain species of the Cichlidae family. It has not been bred in captivity as yet. Sexual dimorphism: not known. Water: 24–26 °C; pH 6.5–7.0; dCH max. 1°.

The fish should be kept in smaller groups. Of the 30 known species of *Distichodus* only a small number are suitable for the aquarium. *D. noboli* is one of the best suited but is generally hard to come by because imports from Zaire are decreasing. The intense red coloration of the caudal fin is found in only some specimens.

Citharinidae

1 ♂

1 ♀

2 juv.

1 Six-barred Distichodus
Distichodus sexfasciatus BOULENGER, 1897

Distribution: central and southwest Africa – Zaire, Angola. Full length: 25 cm. Diet: plant foods augmented with zooplankton. Keeping tank: monospecies, without plants. The species has not been bred in captivity as yet. Sexual dimorphism: not known. Breeding water: 24–26 °C; pH 6.5–7.0; dCH max. 1° (in normal rearing the carbonate hardness [dCH] may be higher); hypothetical values for the development of eggs.

The fish should be kept in a rather small group. They are peaceful and friendly. Young fish are brightly coloured (see illustration), whereas adult fish are coloured grey and yellow, the bright red colouring of the fins being replaced by grey. In view of the fish's high rate of metabolism the water in the tank must be well filtered and kept thoroughly clean. A regular supply of fresh water promotes their well-being.

2 Long-nosed Distichodus
Distichodus lusosso SCHILTHUIS, 1891

Distribution: Cameroon, Zaire, Angola, Zambia. Full length: 40 cm. Diet: plant foods augmented by zooplankton. Monospecies keeping tank. The species has not been bred in captivity as yet. Sexual dimorphism: not known. Water: 24–26 °C; pH 6.5–7.0; dCH max. 1° (hypothetical values for the development of eggs).

The fish should be kept in a rather small group. Only the largest aquariums or pools are suitable for this species. Because of its size *D. lusosso* is not an aquarium fish in the true sense – in other words not for standard aquariums. It may be bred only in a facility which has pools, a sufficient number of breeding fish, and the possibility of performing hypophysation and artificial fertilization – in the future apparently in African countries interested in the fish as an item of commerce (on a commercial scale).

Citharinidae

1 juv.

2 juv.

The so-called South American 'knife fish' inhabit gently-flowing waters, lagoons and shallow lakes with dense vegetation. They are crepuscular fish that resemble the 'knife fish' of Africa (family Notopteridae). The long anal fin forms a border extending the length of the body and promotes swimming – both forward and backward – by means of waving movements. Many species reach a great length but their growth is slow. Most are quarrelsome towards others of their own kind.

1 Green Knife Fish
Eigenmannia virescens (VALENCIENNES, 1849)

Syn. *Sternarchus virescens, Cryptops humboldti, C. lineatus, C. virescens, Eigenmannia humboldti, Sternopygus humboldti, S. limbatus, S. lineatus, S. microstomus, S. tumifrons, S. virescens*

Rhamphichthyidae

Distribution: large part of South America from the Magdalena River, Colombia, in the north to the Río de la Plata in the south (only in fresh waters). Full length: male 35–45 cm, female – 20 cm. Diet: live food of all kinds, chiefly mosquito larvae. Monospecies keeping tank. Breeding tank: of 300- to 500 litre capacity with dim light, plenty of floating plants on the surface. Sexual dimorphism: the male is much larger, the female has a greatly enlarged body during the spawning period. Sex ratio: put a large shoal of fish in the tank for spawning with a preponderance of females. Breeding water: 27 °C; pH 5.5–7.0; dCH < 1°; dGH 6°. Eggs: sticky, $\varnothing$ 1.5 mm, incubation period three days. Feeding of fry: brine shrimp nauplii.

Unlike most species belonging to this family *E. virescens* is a gregarious fish with others of its own kind (species); a group of such fish has a firm social structure. Spawning in nature takes place only during the rainy season. The attainment of sexual maturity depends primarily on the gradual decrease in the concentration of salt in the water (conductivity in µS), to a lesser extent on a lowering of the pH and rise in the height of the water column. Therefore a prerequisite for successful breeding is thorough preparation of the brood fish (by simulating periods of drought and rain) for a period of at least two months. The first successful attempt at breeding this fish was an experimental one, performed in a West German laboratory circa in the late seventies. The fish spawn at night; during the spawning period the female deposits 100 to 200 eggs in the roots of floating plants. The eleutherembryos are 6 mm long; endogenous nutrition from the yolk sac lasts eight days. The young fish grow rapidly and on reaching a length of 2 cm resemble the adults. The male attains sexual maturity on reaching a length of 13 cm, the female on reaching a length of 10 cm.

Family Cyprinidae

The Carp family is found in fresh waters throughout the world. The fish do not have an adipose fin. The mouth is more or less protractile, the jaws toothless. However, there are rows of pharyngeal teeth on the throat bones for chewing food. The length of the various species ranges from 2 cm to more than 2 m.

The genus *Barbus,* the only name sometimes used in the UK, established in 1816 by Cuvier and Cloquet, included a great many widely diverse species. In 1822 Hamilton used the generic name *Puntius* for the first time. In 1957 L. P. Schultz revised the genus *Barbus* and divided it into the following four genera: *Barbus, Barbodes, Capoeta* and *Puntius.*

1 Zebra Danio
Brachydanio rerio (HAMILTON-BUCHANAN, 1822)
Syn. *Cyprinus rerio, Perilampus striatus, Danio rerio*

Cyprinidae

Distribution: eastern India. Full length: 6 cm. Diet: live as well as artificial foods. Community tank. Breeding tank: of at least 6-litre capacity with spawning grid, light to sun-flooded. Sexual dimorphism: the female is markedly plumper. Sex ratio: 2 males : 1 female. Breeding water: 22–24 °C; pH 7.0; dCH max. 2°; fresh. Eggs: incubation period 62 hrs./27 °C; becomes longer as the temperature drops. Feeding of fry: 5–7 days *Paramecium caudatum,* rotatoria, aqueous suspension of fry foods, then *Cyclops* and brine shrimp nauplii.

Separate the males and females for 7 to 14 days prior to spawning. Spawning takes place in the morning. The female deposits up to 2,000 eggs. When spawning is over take out the parent fish, remove the spawning grid, replace half of the water with fresh water and treat the eggs with methylene blue. The young fish grow well and quickly in rather shallow, flat tanks.

2 *Brachydanio rerio* – veil-finned form

Cyprinidae

Selectively bred apparently during the seventies in the USSR but not yet fully fixed genetically.

3 Leopard Danio
Brachydanio frankei MEINKEN, 1963
Syn. *Danio frankei*

Cyprinidae

Distribution: unknown. Full length: 5 cm. Otherwise see *B. rerio.*

When describing the species Dr. Meinken was informed by the Bremen importer H. Espe that he had imported these fish from Kampuchea. Such an import was never repeated and aquarists voiced the opinion that *B. frankei* is an aquarium-bred mutation of *B. rerio. B. frankei* interbreeds prolifically with *B. rerio* and the ensuing generations are also fertile. Studies by Meinken (1963, 1967) and Frank (1966), however, indicate that in terms of morphological-anatomical characteristics *B. frankei* is much more closely related to *B. tweediei* and *B. nigrofasciatus* (Hamilton – Buchanan, 1822) than to *B. rerio.*

4 *Brachydanio frankei* – veil-finned form

Cyprinidae

The veil-finned form of *B. frankei* appeared at the same time as the veil-finned form of *B. rerio.* In all probability it likewise originated in the USSR in the seventies.

1 ♂

1 ♀

2 ♂

4 ♂

3 ♂

1 Pearl Danio
Brachydanio albolineatus (BLYTH, 1860)
Syn. *Nuria albolineata, Danio albolineata*   Cyprinidae

Distribution: Burma, Thailand, Malay Peninsula, Sumatra. Full length: 6 cm. Diet: live as well as artificial foods. Community tank, well covered. Breeding tank: of 30- to 50-litre capacity with spawning grid, finely-leaved plants, 10 to 15 cm high water column, elongate, light to sun-flooded. Sexual dimorphism: the male is slimmer, more vividly coloured, the female larger, more robust. Sex ratio: 2–3 males : 1 female breed the fish in a shoal. Breeding water: 24–26 °C; pH 6.5–7.5; dCH max. 2°; fresh. Eggs: incubation period three days/26 °C. Feeding of fry: five to seven days *Paramecium caudatum*, artificial fry foods, then *Cyclops* or brine shrimp nauplii.

A school fish dwelling in the upper layers of water. The males and females should be separated for a week before spawning. Females that are not given the opportunity to spawn become infertile or may even die. Endogenous nutrition lasts five to seven days. Growth of the fry is irregular.

2 Kerr's Danio
Brachydanio kerri (SMITH, 1931)
Syn. *Danio kerri*   Cyprinidae

Distribution: southern Thailand, jungle streams without aquatic vegetation. Full length: 5 cm. Diet, tank, breeding tank, sexual dimorphism, sex ratio and feeding of the fry: same as for *B. albolineatus*. Breeding water: 24 °C; pH 7.0; dCH < 2°; dGH max. 10°; fresh, oxygen-rich. Eggs: incubation period four days.

Peaceful school fish with two pairs of relatively long barbels. Spawning takes place in open water near the bottom. The female deposits up to 400 eggs.

3 Spotted Danio
Brachydanio nigrofasciatus (HAMILTON-BUCHANAN, 1822)
Syn. *Barilius nigrofasciatus, Brachydanio analipunctatus, Danio nigrofasciatus*   Cyprinidae

Distribution: Burma – in rivers, streams and rice-paddies. Full length: 4.5 cm. Diet: live as well as artificial foods. Community tank. Breeding tank: of 6- to 10-litre capacity with spawning grid. Sexual dimorphism: the male is slimmer, his anal fin has a light brown border on the lower edge; the female is more robust. Sex ratio: 2 males : 1 female. Breeding water: 26–28 °C; pH 7.0; dCH max. 2°; fresh. Eggs: incubation period three days. Feeding of fry: as for *B. albolineatus*.

School fish, like a little more warmth than the other species of *Brachydanio.* They like light tanks flooded by the morning sun. The males and females should be separated for about three weeks before spawning. The female deposits a maximum of 300 eggs on plants. The parent fish should be removed after spawning. The fry become free-swimming in three days and assemble close to the surface. Their growth is rapid.

1 ♂

1 ♀

2

3

1 Giant Danio
Danio aequipinnatus (McClelland, 1839)
Syn. *Perilampus malabaricus, P. aurolineatus, P. canarensis, P. mysorius,*
Paradanio aurolineatus, Danio alburnus, D. aurolineatus, D. lineolatus, D. micronema,
D. osteographus, D. malabaricus, Leuciscus lineolatus

Cyprinidae

○ ◐ Distribution: west coast of India and Sri Lanka. Full length: 12 cm. Diet: live as well as artificial foods. Community tank. Breeding tank: of 50- to 100-litre capacity depending on the number of fish, with spawning grid, well-covered with glass, light to sun-flooded. Sexual dimorphism: the male has a greater amount of golden-brown colouring, the female is fuller in the body. Sex ratio: 2 males : 1 female (set the fish up in a shoal for spawning). Breeding water: 23−26 °C; pH 7.0; dCH max. 2°; fresh. Eggs: incubation period 30 hrs./26 °C. Feeding of fry: *Paramecium caudatum,* aqueous suspension of artificial fry foods, later nauplii of brine shrimp or *Cyclops.*

The brood fish are set up for spawning in the evening before putting out the light. Spawning generally takes place in the morning hours of the following day. There is usually a large number of eggs. After spawning the parent fish are taken out and the grid removed, a third to half of the water is replaced by fresh water, and the water is slightly coloured with methylene blue. On hatching the embryos suspend themselves from the glass sides of the tank with a sticky secretion from cutaneous glands. *D. aequipinnatus* is a lively school fish that is fond of sunlight. The fish may be put out in garden pools from June till September (in congenial years). In cooler summers they tolerate even lengthier spells of low temperatures down to 10 °C but do not grow. However, after being moved to a warm aquarium in the autumn they rapidly make up for the temporary halt in growth.

2 Bengal Danio
Danio devario (Hamilton-Buchanan, 1822)
Syn. *Cyprinus devario*

Cyprinidae

○ ◐ Distribution: Pakistan, northern India and Bangladesh to Assam. Full length: 10 cm. Diet: live as well as artificial foods. Community tank. Breeding tank: of 50- to 100-litre capacity depending on the number of fish, with spawning grid, light to sun-flooded, well covered with glass. Sexual dimorphism: the female is larger, deeper and fuller in the body. Sex ratio: 2 males : 1 female (the fish spawn in a shoal). Breeding water: 23−26 °C; pH 7.0; dCH max. 2°. Eggs: ∅ *c.* 1.5 mm, incubation period 30 hrs. Feeding of fry: *Paramecium caudatum,* aqueous suspension of artificial fry foods, nauplii of brine shrimp or *Cyclops.*

School fish. Readily interbreeds with *D. aequipinnatus.* The hybrid offspring resemble the males of *D. aequipinnatus* and are infertile. The fish stand up well to lower temperatures (15 °C) and may therefore be put in garden pools in the summer. The eleutherembryos hang from surrounding objects or else rest on the bottom. The fry grow rapidly and the young fish attain maturity at the age of six to eight months.

Cyprinidae

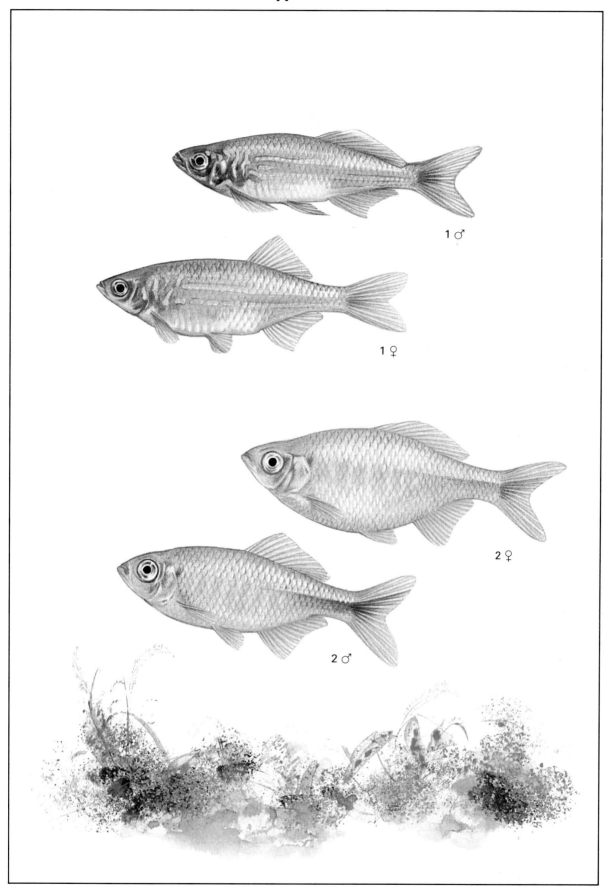

1 ♂

1 ♀

2 ♀

2 ♂

1 Bala 'Shark'
Balantiocheilus melanopterus (BLEEKER, 1850)
Syn. *Barbus melanopterus, Puntius melanopterus, Systomus melanopterus*

Cyprinidae

Distribution: Thailand, Malay Peninsula, Sumatra, Borneo. Full length: 35 cm. Diet: live as well as artificial foods. Community tank of 500- to 1000-litre capacity, or heated pools. Breeding tank: of 500-litre capacity with spawning grid. Sexual dimorphism: the male has more highly coloured fins, the ripe female is fuller in the body. Sex ratio: 2 males : 1 female (in a shoal). Breeding water: 25–26 °C; pH 6.4–7.0; dCH < 2°; dGH < 10°. Eggs: incubation period? Feeding of fry: brine shrimp nauplii.

School fish, rapid and expert swimmers. They should be kept in light and well covered tanks. Sexual maturity is attained on reaching a length of 15 cm.

This species is intensively propagated in Singapore breeding farms, but in all probability there is no record of its having been bred in aquarium conditions.

2 Gambian Barb
Barbodes ablabes (BLEEKER, 1863)
Syn. *Barbodes gambiensis, Barbus gambiensis*

Cyprinidae

Distribution: Guinea. Full length: 10 cm. Diet: live as well as artificial foods. Community tank. Breeding tank: of 50-litre capacity with spawning grid, finely-leaved plants. Sexual dimorphism: the male is smaller, slimmer, the orange colour on the fins is brighter. Sex ratio: 1:1. Breeding water: 24 °C; pH 6.5–7.0; dCH < 2°. Eggs: ∅ 1 mm, incubation period 18–24 hrs. Feeding of fry: nauplii of brine shrimp or *Cyclops.*

Very prolific species. After spawning take out the parent fish and add methylene blue to the water with the eggs. The first week the fry should also be fed at night under faint illumination. Growth is rapid in the first three weeks but then slows.

3 Five-banded Barb
Barbodes pentazona pentazona BOULENGER, 1894
Syn. *Puntius pentazona, Barbus pentazona*

Cyprinidae

Distribution: Malay Peninsula, Singapore, Sumatra, Borneo, calm waters in the lowlands. Full length: 5 cm. Diet: live as well as artificial foods. Community tank. Breeding tank: of 10-litre capacity with spawning grid, finely-leaved plants. Sexual dimorphism: the male is smaller, slimmer, more highly coloured, the ripe female is very full in the body. Sex ratio: 1:1. Breeding water: 26 °C; pH 6.0–7.0; dCH max. 1°; dGH 8–10°. Eggs: large, yellow to orange, incubation period 26–30 hrs. Feeding of fry: nauplii of brine shrimp or *Cyclops.*

Not every pair is willing to spawn. Separating the males and females is not recommended. The female deposits 300 to 400 eggs during spawning. After spawning the parent fish should be removed from the tank. Endogenous nutrition lasts six days. The fry grow rapidly at first, but at the age of two to three months their growth slows. Sexual maturity is attained at 10 to 12 months.

Cyprinidae

1 Clown Barb
Barbodes everetti BOULENGER, 1894
Syn. *Puntius everetti*

☐
◑ Distribution: Singapore, Borneo, Kalimantan Island. Full length: 13 cm. Diet: live, artificial and plant foods. Community tank. Breeding tank: of 100-litre capacity, shallow with large expanse of water, light to sun-flooded, finely-leaved plants, spawning grid. Sexual dimorphism: the male is more vividly coloured, the female noticeably fuller in the body. Sex ratio: 1:1 or 2 males : 1 female. Breeding water: 26−28 °C; pH 6.0−7.0; dCH < 2°; dGH < 10°. Eggs: incubation period 26−30 hrs.

Peaceful school fish. In small tanks they are shy and refuse to spawn. Before spawning the males and females should be separated for about 14 days. It is recommended to put in older males for spawning because they are not sexually mature until the age of 18 months, whereas females attain sexual maturity at 12 months.

2 *Barbodes bariloides* BOULENGER, 1914
Syn. *Barbus bariloides*

○
◑ Distribution: Angola, Zambia, Zaire − smaller waters overgrown with plants. Full length: 5 cm. Diet: live as well as artificial foods. Community tank. Breeding tank: of 10-litre capacity with spawning grid, finely-leaved plants. Sexual dimorphism: the male is deep rufous red with 12 to 15 bluish to black transverse stripes, the female is more robust, plainer in colour. Sex ratio: 1:1. Breeding water: 24 °C; pH 7.0; dCH < 1°. Eggs:

incubation period 24 hrs. Feeding of fry: nauplii of brine shrimp or *Cyclops*.

If the weather conditions are congenial young fish may be put outdoors in garden pools from June till September. They attain sexual maturity in four months. They should be kept in a large shoal.

3 *Barbodes eugrammus* SILAS, 1956
Syn. *Barbus eugrammus, Puntius eugrammus*

☐
◑ Distribution: Malay Peninsula, Sumatra, Borneo. Full length: 14 cm. Diet: live as well as artificial foods with occasional plant foods. Community tank. Breeding tank: of 50- to 100-litre capacity with spawning grid, plants; recommended height of water column − 20 cm. Sexual dimorphism: the female has fainter longitudinal stripes, is more high-backed and fuller in the body. Sex ratio: 1:1. Breeding water: 25−26 °C; pH 6.0−6.5; dCH < 1°; dGH max. 5°. Eggs: incubation period 24−30 hrs. Feeding of fry: nauplii of brine shrimp or *Cyclops*.

This longitudinally-striped barb with barbels was described as early as 1853 by Bleeker as *Barbus fasciatus.* However, because another fish (transversely-striped and without barbels) had been described as *Cirrhinus (Barbus) fasciatus* by Jerdon four years earlier the scientific name given to the species described by Bleeker later became invalid (secondary homonym) and 100 years later it was described again and given another name − *Barbodes eugrammus.*

Cyprinidae

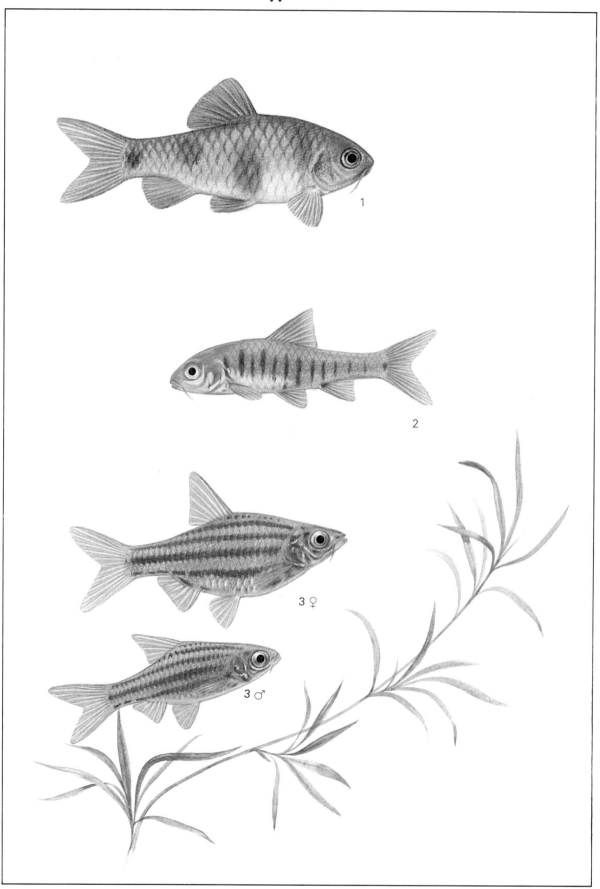

1

2

3 ♀

3 ♂

1 Black Ruby Barb or Purple-headed Barb

Puntius nigrofasciatus GÜNTHER, 1868

Syn. *Barbus nigrofasciatus*   Cyprinidae

Distribution: southern Sri Lanka, shallow, calm-flowing waters with dense vegetation. Full length: 6.5 cm. Diet: live as well as artificial foods. Community tank. Breeding tank: of 10-litre capacity with spawning grid, finely-leaved plants, subdued light. Sexual dimorphism: the male is higher in the back, larger and more intensely coloured. Sex ratio: 1:1. Breeding water: 24 °C; pH 6.5–7.0; dCH max. 1°; dGH 8–10°. Eggs: incubation period 24 hrs. Feeding of fry: *Cyclops* or brine shrimp nauplii, artificial fry foods.

Peaceful school fish, becoming aggressive only if they do not have enough room; in a tank with too much light and with a light bottom the fish are shy and pale. Spawning generally takes place in the morning hours. The fish spawn amidst plants for about two hours, after which they should be taken out. Endogenous nutrition lasts seven days. Some aquarists recommend keeping the fish at a low temperature of 14 to 16 °C during the winter. In spring such fish are then very willing to spawn at temperatures of 18 to 22 °C. Fish kept permanently at a high temperature are less coloured and reluctant to spawn.

2 Two-spot Barb

Puntius ticto stoliczkae (DAY, 1869)

Syn. *Barbus ticto stoliczkae*
(incorrect designation: *Puntius stoliczkanus, Barbus stoliczkanus*)   Cyprinidae

Distribution: southern Burma, Irrawaddy river region. Full length: 6 cm. Diet: live as well as artificial foods. Community tank. Breeding tank: of 10-litre capacity with spawning grid, finely-leaved plants. Sexual dimorphism: the dorsal fin of the male is coloured red, edged with black at the top and with a dark, sickle-shaped spot or several dark spots in the centre: the dorsal fin of the female is merely tinged with red. The other fins are transparent and she is fuller in the body. Sex ratio: 1:1. Breeding water: 24–26 °C; pH 6.5–7.0; dCH < 2°. Eggs: Ø 1–1.2 mm, brownish or greyish-yellow, clear, incubation period 24–30 hrs. Feeding of fry: the first three to four days *Paramecium caudatum* or *Cyclops* nauplii, later brine shrimp nauplii.

This species is not firmly established in terms of nomenclature. *P. ticto stoliczkae* apparently differs only by the number of scales in the transverse row from the nominate form *P. ticto ticto* (Hamilton-Buchanan, 1822), which reaches a length of 10 cm and inhabits the waters of India and Sri Lanka. It is thus quite possible that this is merely an ecotype of *Puntius ticto*. The eggs are small and glassily transparent. Endogenous nutrition lasts five days. The fry grow rapidly; in three months they reach a length of 4 cm and sexual differentiation begins. The fish attain sexual maturity in seven months. *P. ticto stoliczkae* is a school fish, the same as *P. conchonius*, with which it also interbreeds in artificially prepared conditions.

1 ♀

1 ♂

2 ♂

2 ♀

1 Rosy Barb
Puntius conchonius (HAMILTON-BUCHANAN, 1822)
Syn. *Cyprinus conchonius, Systomus conchonius, Barbus conchonius*   Cyprinidae

Distribution: northern India, Bangladesh, Assam, in rivers, ponds and pools; it is possible that it has also been introduced to places outside its original range. Full length: 15 cm. Diet: live as well as artificial foods, with occasional vegetable food. Community tank. Breeding tank: capacity of 20–100 litres depending on the size and number of fish, with spawning grid. Sexual dimorphism: the male is purplish-red with dorsal, ventral and anal fins coloured black, the female is less colourful, fuller in the body. Sex ratio: 1:1, the fish may also be bred in a shoal with a slight preponderance of males. Breeding water: 24 °C; pH 7.0; dCH max. 2°. Eggs: glassy, very sticky, incubation period 24 hrs. Feeding of fry: nauplii of brine shrimp or *Cyclops* and artificial fry foods.

Aquarium fish are generally smaller. Due to lengthy inbreeding and unfavourable conditions many populations are stunted and attain sexual maturity when they are only 4 cm long. After spawning the parent fish should be removed and half the water replaced by fresh water. The eggs should be treated with methylene blue. Free-swimming fry should be fed intensively three to four times a day, with an additional feeding at night, the first week under faint light. In roomy tanks the fry grow rapidly. When the young fish reach a length of 1 cm they may be put outdoors in garden pools (June to September). They tolerate brief spells of low temperature (down to 10 °C) without harm. Young fish kept in pools can be expected to attain optimum size.

2 *Puntius conchonius* – veil-finned form
Cyprinidae

This mutation was bred and genetically fixed in the USSR in the late sixties. As a result of inbreeding these fish are stunted, reaching a maximum length of 5 cm.

3 *Puntius conchonius* – xanthoristic (xanthistic) (golden) form
Cyprinidae

This form was bred and genetically fixed in the German Democratic Republic and Czechoslovakia. It reaches a maximum length of only 5 cm. The fish are more thermophilous (like more warmth).

4 *Puntius conchonius* – xanthoristic (xanthistic) (golden), veil-finned form
Cyprinidae

In the early seventies breeders were successful in obtaining these attractive fish by crossing veil-finned forms with the short-finned xanthoristic form. Further selective breeding was carried out in the USSR, GDR, and Czechoslovakia. It seems that the long fins have not been absolutely genetically fixed as yet. Maximum length 5 cm, more thermophilous (warmth-loving) fish.

None of these forms should be cross-bred with the original wild form, whose characteristics are dominant.

1 ♂
1 ♀
2 ♂
3 ♂
3 ♀
4 ♂

1 Black-spot Barb

Puntius filamentosus (CUVIER and VALENCIENNES, 1844)

Syn. *Leuciscus filamentosus, Barbus mahecola, B. filamentosus, Systomus assimilis*   Cyprinidae

Distribution: southern and southwest India, Sri Lanka, mountain streams. Full length: 15 cm. Diet: live as well as artificial foods. Community tank (together with larger, lively species of fish). Breeding tank: with capacity of 100—200 litres, spawning grid. Sexual dimorphism: conspicuous; the male has the dorsal fin rays extended, terminating in a pectinate elongation, and a spawning rash on the snout above the upper jaw. Sex ratio: 1 : 1 or a slight preponderance of females (artificial fertilization is also possible). Breeding water: 26 °C; pH 7.0; dCH max. 1°. Eggs: minute, yellowish, slightly adhesive, incubation period 48 hrs. Feeding of fry: nauplii of brine shrimp or *Cyclops*.

Breeder fish attain sexual maturity at approximately 18 months. Spawning takes place among plants at the surface and is very vigorous. During the extremely brief act of mating the male is pressed against the female and lightly entwines her body with his tail fin.

Inasmuch as *P. filamentosus* is a rather robust fish it is possible to perform artificial fertilization. A must, when doing this, is gentle handling of the breeder fish and absolute cleanliness of all equipment. Artificial fertilization by the dry method must be done calmly, quickly, skilfully, and without damaging the fish. Artificial fertilization should always be performed at the beginning of the natural spawning period. The egg must not come in contact with water before it is joined with the sperm (the procedure of artificial fertilization is described under *Carassius auratus*).

The number of eggs released by the female is very large. When spawning is over the parent fish should be removed from the tank and half the water should be replaced by fresh water of the same composition and temperature. Colour the water faintly with methylene blue. Because of the great number of young fish make sure they have sufficient food and fresh water. Later sort them according to size to promote regular and rapid growth. Young fish have a typical juvenile coloration that is quite different from that of the adult fish. This colouring disappears at about seven months and the third transverse band is transformed into a blotch resembling a teardrop.

1 ♂

1 ♀

1 juv.

1 Two-spot Barb
Capoeta bimaculata (BLEEKER, 1864)
Syn. *Barbus bimaculatus, Barbodes bimaculatus*

Cyprinidae

Distribution: Sri Lanka. Full length: 7 cm. Diet: live, artificial and plant foods. Community tank. Breeding tank: of 9- to 10-litre capacity with spawning grid, finely-leaved plants, light to sun-flooded. Sexual dimorphism: the male is slimmer, smaller, faintly reddish on the sides. Sex ratio: 1:1 (the fish may be bred in a shoal in larger tanks). Breeding water: 24 °C; pH 6.5−7.0; dCH max. 2°. Eggs: small, glassy and sticky; incubation period 24 hrs. Feeding of fry: the first two days *Paramecium caudatum,* then nauplii of brine shrimp or *Cyclops.*

The fish spawn most frequently in the morning. The female is very prolific and in two hours deposits several hundred eggs. About 500 young fish may be reared from a single female and single spawning. The eleutherembryos hang from the glass sides of the tank and other firm objects. Endogenous nutrition lasts two days after which the fry become free-swimming. The young fish grow slowly. In view of their great number they must be transferred in time to roomy tanks. During growth the best temperature is 20 to 22 °C. Provide strained spinach as auxiliary food. When water is added to the tank the young fish jump, making long leaps counter to the flow of the water. In calm water they do not jump from the tank.

2 Odessa Barb
Puntius sp. 'Odessa'

Cyprinidae

Origin unknown. (Among other theories, Dr. H. R. Axelrod believes the fish are from North Vietnam). Full length: 6 cm. Diet: live as well as artificial foods. Community tank. Breeding tank: of 10- to 50-litre capacity with spawning grid, finely-leaved plants. Sexual dimorphism: the male has a prominent red longitudinal band on either side, the female is fuller in the body. Sex ratio: 1:1 (the fish may be bred in pairs as well as in a shoal). Breeding water: 25 °C; pH 7.0; dCH 2° (according to some breeders the eggs develop even at dCH 7°). Eggs: ∅ 0.9 mm, incubation period 18−20 hrs/28 °C, 24 hrs/25 °C. Feeding of fry: brine shrimp nauplii.

The fish are very prolific. Rearing is simple. The growth of young fish is more rapid if there are fewer fish in the tank.

Cyprinidae

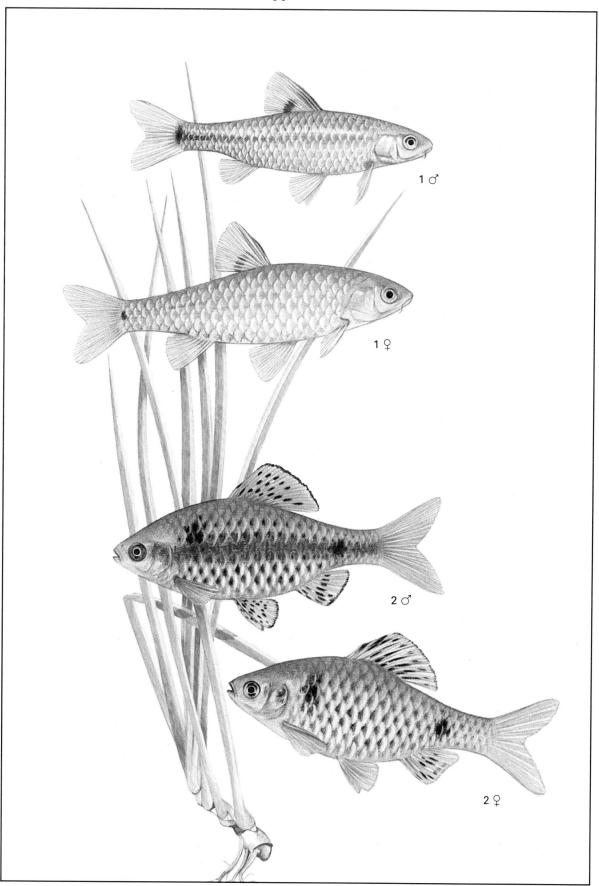

1 ♂

1 ♀

2 ♂

2 ♀

1 **T-barb** or **Spanner Barb**

Barbodes lateristriga CUVIER and VALENCIENNES, 1844

Syn. *Barbus zelleri, B. lateristriga, Systomus lateristriga, Puntius lateristriga*   Cyprinidae

Distribution: southeast Asia – Thailand, Singapore, Sumatra, Java, Borneo and other islands, Malay Peninsula – clear flowing waters and ponds. Full length: 20 cm. Diet: live as well as artificial foods with occasional vegetable food. Community tank; but only if kept together with fish of similar size and like requirements. Breeding tank: of 100- to 200-litre capacity with spawning grid, thickets of plants, water column 25–30 cm high. Sexual dimorphism: the male is more slender and more vividly coloured. Sex ratio: 1:1 (several pairs may be put in the tank for spawning). Breeding water: 26–28 °C; pH 6.5–7.0; dCH < 2°; dGH max. 10°. Eggs: sticky, incubation period 48 hrs. Feeding of fry: brine shrimp nauplii, finely sifted zooplankton.

Lively, undemanding, robust fish. Young fish assemble in shoals, older fish tend to be solitary. The female deposits several hundred eggs during a single spawning. Spawning generally takes place in the early morning in plant thickets with the males vigorously chasing the females. The parent fish should be removed after spawning. The young fish should be graded according to size during growth and their number thinned by putting them into several separate tanks. Spacious heated pools are well suited for rearing young fish.

2 **Longfin Barb**

Capoeta arulia (JERDON, 1849)

Syn. *Barbus arulius, Puntius arulius*   Cyprinidae

Distribution: southeastern India. Full length: 12 cm. Diet: live as well as artificial foods with occasional vegetable food. Community tank. Breeding tank: with capacity of 100 litres per pair, spawning grid, finely-leaved plants, diffused light. Sexual dimorphism: the male is slimmer and slightly smaller, with dorsal rays lengthened in fan-like fashion and with a spawning rash round the mouth. Sex ratio: 1:1 (the fish may also be bred in a shoal). Breeding water: 24–26 °C; pH 6.5–7.0; dCH < 2°. Eggs: slightly adhesive, the colour of tea, ∅ 1.5 mm, incubation period 35 hrs/26 °C. Feeding of fry: *Cyclops* or brine shrimp nauplii.

Lively school fish. Spawning takes place at dusk on the bottom both amidst plants as well as in open water. When there is insufficient space the male may thrash the female to death. During the period of endogenous nutrition the embryos are suspended on plants and on the sides of the tank in darker places. Seven days after becoming free-swimming the fry attain a length of 3.5 mm. Their growth is relatively rapid.

1 ♀

1

1

2 ♂

2 ♀

1 Checker Barb, Island Barb or Iridescent Barb
Capoeta oligolepis (BLEEKER, 1853)
Syn. *Barbus oligolepis, Puntius oligolepis, Systomus oligolepis*   Cyprinidae

Distribution: water systems of Sumatra. Full length: 1.5 cm. Diet: live as well as artificial foods. Community tank. Breeding tank: of 10- to 50-litre capacity (depending on the number of parent fish) with spawning grid, finely-leaved plants. Sexual dimorphism: the male is slimmer with fins coloured brick-red edged with black and prominent border on the dorsal and anal fin. Sex ratio: 1:1 (the fish may also be bred in a shoal). Breeding water: 24 °C; pH 6.5; dCH < 2°. Eggs: incubation period 36 hrs. Feeding of fry: brine shrimp nauplii.

The fish should be kept in a shoal. Rearing is not difficult.
According to some sources a great many hybrids have been obtained by crossing *C. oligolepis* × *Puntius conchonius, Barbus dunckeri, Capoeta semifasciolata, Puntius ticto stoliczkae, P. ticto ticto, P. vittatus, Brachydanio albolineatus, B. rerio, Danio aequipinnatus.* According to H. Frey the fish may have two or four barbels. In aquarium conditions aquarists have succeeded in developing a xanthoristic form that is genetically fixed.

2 Cherry Barb
Capoeta titteya (DERANIYAGALA, 1929)
Syn. *Barbus frenatus, B. titteya, Puntius titteya*   Cyprinidae

Distribution: shaded brooks and lowland rivers of Sri Lanka. Full length: 5 cm. Diet: small, live as well as artificial foods with occasional plant foods. Spacious monospecies keeping tank. In mixed aquariums the fish are shy and their behaviour unnatural. Breeding tank: of 10-litre capacity with spawning grid, finely-leaved plants, dark bottom, light diffused through floating plants, water column *c.* 10–15 cm high. Sexual dimorphism: the male is red, the female brownish with conspicuous longitudinal stripe. Sex ratio: 1:1. Breeding water: 25–27 °C; pH 6.5–7.0; dCH < 2°. Eggs: the colour of tea, attached to plants by filaments, incubation period 24 hrs. Feeding of fry: nauplii of brine shrimp or *Cyclops.*

Populations from native waters as well as from aquariums are variable in coloration. Peaceable fish tending to remain scattered rather than assembling in shoals. Males are quarrelsome towards one another. The act of spawning lasts about three hours, with the female releasing one or two eggs at each mating and up to 300 in all. During the period of endogenous nutrition the larvae generally rest on the bottom. When the fry become free-swimming the level of the water should be lowered to about 5 cm and then gradually increased as the young fish grow.

Cyprinidae

1 ♂

1 ♀

2 ♂

2 ♀

1 Half-banded Barb, Chinese Barb or Green Barb

Capoeta semifasciolata GÜNTHER, 1868

Syn. *Capoeta guentheri, Puntius guentheri, P. semifasciolatus, Barbus semifasciolatus*

Cyprinidae

○
◑

Distribution: southeastern China from Hong Kong to the island of Hainan. Full length: 10 cm. Diet: live as well as artificial foods. Community tank. Breeding tank: of 10- to 50-litre capacity depending on the number of parent fish, with spawning grid, finely-leaved plants. Sexual dimorphism: the male is more vividly coloured, the female robust, markedly fuller in the body. Sex ratio: 1:1 (several pairs of fish may be put in the tank for spawning). Breeding water: 24 °C; pH 6.5–7.0; dCH < 2°. Eggs: sticky, incubation period 30–36 hrs. Feeding of fry: nauplii of brine shrimp or *Cyclops.*

Spawning takes place mostly in the morning hours. It is very tempestuous; the female deposits approximately 300 eggs. The parent fish should be taken out after spawning and methylene blue added to the water with the egs. The grid should also be removed but not until the fry become free-swimming. Rearing is simple.

2 Gold Barb

Capoeta semifasciolata 'schuberti'

Commercial name: *Barbus 'schuberti', Puntius 'schuberti'*
Care and breeding the same as for *Capoeta semifasciolata.*

Cyprinidae

○
◑

In 1868 Günther described the species *Capoeta semifasciolata* and in 1923 E. Ahl described the species *Puntius sachsi.* The two are practically identical. They are distinguished only according to their origin and variable coloration; *C. semifasciolata* has two barbels, *P. sachsi* has none. *C. s. 'schuberti'* was considered to be a xanthoristic form of both the aforesaid species. In fact, however, there exist three forms of *C. 'schuberti'.* The first is not typically xanthoristic because it has black spots (see illustration). The second form is derived from populations reared in captivity in Europe — it is yellow-orange, without spots, and with dark eyes, in other words a typical xanthoristic form. The third form has red eyes and is thus albinistic. It was determined that all three are colour aberrations of *Capoeta semifasciolata;* in no case are they aberrations of *Puntius sachsi.*

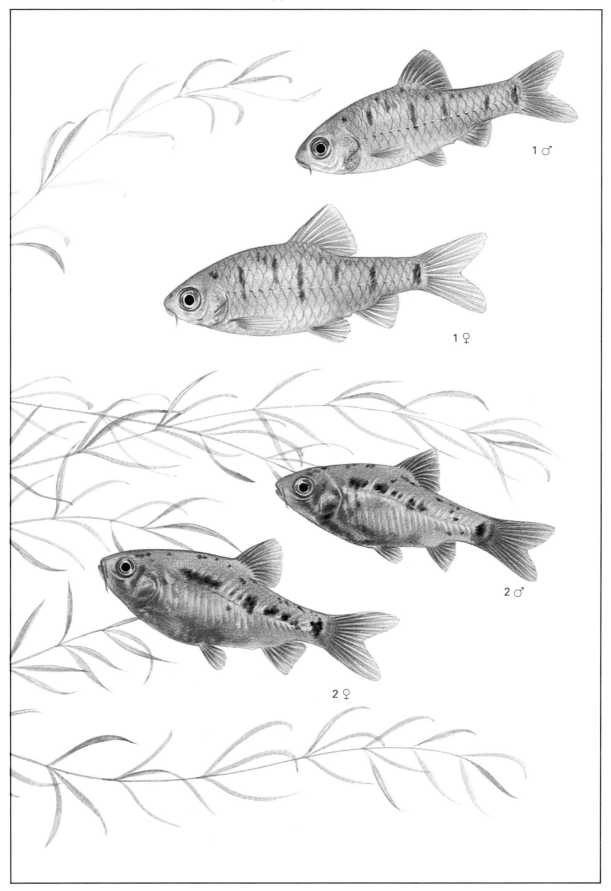

1 ♂

1 ♀

2 ♂

2 ♀

1 **Sumatra Barb** or **Tiger Barb**

Capoeta tetrazona tetrazona (BLEEKER, 1855)
Syn. *Puntius tetrazona, Barbus tetrazona*

Cyprinidae

Distribution: Indonesia — Sumatra, Borneo. Full length: 7 cm. Diet: live as well as artificial foods. Community tank (neither with slower, peaceful fish, nor with long-finned fish). Breeding tank: with capacity of 10 litres per pair, spawning grid, finely-leaved plants. Sexual dimorphism: the ventral fins of the male are deep red to the margins, the upper snout is reddish, the dorsal fin is edged with vivid red, the female is fuller, with duller colouring and ventral fins transparent on the margins. Sex ratio: 1:1. Breeding water: 26 °C; pH 6.5—7.0; dCH < 1° (peat extract may be added). Eggs: $\varnothing$ 1 mm, sticky, incubation period 36 hrs. Feeding of fry: nauplii of brine shrimp or *Cyclops*.

The males are aggressive during the spawning period and in a small aquarium may thrash unripe females to death. This does not happen if the fish are in a shoal and in a large aquarium. Therefore in a smaller breeding tank if the fish do not spawn within 24 hours it is recommended to take the pair out and repeat the process later. As with other species of fish successful breeding depends on the carbonate hardnes dCH; if the dCH is less than 1° the percentage of undeveloped eggs increases. The females are prolific, particularly those that are regularly spawned. Young fish grow rapidly; in 14 days they reach a length of 1 cm and are conspicuously banded. This species is prone to various diseases.

2 *Capoeta tetrazona* — mossy form

Cyprinidae

In 1975 the West German company Gustav Struck-Manching imported an interesting colour mutation called the 'mossy barb'. The parent generation, apparently from Asian breeding enterprises, was not fully fixed genetically and this became evident after the first spawning. The offspring of the imported fish varied widely in coloration (dissimilar hereditary traits) — they included the wild form, specimens with atypical bands, the albinistic and xanthoristic 'Hong Kong' forms, and the slowest-growing mossy form. During the course of lengthier selective breeding in Czechoslovakia and the German Democratic Republic the purity of the populations was greatly improved. In selecting fish for spawning it is necessary to exclude all atypical fish and those that are not well and fully coloured because black colouring is recessively hereditary (in offspring it is often suppressed and readily gives way to the dominant wild colouring). Care and breeding are the same as for the wild form, but the females deposit fewer eggs and the growth of the young fish is much slower than in the wild form.

Cyprinidae

1 ♂

1 ♀

2 ♂

2 ♀

149

1 *Capoeta tetrazona,* albinistic form

Selectively bred form with full set of scales. In selecting fish for spawning it is necessary to exclude specimens coloured like the wild form or with coloration in any way different from the albinotic form.

2 *Capoeta tetrazona* – xanthoristic 'Hong Kong' form

This form was apparently bred in Asia. It is distinguished by being flesh-coloured and without any indication of bands. In substance it is a xanthoristic form without scales or with only a few scales. Specimens bred in Asia (Singapore) are genetically fixed and deviations from this form are practically non-existent.

3 **Butterfly Barb**
Capoeta hulstaerti (POOL, 1945)
Syn. *Barbus hulstaerti*

Distribution: Africa: region of the lower Zaire (Congo) river, Pool Malebo (Stanley Pool), and Angola. Full length: 3.5 cm. Diet: live as well as artificial foods with occasional vegetable food. Monospecies keeping tank. Breeding tank: of 10- to 20-litre capacity with spawning grid, finely-leaved plants, shaded to dark. Sexual dimorphism: the male is slimmer, the forward spot on the sides is comma-shaped, the forward spot is less distinct and rounded. Sex ratio: 1:1 or in a shoal with a slight preponderance of males. Breeding water: 24 °C; pH 6.0–6.5; dCH 0°; dGH 5°; (according to some sources the top temperature limit of the water for the fry is 22 °C). Eggs: incubation period ?. Feeding of fry: ?.

Reports about the care and breeding of this species are few. The fish should always be kept in a large shoal. Some authorities recommend that the substrate on the bottom of the tank be alternately light and dark. The fish purportedly spawn in the darkest parts of the tank. They are sensitive to fluctuations in the chemical composition of the water. In mixed aquariums with other species of fish they are generally shy and inactive.

1 – *Barbodes pentazona pentazona*
2 – *Barbodes pentazona kahajani*
3 – *Barbodes pentazona hexazona*
4 – *Capoeta tetrazona partipentazona*

Cyprinidae

1 ♂

2 ♂

2 ♀

3 ♀

3 ♂

There are over 100 varieties of goldfish of which only a few are mentioned here.

1 *Carassius auratus* (LINNAEUS, 1758)
Syn. *Cyprinus auratus*

Distribution: Far East – Japan, Korea and China, Sakhalin, the region of the Amur River, Siberia, and the whole of the Soviet Union. It is also found in central Asia and is currently penetrating into central Europe. After 1960 it was introduced into ponds in Hungary and Romania and has migrated to the Tisa and Danube Rivers basins; as of 1970 its spread took on the form of an invasion with the species penetrating as far as the waters of the Morava, Svratka and Dyje Rivers basins in Czechoslovakia. Besides this, in certain congenial localities, domesticated ornamental forms have reverted to the wild. Full length: 36 cm. Diet: live, artificial and plant foods. Monospecies keeping tank. Breeding tank: spacious, stocked with plant thickets. Sexual dimorphism: the male has a rash on the gill covers during the spawning period. In some colour strains, however, e.g. white or black, this spawning rash is barely discernible. The male may also be identified by his violent chasing of the ripe female. Sex ratio: 2 males : 1 female (1 male and several females in the case of artificial insemination). Breeding water: 18–25 °C; pH 7.0; dCH max. 2°. Eggs: $\varnothing$ c. 1 mm, sticky, incubation period 72 hrs/25 °C. The hatching of the embryos may take several hours longer; they hatch in succession (this applies to all other forms as well). Cultivated in Europe as an ornamental fish since the 17th century.

The species is differentiated into two types of population: a) fast growing, with only so-called gynogamic females, and b) slow-growing, with the proportion of males and females about equal. There are no visible morphological differences between the two populations and hence the original division into the subspecies *C. auratus gibelio* and *C. auratus auratus* is open to question. Gynogamic females spawn with males of other species of cyprinid fish such as the Common Bream (*Abramis brama*), Silver Bream (*Blicca bjoerkna*), Carp (*Cyprinus carpio*), Crucian Carp (*Carassius carassius*), Roach (*Rutilus rutilus*), Chub (*Leuciscus cephalus*), Ide (*Leuciscus idus*), and Tench (*Tinca tinca*), and the offspring are all gynogamic females. This is a case of so-called merospermatic fertilization in which the sperm of another, different species penetrates the egg but the nuclei of the two do not fuse and the sperm nucleus dies. The egg nucleus undergoes cleavage with the participation of the sperm centriole (a body in the head of the sperm that develops into the whip-like tail). The alien sperm thus merely activates the egg. This, then, is not a crossing of two species in the ordinary sense, nor is it explicitly parthenogenesis (development of an unfertilized ovum possessing only the characteristics of the mother), for the resulting population possesses the occasional paternal characteristic, e.g. barbels inherited from male carp. This unusual method of reproduction is called gynogenesis and occurs, for example, in *C. auratus* populations from the Amur River.

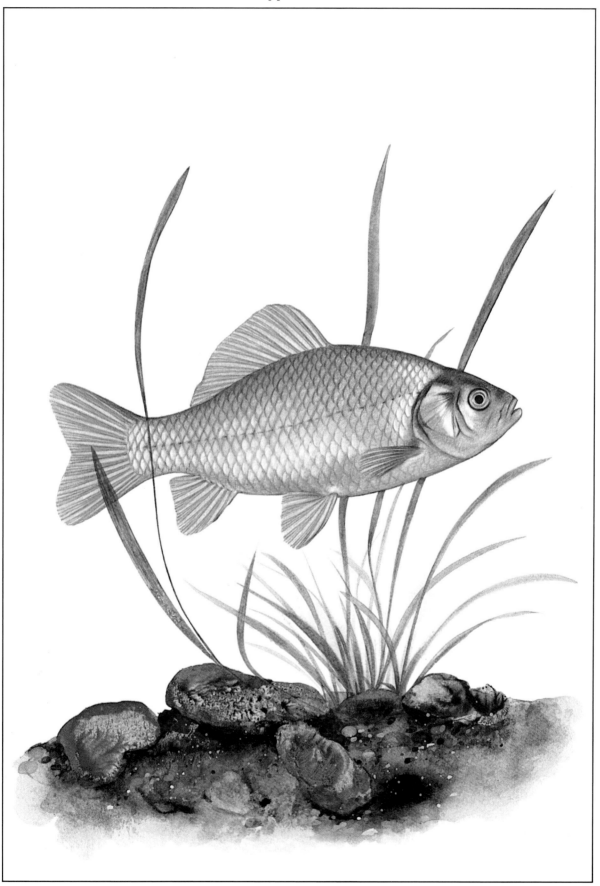

□
●

The Chinese found the golden form of *C. auratus,* the Goldfish, so attractive that they kept it in special pools and made it the object of a cult. By selective breeding in captivity for over a thousand years they developed the fish known today as veiltails – *C. auratus* var. *bicaudatus.* It may be said that the goldfish, which for centuries now has been kept by man in household aquariums, has been fully domesticated, even though it cannot be called a household pet. During this time there appeared many different forms which man reproduced and cross-bred, haphazardly at first and later systematically, so that the final outcome is a vast number of forms for whose preservation we are indebted to the skill and knowledge of Far East breeders. Wild forms are reproduced in vast quantities at farms in the USA and supplied as food fish. Breeding fish should be overwintered at a temperature of about 10 °C; this applies particularly to certain rather sensitive forms such as the black telescope. Other forms will survive the winter outdoors under a layer of ice and often attain relatively large proportions. The fish become sexually mature at the age of two years, on the rare occasion at one year. Some older females may deposit as many as 400,000 eggs.

Diet, tank, water, care and breeding are the same as for *C. auratus auratus.*

□
●

This form was developed in China apparently as late as the beginning of the 20th century. The body is egg-shaped and scaly. The dorsal fin is absent, the caudal fin is short, forked and quadripartite, the anal fin double. The eye is normal with the typical fluid-filled leathery bubble. The colour is variable – silvery white, gold, orange, mottled, brown, or cinnamon. The length of the body is 70 to 80 mm, the length of the caudal fin 50 to 60 mm.

The only way to ensure the purity of specific forms of veiltails is by artificial insemination. For this it is necessary to obtain eggs and milt from fully ripe breeding fish, which should be done at the beginning of the natural spawning period. The method that has proved most successful is the so-called dry method of artificial insemination where first the eggs and then the milt are collected in a dry dish. These are then mixed together with a goose or chicken quill and covered with water. In the water the sperm then become mobile and fertilization takes place. The motility of the sperm lasts only seconds and depends on the temperature and physico-chemical properties of the water. Equally brief is the time it takes for the micropyle of the egg (the minute opening through which the sperm enters) to open. On contact with water the eggs become very sticky. After 24 hours rinse off the slime with a stream of water of the same composition and temperature. Colouring the water faintly with methylene blue will prevent the spread of fungi. Fertilization is almost 100 per cent successful by this method, whereas by the so-called wet method of artificial insemination in water the rate of success is only 40 to 70 per cent.

Diet, tank, water, care and breeding are the same as for *C. auratus auratus.*

1 *Carassius auratus* var. *bicaudatus* – 'Red Cap'

This form originated in China, probably in the years 1547–1643. Present-day 'Red Caps' have an egg-shaped body covered with scales without a dorsal fin, the anal fin double, the caudal fin forked and quadripartite. The body colour is whitish-silvery with a metallic glint, the fins are opaque to transparent. On top of the head is an orange to red-coloured 'cap' from which this form takes its name. The body measures 70 to 80 mm in length, the caudal fin 50 to 70 mm or even more. Similarly coloured fish with a fully developed dorsal fin are imported from Japan and have been bred for some time past by European breeders as well.

2 *Carassius auratus* var. *bicaudatus* – 'Red form'

The breeding of red-coloured fish with a forked caudal fin was begun in China apparently after 1644. The red colour occurs in veiltails very frequently, both in the classic as well as in numerous other forms.

Diet, tank, water, care and breeding are the same as for *C. auratus auratus*.

3 *Carassius auratus* var. *bicaudatus* – 'Calico'

So-called 'Tiger Fish' appeared in China apparently between 1547 and 1643. No more was heard about them until 1900, when the 'Tiger Fish', also called 'Calico' (Shubunkin), appeared once again in Japan. This form was developed by a goldfish dealer in Tokyo by cross-breeding the 'Wakin' form and the 'Hibuna' form of the 'Calico' telescope fish. (The 'Wakin' is a robust, 30 cm long, hardy form with simple caudal fin – a form closest to the original veiltail. It may be coloured red, red-and-white, or white. 'Hibuna' is a scarlet-coloured, elongated form with simple fin.) 'Calico' (Shubunkin) is a scaleless form with simple, veil-like tail fin. It is irregularly spotted in a combination of the classic colours red, yellow and black, plus grey and blue. 'Shubunkin' also includes single-coloured as well as multi-coloured forms, e.g. blue, brown-and-red, black-and-white, red-and-black, black-white-and-red, black-white-and-gold, red-black-and-blue. They are considered to be the most suitable for garden ponds and pools.

The illustrated form 'Calico' (Shubunkin), imported from Japan, has the classic veiltail shape. Similarly coloured is 'Azuma Nishiki' (the Dutch Calico) with a body like that of a 'Lionhead', bred in Japan round 1920.

Diet, care and breeding are the same as for *C. auratus auratus*.

1 *Carassius auratus* var. *bicaudatus* – Telescope

Cyprinidae

Fish of this variety with telescope eyes were developed in China in the years 1547–1643. In Japan this form was widely bred in various colours. Those cultivated included red-coloured fish, variously mottled (calico) fish, and ones with transparent scales. Typical of telescope fish are the greatly protruding eyes, projecting in the line of the optic axis symmetrically on both sides. Such eyes are the result of retina degeneration caused by hormones secreted by the thyroid gland. The body is relatively short, the caudal fin was originally short but in recent years has become longer through breeding. The black telescope fish was developed in China in the years 1848–1925 and is also widespread and bred in Japan.

Diet, tank, water, care and breeding are the same as for *C. auratus auratus*.

2 *Carassius auratus* var. *bicaudatus* – Skygazer

Cyprinidae

This form was developed in China round 1895. It was then further bred in Japan.

Diet, tank, water, care and breeding are the same as for *C. auratus auratus*.

3 *Carassius auratus* var. *bicaudatus* – Oranda

Cyprinidae

The Oranda, or so-called Dutch Lionhead, is one of the largest forms of this variety. It reaches a length of 60 cm, with the length of the tail equalling that of the head and body combined. All the fins are long. The Dutch Lionhead was apparently brought from China to Japan (Nagasaki) by Dutch merchants in the 17th century and bred further in that country. Unlike the Chinese Lionheads, bred in China apparently round 1846, which had an egg-shaped body without a dorsal fin, this form has a developed dorsal fin and deeply forked caudal fin which may be quadripartite and fringe-like. The sponge-like skin excrescences around the head do not begin to develop until the second year. Orandas have been bred in various colours – they may be yellow, orange, and various shades of red and black.

Diet, tank, water, care and breeding are the same as for *C. auratus auratus*.

There are many species of Carp of which only a few are mentioned here.

Carp
1 *Cyprinus carpio carpio* LINNAEUS, 1758
Syn. *Cyprinus acuminiatus, C. coriaceus, C. elatus, C. hungaricus, C. macrolepidotus, C. regina, C. rex cyprinorum, C. specularis*

Distribution: the wild form – Sazan – inhabits the tributaries of the Mediterranean, Black, Caspian and Aral seas. The body is elongate, measuring three and a half to four times less in height than in length. It reaches a total length of 100 cm. A cultivated high-backed form measuring only two and a half to three times less in height than in length and an ornamental form, *C. carpio* var. Koi, bred in Japan, were derived from this wild form. The latter has the elongated build of the wild form. According to various reports it has run wild in some European waters.

Diet: because the fish readily become fat their diet should contain 70 per cent protein (live foods), 20 per cent carbohydrates (rolled oats, pasta), nine per cent vegetable food and one per cent minerals. At higher temperatures during the summer months feed them more frequently, at temperatures below 15 °C reduce the proportion of proteins, at temperatures of below 8 °C cease feeding them entirely – their metabolism is greatly suppressed. Tank: ornamental pools and ponds slanting slightly to one side, 80–120 cm deep, with firm bottom and sediment bowl; plant with water-lilies. Breeding tank: small, well-planted ponds. The fish may be spawned artificially. Sexual dimorphism: viewed from above the female is more robust, the male has a faint spawning rash. Sex ratio: set up the fish to spawn in groups with a slight preponderance of males. Breeding water: 15–20 °C; pH 7.0–7.5; dCH 2°; dGH 10–15°, fresh, rich in oxygen. Eggs: ∅ *c.* 1 mm, sticky, incubation period five days/15 °C, three days/20 °C. Feeding of fry: finely sifted zooplankton.

The fish attain sexual maturity at the age of two to four years, the males earlier than the females. The female deposits the eggs on aquatic or submerged plants. She may deposit up to 1,500,000 eggs. The newly-hatched fry hang from plants with the aid of the sticky glands on the head. Endogenous nutrition lasts approximately 10 days. The fish must be handled with care; use the largest possible net of the finest mesh. The optimum temperature range for Koi is 16 to 20 °C. At higher temperatures the pool should be shaded and part of the water replaced by fresh water, and in winter it is recommended to keep the fish indoors.

The recorded history of carps is very old. In a preserved third-century manuscript we find mention of red, white and blue carp. The various colour forms as we know them today, however, were not bred until the late 19th century. Koi are divided into two basic types according to body build:

A) slender fish of the Asian line probably derived in part from the Asian subspecies *C. carpio haematopterus;*

B) broader fish of the European line, originating chiefly in Germany. The systematic breeding and crossing of the individual forms produced a whole range of magnificent colours from which the various Koi carps take their name. The following are three of the many forms: a – Taisho Sanke – red, black, white; b – Tancho Sanke – white, black plus a red patch on the head, and c – Kin Showa – red with orange and black markings.

Cyprinidae

1 a

1 b

1 c

1 Trunk Barb or Flying Fox

Epalzeorhynchus kallopterus (Bleeker, 1850)

Syn. *Barbus kallopterus*

Cyprinidae

Distribution: southeast Asia — Indonesia: Thailand, Sumatra and Borneo, flowing waters. Full length: 16 cm. Diet: live, artificial foods augmented by vegetable foods. Monospecies keeping tank. Sexual differences and manner of reproducing are not yet known. Water: 24–26 °C; pH 6.5–7.0; dCH max. 1°; dGH 5–8°.

The fish should be kept in a large tank of about 500-litre capacity with a relatively small number of specimens so they have plenty of room. It is necessary to provide them with plenty of hiding places. Older specimens are aggressive and defend their territories, particularly against others of their own kind. They dwell on the bottom, where they also search for food. The mouth is provided with two pairs of barbels. When at rest they like to lie on the bottom propped up on their pectoral fins. They purportedly also feed on planarians.

2 Siamese Flying Fox

Epalzeorhynchus siamensis Smith, 1931

Cyprinidae

Distribution: Thailand and Malay Peninsula, flowing waters. Full length: 14 cm. Diet: live, artificial and plant foods, chiefly algae. Monospecies keeping tank, richly planted in places, with mineralized wood from moors. Sexual dimorphism: not known. Water: 24–26 °C; pH 6.5–7.0; dCH max. 1°; dGH 5–8°; oxygen-rich. This species has not been bred in captivity as yet; it seems that it will be possible to use the experience gained in breeding fish of the genus *Labeo* as a guideline.

The fish are aggressive towards others of their own kind and should therefore be kept in a roomy tank containing relatively few specimens and provided with plenty of hiding places.

Unlike the similar *E. kallopterus*, *E. siamensis* has transparent fins with delicate white shading and the broad dark band along the body ends at the base of the tail (in *E. kallopterus* it extends into the tail). The body beneath the band is white. The mouth is subterminal and provided with two pairs of barbels on the upper jaw. The fish specialize in grazing off algae, also consuming thread-like algae; they take no notice of higher plants. They also eat planarians, a fact that may be used to good advantage in controlling these unwelcome aquarium guests. In its home countries this species is used as a food fish.

1 Indian Hatchet Fish
Chela laubuca (Hamilton-Buchanan, 1822)
Syn. *Cyprinus laubuca, Laubuca laubuca, L. siamensis, Leuciscus laubuca, Perilampus guttatus, P. laubuca*

Cyprinidae

Distribution: Sri Lanka, Burma, Thailand, Malay Peninsula, Sumatra. Full length: 6 cm. Diet: live as well as artificial foods. Community tank. Breeding tank: of 50-litre capacity with spawning grid, elongate, light to sun-flooded, well covered, water column 12–20 cm high. Sexual dimorphism: the male is slimmer, the female fuller and more robust. Sex ratio: 2 males : 1 female (the fish should be set up in a shoal for spawning). Breeding water: 24–26 °C; pH 6.5; dCH < 2°; fresh. Eggs: incubation period 24 hrs/24 °C. Feeding of fry: *Paramecium caudatum*, extremely fine *Cyclops* or brine shrimp nauplii (aqueous suspension of artificial fry foods).

Spawning takes place before dusk. The female deposits several hundred eggs. Endogenous nutrition lasts three days. Both young and adult fish should be given food several times a day in smaller quantities. If given too much food serious health disorders may ensue and the fish may even die.

2 Flying Barb
Esomus danrica (Hamilton-Buchanan, 1822)
Syn. *Nuria danrica*

Cyprinidae

Distribution: India, Sri Lanka, Thailand, shallow waters with large surface area, also rice paddies. Full length: 15 cm. Diet: live as well as artificial foods. Community tank. Breeding tank: of 200-litre capacity with spawning grid, wide, elongate, water column *c.* 30 cm, finely-leaved plants. Sexual dimorphism: the male is smaller, slimmer. Sex ratio: 1:1 (or 2 males : 1 female), the fish are set up in a shoal for spawning. Breeding water: 25–28 °C; pH 6.5–7.0; dCH max. 2°. Eggs: transparent, small, incubation period 20 hrs. Feeding of fry: *Paramecium caudatum*, extremely fine *Cyclops* nauplii or rotatoria, brine shrimp nauplii (artificial fry foods).

Surface school fish that are accomplished swimmers and jumpers. They have highly developed pectoral fins which enable them to leap above the surface for food (insects). Before spawning the males and females should be separated for about 14 days. Spawning takes place in the early morning, often at dawn. The act of spawning lasts about two hours and the female deposits up to 700 eggs. Afterwards the parent fish should be removed. As soon as the fry become free-swimming the water level should be lowered to about 5 cm. The young fish grow rapidly and attain sexual maturity at the age of four months. Fresh, clean, oxygen-rich water promotes growth as well as the good condition of the fish.

3 Malayan Flying Barb
Esomus malayensis (Mandée, 1909)
Syn. *Nuria danrica* var. *malayensis*

Cyprinidae

Distribution: southeast Asia and Malay Peninsula. Full length: 8 cm. Diet, tanks as well as breeding are the same as for *E. danrica.*

Cyprinidae

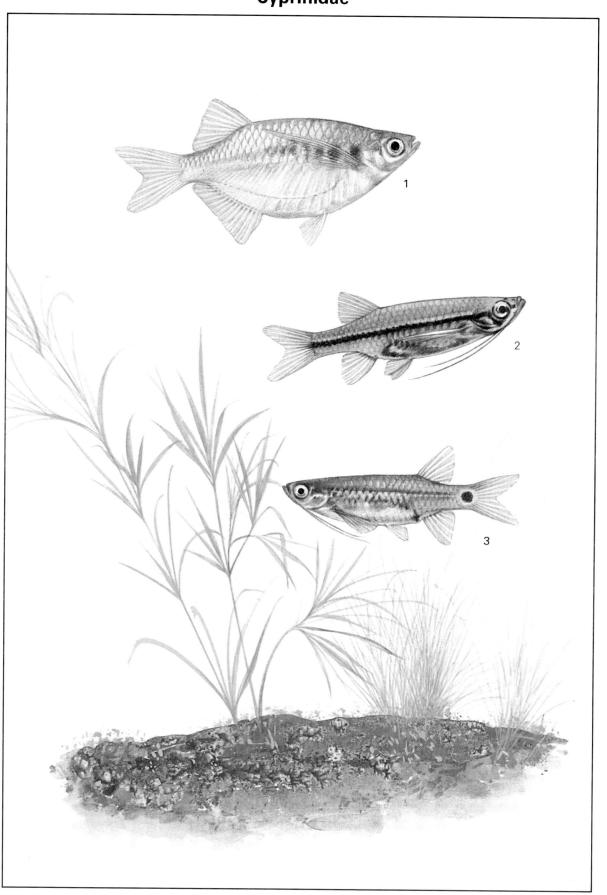

1

2

3

1 Red-tailed Black Shark
Labeo bicolor SMITH, 1931

Distribution: Thailand — swiftly-flowing tributaries of the Menam River. Full length: 12 cm. Diet: live as well as artificial foods, augmented by plant foods. Monospecies keeping tank. Breeding tank: of at least 200-litre capacity with hiding places and plant thickets; provide streaming of water with a forced circulation filter. Sexual dimorphism: the male's caudal fin is a more vivid red; the female is larger and fuller in the body before spawning, her caudal fin is less vividly coloured. Sex ratio: 1:1. Breeding water: 22–24 °C; pH 6.5–7.0; dCH max. 1°. Eggs: non-adhesive, incubation period 14 hrs/22 °C. Feeding of fry: *Paramecium caudatum*, later fine *Cyclops* nauplii and then brine shrimp nauplii.

Aggressive and territorial fish. Breeding in captivity was successful only after injecting the brood fish with carp hypophysis (2 mg hypophysis per 100 g live weight). The hypophysis must be applied when the fish's ripeness is at its peak. If the hypophysation succeeds, spawning takes place within 24 hours without fail. At first the paired fish display to one another and swim to a strong stream of water. A few hours later they begin spawning. The female deposits up to 1,000 eggs. After spawning the eggs float freely in the water; those that sink do not develop further. Siphon off the eggs with a small rubber tube and transfer them to a separate tank, where they should be kept in constant motion by strong aeration. The newly-hatched fry are small and coloured blue-grey. After 24 hours they switch over to exogenous nutrition. From the time they are a month old provide the young fish with occasional vegetable food.

2 Bridle Shark
Labeo frenatus FOWLER, 1934

Distribution: northern Thailand. Full length: 15 cm. Diet: live as well as artificial foods augmented by plant foods. Other requirements are the same as for *L. bicolor*. Sexual dimorphism: the male is slimmer, his anal fin is edged with black. The fish were successfully bred in Czechoslovakia in the early eighties.

Unlike *L. bicolor* these fish are not quarrelsome. But they, too, must be subjected to hypophysation to spawn in captivity. Take the hypophysis from food carp sold on the market, or better still from culled brood carp, regardless of sex. Before using it rub the hypophysis to a powder in a porcelain dish and dilute it with a physiological solution (0.65 g NaCl per 100 cc distilled water or 6.5 NaCl per 1 litre of distilled water boiled for 20 minutes in a laboratory glass vessel). Put 1 hypophysis in 2 ml of the solution. The emulsion must be well mixed. Using a hypodermic inject the required amount under the first to third ray of the dorsal fin in the direction of the head. All equipment must be sterilized (30 minutes in boiling water) and thoroughly dried. An overdose of hypophysis is dangerous and may cause death.

Cyprinidae

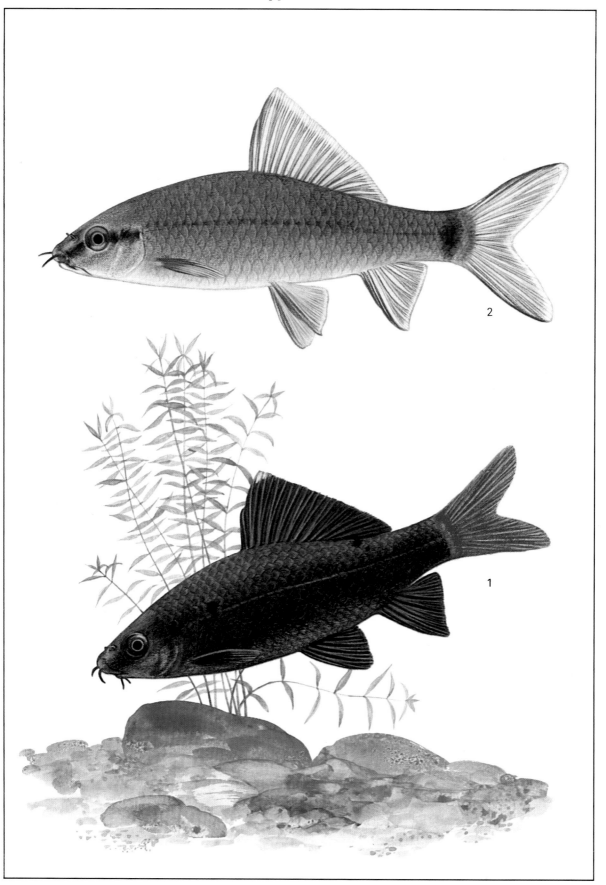

1 Redtailed Rasbora
Rasbora borapetensis H. M. SMITH, 1934 Cyprinidae

Distribution: Thailand (Bung Borat), western Malaysia. Full length: 5 cm. Diet: live as well as artificial foods. Community tank. Breeding tank: of 10-litre capacity with spawning grid and finely-leaved plants. Sexual dimorphism: the male is slimmer, slightly smaller. Sex ratio: 1:1. Breeding water: 26–28 °C; pH 7.0; dCH 2°; dGH 4°; add peat extract. Eggs: ∅ 0.5 mm, glassy, non-adhesive, incubation period 23–24 hrs. Feeding of fry: first seven days *Paramecium caudatum,* then the finest *Cyclops* nauplii or rotatoria; after four weeks brine shrimp nauplii.

School fish. The female sometimes deposits more than 500 eggs. Remove the parent fish after spawning. The newly-hatched fry hang from the sides of the tank. They have a relatively large yolk sac and become free-swimming three days after hatching. They are very minute. Feeding them artificial fry foods has not proved successful! Their growth is slow at first, becoming more rapid after the first critical month and at the age of five months the fish begin to mature sexually.

2 *Rasbora hengeli* MEINKEN, 1956 Cyprinidae

Distribution: Sumatra. Full length: 3.5 cm. Diet: live as well as artificial foods, preferably small live foods. Monospecies keeping tank (or in a mixed aquarium together with small, peaceful species). Breeding tank: of 6- to 10-litre capacity with spawning grid, dim light, and a *Cryptocoryne* plant. Sexual dimorphism: the male is slimmer and more intensely coloured, the female more high-backed. Breeding water: 26–28 °C; pH 6.0–6.5; dCH 0°; dGH max. 6°; add peat extract. Eggs: incubation period 24 hrs/26 °C. Feeding of fry: four to five days *Paramecium caudatum,* then newly-hatched brine shrimp nauplii.

The fish are very similar to *R. heteromorpha* but more slender and less vividly coloured. Meinken observed interesting social behaviour in these fish which he called 'placing of sentries'. Whenever a school of fish stops swimming several individuals turn face outward from the school and keep on the lookout. If danger threatens they immediately raise the alarm and the whole school flees.

3 Eye-spot Rasbora
Rasbora dorsiocellata dorsiocellata DUNCKER, 1904 Cyprinidae

Distribution: Malay Peninsula, Sumatra. Full length: 6.5 cm. Diet, keeping tank, breeding tank, sexual dimorphism, sex ratio and breeding water the same as for *R. borapetensis.* Eggs: ∅ 1 mm, glassy, non-adhesive, incubation period 24 hrs. Feeding of fry: seven days *Paramecium caudatum,* then *Cyclops;* after 14 days brine shrimp nauplii.

School fish. It is recommended to keep the water level low, about 8 to 10 cm above the grid, so that the eggs can drop below the grid before the parent fish can eat them. After spawning is over remove the parent fish. Endogenous nutrition lasts three days. The subspecies *R. dorsiocellata macrophthalma* Meinken, 1951 (Leuchlangen Rasbora) reaches a total length of 3.5 cm.

Cyprinidae

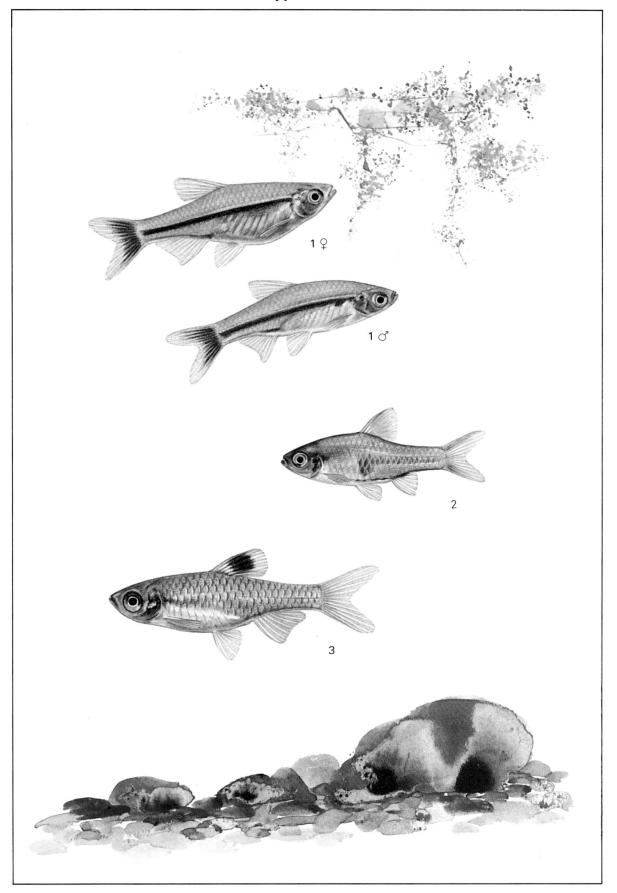

1 ♀

1 ♂

2

3

1 Harlequin Rasbora
Rasbora heteromorpha DUNCKER, 1904

Cyprinidae

Distribution: southeast Asia — southeastern Thailand, Malay Peninsula, Singapore, Sumatra. Full length: 4.5 cm. Diet: live as well as artificial foods. Community tank. Breeding tank: of 6-litre capacity with spawning grid, a bunch of *Cryptocoryne* or other broad-leaved plants. Sexual dimorphism: the male is slimmer and has the lower tip of the wedge extended downward to the central line of the belly. Sex ratio: 1:1 (the fish may be bred in a shoal). Breeding water: 26–28 °C; pH 6.5; dCH 0°; dGH 6°; filtered through peat. Eggs: incubation period 24 hrs/28 °C. Feeding of fry: nauplii of brine shrimp or *Cyclops*.

Fish that are fully acclimatized in captivity are easily reared. They may be kept in large shoals in large tanks but the males and females should be separated for 10 to 14 days before spawning. The female deposits the eggs on the underside of plant leaves; some fall to the bottom. The eleutherembryos are relatively large — 4 mm. Endogenous nutrition lasts five days. In the initial stage of rearing the fry the water column should be approximately 5 to 10 cm high. Normal water is then added to the tank gradually to condition the fry to harder water. After 14 days the first indications of the wedge appear in the colouring of the young fish. At three months the fish are 3 cm long. They are often attacked by large numbers of unicellular parasites of the genus *Oodinium*.

2 Big-spot Rasbora
Rasbora kalochroma (BLEEKER, 1850)
Syn. *Leuciscus kalochroma*

Cyprinidae

Distribution: Malay Peninsula, Sumatra and Borneo. Full length: 5 cm (10 cm?). Diet: live as well as artificial foods. Community tank. A species that has not been bred in captivity as yet. Pre-supposed parameters of the breeding tank: capacity of 20–50 litres, elongate, with spawning grid, finely-leaved as well as broadleaved plants, diffused light. Sexual dimorphism: the male is slimmer, more vividly coloured. Sex ratio: 1:1. Pre-supposed characteristics of the breeding water: 26–28 °C; pH 6.0–6.5; dCH 0° (1°); dGH 5–10°; filtered through peat.

Peaceful fish assembling in shoals when young, tending to scatter when older. According to Meinken individual fish establish small territories 30 to 35 cm in diameter from which they chase all other fish, including members of their own species. *Rasbora elegans* Volz, 1903, is a similar, less coloured species.

Cyprinidae

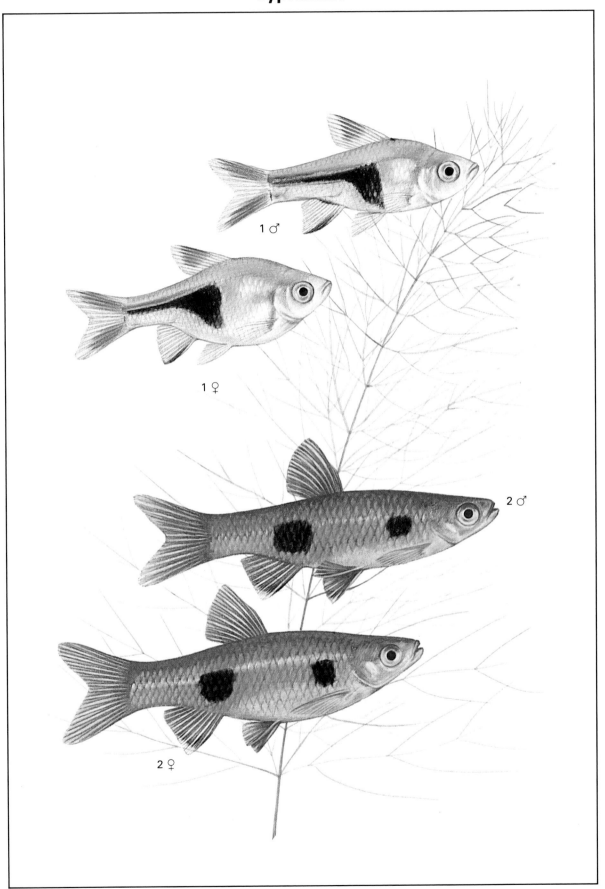

1 ♂

1 ♀

2 ♂

2 ♀

1 Red-striped Rasbora
Rasbora pauciperforata WEBER and DE BEAUFORT, 1916
Syn. *Rasbora leptosoma*   Cyprinidae

○
◑ Distribution: Greater Sunda Islands. Full length: 7 cm. Diet: live as well as artificial foods. Community tank, only with fish of like characteristics. Breeding tank: elongate, with capacity of 100 litres, spawning grid, thickets of finely-leaved plants here and there, diffused lighting, dark bottom, well covered with glass. Sexual dimorphism: the male is slimmer. Sex ratio: for spawning set up the fish in a shoal with a slight preponderance of males. Breeding water: 24–26 °C; pH 6.0–6.5; dCH < 1°; dGH max. 5°; filtered through peat or with an addition of peat extract. Eggs: incubation period 24–30 hrs.

Feeding of fry: finest *Cyclops* or brine shrimp nauplii.

Timid, school fish. In a school of young fish individuals select partners according to preference. As soon as spawning is over remove the parent fish. *R. pauciperforata* is a typical representative of the group of slender rasboras with reduced lateral line and dark longitudinal stripe. Their number includes *R. urophthalma, R. beauforti, R. wegae, R. palustris* and *R. semilineata*.

2 Scissor-tailed Rasbora
Rasbora trilineata STEINDACHNER, 1870
Syn. *Rasbora calliura, R. stigmatura*   Cyprinidae

○
◑ Distribution: Malay Peninsula, Sumatra and Borneo. Full length: 15 cm. Diet: live as well as artificial foods. Community tank. Breeding tank: of 50-litre capacity with spawning grid and finely-leaved plants. Sexual dimorphism: the male is smaller and slimmer. Sex ratio: 1:1, or with a slight preponderance of males. Breeding water: 25–28 °C; pH 6.5–7.0; dCH < 2°. Eggs: incubation period 18–20 hrs/28 °C. Feeding of fry: brine shrimp nauplii.

Before spawning separate the males and females for about 14 days. Spawning is generally triggered by an increase in the temperature of the water to 28–30 °C. A carbonate hardness with dCH value higher than 2° causes disorders in the development of the eggs and fry resulting in deformed populations. *R. trilineata* is a very prolific species. Growth of the young fish is rapid.

3 Ceylonese Fire Barb
Rasbora vaterifloris DERANIYAGALA, 1930
                                                            Cyprinidae

○
● Distribution: Sri Lanka, southern part, in swiftly-flowing waters. Full length: 4 cm. Diet: live as well as artificial foods. Monospecies keeping tank. Breeding tank: elongate, with capacity of 30–50 litres, spawning grid, and finely-leaved plants. Sexual dimorphism: the dorsal and anal fins of the male are broader and more intensely coloured; the female is fuller in the body. Sex ratio: set up the fish to spawn in a shoal with a slight preponderance of males. Breeding water: 22–24 °C; pH 6.5–7.0; dCH 0°; dGH 5–8°; provide streaming water. Eggs: incubation

period 26–40 hrs. Feeding of fry: *Cyclops* or very fine brine shrimp nauplii.

School fish. Separate the males and females for about 14 days before spawning. Because in their native habitats the fish spawn during the rainy season when relatively cold water flows down from the mountains a temperature higher than 26 °C disrupts or entirely halts the development of the eggs. Every 14 days replace between quarter and half the water with fresh water.

Cyprinidae

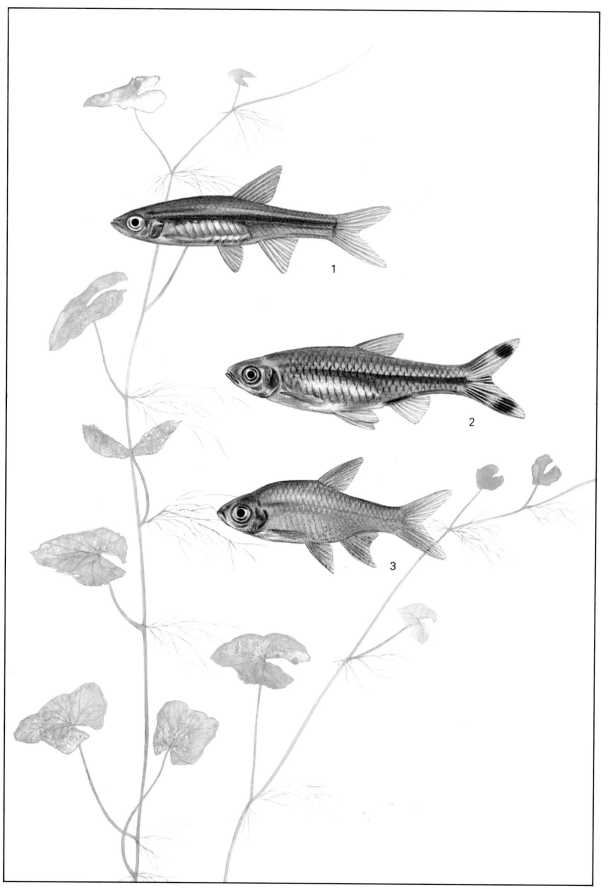

1 Spotted Rasbora or Dwarf Rasbora
Rasbora maculata DUNCKER, 1904

Cyprinidae

Distribution: southeast Asia, Malay Peninsula, Sumatra, Singapore, flowing as well as standing waters, pools and small ditches. Full length: 2.5 cm. Diet: live as well as artificial foods. Monospecies keeping tank (or with other small species of fish). Breeding tank: of 3 to 6-litre capacity with spawning grid. Sex ratio: 1:1. Breeding water: 26–28 °C; pH 6.5; dCH 0°. Eggs: incubation period 24 hrs/28 °C. Feeding of fry: first four to five days *Paramecium caudatum,* then *Cyclops* nauplii or rotatoria, after seven days brine shrimp nauplii.

Rasbora maculata is one of the smallest members of the family Cyprinidae. On the Malay Peninsula it was often observed in the company of large shoals of *Capoeta tetrazona.* Before spawning the males should be separated from the females and the fish should be generously fed. As soon as the females are well-rounded set up one or two pairs for spawning. The fish spawn in subdued light amidst finely-leaved plants. The female deposits 30 to 200 eggs during spawning. When this is over the parent fish should be taken out of the tank. The fry become free-swimming four days after hatching; they shun light and keep to the bottom, they readily escape notice. Young fish grow rapidly and attain sexual maturity at the age of ten weeks.

2 Dotted-tail Rasbora
Rasbora urophthalma AHL, 1922

Cyprinidae

Distribution: Sumatra, possibly also in Vietnam near Ho Chi Minh City (formerly Saigon). Full length: 3.5 cm. Diet: live as well as artificial foods. Monospecies keeping tank (or with peaceful fish of the same size). Breeding tank: of 3- to 6-litre capacity with spawning grid, several small Cryptocorynes or other plants with wide leaves, diffused light. Sexual dimorphism: the male is smaller, slimmer and more vividly coloured, with a whitish spot topped by a black stripe at the base of the dorsal fin. Sex ratio: 1:1. Breeding water: 26–28 °C; pH 6.5; dCH 0°; fresh, filtered through peat. Eggs: incubation period 48 hrs. Feeding of fry: *Paramecium caudatum,* extremely fine nauplii of brine shrimp or *Cyclops.*

Brood fish are kept in a large shoal in well overgrown aquariums. Before spawning the males should be separated from the females until the latter are noticeably ripe. During spawning the female deposits 50 eggs on the underside of leaves. The parent fish should be removed after spawning. The free-swimming fry are sensitive to light and readily escape notice. The growth of the young fish is relatively rapid.

1 ♂

1 ♀

2

1 Bitterling

Rhodeus sericeus amarus (BLOCH, 1782)

Syn. *Rhodeus amarus*

Cyprinidae

○
●

Distribution: excepting Italy, Spain, Great Britain, Ireland, Denmark and Scandinavia (in other words the southernmost and northernmost parts of the continent) distributed throughout Europe to the Urals. Full length: 7–10 cm. Diet: live as well as artificial foods. Monospecies keeping tank. Breeding tank: of 100-litre capacity; on the bottom put a tall dish with coarse gravel containing a live mussel. Sexual dimorphism: the male is more colourful, slimmer, during the spawning period he has a spawning rash on the snout and above the eyes; during the spawning period the female develops a long ovipositor from the urogenital papilla, a tube that is often longer than her. Sex ratio: 1:1. Breeding water: 18–21 °C; pH 7.0–7.5; dCH 2°. Eggs: incubation period three to four weeks. Feeding of fry: *Cyclops* nauplii, finely sifted zooplankton.

The Bitterling is a suitable fish for larger cold-water aquariums. It can be propagated in captivity if provided with congenial conditions.

The spawning period is in April to May. With the aid of the long ovipositor the female inserts 30 to 40 eggs between the gills of the mussel. The male then ejects his sperm into the water above the mollusc. This is inhaled by the mollusc through the intake valve with the stream of water which constantly passes through its gills where it fertilizes the eggs. The fry hatch among the gills of the mollusc and remain there for some time, until they complete their development. As soon as the fry are capable of fending for themselves they leave their host through its intake valve. This is a good time to remove the mollusc from the aquarium and thus prevent the development of the mollusc larvae (glochidia) on the fish. The mollusc may release its larvae, which cling by sticky threads to the gills and fins of the fish. There they remain encapsulated for several weeks until they finish the larval stage, after which they leave the fish for the open water. If strongly attacked by glochidia young fish may suffer serious health problems.

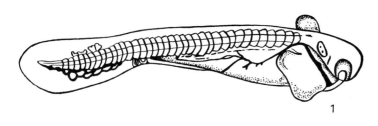

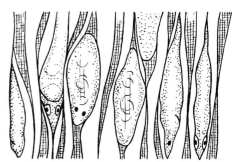

1 – embryo of bitterling
2 – embryos between the gill filaments of a bivalve

1 ♂

1 ♀

1 White Cloud Mountain Fish
Tanichthys albonubes LIN SHU-YEN, 1932
Syn. *Aphyocypris pooni*

Distribution: southern China, streams in the vicinity of Canton and Hong Kong. Full length: 4 cm. Diet: live as well as artificial foods. Monospecies keeping tank. Breeding tank: of 50 to 100 litre capacity with thickets of aquatic vegetation. Sexual dimorphism: the male is slimmer, more vividly coloured, and has a larger dorsal and anal fin. Sex ratio: 1:1; the fish may be bred in a shoal with a slight preponderance of males. Breeding water: 20–22 °C; pH 7.0; dCH 2°. Eggs: small, yellowish, incubation period 72 hrs. Feeding of fry: *Paramecium caudatum*, later nauplii of brine shrimp or *Cyclops*, artificial fry food.

The parent fish may be left in the tank; remove only larger, more developed fry. There must be no gastropods, hydrozoans or planarians in the tank. The characteristic juvenile coloration of the young with longitudinal band glistening with a neon sheen gave rise to the name 'false neon fish'. These fish are suitable for putting outdoors in a garden pool in summer.

2 *Tanichthys albonubes* – veil-finned form

Bred and genetically fixed in the second half of the sixties, probably in Poland. Long-term and unsuitable interbreeding with the wild form, low prices and low demand on the market are the reasons why genetically fixed strains nowadays occur rarely or not at all. Breeding and rearing of the veil-finned form is the same as for the wild form. Removal of all short-finned specimens from the tank during breeding is essential.

Family Gyrinocheilidae

Typical of this family is the skin extension of the gill cover edge forming an opening for the intake of water at the upper end of the gill cover and an opening at the lower end of the gill cover for the discharge of water flowing through and washing the gills. There are no pharyngeal teeth. The mouth is transformed into a sucking disc and the thick lips are provided with rasp-like folds for scraping off algae or for holding the fish fast to the substrate.

3 Chinese Algae-eater
Gyrinocheilus aymonieri (TIRANT, 1883)
Syn. *Psilorhynchus aymonieri, Gyrinocheilus kaznakovi?*

Distribution: Thailand. Full length: 27 cm. Diet: live, artificial and plant foods. Monospecies keeping tank. This species has not been bred in captivity as yet. Sexual dimorphism: the male has spawning tubercles on the head, the female is larger and stronger. The optimum ratio of the sexes is not known. Water: 20–25 °C; pH 6.5–7.0; dCH max. 2°; dGH max. 10°.

The fish are territorial and aggressive. They may be kept in a shoal providing they are scattered throughout a large space. There are many unclear points in the systematic classification of the genus *Gyrinocheilus*. At present it includes four species: *G. kaznakovi* Berg, 1906, *G. aymonieri* (Tirant, 1883), *G. pustulosus* Vaillant, 1902, and *G. pennocki* Fowler, 1937. Purportedly only the species *G. kaznakovi* is imported on a mass scale. Some contemporary literature, however, states that *G. kaznakovi* is a synonym for *G. aymonieri*.

1 ♀

1 ♂

2 ♂

3

The members of this family are distributed throughout Eurasia. They are closely related to the Cyprinidae family. They are bottom fish that live in flowing as well as standing waters. Some species bury themselves in the muddy bottom, others hide under stones and branches. They become active at twilight. The body is either naked, without scales, or with small scales deeply imbedded in the skin. The mouth is generally protractile and surrounded by 6 to 12 barbels. Sometimes there are spines beneath the eyes that can be erected and which serve as a defence against enemies. In some species the intestine is used as an accessory respiratory organ.

1 Clown Loach or Tiger Botia
Botia macracantha (BLEEKER, 1852)
Syn. *Cobitis macracanthus, Hymenophysa macracantha*   Cobitidae

Distribution: Sumatra, Borneo. Full length: 30 cm. Diet: live as well as artificial foods. Monospecies keeping tank: of 300- to 500-litre capacity with sufficient hiding places, but usually kept in a mixed tank. Sexual differences and manner of reproducing are not known. Breeding water (hypothetical): 24–26 °C; pH 6.5–7.0; dCH max. 1°; dGH max. 10°; fresh, rich in oxygen.

According to report this species has been successfully bred in the USSR but the results have not been published. In the wild the fish spawn at the beginning of the rainy season in fast-flowing streams with rapids. Young fish assemble in large schools and develop in the calmer waters where these streams flow into rivers. Adult fish form only small groups.

2 Reticulated Loach
Botia lohachata CHAUDHURI, 1912   Cobitidae

Distribution: northern India. Full length: 10 cm. Diet: chiefly live foods (worms), may be augmented by artificial foods. Monospecies keeping tank (but normally kept in mixed aquariums): spacious. Sexual differences and manner of reproducing are not known.

A school fish that is active at night. Unlike other species of *Botia,* however, it does not hide much and also appears during the daytime.

3 *Botia sidthimuntki* KLAUZEWITZ, 1959   Cobitidae

Distribution: northern Thailand. Dwells in small, muddy waters. Full length: up to 6 cm. Diet: live as well as artificial foods. Monospecies keeping tank (but normally kept in mixed aquariums): of about 200-litre capacity with water column 30 cm high, open space and sufficient hiding places. Sex differences and manner of reproducing are not known.

The chequered coloration of the fish is variable. Dark or dingy coloured fish are in poor health. Imported young fish are often cachectic, infested by the ectoparasitic infusorian *Ichthyophthirius multifiliis,* and soon die. Healthy fish may do well in captivity for a number of years. Lighting and its intensity, the chemical composition of the water and changes in this composition, the temperature of the water and changes in temperature, the diet for successful breeding in captivity are not yet known.

1 Blue Loach
Botia modesta BLEEKER, 1864 Cobitidae

Distribution: Malaysia, Thailand to Vietnam. Full length: 24 cm. Diet: mostly live foods (worms), may be augmented by artificial foods. Monospecies keeping tank, roomy with sufficient hiding possibilities but normally kept in mixed aquariums. Nothing is known about the manner of reproduction and sexual dimorphism. Breeding water (hypothetical): 24–26 °C; ph 6.5–7.0; dCH max. 1°; dGH max. 10°; fresh, rich in oxygen.

Twilight fish that are active at night. Easily confused with *B. lecontei*. In its native home *B. modesta* is a food fish, called *pla mu khao* (meaning white pig fish) by the local population.

2 Tiger Loach
Botia hymenophysa (BLEEKER, 1852) Cobitidae

Distribution: India, Malay peninsula, Greater Sunda Islands. Full length: 20 cm. Diet: primarily live foods (worms), may be augmented by artificial foods. Monospecies keeping tank, roomy, with sufficient hiding possibilities, but normally kept in mixed aquariums. Nothing is known about the manner of reproduction and sexual dimorphism. Water: see *B. modesta.*

Compared with the other members of the genus *Botia*, *B. hymenophysa* has a more elongate body with broader tail end, like *B. berdmorei* (Blyth, 1860). The fish should be kept in a large community. Solitary specimens and groups of only a few fish are shy and quarrelsome.

3 Leconte's Loach
Botia lecontei FOWLER, 1937 Cobitidae

Distribution: Thailand. Full length: 7 cm. Diet: mainly live foods (worms), may be augmented by artificial foods. Normally kept in mixed aquariums. Nothing is known about the manner of reproduction and sexual dimorphism of this species. Water: see *B. modesta;* adult fish may be kept in water with a greater carbonate hardness – dCH *c.* 2°.

Peaceable, school fish that are active at twilight. They remain hidden during the daytime. Their coloration resembles that of *B. modesta.* Both species are a mousy grey, *B. lecontei* has a faint red sheen, *B. modesta* a blue-violet sheen. The reddish-orange colour of the fins varies in intensity in both species, but the fins of *B. modesta* are generally paler and shade into yellowish tints. *B. lecontei* has a straighter ventral contour, in *B. modesta* this contour is more convex (see illustration). *B. lecontei* has a large round spot on the root of the tail, in *B. modesta* the tail root bears a wide, dark ring-like mark. The intensity of the spot or ring varies according to the fish's mood.

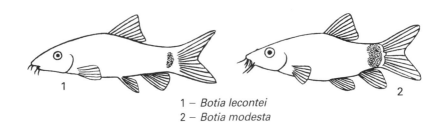

1 – *Botia lecontei*
2 – *Botia modesta*

Cobitidae

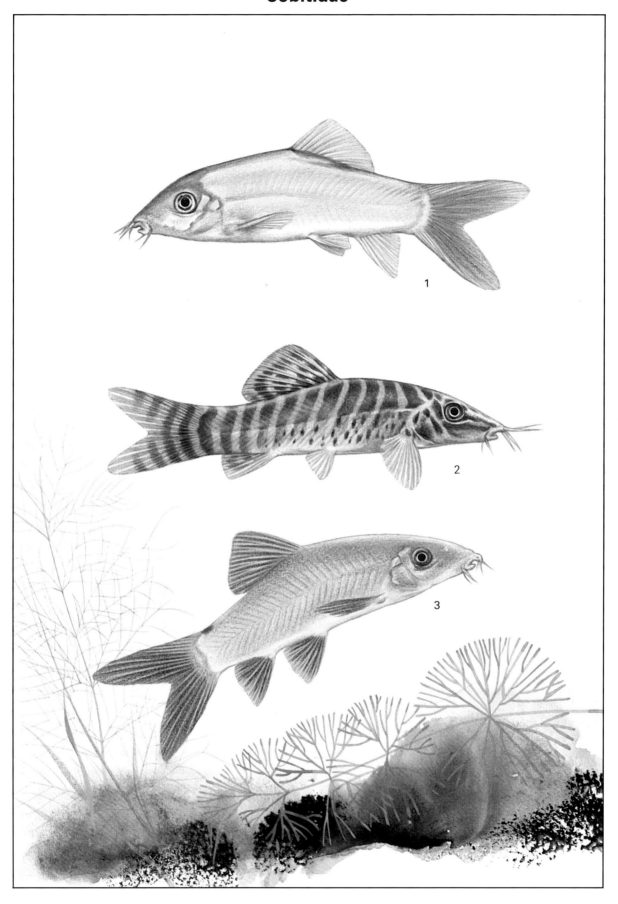

1 Hora's Loach
Botia horae SMITH, 1931
Syn. *Botia modesta* (not Bleeker)

Cobitidae

Distribution: Thailand. Full length: 10 cm. Diet: live foods that fall to the bottom (it is benthophagous). Community tank: with subdued light, floating plants, bottom covered with fine sand and provided with sufficient hiding places. Breeding tank: containing only this species of fish, otherwise the same as the community tank. Sexual dimorphism: not known. This species has not been bred in captivity so far.

These are peaceful fish that become active at twilight. *Botia horae* differs from the other members of the genus by its coloration and the black longitudinal stripe which extends from the mouth along the dorsal ridge, turns downward at the tail root into a broad transverse band and simultaneously continues on into the marginal rays of the upper lobe of the caudal fin. Pale cross stripes appear and vanish on the sides of the body according to the fish's mood.

2 Long-nosed Loach
Acanthopsis choirorhynchus (BLEEKER, 1854)
Syn. *Cobitis choirorhynchus, Acanthopsis choerorhynchus, A. biaculeata, A. diazona*

Cobitidae

Distribution: extensive water systems of southeast Asia, the Sunda Islands. Full length: 22 cm. Diet: any foods that fall to the bottom (it is benthophagous), chiefly worms and the larvae of aquatic insects. Monospecies keeping tank: with 5 to 10 cm layer of fine sand on the bottom, dim light filtered through floating plants, sufficient hiding places, e.g. mineralized wood from moors covered with Java moss or aquatic ferns (*Bolbitis, Microsorium*). This species has not been bred in captivity so far and sexual differences are unknown. Water: 25–28 °C; pH 6.5–7.0; dCH max. 2°; dGH max. 10°; strongly filtered.

It seems that this is the only species of *Acanthopsis* to be imported. It is a peaceable, solitary, nocturnal fish, variable in coloration, with elongated body and conspicuously large head. It is a poor swimmer. It vigorously digs holes in the sand where it stays with only the close-set eyes on the elongated head visible. The mouth is furnished with three pairs of barbels. Because of the fish's habit of burrowing in the bottom the sand must not be sharp or too coarse. Rooting plants must be put in pots submerged in the sand and surrounded by stones.

This fish is well known in Thailand where it has many vernacular names, e.g. Pla rak kluey, meaning banana fish.

1 juv.

2

1 Slimy Myersi
Acanthophthalmus myersi HARRY, 1949 Cobitidae

Distribution: Thailand, Malay Peninsula, Singapore, Sumatra, Java, Borneo. Full length: 12 cm.
Diet: live foods (worms), may be augmented by artificial foods. Community tank. Breeding tank: of 150- to 200-litre capacity, oblong, with spawning grid, diffused lighting, islands of floating plants. Sexual dimorphism: the male is slender, the female markedly fuller in the body when ripe with visible green ovaries. Sex ratio: 1:1 (a greater number of fish may be set up for spawning). Breeding water: 26 °C; pH 6.5; dCH max. 1°; dGH max. 10°. Eggs: greenish, $\varnothing$ 1 mm, incubation period 24 hrs. Feeding of fry: brine shrimp nauplii, later chopped tubifex worms. First breeding: 1975, Lev Gudkov, USSR.

According to Klauzewitz this is a subspecies of *A. kuhli* and the correct name would then be *A. kuhli myersi*.
Spawning is provoked by the intramuscular injection of synthetic gonadotrophin. Also recommended is hypophysation of the male with natural carp hypophysis when the female is fully ripe — this is indicated by a greatly bulging belly and by the restless swimming of the female along the sides of the tank. (Some females spawn spontaneously by slowly swimming through plant thickets). The fish are more likely to spawn when there is a drop in atmospheric pressure. When spawning, the male and female rise to the surface where they swim rapidly side by side causing waves and eddies on the water surface. On releasing the eggs and milt they plunge suddenly to the bottom in a stream of air bubbles. This is repeated at five to ten-minute intervals for two to four hours. The females deposit more than 1,000 eggs. Remove the parent fish after spawning. The newly-hatched fry are furnished with external fruticose gills which disappear within a fortnight.

2 Coolie Loach
Acanthophthalmus kuhli sumatranus FRASER-BRUNNER, 1940 Cobitidae

Distribution: Sumatra. Full length: 8 cm. Other requirements same as for *A. myersi*.

Twilight fish that are active at night, remaining hidden during the daytime. They interbreed well with *A. myersi*.

3 Shelford's Loach
Acanthophthalmus shelfordi POPTA, 1901 Cobitidae

Distribution: Borneo, Sarawak (eastern Malaysia). Full length: 8 cm. Other requirements same as for *A. myersi*. First import: 1939.

This species is sometimes classed in the 'kuhli' group, which includes *A. kuhli, A. semicinctus, A. myersi* and *A. shelfordi* — all bigger fish.

Members of the *'cuneovirgatus'* group, which includes *A. cuneovirgatus* and *A. robiginosus*, are smaller fish and differ from the former by the shape of the scales. The scales of the *'kuhli'* group are almost round whereas those of the *'cuneovirgatus'* group are elliptic.

Cobitidae

1

2

Family Bagridae

The members of this family are found in various types of water in Africa and Asia, including the Malayan archipelago. When danger threatens they emit croaking or chirping sounds. The body has no scales (the skin is completely naked). The upper and lower jaw and often the palatal bone are equipped with teeth. There are two to four pairs of barbels on the upper and lower lip. The dorsal fin inserts relatively near the front end, the first ray of the dorsal fin is transformed into a strong spine that is often saw-edged. The adipose fin may be small or big and extended lengthwise; the anal fin is small. The eyes are also small and often covered with skin. This family includes a large number of species.

1 Striped Catfish
Mystus vittatus (BLOCH, 1794)
Syn. *Silurus vittatus, Macrones tengara, Mystus tengara, M. atrifasciatus, Hypselobagrus tengara*   Bagridae

Distribution: India and Pakistan, Burma. Full length: 20 cm. Diet: live as well as artificial foods, including live fish. Community tank, with fish bigger than 8 cm. Brood fish should be kept only with others of their own kind in a tank with a capacity of at least 200 litres and provided with sufficient hiding places and dim lighting. Breeding tank: same as monospecies keeping tank.

Sexual dimorphism: not known. So far the species has not been bred in captivity. Water: 24–28 °C; pH 7.0; dCH max. 2°.

M. vittatus is a catfish that is active during the daytime. Spawning in the wild takes place amidst the tangle of roots and aquatic plants on the bottom, where the female deposits eggs.

Family Siluridae

The members of this family, so-called genuine catfish, are distributed from central Europe through central, southern and southeast Asia to east Asia. They have completely naked skin and one to six pairs of long barbels. The dorsal fin is either very small or entirely absent. The anal fin is very prolonged and often connects with the caudal fin. There is no adipose fin. The eyes are small. Many species resemble members of the Schilbeidae family.

2 Indian Glass Catfish
Kryptopterus bicirrhis CUVIER and VALENCIENNES, 1839
Syn. *Cryptopterichthys bicirrhis, Cryptopterus amboinensis, Kryptopterichthys palembangensis, Silurus bicirrhis, S. palembangensis*   Siluridae

Distribution: southeast Asia from Thailand to the Greater Sunda Islands, exclusively in fresh waters. Full length: male 10 cm, female 15 cm. Diet: small live foods, may be augmented by artificial foods. Community tank, together with small and peaceful species of fish. Brood fish should be kept by themselves in a monospecies tank. Breeding tank: of 100–200-litre capacity, light, with dark bottom, plant thickets here and there, floating plants, and streaming water provided by a forced circulation filter. Sexual dimorphism: monomorphic fish. Sex ratio: set up the fish in a larger shoal. Breeding water: 25–28 °C; pH 7.0; dCH max 2°; dGH max 10° ?

Peaceable school fish. Warmth-loving, lowest temperature limit of the water is 20 °C.

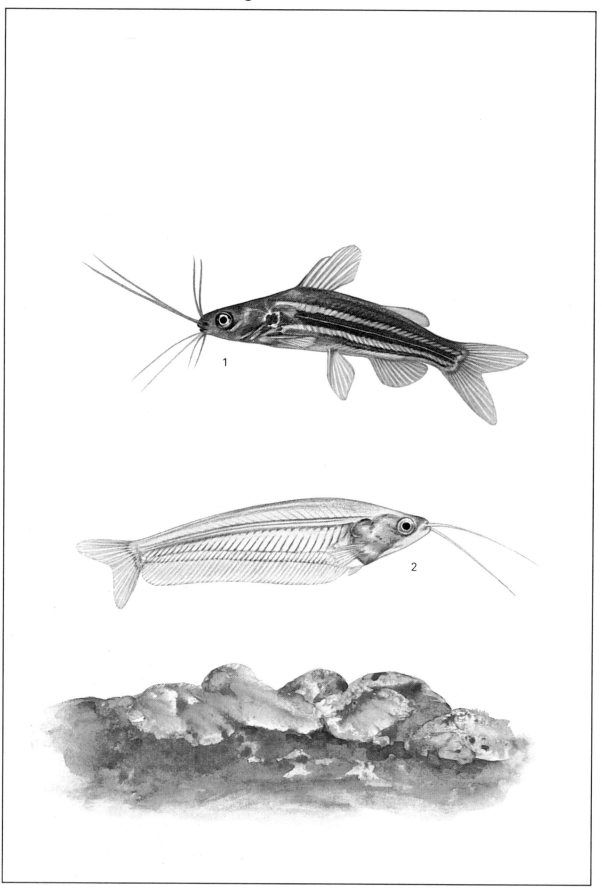

Family Schilbeidae

The members of this family are distributed in Africa and Asia. They are good swimmers. The body is elongate and regularly flattened laterally. The short dorsal fin inserts towards the front and is furnished with a strong, sharp spine, which may be absent in some species. The pectoral fins are also furnished with a strong spine. The anal fin is very long. The caudal fin is generally indented. Some species possess an adipose fin. The eye is located practically in line with the mouth. Many species are also active during the daytime.

1 Three-striped Glass Catfish
Eutropiellus debauwi (BOULENGER, 1900)
Syn. *Eutropius debauwi*   Schilbeidae

Distribution: the Zaire (Congo) River region, Pool Malebo (Stanley Pool). Full length: 8 cm. Diet: live foods, may be augmented by artificial foods. Community tank — only together with peaceful species of fish. Breeding tank: with capacity of 200 litres or more, open space, dark bottom, diffused lighting, and forced circulation filter to provide streaming water. Sexual dimorphism: the female is fuller in the body and with lighter longitudinal bands. Sex ratio: 1:1, or with a slight preponderance of females. Breeding water: 24 °C; pH 6.0–7.0; dCH max. 2°; dGH max. 10°; rich in oxygen, filtered through peat. Bred by A. Kochetov in 1984 — Moscow zoo.

Definitely a school fish; specimens kept singly do poorly. The fish are active during the daytime, being constantly on the move in all layers of water. They swim in a slightly slanting position with continually waving caudal fin pointing downward. There is a developed adipose fin and three pairs of long barbels round the mouth.

Family Pangasiidae

Catfish-like fish related to the Schilbeidae family. Adult specimens are toothless, whereas young and half-grown fish have fully developed teeth.

2 Siamese Shark
Pangasius sutchi FOWLER, 1937   Pangasiidae

Distribution: Thailand round Bangkok — Menam River (now the Chao Phraya River). Full length: up to 1 metre. Diet: live foods of all kinds, including small fish, varied plant foods (also boiled rice, maize, and pieces of banana). Adult fish lose their teeth and take mostly vegetable foods. Monospecies keeping tank of large size. Nothing is known about the breeding and sexual dimorphism of this species. Water: 22–28 °C; pH 6.5–7.5; dCH 2°; dGH 10°; fresh (the fish are not comfortable in water that is too soft).

Young fish assemble in shoals and for that reason should never be kept singly. They are constantly on the move in all layers of the water. When startled they swim distraughtly about bumping into surrounding objects and finally sinking to the bottom where they remain lying still for a while. Because the fish breathe in air at the surface it is believed they have an accessory respiratory organ. Its function, however, has apparently not been studied as yet nor have any reports been published on the subject. Though the eyes are small the other sensory organs, including the barbels, are very well developed — the fish react to the presence of food from a great distance.

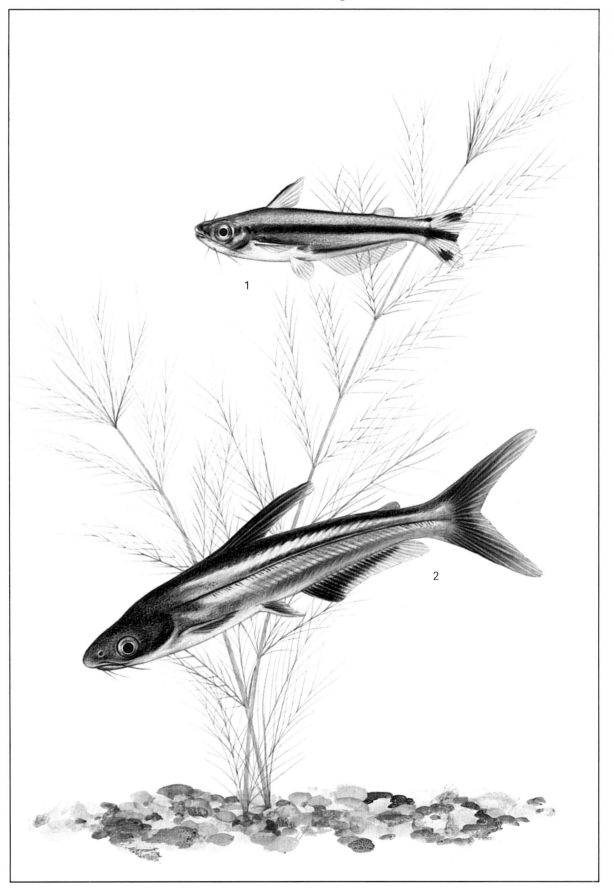

Family Mochokidae

The native waters of this family are African rivers and lagoons south of the Sahara. The family includes a great number of species, some of which reach a length of 60 cm. In nature the fish assemble in large shoals. They are active at night. The adipose fin is well developed. The mouth is provided with three pairs of barbels. The pair of barbels on the upper lip is remarkably long, the two pairs on the lower lip are often richly branched (feathered). There are now numerous species available, of which two are described below.

1 Congo Back-swimmer or Upside-down Catfish
Synodontis nigriventris DAVID, 1938
Syn. *Synodontis ornatipinnis* (not Boulenger, 1899) — Mochokidae

Distribution: Zaire — basin from Kinshasy to Bosong. Full length: male — 8 cm, female — 10 cm. Diet: live as well as artificial foods. Community tank. Breeding tank: of 50-litre capacity per pair, with subdued lighting, floating plants on the surface, drainage pipe placed on the bottom. Sexual dimorphism: the male is smaller and slender, the female has a noticeably enlarged belly. Sex ratio: 1:1. Breeding water: 24–26 °C; pH 6.5–7.5; dCH < 2°. Eggs: small, faintly yellowish, incubation period seven days. Feeding of fry: brine shrimp nauplii.

Fish that become active at twilight. Spawning sites are located in cavities. Shortly before spawning the fish change colour from light brown to blue-green. The male and female both tend the spawning site. Endogenous nutrition lasts four days. The larvae already have barbels on the upper lip; they are a yellowish colour and their growth is slow. Barbels appear on the lower lip at the age of four weeks. From the age of seven weeks the young fish begin swimming on their backs and acquire the typical protective coloration — the back is paler, the belly dark to black. Young fish assemble in shoals. They attain sexual maturity at the age of three to four years, some individuals even later. In captivity the fish breed only occasionally, as many females never attain sexual maturity in aquariums.

2 Polka-dot African Catfish
Synodontis angelicus SCHILTHUIS, 1891 — Mochokidae

Distribution: Zaire, Cameroon. Full length: 18 cm. Diet: live foods, chiefly worms and the larvae of midges. The fish should be given food before dusk. Monospecies keeping tank: spacious, with a layer of fine, rather dark sand on the bottom, sufficient crevices and cavities (mineralized wood from moors), diffused light. Sexual differences and manner of reproducing are not known. Water: 24 °C; pH 6.5–7.0; dCH max. 2°; dGH max. 10°; fresh, settled; a circulating filter with activated coal is used to simulate streaming of water.

Fish that are active by night, remain hidden during the daytime. The body is covered with a thick layer of mucus, the mouth is furnished with three pairs of barbels — the feathered barbels on the lower lip are shorter. Catfish are fond of streaming water and digging in the bottom. They are sensitive to chemicals, particularly chlorine and higher concentrations of nitrates and nitrites. Restless swimming of the fish in the daytime indicates that they do not feel well. The high prices demanded for these fish are due to the fact that capturing them in the wild is not only difficult but prohibited, and breeding them in captivity has not been successful as yet.

Family Doradidae

Catfish-like fish distributed in South America. They are active at twilight and at night, some species also during the daytime. They have a greatly developed sense of touch and smell. The large head is very bony, the eyes are small. The mouth is furnished with three pairs of relatively long barbels. The sides of the body are either naked or equipped with rows of bony plates and also erectile spines furnished with hooks. The first rays of the dorsal and pectoral fins are transformed into strong bony spines, often saw-edged. There is a developed adipose fin. Many species are capable of burying themselves swiftly in the bottom when danger threatens, others express fright by producing grunting sounds.

1 Hancock's Amblydoras
Amblydoras hancocki CUVIER and VALENCIENNES, 1840
Syn. *Amblydoras affinis, Doras affinis, D. costatus, D. hancocki, D. truncatus*   Doradidae

Distribution: Brazil — Branco and Guaporé rivers, shallow side arms of the rivers with dense algal growths. In some localities the fish live in shoals numbering thousands of individuals. Full length: 15 cm. Diet: live as well as artificial foods (earthworms, robust zooplankton, quality granulated food, etc.). Monospecies keeping tank with capacity of 100 to 300 litres, height of water column about 30 cm, sufficient hiding possibilities, dim lighting. Breeding tank: same as keeping tank. Sexual dimorphism: the male has brown spots on the ventral side, the female has a dingy white belly. Sex ratio: 1:1 (in a shoal).

Water: 24–26 °C; pH 6.5–7.0; dCH max. 2°; dGH max. 10°. The fish have not been bred in an aquarium so far.

Because the fish are active at night they should be given food at nightfall. They are very voracious. Younger specimens seek food often even during the daytime. In the wild *A. hancocki* builds a nest of plant matter and bubbles on the water surface. The spawning site is watched over by the male. When taken out of the water the fish emit croaking sounds.

2 Spiny Catfish or Talking Catfish
Acanthodoras spinosissimus (EIGENMANN and EIGENMANN, 1888)
Syn. *Doras spinosissimus*   Doradidae

Distribution: middle Amazon region, larger water courses and flooded land. Full length: 15 cm. Diet: live as well as artificial foods (earthworms, granules, etc.). Community tank. Breeding tank: with capacity of 100 to 200 litres, cavities, drainage pipes, mineralized wood from moors, subdued light. Sexual dimorphism: the male is slimmer in the body and has a marbled belly, the female's belly is a uniform brown. Sex ratio: 1:1, or with a slight preponderance of males — in a shoal. Water: 24–26 °C; pH 6.5–7.0; dCH max. 2°; dGH max. 10°; filtered through peat. The species has not been bred in an aquarium as yet.

Fish that are active at night, in youth also during the daytime. The bony plates covering the body as well as the dorsal and pectoral fins are equipped with spines. A chance attacker may be startled for a moment when squeezed hard between the strong spine of the pectoral fin and the fish's body thereby giving the fish time to escape. If the fish gets entangled in a net do not try to free it by force; turn the net so that the fish is on the outside and submerge it in water. The fish will free itself after a while.

Doradidae

Family Aspredinidae

The members of this family are native to the Amazon River region. The body build is unusual; – it is short, very wide and flattened at the head and shoulder belt with a very long tail section slightly compressed from the side. The adipose fin is missing. The skin is naked and covered with large warts. The eyes are very small. The mouth is furnished with barbels. The sense of smell and touch is highly developed – the fish are active mainly at night. The family is divided into two subfamilies: the Aspredininae and the Bunocephalinae. It is very difficult to distinguish between the species according to their external characteristics and in commercial practice many are not differentiated at all.

1 Banjo Catfish
Bunocephalus bicolor STEINDACHNER, 1882   Aspredinidae

◁
●

Distribution: Amazon region to La Plata. Full length: female 15 cm, the male is smaller. Diet: tubifex worms, chopped earthworms, granulated food. Usually kept in mixed aquariums. Breeding tank: of 100-litre capacity with hollow bricks on the bottom, water level about 30 cm, dim lighting. Sexual dimorphism: the female is fuller in the body. Sex ratio: 1:1; set up the fish in a small shoal. Breeding water: 24–26 °C; pH 6.5–7.0; dCH < 2°; dGH < 10°; filtered through peat. Eggs: ∅ 1 mm, greyish white, protected by a coat of clear, soft, gelatinous, slightly sticky secretion; incubation period 50–72 hrs. Feeding of fry: Only brine shrimp nauplii, do not overfeed! Twice during the day, once before turning off the light. First breeding: January 1985 – I. Petrovický (author of this book), Prague.

Nocturnal fish that take food only at night, also in very subdued light (glow discharge tube). A characteristic peculiar to this fish is the renewal of the delicate cuticle by regular moulting. The organs of taste are highly developed and make up for the fish's weak sight. They are located chiefly in and round the mouth and on the three pairs of barbels. Food cast into the tank (always before turning off the light) immediately elicits a response in the form of opening and closing of the mouth followed shortly after by the fish's swimming directly to the spot where the food is located. Sexual maturity is attained at the age of two years. Spawning of mature fish is triggered off by fresh, slightly cooler water (3 to 4 °C lower) and a sudden drop in atmospheric pressure. The fish spawn at night or shortly before dawn. The female deposits several hundred eggs scattered freely on the bottom – they are not cared for by the parent fish. Draw off the eggs with a rubber hose 3 mm in diameter, treat them with methylene blue, and shade the tank. The newly-hatched fry are glassily transparent and 5 mm long. They keep to the dark parts of the tank. Endogenous nutrition ends two days after hatching and on the third day the fish begin taking food; feed them even during the day. At the age of 10 days they measure 10 mm in length and greatly resemble the adult fish; during the daytime they already assume a static position, reacting to food only in the immediate vicinity. When they reach a length of 15 mm they may be fed finely chopped tubifex worms, but only in careful doses. Food residues on the bottom of the tank may cause fungus diseases and skin inflammations in adult as well as young fish.

Family Pimelodidae

The fish of this family are distributed from southern Mexico to and in South America excepting the southernmost regions. Most species reach a great length. The body is generally elongate and laterally compressed. The body is not armoured, the skin is naked, without scales. All members of the family are good swimmers. The first ray of the pectoral fins is transformed into a strong bony thorn. The dorsal fin inserts far to the front. The anal fin is short, the adipose fin is developed and quite long in some species. The mouth is provided with three pairs of barbels which generally point rigidly forward. The jaws are toothed. There are now numerous species imported into the UK.

1 Shovel-nose Catfish
Sorubim lima (BLOCH and SCHNEIDER, 1806)
Syn. *Platystoma lima, P. luceri, Silurus gerupensis, S. lima, Sorubim infraocularis, S. luceri*   Pimelodidae

Distribution: Amazon region, rivers in the La Plata region. Full length: 60 cm. Diet: live foods in great quantities — small fish, earthworms, larvae of aquatic insects, coarser zooplankton, etc.; may be augmented by pieces of beef and fish meat, beef heart, and granulated food. Monospecies keeping tank: of 500 to 1000-litre capacity; the fish should be kept in a rather small shoal. Manner of reproducing is not known. Sexual dimorphism: ?. Water: 24−28 °C; pH 6.5−7.0; dCH max. 2°; dGH max. 10°.

S. *lima* is a crepuscular and nocturnal fish. It requires sufficient hiding places amongst plants and subdued lighting. It is a solitary, predaceous fish. At night the fish hunt food and are capable of digging into the bottom to depths of 5 cm, keeping the barbels pressed close to the body. The belly is nearly snow white. The skin is rough, like fine emery paper. The fish utters growling sounds when taken out of the water. The mouth is furnished with small teeth, the upper jaw extends markedly beyond the lower jaw. The large adipose fin inserts in line with the anal fin. The first ray of the pectoral fins is equipped with teeth, (hence the specific name *lima,* which is the Latin word meaning file).

2 Dwarf Marbled Catfish
Microglanis parahybae (STEINDACHNER, 1880)
Syn. *Pseudopimelodus parahybae*   Pimelodidae

Distribution: southeastern Brazil, Paraguay, northern Argentina. Full length: 8 cm. Diet: live foods, chiefly worms and larvae of aquatic insects. Monospecies keeping tank: of 100- to 200-litre capacity with sufficient hiding places, floating plants. Sexual dimorphism: unknown. Sex ratio: keep in a small shoal. Water: 24−28 °C; pH 6.5−7.0; dCH max. 2°; dGH max. 10°. There is no record of its having been bred.

Fish that is lively in the evening and at night, lying motionless in hiding places during the daytime. The colouring and markings of the fish are variable; they may be yellow-brown with irregular bands or rows of spots. The head is large and flat, the eyes are small, directed forward and covered with a translucent skin. The naked body without scales is laterally compressed, less strongly in the front part, more so in the rear. The adipose fin is low and long-stretched. The first ray of the dorsal and anal fins is transformed into a strong spine equipped with saw-like teeth.

198

Pimelodidae

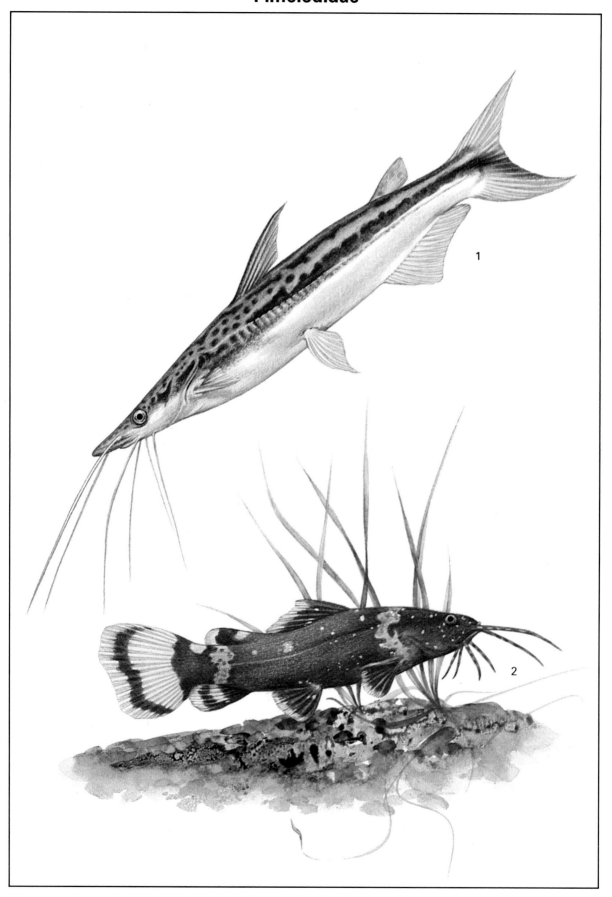

Family Callichthyidae

Small catfish, active at twilight, distributed in tropical and subtropical South America. The ventral contour is flat, the dorsal outline arched; behind the dorsal fin is a typical adipose fin. The pectoral fins with first ray transformed into a strong sharp spine play an important role in reproduction. The sides of the fish are covered with bony plates, one overlapping the other. This armour also covers the head and back. The fish are divided into two groups according to their armour and body shape: 1) the genera *Callichthys, Cascadura, Dianema* and *Hoplosternum,* 2) the genera *Aspidoras, Brochis, Chaenothorax* and *Corydoras.* The family is further characterized by having one pair of barbels on the upper jaw and one or two pairs on the lower one. The eyes in most members are large and very motile. These Catfish are bottom-dwelling fish. *Corydoras* is the genus with the greatest number of species (nearly 100). However, they are often difficult to identify because the differences between them are slight and the individual characteristics exhibit marked variability. Closely related to *Corydoras* is the genus *Brochis* with two species, differing in the number of rays in the dorsal fin.

Fish of the family Callichthyidae are able to survive in water that is poor in oxygen with the aid of the intestine which is used as an auxiliary organ of breathing. Atmospheric air is swallowed and rapidly pushed all the way to the anus, the oxygen being absorbed into the blood stream through the lining of the intestine. All members of the family are school fish.

1 Head-stripe Corydoras
Corydoras punctatus (BLOCH, 1794)
Syn. *Cataphractus punctatus, Corydoras geoffroy, C. punctatus julii*

Callichthyidae

Distribution: Orinoco, Essequibo, Amazon. Full length: 6 cm. Diet: live as well as artificial foods. Community tank. Breeding tank: with capacity of 50 litres or more, dim lighting. Sexual dimorphism: the male is slimmer and smaller. Sex ratio: 2−3 males : 1 female. So far it is not known if this species has been bred. Water: 24−28 °C; pH 6.0−7.0; dCH max. 2°; dGH max. 10°.

The dark mottlings and spots are extremely variable. *C. punctatus* is closely related to *C. julii;* the dark spot on its dorsal fin, however, is bigger. Both species have more intense markings on the lateral line.

2 *Corydoras melini* LÖNNBERG and RENDAHL, 1930

Callichthyidae

Distribution: northwestern basin of the Negro River, also upstream where the Vaupés River forms the boundary between Brazil and Colombia. Full length: 6 cm. Diet: live as well as artificial foods. Community tank. Sexual dimorphism: not known. Water: 22−26 °C; pH 6.0−7.0; dCH max. 2°; dGH max. 10°. So far it is not known if this species has been bred; however should this be attempted the carbonate hardness (dCH) should probably be lower for the development of the eggs, i.e. dCH < 1°; the general hardness dGH < 10°.

Very similar to and readily confused with *C. metae.* This led Hoedeman to conclude, in 1952, that *C. melini* is a subspecies of *C. metae,* but he later changed his opinion.

1 Network Catfish
Corydoras reticulatus FRASER-BRUNNER, 1938

Callichthyidae

Distribution: Amazon region in Monte Alegre. Full length: 7 cm. Diet: live as well as artificial foods. Community tank. Breeding tank: with capacity of 50 litres or more, dim lighting. Sexual dimorphism: the male is more colourful and has a high, pointed dorsal fin with rows of black stripes and extraordinarily long ventral fins drawn out into a point; the female is darker, her dorsal fin is lower and without markings, the ventral fins shorter and broader. Sex ratio: 2 males : 1 female. Breeding water: 26 °C; pH 6.5−7.0; dCH max. 2°: Eggs: incubation period 3 days. Feeding of fry: brine shrimp nauplii.

The males clean the underside of leaves. During the act of spawning the female sucks on to the male above his ventral fin for a while. When she lets go she expels the eggs into a pouch formed by the ventral fins of the male. Then she anchors the sticky eggs to the leaves of plants. Transfer the plant stems or leaves with the eggs to a nursery tank. The fry thrive, particularly during the first three weeks, in flow-through aquariums with large bottom area and low water level.

2 Schwartz's Corydoras
Corydoras schwartzi RÖSSEL, 1963

Callichthyidae

Distribution: mouths of rivers where they enter the Amazon (Brazil). Full length: 6.5 cm. Diet: live as well as artificial foods. Community tank with dim lighting. Breeding tank: of 50- to 100-litre capacity. Sexual dimorphism: the male is slimmer and smaller. Sex ratio: 2−3 males : 1 female. The species has not been bred in captivity so far. Water: 22−26°; pH 6.0−7.0; dCH max. 2°.

A very variable species.

3 Pygmy Corydoras
Corydoras pygmaeus KNAAK, 1966
Syn. *Corydoras hastatus australe*

Callichthyidae

Distribution: Brazil, Madeira River and its tributaries. Full length: 2.5 cm. Diet: live as well as artificial foods. Community tank (only together with small species of fish). Breeding tank: of 10- to 50-litre capacity. Sexual dimorphism: the male is smaller and slimmer. Sex ratio: 2−3 males : 1 female. Breeding water: 24 °C; pH 6.5−7.0; dCH max. 2°. Eggs: $\emptyset$ 1.2 mm, milky cloudy, sticky, incubation period 6 days. Feeding of fry: newly-hatched brine shrimp nauplii.

One of the smallest species of Callichthyidae. It is very similar to *C. hastatus,* the manner of spawning being the same as well. The most striking character of identification differentiating the two is the longitudinal band on the sides which is much more pronounced in *C. pygmaeus* and the spot in the caudal fin, which in *C. pygmaeus* is smaller and without the lighter spots. Unlike other species these catfish occasionally swim in a swarm in the middle reaches of the tank. The newly-hatched fry are minute and glassy. Siphon them up with a rubber tube 3 mm in diameter and transfer them to a nursery tank. Fry mortality may be lowered by adding 1 teaspoon NaCl for every 10 litres of water and by lowering the water level to 1 cm. During the critical period (the first 10 days) the fry may also be kept in roomy wooden frames covered with nylon fabric on the bottom. Let these, together with the fry, float on the surface of a large tank. After 10 days slowly begin to raise the water level − the young fish will grow quickly and without any problems.

1 Elegant Corydoras
Corydoras elegans STEINDACHNER, 1877

Syn. *Gastrodermus elegans, Corydoras pestai*

Callichthyidae

Distribution: water system of the middle Amazon. Full length: 6 cm. Diet: live as well as artificial foods. Community tank. Breeding tank: of 60-litre capacity with strongly dimmed lighting. Sexual dimorphism: in the male the band which runs along the upper edge of the body is an intense metallic green, in the female it is black-green; the female is fuller in the body. Sex ratio: 2–3 males : 1 female. Breeding water: 20–24 °C; pH 6.5–7.0; dCH max. 2°. Eggs: incubation period 4 days. Feeding of fry: brine shrimp nauplii.

Only little is known about the care and breeding of this species. It is similar to that of *C. arcuatus* (see below).

2 Stream-lined Corydoras or Tabatinga Catfish
Corydoras arcuatus ELWIN, 1939

Callichthyidae

Distribution: Brazil — central region of the Amazon, round Tefé. Full length: 5 cm. Diet: live as well as artificial foods. Community tank, dim lighting. Breeding tank: of 50- to 100-litre capacity. Sexual dimorphism: the male is smaller, his dorsal fin pointed. Sex ratio: 2–3 males: 1 female. Nothing is known about the breeding of this species. Water: 25–28 °C; pH 6.0–7.0; dCH max. 2°; dGH max. 10°.

The male is timid and readily frightened, sensitive to drops in temperature. This species also includes a type with entirely different coloration, the dark band broken up into spots and the caudal fin also spotted. Decisive factors in the propagation of these fish include not only proper composition and temperature of the water, but also the season of the year, alternating changes in atmospheric pressure, gradual changes in the chemical composition of the water, alternating changes in the temperature of the water, make-up of the diet, etc. In less plastic species, of which *C. arcuatus* is one, these factors are firmly coded in the organism and providing them under artificial conditions is very difficult. That is why many species cannot be successfully bred as yet. If we succeed in surmounting these obstacles there is hope that the species will slowly become acclimatized and adapted to the new environment.

3 *Corydoras axelrodi* RÖSSEL, 1962

Callychthyidae

Distribution: Meta River in Colombia. Full length: 5 cm. Diet: live as well as artificial foods. Community tank. Little known species; so far nothing is known of its having been bred in captivity. The fish should be kept in a shoal. Water: 22–26 °C; pH 6.0–7.0; dCH max. 2°; dGH max. 10° (hypothetical values for the development of the eggs; for adult fish in a keeping tank the dCH and dGH may be slightly higher).

A character of identification distinguishing this species from other species is the slanting longitudinal band which runs along the upper edge of the body extending to the lower base of the caudal fin and continuing on into the bottom rays of the caudal fin.

1 Bronze Catfish

Corydoras aeneus (Gill, 1858)

Syn. *Hoplosternum aeneum, Callichthys aeneus, Corydoras macrosteus,*
C. microps, C. venezuelanus, C. schultzei

Distribution: water systems in Venezuela, Trinidad, small tributaries of the Amazon in Brazil and farther south to the La Plata in Argentina. Full length: 7 cm. Diet: live as well as artificial foods. Community tank. Breeding tank: with capacity of 50 litres or more, dim lighting. Sexual dimorphism: the male is slimmer, smaller. Sex ratio: 2—3 males : 1 female, basic breeding group; the fish may also be bred in a shoal. Breeding water: 20—24 °C; pH 7.0; dCH max. 2°. Eggs: $\emptyset$ 1.5 mm, incubation period 4 days. Feeding of fry: brine shrimp nauplii.

This species is variable in coloration, particularly as regards the width of the dark band. That is why *C. schultzei* was long considered to be a separate species. An albinistic form as well as one with prolonged dorsal and anal fins have been bred by Asian breeders. It is difficult to tell when the spawning period occurs. Spawning is generally triggered by a drop in atmospheric pressure followed by rain. Such an impulse may be provided by adding fresh, cooler water to the tank so that the temperature drops by about 5 °C. The act of spawning is the same as in other species of *Corydoras* (see *C. paleatus*). The strongly adhesive eggs are deposited mostly in the upper part of the tank close to the surface. When the fry have hatched the water column should be lowered to approximately 10 cm. Feeding them free-floating zooplankton is not advisable for the fry have difficulty catching hold of it. Zooplankton should, therefore, be provided either frozen or killed with warm water. The fry feed not only on the bottom but also at the surface, where they swim rapidly belly-side up. If it is necessary the eggs may be scraped off the side panes of the aquarium with a razor blade or, in the case of rounded objects, removed with the thumb and forefinger; the eggs are blunt and hardy. Eggs so removed may be affixed to the side panes of the nursery tank by pressing lightly with the forefinger (the eggs shouldn't touch one another). Introduce aeration and colour the water faintly with methylene blue. The addition of one teaspoon of NaCl for every 50 litres of water will lower the mortality of the eggs and fry. The regular exchange (weekly or fortnightly) of two-thirds of the water with fresh water promotes the growth of the young fish. However, the fry are sensitive to some kinds of treated tapwater. To prevent pronounced mortality of the fish allow the fresh tapwater to stand 24 hours before putting it in the tank.

1 ♀

1 ♂

1 ♂

1 ♀

1 Dwarf Corydoras or Rabaut's Corydoras
Corydoras rabauti LA MONTE, 1941
Syn. *Corydoras myersi, C. zygatus*   Callichthyidae

Distribution: tributaries of the Amazon above the mouth of the Negro River. Full length: 6 cm. Diet: live as well as artificial foods. Community tank. Breeding tank: with capacity of 50 litres or more, greatly subdued light. Sexual dimorphism: the female is larger, more robust. Sex ratio: 2–3 males : 1 female. Breeding water: 24 °C; pH 6.5–7.0; dCH max. 2°. Eggs: greyish-opaque, incubation period 4 days. Feeding of fry: brine shrimp nauplii.

Breeding this species in an aquarium is problematic in that the fish spawn only rarely or not at all. A group of fish under observation that attained sexual maturity in 1976 spawned for the first time in 1977 during a sudden drop in atmospheric pressure. Approximately 200 eggs were deposited by four females on the side panes of the aquarium. The fertilized eggs were treated with methylene blue; the fry started exogenous nutrition nine days after spawning and were reared without any problems. In three months the young fish reached a length of 2.5 cm. The group of six males and four females spawned again after an interval of three months. The number of eggs deposited was about the same. From then until 1984 the fish did not spawn at all, even though the females were clearly full all the time but apparently no longer able to reproduce. It has been reported on occasion that full females deposit unfertilized eggs in the absence of males; this did not happen in the group of fish under observation.

2 Masked Corydoras or Bandit Catfish
Corydoras metae EIGENMANN, 1914   Callichthyidae

Distribution: Colombia, – Meta River. Full length: 5.5 cm. Community tank. Breeding tank: of 50-litre capacity with dim light. Sexual dimorphism: the male is slimmer and smaller. Sex ratio: 2–3 males : 1 female. Water: 23–26 °C; pH 6.0–7.0; dCH max. 2°; dGH up to 10°. Breeding in captivity seems not to have succeeded as yet.

A group of fish was observed for a period of six years. Changes were made in their environment – in the temperature of the water, the chemical composition of the water, the intensity of lighting – but without effect. Hypophysation by injection likewise had no effect: the fish did not spawn. At the end of the six-year period several fish were dissected. Male sexual organs were found in smaller specimens, larger specimens were sexually undifferentiated, probably females that for unknown reasons did not attain sexual maturity in captivity.

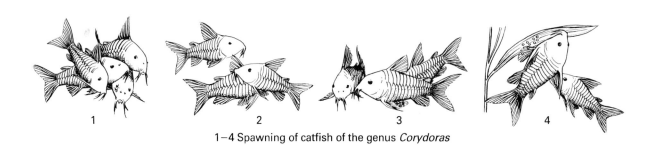

1–4 Spawning of catfish of the genus *Corydoras*

1 ♂

1 ♀

2 ♂

2 ♀

1 Dwarf Catfish or Pygmy Catfish
Corydoras hastatus EIGENMANN and EIGENMANN, 1888

Syn. *Microcorydoras hastatus, Corydoras australe*

Callichthyidae

Distribution: Brazil. Full length: 3 cm. Diet: live as well as artificial foods. Community tank (only together with small species of fish). Breeding tank: with capacity of 10 to 50 litres (depending on the number of fish). Sexual dimorphism: the male is smaller and more slender. Sex ratio: 2–3 males : 1 female. Breeding water: 24 °C; pH 6.5–7.0; dCH max. 2°. Eggs: minute, milky, incubation period 6 days. Feeding of fry: brine shrimp nauplii.

The fish generally spawn in a shoal at the close of the day. The males swim round the females with a fluttering movement of the caudal fin. Immediately before the act of mating the male bends its body sideways in an arc with the outside curve in front of the female's mouth and then reverses his position, with the female's mouth thus inside the arc formed by his body; as soon as the male catches hold of the female's barbels with his pectoral fins and presses her to his body he twists into an S-shape. Into the pouch formed by her ventral fins the female expels a single egg which is immediately fertilized. After a brief interval the female anchors the egg to the bottom, to a glass pane, to a rock, or to a plant. The above performance is repeated constantly until the female is depleted. There are not many eggs. As soon as the school of fish cease spawning they should be transferred to another, similar tank. The newly-hatched fry are large, measuring 4.8 mm in length. For the first 10 days the level of water in the tank must not be higher than 2 cm. Growth of the fry is rapid and regular. The fish are very similar to *C. pygmaeus;* the most conspicuous character of identification is the spot at the tail base – in *C. hastatus* there are two small lighter spots inside the black spot.

2 Leopard Corydoras
Corydoras julii STEINDACHNER, 1906

Callichthyidae

Distribution: upper Amazon and its tributaries. Full length: 6 cm. Diet: live as well as artificial foods. Community tank. Breeding tank: of 50- to 100-litre capacity. Sexual dimorphism: the male is smaller, more slender. Sex ratio: 2–3 males : 1 female. Water: 25–28 °C; pH 6.0–7.0; dCH max. 2°; dGH max. 10° (it seems that the species has not yet been bred).

Shy species, requires more warmth. Often confused with *C. trilineatus* which is extremely variable in coloration.

3 Spotted Catfish
Corydoras melanistius melanistius REGAN, 1912

Callichthyidae

Distribution: French Guiana. Full length: 6 cm. Diet: live as well as artificial foods. Community tank. Breeding tank: of 50- to 100-litre capacity. Sexual dimorphism: the male is smaller, more slender. Sex ratio: 2–3 males: 1 female. Water 25–28 °C; pH 6.0–7.0; dCH max. 2°; dGH max. 10°. So far it is not known if this species has been bred.

Very variable species. In 1974 Fraser-Brunner described the subspecies *C. melanistius brevirostris* (syn. *C. wotroi*).

1 Peppered Catfish
Corydoras paleatus (JENYNS, 1842)
Syn. *Callichthys paleatus, Corydoras marmoratus, C. maculatus,*
C. punctatus var. *argentina, C. microcephalus*

Callichthyidae

Distribution: southeastern Brazil and Uruguay. Full length: 7 cm. Diet: live as well as artificial foods. Community tank. Breeding tank: with capacity of 50 litres or more, dim light. Sexual dimorphism: the male is slimmer, his dorsal fin has a prolonged ray, the female is more robust. Sex ratio: 2−3 males : 1 female. Breeding water: 20−24 °C; pH 6.5−7.0; dCH max. 2°; Eggs: incubation period 4 days. Feeding of fry: brine shrimp nauplii. Propagated in 1878 by Carbonnier in Paris.

Before spawning the males swim nervously about the tank. Prior to the act of mating the female descends to the bottom pursued by several males. One of the males positions himself with his side at right angles to the head of the female and presses her by the barbels to his belly with his pectoral fin − the position of the two resembles the letter 'T'. With bodies quivering strongly the male releases the sperm and the female the eggs into a pouch formed by her ventral fins. In the pouch is a slit through which the sperm reach the eggs. The female then swims to a suitable place which she first feels with her whiskers and cleans, after which she opens the fin-pouch and with swaying movements of the body sticks the fertilized eggs onto the surface. After a short interval the act of mating is repeated. The spawning period often lasts several weeks with the female depositing as many as 50 eggs a day.

2 Bristly Corydoras
Corydoras barbatus (QUOY and GAIMARD, 1824)
Syn. *Callichthys barbatus, Scleromystae barbatus, S. kronei, Corydoras eigenmanni, C. kronei*

Callichthyidae

Distribution: region between Rio de Janeiro and Sao Paulo. Full length: 12 cm. Diet: live as well as artificial foods. Community tank. There are no reports of its being bred in captivity nor of sexual differences. The fish should be kept in a shoal. Water: 22−26 °C; pH 6.0−7.0; dCH max. 2°; dGH max. 10°.

C. barbatus has a remarkably slender body and elongated head. The markings are extremely variable, being different in young and older fish as well as in fish from various localities.

3 Emerald Brochis
Brochis splendens (DE CASTENAU, 1855)
Syn. *Brochis coeruleus, B. dipterus, Callichthys splendens,*
Chaenothorax bicarinatus, Ch. semiscutatus

Callychthyidae

Distribution: Ecuador, Peru, Brazil. Full length: 8 cm. Diet: live as well as artificial foods. Community tank. Breeding tank: of 50- to 100-litre capacity. Sexual dimorphism: ? Sex ratio: 2−3 males : 1 female. Water: 22−28 °C; pH 6.0−7.0; dCH max. 2°; dGH max. 10°. (It seems that breeding has not yet been successful).

The genus *Brochis* is closely related to the genus *Corydoras,* but differs by the armoured snout furnished with bony plates and the dorsal fin with a longer-stretched base and greater number of rays. *B. splendens* is very variable in coloration; colour deviations are caused by differences in pH in the separate localities.

1 Porthole Catfish
Dianema longibarbis COPE, 1871
Syn. *Callichthys adspersus, Decapogon adspersus*　　　　　　　　　　　　　Callichthyidae

○
◑ Distribution: Colombia, Peru and Brazil. Full length: 9 cm. Diet: live as well as artificial foods. Community tank. Breeding tank: of at least 50-litre capacity with dim light; place an inverted plastic dish resembling a broad leaf on the surface. Sexual dimorphism: the male is slimmer, smaller, the female is more robust. Sex ratio: for spawning put a rather large shoal in the tank with a slight preponderance of males. Breeding water: 24 °C; pH 7.0; dCH max. 2°. Eggs: yellowish, ∅ 1.5 mm, incubation period 5 days. Feeding of fry: brine shrimp nauplii.

The male builds a bubble nest on the underside of the leaves of aquatic plants. Spawning usually takes place when there is a drop in atmospheric pressure. The female deposits about 300 eggs in the nest. The nest is cared for by the male. The foam bubbles contain protective substances important for the initial development of the eggs. As soon as the eggs turn a darker colour transfer the nest with the eggs to a nursery tank. The embryos hatch within 24 hours. In the first days of life the fry are often attacked by mould and perish. This can be held in check by adding methylene blue to the water already in the egg stage, plus a teaspoon of NaCl for each 10 litres of water and by keeping the temperature of the water constant. The first two weeks the water column should be kept at a height of 2 to 3 cm. Once the fry overcome the critical period their growth is rapid.

2 Stripe-tailed Catfish
Dianema urostriata MIRANDA RIBERIO, 1912
Syn. *Decapogon urostriatum*　　　　　　　　　　　　　　　　　　　　　　Callichthyidae

○
◑ Distribution: Brazil − Amazon River and its tributaries round Manaus. Full length: 10 cm. Diet: live as well as artificial foods. Community tank. Breeding tank: the same as for *Dianema longibarbis.* Sexual dimorphism: ? Breeding it in captivity has apparently been unsuccessful.

A peaceable school fish. Imported only occasionally.

3 Port Hoplo or Atipa
Hoplosternum thoracatum (CUVIER and VALENCIENNES, 1840)
Syn. *Callichthys thoracatus, C. longifilis, C. personatus, C. exaratus, Hoplosternum thorae, H. longifilis*　　Callichthyidae

○
◑ Distribution: Trinidad, Guyana, Martinique, Venezuela, Brazil, Peru, Paraguay, in flat expanses of muddy waters greatly overgrown with vegetation. Full length: 18 cm. Diet: live as well as artificial foods. Community tank. Breeding tank: the same as for *D. longibarbis.* Sexual dimorphism: the male is coloured greyish-violet on the underside and the first rays of the pectoral fins are modified into a strong bony spine covered with minute teeth. The female is coloured white with round dark patches on the underside. Sex ratio: 1:1, or several specimens with a slight preponderance of males. Breeding water: 24 °C; pH 6.5−7.0; dCH max. 2°. Eggs: ∅ c. 2.5 mm, faintly yellowish, incubation period 3−5 days. Feeding of fry: brine shrimp nauplii.

The male builds a large bubblenest on the underside of leaves floating on the surface. The female may deposit as many as 1000 eggs. The male vigorously protects the spawning site. The embryos are 6 mm long, have developed fins and barbels, and rapidly consume the yolk sac. The fry become free-swimming in 48 hrs. They are sensitive to light and seek shelter.

Family Loricariidae

The fish of this family inhabit the mountain streams of South America. Only few erudite authorities are capable of distinguishing the various species. Some have a typical coloration that may be confused with the juvenile coloration of other species, or else fish of the same species but from different biotopes may be differently coloured. That is why colouring and markings are not a decisive means of identification and differentiation is possible only on the basis of morphological-anatomical characters. One such character, for instance, is the arrangement of the bony plates on the belly, the arrangement and shape of the dorsal and anal fins, etc. Apart from a few exceptions these armoured catfish are greatly compressed from above (dorso-ventrally). In some the skin is totally covered with bony plates, in others the belly is unarmoured, and some genera have no armour whatsoever. The mouth is subterminal and enclosed by thick lips furnished with horny papillae. This enables the fish to rasp off growths from firm objects. Many species live in swiftly-flowing water and therefore their mouth is furnished with a sucking apparatus. Because of the way the body is flattened, the gill slits are located on the underside of the head. Except for the caudal fin, all the fins possess strong spines.

1 *Ancistrus multispinnis* (REGAN, 1912)
Syn. *Xenocara multispinnis*

Loricariidae

Distribution: Brazil and Guyana – in rapids. Full length: 15 cm. Diet: live and plant foods, may be augmented by artificial foods (flakes). Community tank. Breeding tank: with capacity of 50- to 100 litres, drainage pipes *c.* 40 mm in diameter on the bottom, and diffused lighting. Sexual dimorphism: the male has branched tentacles on the head and round the upper jaw, in the female they are little-developed or completely absent. Sex ratio: 1:1, or with a slight preponderance of females. Breeding water: 24 °C; pH 7.0; dCH 2°; dGH 10°. Eggs: ⌀ 3 mm, yellow to orange, sticky, incubation period 6 days. Feeding of fry: brine shrimp nauplii. First breeding: apparently in Czechoslovakia in 1977.

Twilight fish. During the daytime they remain hidden in cavities, cracks and burrows which they dig under stones and where the spawning sites, that the males defend vigorously, are located. The eggs are cared for by the male. The female deposits grape-like clusters of 50 to 100 eggs. Remove the individual egg clusters and incubate them separately.

2 Pearl Sucker
Ancistrus hoplogenys (GÜNTHER, ?)

Loricariidae

Distribution: a rarely-seen catfish with range extending from Guyana to the Paraguay River. Full length: 12 cm. Diet: live and artificial foods, augmented by plant foods. Keeping tank: because these fish are so rare they should be kept in a monospecies tank with dim lighting and sufficient hiding possibilities. Breeding tank: same as keeping tank. Sexual dimorphism: the male has more, longer tentacles on the head.

Sex ratio: 1:1; or with a slight preponderance of females. Water: 20–24 °C; pH 7.0; dCH 2°, slight deviations do not matter. So far there are no reports about the breeding of these fish.

Fish that are active at night. They are among the most colourful members of this genus.

1 ♂

2

1 Bristle-mouth

Ancistrus dolichopterus KNER, 1854

Syn. *Ancistrus cirrhosus* (not Valenciennes), *A. temmincki* (not Valenciennes),
Chaetostomus delochopterus, Xenocara dolichopterus

Distribution: Guyana, Amazonia and Mato Grosso, strongly flowing streams. Full length: 13 cm. Diet: live and plant foods, may be augmented by artificial foods. Community tank. Breeding tank: of 50- to 100-litre capacity with drainage pipes or PVC tubes on the bottom, diffused light. Sexual dimorphism: the male is paler and has large tentacles on the head and round the upper jaw, some of which may be branched, others fork-like at the end; in the female these tentacles are only slightly developed and arranged in a single row round the mouth. Sex ratio: 1:1 (or 1 male : 2–3 females). Breeding water: 24 °C; pH 7.0; dCH 2° (slight deviations do not matter). Eggs: incubation period 5 days. Feeding of fry: brine shrimp nauplii, flaked plant foods; after a week also strained spinach.

Fish that are active by night, remaining hidden during the daytime. They spawn in cavities which they dig beneath stones or pieces of wood. The male cares for the eggs, but his presence is not necessary. Like many members of the genus *A. dolichopterus* feeds in the aquarium on organic remnants and algae.

2 Panaque

Panaque nigrolineatus (PETERS, 1877)

Syn. *Cochliodon nigrolineatus, Chaetostomus nigrolineatus*

Distribution: Colombia, Brazil and Venezuela. Full length: ?, in aquariums 25 cm. Diet: live as well as plant foods; may be augmented by artificial foods. Community tank (only together with peaceful species of fish). Breeding tank: with capacity of 500 litres or more, sufficient hiding places and diffused light. Sexual dimorphism: ? Sex ratio: 1:1. In captivity spawning is a chance occurrence, as, for instance, in 1974 in the showroom aquarium of the Gustav Struck Co. in Manching. However, more detailed information about breeding conditions is lacking. Water: 24 °C; pH 6.5–7.5; dCH 2°; dGH max. 15°.

Fish that are active at night. They are variable in coloration, the ground colour ranging from greyish to brown to greenish-brown, not particularly attractive as a rule. The reddish-brown or completely red eyes are striking. In the aquarium the fish graze off algae. In a mixed aquarium, in the company of other fish, they lose their inherent shyness. They establish territories which they defend against members of their own species. They are imported only very occasionally.

1 ♂

2

1 Dwarf Otocinclus
Otocinclus affinis STEINDACHNER, 1877 Loricariidae

Distribution: southeastern Brazil, in the region of Rio de Janeiro, clean, swift-flowing streams with aquatic plants and algal growths. Full length: 4 cm. Diet: live, artificial and plant foods (algal growths and benthic organisms contained therein). Community tank. Breeding tank: with capacity of 50 litres or more, well-lit in part, otherwise with dim lighting. Sexual dimorphism: the male is slimmer and smaller. Sex ratio: the fish are bred in a shoal with a preponderance of males. Breeding water: 20–23 °C; pH 6.5; dCH < 2°; dGH max. 10°; fresh, oxygen-rich, streaming water provided by circulating activated-coal filters. Eggs: small, sticky, incubation period 2–3 days/20 °C. Feeding of fry: *Paramecium caudatum* and newly hatched brine shrimp nauplii.

Crepuscular fish that are also active during the daytime. The females are not particularly prolific; they stick the eggs on plants, stones and the glass sides of the aquarium. The eleutherembryos should be sucked up with a tube 3 mm in diameter and transferred to flat nursery tanks with water column 3 to 5 cm high. Young fish seek out streaming water.

2 Sucker Catfish
Otocinclus vittatus REGAN, 1904 Loricariidae

Distribution: region of Mato Grosso and of the Paraguay River – flowing waters. Full length: 5.5–6 cm. Diet: live, artificial and plant foods (algae and small benthic organisms). Community tank. Breeding tank: of 50-litre capacity, bottom with dark areas, plant thickets. Sexual dimorphism: the male is slimmer, the female fuller in the body. Sex ratio: the fish are bred in a shoal with a preponderance of males. Breeding water: 20–23 °C; pH 6.5; dCH < 2°; dGH max. 10°; streaming water provided by circulating activated-coal filters. Eggs: small, sticky, incubation period 2–3 days. Feeding of fry: extremely fine live and artificial foods (*Paramecium caudatum,* fine sorts of brine shrimp nauplii, e.g. South American species).

Fish that are active by night but may be seen even during the daytime. They are fond of flowing water and dense growths of algae. The female sticks the eggs on the glass sides of the aquarium and on plants. Endogenous nutrition lasts three days. Free-swimming fry lead a hidden existence.

Twenty species of *Otocinclus* have been described so far, some of them very similar and often confused. Only few populations are aquarium-bred: most fish are obtained in the wild, e.g. *O. flexilis* Cope, 1894, *O. maculicauda* Steindachner, 1876, *O. maculipinnis* Regan, 1912, *O. nigricauda* Boulenger, 1891. The individual species cannot be distinguished by sight, the names under which they are sold in shops are usually not authoritative and so in many instances we don't know which species we have in the aquarium.

Loricariidae

1

2

☐
● Distribution: Colombia (Caqueta, Cauca and Japura rivers). Full length: 20 cm. Diet: in their native waters the fish graze off algae and the benthic organisms in their midst, in aquariums they are fed strained spinach, FD tablets and lyophilized flaked foods. Monospecies keeping tank: of 100- to 200-litre capacity, well overgrown with floating plants and with dark bottom. Breeding tank: same as keeping tank. Sexual dimorphism: unknown. Sex ratio: the fish are bred in a small group. Water: 22−26 °C; pH 6.5−7.0; dCH max. 2°; dGH max. 10°; fresh but settled, oxygen-rich and filtered through peat. Breeding in captivity has not succeeded apparently.

Some species of *Farlowella* have already been successfully propagated and reared. *F. gracilis,* however, is a species that is sensitive to changes in the environment and requires a long time for acclimatization. They are peaceful, bottom-dwelling fish, with a very slender body. A distinguishing characteristic and means of identifying the various species is the arrangement of the rows of plates on the belly. Members of the genus *Farlowella* differ from those belonging to the genus *Dasyloricaria* by the position of the dorsal fin. In *Farlowella* the dorsal fin inserts in line with the anal fin whereas in *Dasyloricaria* it inserts farther forward, ahead of the anal fin.

2 Whiptail
Dasyloricaria filamentosa (STEINDACHNER, 1878)
Syn. *Loricaria filamentosa*   Loricariidae

○
◑ Distribution: Colombia − Magdalena River region. Full length: 25 cm. Diet: live as well as artificial foods. Community tank. Breeding tank: of 30- to 50-litre capacity, with plastic tubes about 30 mm in diameter on the bottom. Sexual dimorphism: the male has bristles on the pectoral fins. Sex ratio: 1:1. Breeding water: 24 °C; pH 7.0; dCH 2°; fresh. Eggs: ∅ 2 mm, incubation period 9 days. Feeding of fry: brine shrimp nauplii.

It is difficult to identify the individual species. One guideline is the arrangement of the bony plates on the belly. *D. filamentosa* has the upper ray of the caudal fin prolonged in threadlike fashion, other species have the lower ray prolonged as well and in some species the rays of the caudal fin are not prolonged at all. The fish become active at twilight, remaining hidden during the daytime. The main and often only spawning period is during the winter months. The brood fish seek narrow cavities for spawning. The male cares for the eggs and he may be transferred to the nursery tank together with the tube. When the fry become free-swimming the male should be removed. The free-swimming fry are 7 mm long and very sensitive to the presence of protein substances in the water. For this reason it is absolutely necessary to filter the water through activated coal and replace the water with fresh water of the same composition and temperature every second day. Ordinary tapwater will generally suffice. The height of the water column should be kept at about 10 cm at first. The fry grow rapidly and they gradually lose their sensitivity to pollution of the water.

1

2

Family Atherinidae

Most members of this family inhabit the shallow shoreline waters of warm seas. Only a few species dwell in brackish waters and the mouths of rivers. These school fish are characterized by having a second, separate dorsal fin. The eggs are large and furnished with sticky filaments by which they adhere to plants.

The ichthyologist Munro divided this originally large family into four separate families: the Atherinidae, Melanotaeniidae, Telmatherinidae and Pseudomugilidae. Authorities, however, differ in their opinion as to the justification for this division.

1 Madagascar Rainbow
Bedotia geayi PELLEGRIN, 1907

Atherinidae

Distribution: Madagascar. Full length: 12–15 cm. Diet: live foods (fruit flies – *Drosophila melanogaster,* small fish) as well as artificial foods. Monospecies keeping tank with dark bottom. Breeding tank: of at least 100-litre capacity with thickets of plants. Sexual dimorphism: the male is larger and more colourful. Sex ratio: 1:1, or a small shoal with a slight preponderance of females. Breeding water: 25–28 °C; pH 7.0–7.5; dCH max. 3°. Eggs: ∅ 1.4 mm, pale yellow, provided with a bundle of filaments, incubation period 6–8 days. Feeding of fry: nauplii of brine shrimp or *Cyclops* nauplii.

Spawning is practically continuous with brief intervals. The fish spawn amidst plants as well as in open water. The eleutherembryos swim in open water in a slanting position with the head upwards, simultaneously filling their gas bladder. Twenty-four hours after hatching the larvae start actively foraging for food. After one week transfer the parent fish to a separate tank or else repeatedly remove plants with eggs and put these in another tank.

Family Melanotaeniidae

The members of this family live mostly in schools in rivers, lakes and swamps in New Guinea and northern Australia. Although the family includes approximately 40 species of fish many of them are incorrectly referred to under the general name *Melanotaenia fluviatilis* or *M. maccullochi.*

Australian Rainbow Fish
2 *Melanotaenia nigrans* (RICHARDSON, 1834)
Syn. *Nematocentris nigrans*

Melanotaeniidae

Distribution: eastern and northern Australia. Full length: 10 cm. Diet: live as well as artificial foods. Community tank. Breeding tank: of 60- to 100-litre capacity with freely-floating finely-leaved plants. Sexual dimorphism: the male is slender, larger, more coloured. Sex ratio: 1 male : 2 females. Breeding water: 20–24 °C; pH 7.0–7.5; dCH max. 2° (1 teaspoon of NaCl per 10 litres of water). Eggs: incubation period 7–10 days. Feeding of fry: *Paramecium caudatum,* later nauplii of brine shrimp or *Cyclops* nauplii.

Spawning takes place on finely-leaved plants. Parent fish only very occasionally eat the eggs and therefore may be left in the tank until the first fry becomes free-swimming, when they should be removed.

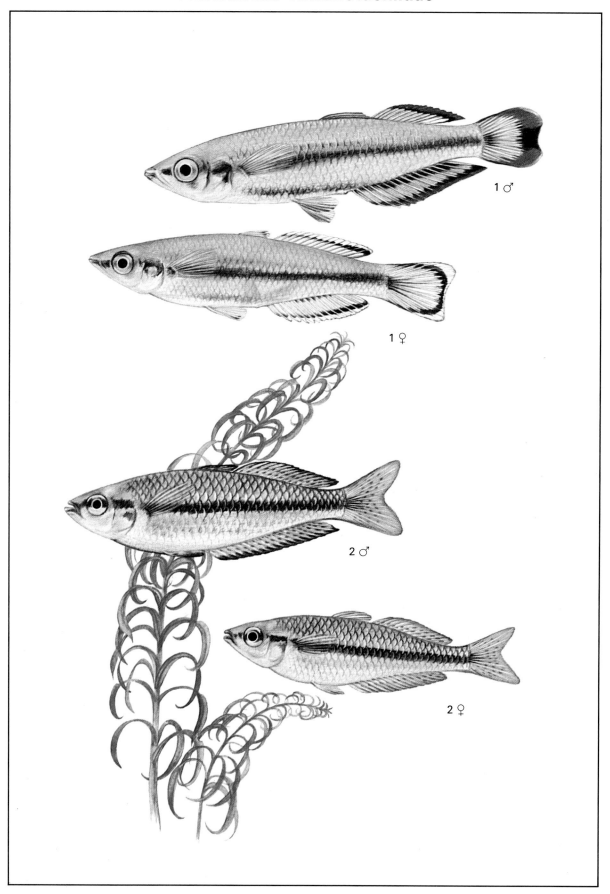

1 ♂

1 ♀

2 ♂

2 ♀

1 Black-lined Rainbow Fish
Melanotaenia maccullochi (OGILBY, 1915)
Syn. *Nematocentris maccullochi*

Distribution: fresh waters in northeastern Australia south to Sydney. Full length: 7 cm. Diet: live as well as artificial foods. Community tank. Breeding tank: with a capacity of 50 litres and more, depending on the number of breeding fish, plenty of light or full sun, and thickets of plants. Sexual dimorphism: the male is slimmer, more colourful. Sex ratio: 1 male : 2 females; put a small shoal in the tank for spawning. Breeding water: 23−25 °C; pH 7.0−7.5; dCH max. 3°; add 1 tablespoon NaCl for every 10 litres of water or 1 litre of sea water for every 50 litres of water. Eggs: incubation period 7−10 days.

Feeding of fry: newly hatched brine shrimp nauplii.

The female deposits approximately 200 eggs during the spawning period. These are attached to plants by short filaments. The dark eggs are also suspended on the tank walls or on plants. After a few days the larvae become free-swimming, keeping close to the surface. The fry are continually on the move. A large number of young fish may be obtained by regularly transferring clumps of plants into a separate tank.

2 Pink-ear Rainbowfish
Melanotaenia fluviatilis CASTELNAU, 1878
Syn. *Nematocentris fluviatilis*

Distribution: northern Australia − Queensland and southern New Guinea. Full length: 10 cm. Diet: live as well as artificial foods. Community tank (together with other species of fish that have the same requirements as to the composition of the water). Breeding tank: with capacity of 60 litres and more, plenty of light (morning sun), clumps of finely-leaved plants. Sexual dimorphism: the male is more colourful, his dorsal and anal fins are pointed and dark-tipped, in the female these fins are more rounded and without dark tips. Sex ratio: 1 male : 2−3 females (the fish may be set up in a larger shoal for spawning). Breeding water: 22−25 °C; pH 7.0−7.5; dCH max. 2°; dGH max. 10°; clear, fresh, oxygen-rich; 1 teaspoon of NaCl for every 10 litres of water may be added. Eggs: incubation period 7−10 days/25 °C. Feeding of fry: first four to five days on infusoria (*Paramecium caudatum*) monoculture, rotatoria, smallest *Cyclops* nauplii, then newly hatched brine shrimp nauplii.

Long confused with the species *M. nigrans*. The dorsal, anal and ventral fins are prominently edged with black, and there is an orange-red spot on the gill covers. In view of the wide geographical distribution of this species the various populations may exhibit differences in coloration. Some may be reddish during the spawning period, others bluish. Always keep a large shoal of fish in the tank. The fish spawn in the upper layers of water. Spawning, which lasts several days, is triggered by the morning sun. The female deposits up to several hundred eggs. The fish spawn throughout the year at shorter or longer intervals. Plants with eggs should be transferred to a separate nursery tank every fifth day.

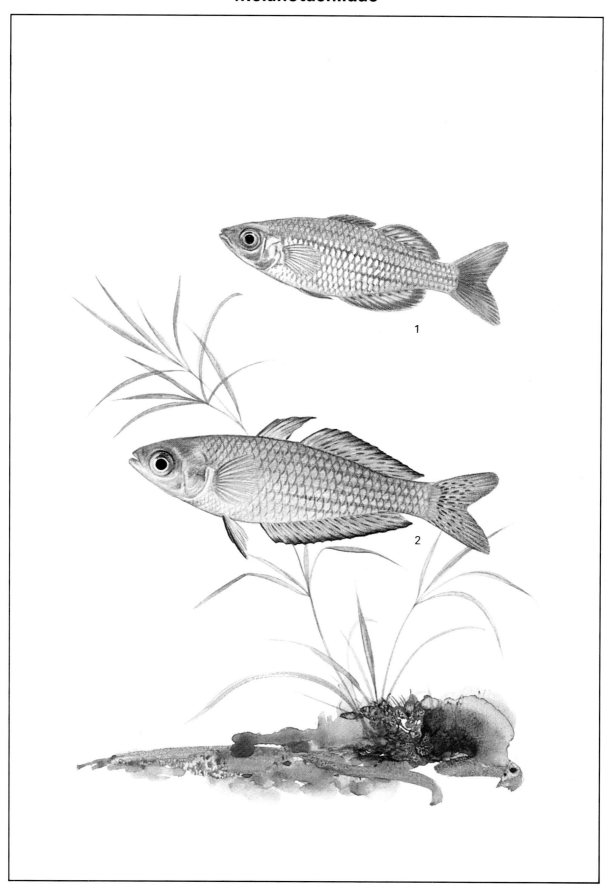

1 Red Rainbowfish
Glossolepis incisus WEBER, 1908   Melanotaeniidae

Distribution: northern New Guinea (Irian), Lake Sentani. Full length: 15 cm. Diet: live as well as artificial foods. Community tank. Breeding tank: of 200-litre capacity with compact bunches of plants. Providing the aquarium with a labyrinth, say of wavy nylon mesh, (at the same time leaving sufficient swimming space for the parent fish) will save a large number of eggs from being eaten by the parents. Sexual dimorphism: the male is larger and coloured red; at the age of two to three years he has a remarkably high body and small, greatly dorsoventrally-flattened head. Sex ratio: the fish are bred in a shoal with a slight preponderance of males. Breeding water: 24 °C; pH 7.0−7.5; dCH 2−3° (1 tablespoon NaCl for every 50 litres of water). Eggs: ∅ 1.3 mm, furnished with 8 to 16 threads rising from a small spot on one pole of the egg case. If the egg comes in contact with a firm object the threads catch hold, contract, and pull the egg to the object. Incubation period 6 days. Feeding of fry: specific genera of rotatoria: *Keratella, Filinia, Brachionus, Polyarthra.* Certain fry foods may also be given; Clark (food for trout fry) finely mixed with water has proved to be good. After 20 days the fry will take brine shrimp nauplii.

The female deposits a relatively small number of eggs (fewer than 70). Before the eggs locate a firm object they float for a time in open water where they may be eaten by the parent fish. That is why it is recommended to fit out the aquarium as stated above. The parent fish are left in the tank for about a week and then moved to another, similarly furnished aquarium. The first free-swimming fry begin to put in an appearance in 10 days. Rearing the fry is difficult, their growth is slow. The fish attain sexual maturity at the age of one year.

2 Green Rainbowfish
Glossolepis wanamensis ALLEN and KAILOLA, 1979   Melanotaeniidae

Glossolepis incisus has been joined by another species with a greenish glitter − *Glossolepis wanamensis,* discovered by Allen. The fish are from Papua New Guinea, from Lake Wanama near the town of Lae in the southeastern part of the island. From the aquaristic viewpoint it is a lovely and attractive species but entirely unknown and one can only hope that it will become widespread. Meanwhile it is presumed that care and breeding will be similar to that of *G. incisus.*

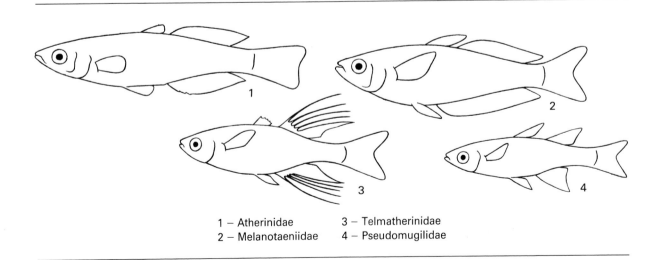

1 − Atherinidae   3 − Telmatherinidae
2 − Melanotaeniidae   4 − Pseudomugilidae

Melanotaeniidae

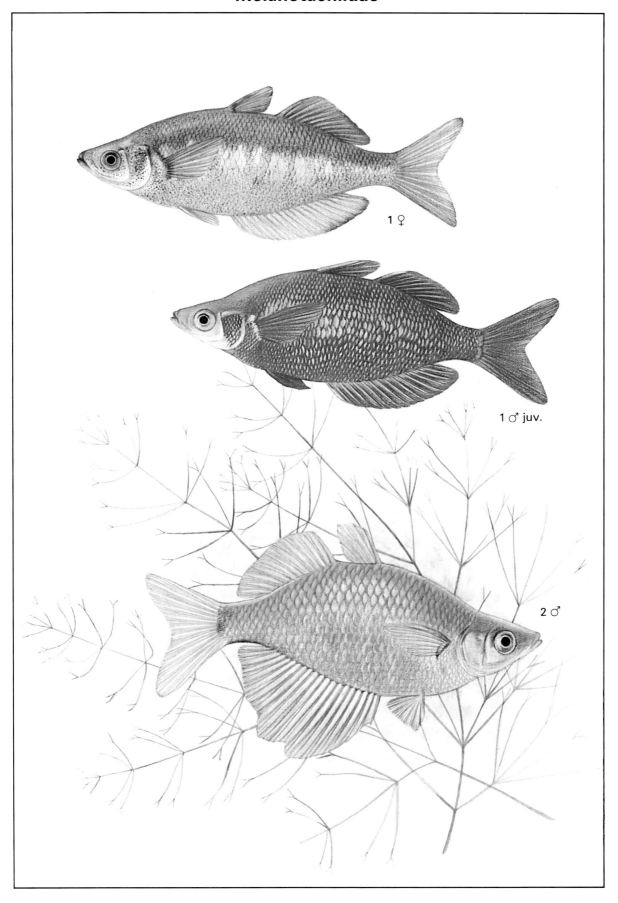

1 ♀

1 ♂ juv.

2 ♂

Family Pseudomugilidae

These secondary freshwater fish inhabit fresh and brackish waters in northern and eastern Australia, New Guinea and the Aru Islands (southwest of New Guinea). The males have longer fins and are more colourful than the females, particularly during spawning. In their native land mosquito-ridden places are often stocked with these fish for they devour mosquito larvae and pupae in enormous numbers. The spawning period lasts up to two months, with the females depositing about 20 large eggs daily. The eggs are furnished with a mucous filament by which they are attached to plants.

1 *Pseudomugil signifer* KNER, 1864
Syn. *Atherina signata, Pseudomugil signatus*   Pseudomugilidae

○
● Distribution: Australia – northern and eastern Queensland. Full length: 4.5 cm. Diet: live as well as artificial foods. Monospecies keeping tank. Breeding tank: of 50-litre capacity with finely-leaved plants. Sexual dimorphism: the male is more colourful. Sex ratio: 1 male : 2–3 females (put a larger shoal of fish in the tank for spawning). Breeding water: 24–26 °C; pH 7.0–8.5; dCH 2°; dGH 11–15°. Add 1 tablespoon of NaCl for every 10 litres of water. Eggs: incubation period 16–20 days. Feeding of fry: brine shrimp nauplii.

The fish spawn on finely-leaved plants throughout the year at short intervals. The free-swimming fry keep close to the surface; they are fond of assembling where the water flows in a stream. They continually 'crawl' in a peculiar manner. They should be taken out and put into a separate tank. Their growth is slow, sexual differentiation begins to be apparent at eight months and sexual maturity is attained at the age of one year.

Family Telmatherinidae

The fish of this family inhabit the Australian-Malayan region including the Indonesian island of Sulawesi (Celebes). The fauna and flora of this region are different from that of the Indo-Malayan region and have characteristics in common with those of New Guinea and Australia. All members of this family are secondary freshwater fish. The only well-known species is the Celebes Rainbow Fish (*Telmatherina ladigesi*).

2 Celebes Rainbow Fish
Telmatherina ladigesi AHL, 1936   Telmatherinidae

○
● Distribution: interior of the island of Sulawesi (Celebes). Full length: 8 cm. Diet: live as well as artificial foods. Monospecies keeping tank. Breeding tank: of 50-litre capacity with thickets of finely-leaved plants. Sexual dimorphism: in the male the rays of the second dorsal fin and anal fin are strongly extended, butterfly-like. Sex ratio: 1 male : 2 females (in a shoal). Breeding water: 24–26 °C; pH 7.5–8.5; dCH 2°; dGH *c.* 11°; filtered through marble gravel and with an addition of 1 tablespoon of NaCl for every 10

litres of water. Eggs: incubation period 10 days. Feeding of fry: brine shrimp nauplii.

The fish spawn in finely-leaved plants at short intervals throughout the year. The free-swimming fry are continually on the move keeping close to the surface. They should be removed regularly and put in a separate nursery tank. Even when fed generously and regularly the young fish grow very slowly. Sexual maturity is attained at the age of seven months.

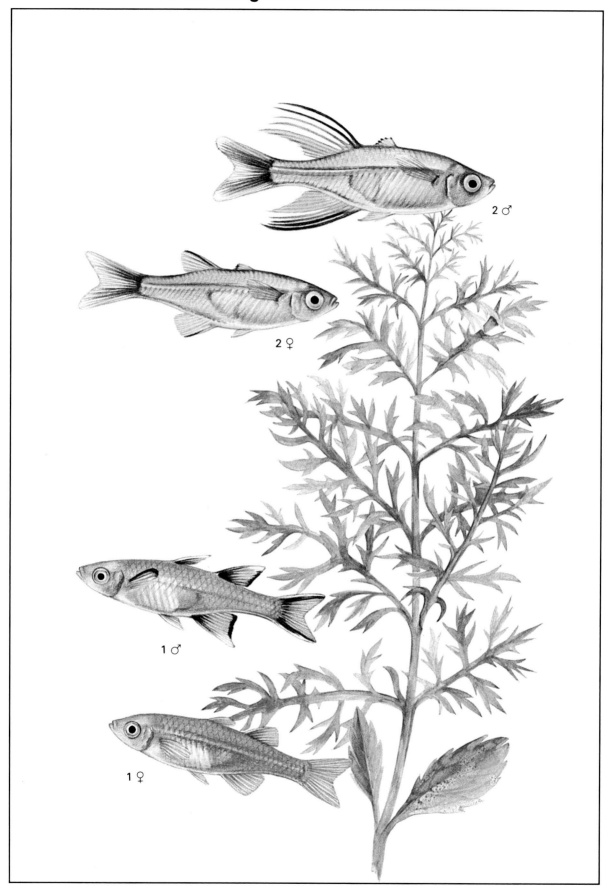

2 ♂

2 ♀

1 ♂

1 ♀

1 Featherfin Rainbow
Iratherina werneri MEINKEN, 1974
Syn. *Iratherina jardinensis*

◁
●
Distribution: island of New Guinea, near the city of Merauke (Irian) north to the Fly River and east to Dar (Papua New Guinea), in Australia on Cape York peninsula in the Jardin River region. Full length: 5 cm. Diet: small live foods (*Cyclops* nauplii are a favourite). Monospecies keeping tank. Breeding tank: of 20- to 50-litre capacity with finely-leaved plants. Sexual dimorphism: in the male the first dorsal fin is high, the fourth ray of the second dorsal fin and fifth ray of the anal fin are greatly extended, the marginal rays of the caudal fin are extended in lyre-like fashion, the female's fins are all shorter. Sex ratio: 1:1 (or the fish may be set up to spawn in a small shoal with a slight preponderance of males). Breeding water: 25 °C; pH 7.5−8.5; dCH 3°; dGH 15°; filtered through marble gravel. Eggs: ∅ 1 mm, glassily transparent, furnished with sticky filaments, incubation period seven days. Feeding of fry: rotatoria, if nothing else is available *Paramecium caudatum*; some artificial foods.

Imported together with *Glossolepis incisus*. At present rarely imported fish; only females are offered on the market. The fish spawn on finely-leaved plants. Five days after spawning the eyes of the embryo are visible inside the egg. Two days later the embryo hatches and the fry immediately begins swimming and actively foraging for food. The fry grow rapidly and at the age of eight weeks it is possible to differentiate the sex of the young fish.

Family Hemirhamphidae

The members of this family are distributed in southeast Asia and dwell in fresh and brackish waters as well as sea water. They are closely related to the fish of the family Belonidae and also have a similar body shape. The lower jaw is much longer than the motile upper jaw. Some genera are viviparous (live-bearing); the copulating organ of the male is markedly different from the gonopodium in structure and is called an andropodium. The first four rays of the anal fin are transformed into the functional part of the andropodium.

2 Celebes Half-beak
Nomorhamphus celebensis WEBER and DE BEAUFORT, 1922

◁
●
Distribution: island of Sulawesi (Celebes) − Lake Poso and some streams near Lappa Kanru. Full length: male − 8 cm, female − 12 cm. Diet: live foods. Monospecies keeping tank. Breeding tank: of 100-litre capacity, elongate, with islets of floating plants. Sexual dimorphism: the male has a slightly elongated lower jaw terminating in a fleshy, hook-like excrescence, and the dorsal, ventral and anal fins edged with black. Sex ratio: 1 male : 2 females. Breeding water: 25 °C; pH 6.5−7.5; dCH max. 10°. Live-bearing fish, interval between litters 28 days. Feeding of fry: finely sifted zooplankton.

The fish generally swim close to the surface of the water; from time to time, however, they also congregate in the middle and bottom layers where they skilfully catch food. Ripe females may be identified by the enlarged body. One female bears 8 to 16 young, 2 to 2.5 cm long and readily distinguished as to sex. Either use a breeding trap or remove the young in time. Young fish prefer larger pieces of food. Their growth is rapid.

1 ♂

2 ♀

2 ♂

1 Malayan Half-beak
Dermogenys pusillus VAN HASSELT, 1823
Syn. *Hemirhamphus fluviatilis*

Hemirhamphidae

◁
◑

Distribution: Thailand, Malaysia, Singapore, Indonesia, in fresh and brackish waters. Full length: male − 6 cm, female − 7 cm. Diet: live foods (a surface fish feeding chiefly on flying insects); fruit flies (*Drosophila melanogaster*), midges, aphids, *Daphnia, Cyclops,* mosquito and midge larvae, plus vitamin D once a week. Community tank. Breeding tank: of 100- to 200-litre capacity, rather shallow, elongate, with open expanse of water. Hang plants at the sides of the tank close to the surface (as a hiding place for the fry). Sexual dimorphism: the male is smaller, his anal fin is transformed into an andropodium. Sex ratio: a larger shoal of fish with a preponderance of females should be put in the tank for spawning. Breeding water: 26−28 °C; pH 7.0−8.0; dCH max. 10°; add 1 tablespoon NaCl for every 10 litres of water, simulate a stream of water with the aid of a filter. Live-bearing fish, interval between each litter 6−8 weeks. Feeding of fry: brine shrimp nauplii, finely sifted zooplankton.

In the wild the fish are exposed to intensive solar radiation which fosters the production of vitamin D. Lack of this vitamin causes defects in the development of the embryo inside the body of the female. The females should not be put in a breeding trap before having their litters for they may hurt (break off) their lower jaws in such a trap; this may also happen in a small tank. One female bears about 50 young. The fry should be removed regularly and put into a separate tank. Young fish grow very rapidly. In the mixed aquarium this species should be kept together with bottom-dwelling fish.

2 Half-beak
Hemirhamphodon pogonognathus BLEEKER, 1853

Hemirhamphidae

◁
●

Distribution: Thailand, Malaysia, Indonesia, in small shallow streams without vegetation. Full length: 9 cm. Diet: live foods, chiefly flying insects, fruit flies (*Drosophila melanogaster*), mosquito larvae and pupae, etc. Zooplankton is also provided as supplementary food. Monospecies keeping tank, shallow, with broad expanse of open water. Sexual dimorphism: the male has an andropodium. The water in the fish's natural habitat is soft, black (large concentration of humic acid from the rotting vegetation on the bottom). The temperature of the water is apparently rather high: 26−28 °C. There is no record of breeding this live-bearing fish in captivity so far. Imports obtained from free nature are made by private individuals.

D. Vogt states that in the locality in the vicinity of Palembang (Sumatra) there are a lot of mosquitoes and that these are probably the main food of these fish. *H. pogonognathus* is more colourful than *Dermogenys pusillus.* The fish should be provided with plenty of space (only a few specimens in the tank) for otherwise they are aggressive, bite one another, and may die as a result of their injuries.

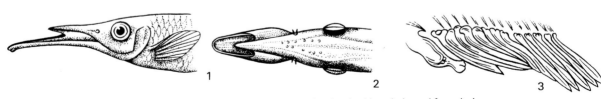

Dermogenys pusillus
1 − beaked head viewed from the side
2 − beaked head viewed from below
3 − andropodium of male

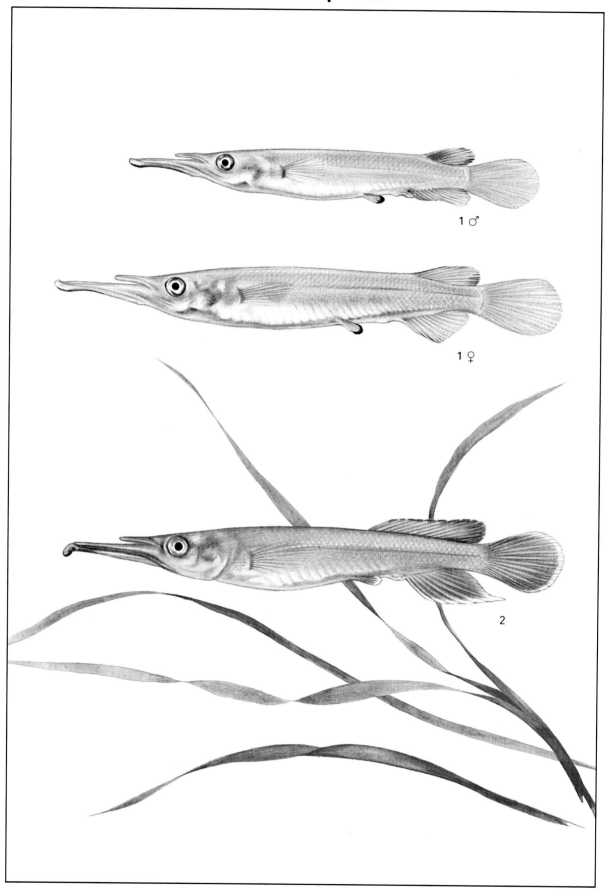

1 ♂

1 ♀

2

Family Belonidae

The members of this family are mostly predaceous sea fish distributed throughout the world. Typical characteristics are the elongated pike-like body and the insertion of the dorsal, ventral and anal fins far to the rear. Further characteristics are the large eyes and the jutting, beak-like, strongly-toothed jaws. Many are large fish of commerce.

1 Indian Freshwater Garfish
Xenotodon cancila (HAMILTON-BUCHANAN, 1822)
Syn. *Esox cancila, Belone cancila, Mastemcembalus cancila*

Belonidae

◁ ● Distribution: fresh and brackish waters in India, Burma, Sri Lanka, Thailand, Malaysia, Borneo and Kampuchea. Full length: 30 cm. Diet: live foods, chiefly fish. Monospecies keeping tank of about 500-litre capacity, elongate, well covered. Breeding tank: with capacity of 200 litres per pair and plant thickets. Sexual dimorphism: the male is more slender. Sex ratio: 1:1. Breeding water: 26 °C; pH 6.5–7.5; dCH max. 2°. Eggs: furnished with 2 mm long filaments, incubation period 9 days. Feeding of fry: brine shrimp nauplii, sifted zooplankton, later mosquito larvae, robust zooplankton and fry of live-bearing fish.

A typical characteristic of the young fish is the upper jaw which is half as long as the lower jaw but later grows to the same length. Young fish mature sexually when they reach a total length of 15 cm. Spawning takes place in plant thickets.

Family Gasterosteidae

The several species of these small, armoured and spiny fish are found in salt, brackish and fresh water in the cold and temperate regions of the northern hemisphere. The individual species differ in the number of spines in front of the dorsal fin, which inserts far to the back and is in line with the anal fin.

2 Three-spined Stickleback
Gasterosteus aculeatus LINNAEUS, 1758
Syn. *Gasterosteus argyropomus, G. biaculeatus, G. brachycentrus,*
G. bispinosus, G. cataphractus, G. cuvieri, G. gymnurus, G. leiurus, G. niger, G. noveboracensis,
G. obolarius, G. ponticus, G. semiarmatus, G. semiloricatus, G. spinulosus, G. teraculeatus,
G. tetracanthus, G. trachurus, Leiurus aculeatus

Gasterosteidae

◁ ● Distribution: along the coasts of Europe, northern Asia and North America. Introduced inland into flowing as well as standing fresh waters. Full length: 12 cm. Diet: live foods. Monospecies keeping tank or garden pool. Breeding tank: with capacity of 100 litres, finely-leaved coldwater plants, and medium-coarse gravel on the bottom. Sexual dimorphism: the male is colourful at spawning time, and slightly smaller; ripe females have a bulging belly. Sex ratio: 1 male : 3–4 females. Breeding water: 18–22 °C; pH 6.5–8.5; dCH 2°. Eggs: incubation period 4–10 days. Feeding of fry: nauplii of brine shrimp or *Cyclops* nauplii, later sifted zooplankton.

The fish spawn from March till July. In cramped quarters the males are aggressive towards one another. The male builds a nest of plant matter on the bottom, which he reinforces with a kidney secretion. He then lures ripe females to the nest. A single female deposits up to 250 eggs. The females should be removed after spawning. The male watches over the nest for a week after the fry have hatched.

1

2 ♀

2 ♂

Family Syngnathidae

Most of the species belonging to this family are sea fish but many may be found also in brackish and fresh waters. They are unusual fish with a typical thin body that is hexagonal in cross-section. The dorsal fin is without spines or is completely absent. The fish are not good swimmers; they swim with the aid of the pectoral fins or with a wavy motion of the dorsal fin. They can hold fast to aquatic plants with the prehensile tail. The eyes move independently of one another and there is a pair of nasal openings, one on either side of the snout. The male has a pouch on the belly for holding the eggs and rearing the fry. In some more primitive species the eggs are attached to the male's skin fold, exposed to the surrounding water, and hence less protected.

1 African Freshwater Pipefish
Syngnathus pulchellus BOULENGER, 1915

Syngnathidae

Distribution: Cameroon, Gabon, Zaire – fresh as well as brackish waters. Full length: 15 cm. Diet: live foods – small mosquito larvae, small Daphnia, newly-hatched fry of live-bearing fish. These foods are an important factor in keeping the fish in good condition. Monospecies keeping tank. Breeding tank: with a capacity of 50 litres or more. Sexual dimorphism: at the age of 5 months the 6 cm long males have a skin fold on either side of the body in line with the first ray of the dorsal fin which broadens their contour when viewed from above. Sex ratio: 1:1, or a slight preponderance of males. Breeding water: 25–28 °C; pH 7.0–7.5; dCH < 2°, fresh, add 1 tablespoon sea salt for every 10 litres of water. Eggs: yellow-orange, quadrangular (shaped like an ashlar stone) with rounded corners; incubation period 18–20 days/25 °C. Feeding of fry: newly-hatched brine shrimp nauplii.

This species occurs in differently coloured populations in separate localities. These are peaceable fish. Their food is sucked in together with water; it is only with difficulty that they catch rapidly-moving organisms. The impetus for spawning comes from the ripe female. She scouts around for a suitable male and then displays to him. Later the two press their bodies together belly to belly. In a short while, approximately within one minute, the female releases the eggs – up to 70 – into the pouch on the male's belly protected by folds of skin. She presses the eggs into the spongy, extremely sticky lining of the pouch. The eggs themselves are not sticky. During the incubation period the skin folds change colour – they turn brown and expand markedly. The fry is 15 mm long and 0.7 mm wide, fully coloured, does not have a yolk sac and resembles the adult fish. The critical period in rearing the fry lasts 14 days. Young fish grow rapidly and attain sexual maturity at the age of eight months.

Syngnathidae

Family Batrachoididae

In the assortment of freshwater fish offered by shops one will occasionally come across members of this family, even though they are actually sea fish. The various species belonging to this family migrate from the sea to the mouths of rivers or even farther upstream to their spawning sites. Though small they are very predaceous and will attack even fish much larger than themselves. This is made possible by the large, deeply-cleft, strongly-toothed mouth. They are bottom-dwelling fish. There are approximately 30 species, some of which are furnished with poison spines. The ventral fins insert ahead of the pectoral fins. There are two dorsal fins. From the aquaristic viewpoint only the species *Halophryne trispinosus* is of interest.

1 Toadfish or Freshwater Lionfish
Halophryne trispinosus (GÜNTHER, 1861)
Syn. *Batrachus grunniens*   Batrachoididae

Distribution: coastal regions of India, Sri Lanka and southeast Asia. Full length: 30 cm. Diet: live foods — fish, earthworms, larger larvae of aquatic insects. Monospecies keeping tank, dim lighting, sufficient hiding places (cavities). Sexual dimorphism: not known. Water: 24 °C; pH 7.5−8; add 1 tablespoon sea salt for every 10 litres of water. The fish were bred in captivity, apparently in the USA, but the fry were not successfully reared.

The fish purportedly spawn in cavities and the large eggs are cared for by the female. *H. trispinosus* is classified in the subfamily Batrachoidinae. It is very closely related to the fish of the subfamily Thalassophryninae, which are poisonous. The individual species of the two subfamilies may be easily confused. The three spines in the dorsal fin are considered to be a good means of identifying the fish of the subfamily Batrachoidinae. Even so it is recommended to be careful when handling these fish. *H. trispinosus* is a predaceous fish that is active by night, remaining hidden during the daytime. It is capable of capturing even quite large fish, including smaller fish of its own kind (species). For that reason it is advisable to put only specimens of about the same size and few in number in a large tank. The lateral line is furnished with spines that catch in nets.

Batrachoididae

Family Cyprinodontidae

The members of this family are found on all continents except Australia. The places they occur in are rain puddles, flooded meadows and ditches.

Unlike the carp fish which they resemble, they have toothed jaws, protrusile mouth, no barbels, and no adipose fin. Some species wait out the dry period in the form of eggs, adult fish die. A major reclassification of this family was done in 1981 by Parenti. Here we adhere to the traditional division into the following groups according to the development of the eggs:

a) Non-annuals: species with a continuous (uninterrupted) development — these inhabit localities where there is water even during the dry season.

b) Annuals: species with a discontinuous (interrupted) development — these live in so-called periodically dry waters. There are two quiescent (dormant) periods — so-called diapauses — in the development of the eggs. The first diapause occurs immediately after fertilization and lasts until the moment the bottom dries up. Development of the embryo is triggered by the increased concentration of oxygen. The second diapause occurs automatically as soon as the development of the embryo is completed but the substrate is not covered with water. As soon as the bottom is flooded with water (the concentration of oxygen is considerably lowered) the second diapause ends and the fry hatches.

c) Semi-annuals: species with an intermediate development living in biotopes where the water dries up to a greater or lesser degree for a short time. These species incline towards one of the above forms of egg development.

1 *Rivulus cryptocallus* HUBER and SEEGERS, 1980

Commercial names: Rivulus NSC 15, Rivulus NSC 13, Rivulus U 13, (U — unknown), *Rivulus* sp. Ravine Villaine, *Rivulus* sp. 'Petit Bourg', Rivulus U 16, *Rivulus* sp. 'Martinique'.

Cyprinodontidae

Distribution: island of Martinique in the Caribbean. Full length: male — 7.5 cm, female — 6.5 cm. Diet: live foods. Monospecies keeping tank, covered. Breeding tank: with capacity of 10 litres and finely-leaved plants (Java moss). Sexual dimorphism: the male is more brightly coloured, the female slender, more or less brown,with black spot on the upper part of the tail root. Sex ratio: 1 male : 2 females. Breeding water: 20–25 °C; pH 6.5; dCH < 2°; dGH < 10°.

Eggs: Ø 1.8–2 mm, yellow-brown, incubation period 2–3 weeks. Feeding of fry: nauplii of brine shrimp of *Cyclops* nauplii.

Let the group of brood fish spawn for a week. The female deposits about 40 eggs. They develop immersed in water but will survive in damp peat so that they may be shipped by mail. The fish attain sexual maturity at the age of six months.

2 Green Rivulus, Brown Rivulus or Cuban Rivulus
Rivulus cylindraceus POEY, 1861

Syn. *Rivulus marmoratus*

Cyprinodontidae

Distribution: Cuba, mountain streams. Full length: 5.5 cm. Diet: live foods. Monospecies keeping tank, well covered. Breeding tank: of 10-litre capacity with finely-leaved plants. Sexual dimorphism: the male is more colourful, the female bigger, with black, light-edged spot on the root of the tail. Sex ratio: 1 male : 2 females.

Breeding water: 23–24 °C; pH 7.0; dCH < 2°. Eggs: Ø c. 3 mm, incubation period 12–14 days. Feeding of fry: brine shrimp nauplii.

Fish that tends to bite. Let brood fish spawn for five to seven days, then separate the sexes for 14 days and let them spawn again. Young fish attain sexual maturity in three months.

Cyprinodontidae

1 ♂

1 ♀

2 ♂

2 ♀

1 Guyana Rivulus

Rivulus holmiae (EIGENMANN, 1909)

Cyprinodontidae

Distribution: Guyana and Surinam. Full length: 10 cm. Diet: live foods, may be augmented with artificial foods. Monospecies keeping tank. Breeding tank: of 20- to 50-litre capacity, elongate, with spawning grid, diffused light, well covered. Sexual dimorphism: the male is a vivid blue, his caudal fin is blue-black edged with orange above and below, the female's caudal fin is blackish, paler towards the base of the tail and without any spot. Sex ratio: 1 male : 3 females. Breeding water: 26 °C; pH 7.0; dCH 2°. Eggs: $\emptyset$ c. 2 mm, incubation period 10–14 days. Feeding of fry: nauplii of brine shrimp or *Cyclops*.

Timid fish. The tank should be only half-filled with water or else well covered with glass, otherwise the fish will jump out. Let the breeding fish spawn for about two days and then transfer them to another tank. The female deposits about 100 eggs, some of which catch in the mesh of the grid and some remain hanging on plants by a thin filament. Therefore the grid must not be removed, but left in the tank until all the fry hatch. The fry keep to the upper layers of the water. Their growth is rapid.

2 Géry's Roloffia

Roloffia geryi (LAMBERT, 1958)

Cyprinodontidae

Distribution: west Africa – Guinea and Sierra Leone, forest and savanna type localities. Full length: 4.5 cm. Diet: live foods. Monospecies keeping tank. Breeding tank: of 6- to 10-litre capacity with spawning grid, finely-leaved plants, water column about 10 cm high. Sexual dimorphism: the male is colourful, the sides and fins have a distinct blue to green glitter, the female is brownish with marbled markings along the length of the lateral line. Sex ratio: 1 male : 3 females. Breeding water: 24 °C; pH 5.5–6.5; dCH max. 1°. Eggs: $\emptyset$ 1.1 mm, development is continuous and lasts 12 days. Feeding of fry: nauplii of brine shrimp or *Cyclops* nauplii.

Let the breeding fish spawn for seven days. They eat the eggs. During spawning it is ideal if the fish can be provided with the larvae and pupae of stinging mosquitoes (so-called black larvae). After seven days remove the parent fish from the tank and separate the males from the females. The grid should be left in place until all the young have hatched, i.e. at least 20 days from the time the fish are put in the tank to spawn. Young fish grow very rapidly, attaining sexual maturity at the age of three months. The parent fish should be generously fed and put to spawn again after about 10 days. The males are very bellicose towards one another.

1 ♀

1 ♂

2 ♂

2 ♀

1 *Roloffia occidentalis* CLAUSEN, 1965

Syn. *Aphyosemion occidentalis*
(the species was long incorrectly designated as *A. sjoestedti*)

◁
●
Distribution: jungle and savanna regions of Sierra Leone. Full length: 9 cm. Diet: live foods. Monospecies keeping tank. Breeding tank: of 20- to 50-litre capacity, with layer of peat on the bottom, diffused light. Sexual dimorphism: the male is brightly coloured,the female is reddish-brown and has transparent fins. Sex ratio: 1 male : 2 females. Water: 22–24 °C; pH 6.5; dCH < 2°; dGH < 10°. Eggs: $\varnothing$ 1.5 mm, development of the eggs is discontinuous with a marked diapause. The period of development differs in the various populations of *R. occidentalis* – from 4 to 9 months – and it is, therefore, necessary to inspect the eggs during this time. Feeding of fry: brine shrimp nauplii.

A very aggressive species. Adult fish are prone to tuberculosis.

Besides the nominate form Clausen described a subspecies with more vivid blue colouring and different markings on the body and fins – *R. occidentalis toddi;* this, however, is currently classified as a separate species – *Aphyosemion toddi* (Clausen, 1966).

2 **Golden Pheasant** or **Blue Gularis**
Aphyosemion sjoestedti (LOENNBERG, 1895)

Syn. *Fundulus sjoestedti, Fundulopanchax sjoestedti, Nothobranchius sjoestedti, Aphyosemion coeruleum*

◁
●
Distribution: west Africa from western Cameroon and southern Nigeria to Ghana, in flooded pools that may but need not dry out periodically. Full length: 12 cm. Diet: larger, live foods, including small fish. Monospecies keeping tank. Breeding tank: of 20-litre capacity with 2 cm thick layer of fibrous peat on the bottom, water column 20–30 cm high, diffused lighting. Sexual dimorphism: the male is larger, more colourful. Sex ratio: 1 male : 2–3 females. Water: 23–25 °C; pH 6.5; dCH max. 2°; dGH max. 12°; add 1/4 teaspoon NaCl to the water. Eggs: amber-coloured, rigid; development of the eggs is discontinuous for a period of 8–10 weeks or continuous for a period of 19–21 days. These figures apply to the summer season. In the spring and autumn months the incubation period is about 5 days longer. Feeding of fry: brine shrimp nauplii or finely sifted zooplankton.

Aggressive fish, extremely variable in coloration. Let the fish spawn for 10 days in well-covered tanks. Then lightly squeeze the water out of the peat, put it in PVC bags, and store the bags in a dark place at a temperature of 18 to 20 °C. After 8 to 10 weeks pour soft water on the peat. Drying out and wetting may be repeated several times at intervals of a week until all the fry have hatched. If fine sand is used instead of peat then put this in a sieve and pour water over it. The sand will be washed off, leaving the eggs in the sieve. These should then be placed on moist polyurethane or peat. The fish attain sexual maturity in two months.

A blue form with prolonged fins has been bred in the USA.

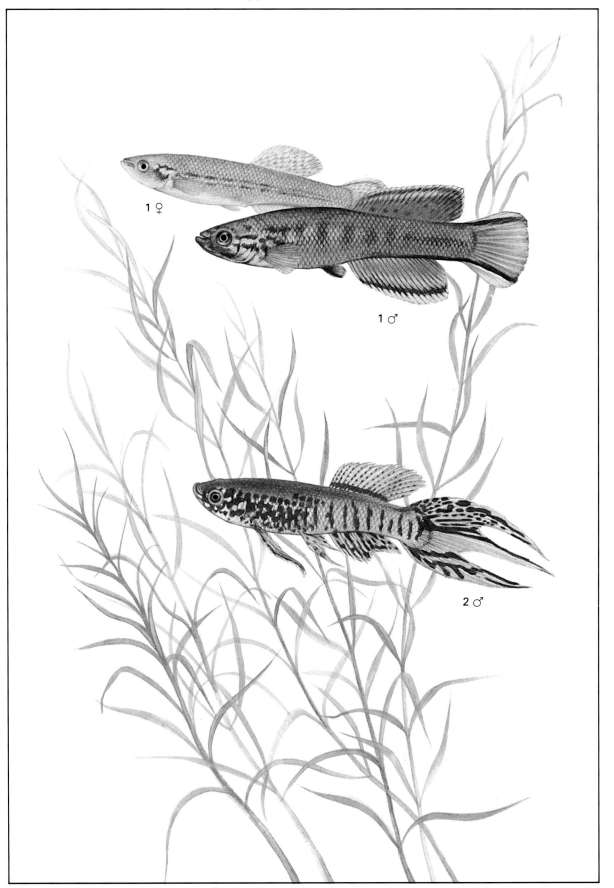

1 Cape Lopez Lyre Tail or Aphyosemion
Aphyosemion australe (RACHOW, 1921)

Syn. *Haplochilus calliurus* var. *australis, H. calliurus, Panchax polychromus, P. australe*   Cyprinodontidae

Distribution: West Africa, muddy coastal waters. Full length: 6 cm (male). Diet: live foods, may be augmented by artificial foods. Monospecies keeping tank. Breeding tank: with capacity of 10 to 15 litres, and spawning grid. Sexual dimorphism: the male is brightly coloured, the female smaller. Sex ratio: 1 male : 3−4 females. Water: 24 °C; pH 6.5−7.0; dCH < 2°. Eggs: development continuous, incubation period 14 days. Feeding of fry: brine shrimp nauplii.

Separate the males and females for about a week before spawning. The fish spawn willingly. Let them spawn for a week. Remove the spawning grid only after the fry have hatched. As soon as the young fish reach a length of 2 cm transfer them to a roomy tank where the temperature may be gradually lowered to 20 °C. Young fish mature sexually in three months. There are also various colour forms of this species.

2 Red Lyre Tail or Red Aphyosemion
Aphyosemion bivittatum (LOENNBERG, 1895)

Syn. *Fundulus bivittatus, Fundulopanchax bivittatum, Aphyosemion bitaeniatum, A. multicolor, A. loennbergi, A. pappenheimi, A. riggenbachi, A. splendopleuris, A. unistrigatum, A. bivittatum holyi*   Cyprinodontidae

Distribution: West Africa − in the waters of virgin forests and savannas. Full length: 7 cm. Diet: live foods. Monospecies keeping tank. Breeding tank: of 15-litre capacity with spawning grid, finely-leaved plants, dim light, and well covered with glass. Sexual dimorphism: the male is very colourful, his dorsal, anal and caudal fins have long tips. Sex ratio: 1 male : 2

females. Breeding water: 20−24 °C; pH 6.5; dCH max. 1°; dGH max. 8°. Eggs: development continuous, incubation period 10−20 days. Feeding of fry: brine shrimp nauplii.

These are peaceful fish. The male woos the female with lively motions. The spawning period lasts approximately three weeks.

3 Walker's Aphyosemion
Aphyosemion walkeri walkeri (BOULENGER, 1911)

Syn. *Haplochilus walkeri, Aphyosemion spurelli, A. litoriseboris*   Cyprinodontidae

Distribution: from the southeastern Ivory Coast to Ghana. Full length: 6.5 cm. Diet: live as well as artificial foods. Monospecies keeping tank. Breeding tank: of 6-litre capacity, well covered, with thin layer of peat on the bottom. Sexual dimorphism: the male is larger, colourful. Sex ratio: 1 male : 2−3 females. Water: 20−24 °C; pH 6.5−7.0; dCH < 1°. Eggs: development discontinuous, incubation period 6−8 weeks. Feeding of fry: brine shrimp nauplii.

Let the brood fish spawn for 10 days. Put the moist peat with the eggs into PVC bags and store at a temperature of 18 to 20 °C. The peat must not become unduly dry! After six weeks lightly crumble the peat, put it in a tank, and pour rain water (15 °C; pH 6.5−7.0; dCH < 1°) over it. Slowly raise the temperature to 22 to 24 °C − most of the fry will hatch within 24 hours. The fish attain sexual maturity at the age of two months.

Cyprinodontidae

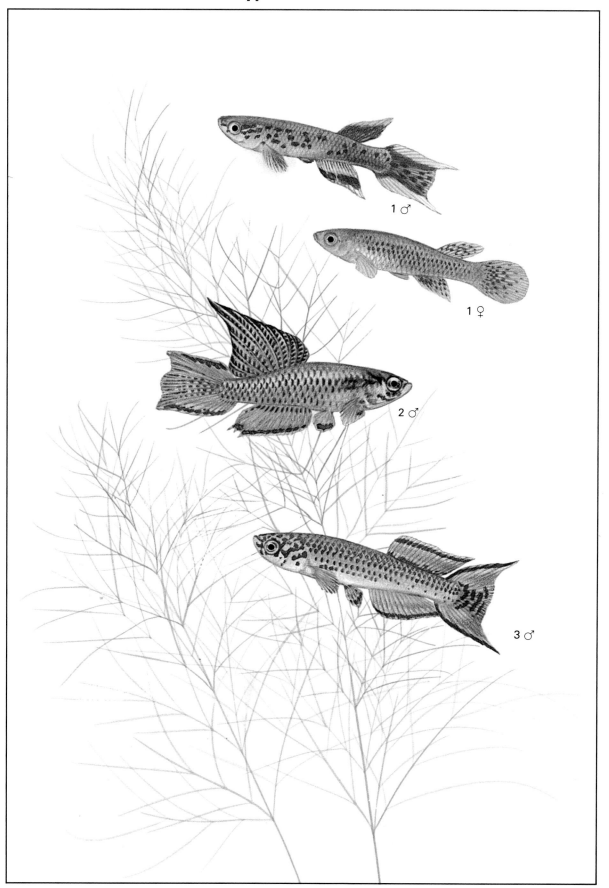

1 *Aphyosemion mirabile* RADDA, 1970

◁
●

Distribution: Cameroon. Full length: 6 cm. Diet: live foods. Monospecies keeping tank. Breeding tank: of 10- to 15-litre capacity, with finely-leaved plants, diffused lighting. Sexual dimorphism: the male is brightly coloured. Sex ratio: 1 male : 2 females. Breeding water: 22–24 °C; pH 6.5; dCH < 2°; dGH < 10°. Eggs: development is continuous, without diapause; incubation of eggs immersed in water lasts 21 days. Feeding of fry: brine shrimp nauplii.

Besides the nominate form Radda divided the species into the following subspecies: *A. mirabile moense, A. mirabile intermitteus,* and *A. mirabile traudeae.* Widespread amongst aquarists who breed tooth carps (family Cyprinodontidae) is the form *A. mirabile* 'TAIKWA', which is apparently the name given to a local population after the place of its occurrence.

2 **Amieti Gardneri**
Aphyosemion amieti RADDA, 1976

○
●

Distribution: west Cameroon, lowland region of the lower Sanaga River near the town of Edes, about 70 km from the Gulf of Guinea – shallow parts of streams and swampy waters of the rain forest. Full length: male – 7.5 cm, female – 6 cm. Diet: live foods, may be augmented by artificial foods. Monospecies keeping tank. Breeding tank: of 6-litre capacity with either a layer of peat on the bottom or finely-leaved plants. Sexual dimorphism: the male is bigger and more colourful, the female yellow-brown with insignificant red spots on the sides along the length of the body and rounded, yellowish-transparent fins (she resembles the female of *A. gardneri* and the two are readily confused). Sex ratio: 1 male : 2–4 females. Breeding water: 23–27 °C; pH 6.0–6.5; dCH 2°; dGH < 10°; fresh. Eggs: their development is intermediary. The incubation period of immersed eggs is 3–5

weeks depending on the temperature; in a moist substrate the incubation period is 6–8 weeks. If flooding of the eggs is delayed by 3–4 months the fry hatch but are incapable of developing. The experience of aquarists is that a greater percentage of eggs will hatch in a moist substrate than in water; the development of the eggs is shorter in the period from April till August, and longer in the period from September till March. Feeding of fry: brine shrimp nauplii.

Peaceable fish, even towards members of their own species. The newly-hatched fry measures 4 mm and its growth is slow. At the age of four weeks the young fish reach a length of 1 cm, at eight weeks the males begin to acquire their specific coloration. The fish attain sexual maturity at 14 weeks and three years is reported to be their maximum life span.

Cyprinodontidae

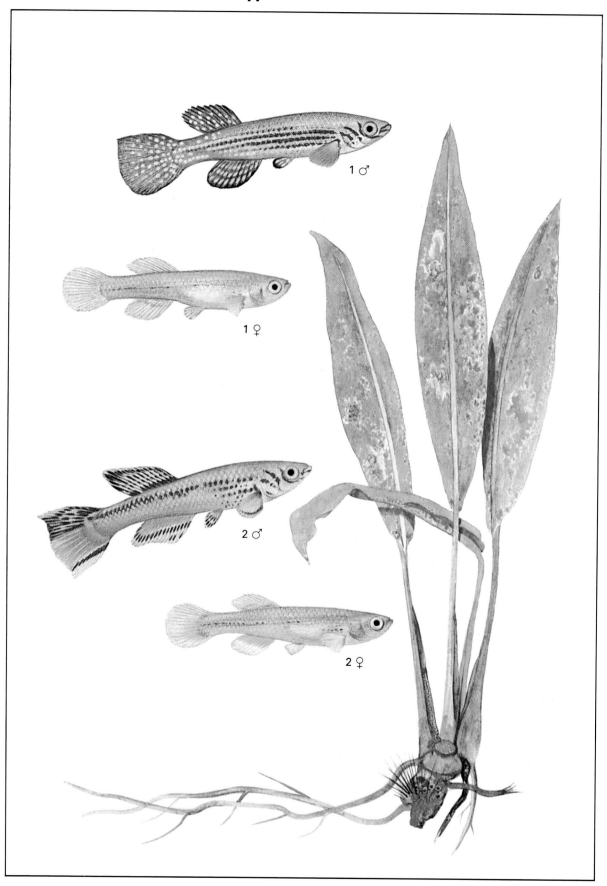

1 ♂

1 ♀

2 ♂

2 ♀

1 Five-lined Killie
Aphyosemion striatum (BOULENGER, 1911)
Syn. *Haplochilus striatus*

◁
●

Distribution: Gabon and central Zaire. Full length: 5 cm. Diet: live foods. Monospecies keeping tank. Breeding tank: with capacity of 6 to 10 litres, diffused light, finely-leaved and floating plants, well covered with glass. Sexual dimorphism: the male is brightly coloured with vivid red spots arranged in longitudinal bands. Sex ratio: 1 male : 3 females. Breeding water: 22–24 °C; pH 6.5; dCH < 2°; dGH < 10°. Eggs: development is continuous; incubation period of submerged eggs is 10–15 days. However, the eggs also tolerate a period of dryness so that they may, for instance, be shipped by mail. They are furnished with filaments by which they become attached to a firm object. Feeding of fry: brine shrimp nauplii.

The spawning period lasts several weeks. Over 12 to 24 hours the female deposits approximately 30 eggs. Related to this species is the similar *A. ogoense* (Pellegrin, 1930) known under the synonym *A. lujae* and also listed as a subspecies of *A. striatum*. The female of *A. ogoense* deposits fewer eggs which can develop only when submerged in water.

2 *Aphyosemion gabuense boehmi* RADDA and HUBER, 1977

◁
●

Distribution: forested region of west Gabon. Full length: male – 5 cm, female – 4 cm. Diet: live foods. Monospecies keeping tank. Breeding tank: of 10-litre capacity, well covered, with fibrous peat on the bottom, diffused light filtered through floating plants. Sexual dimorphism: the male is vividly coloured with lyre-shaped caudal fin, the female is light brown with transparent fins and may have nondescript red spots on the sides of the body and on the dorsal fin. Sex ratio: 1 male : 3 females. Breeding water: 22–26 °C; pH 6.5–7.5; dCH max. 2° (a lower, more acid pH value prolongs the development of the eggs). Eggs: development is continuous, incubation period is 14–18 days/22 °C; 8–10 days/26 °C. Feeding of fry: brine shrimp nauplii.

This species is differentiated into three subspecies: *A. gabuense gabuense, A. gabuense marginatum,* and *A. gabuense boehmi.* It is relatively little fertile. Let the fish spawn for a day and then again after an interval of several days, during which time, however, the males must be separated from the females. The newly-hatched fry measure about 3 mm in length; their growth is slow – in four weeks their length is about 10 mm. The fish attain sexual maturity in 14 to 16 weeks and their maximum length at the age of six months.

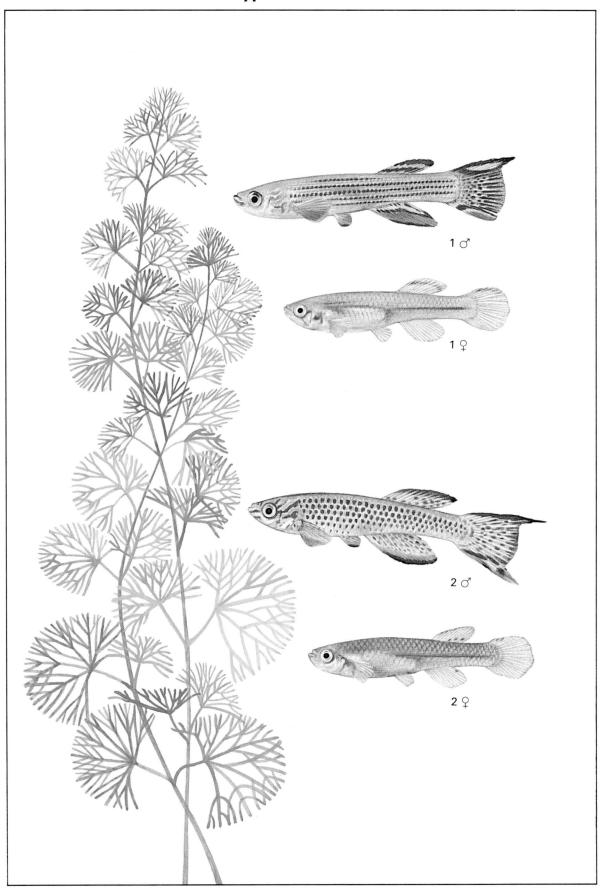

1 ♂

1 ♀

2 ♂

2 ♀

1 Cinnamon Killie

Aphyosemion cinnamomeum CLAUSEN, 1963

Distribution: highlands of western Cameroon. Full length: 5 cm. Diet: live foods. Monospecies keeping tank. Breeding tank: of 10- 15-litre capacity, with layer of peat on the bottom, diffused light. Sexual dimorphism: the male is more brightly coloured. Sex ratio: 1 male : 2 females. Breeding water: 20–24 °C; pH 6.5; dCH max. 1°; dGH max. 8°. Eggs: development is intermediary, incubation of immersed eggs lasts 3–4 weeks. Feeding of fry: brine shrimp nauplii.

A. cinnamomeum is found in a relatively limited area in the mountain region of Cameroon. It resembles none of the species of the genus *Roloffia* or *Aphyosemion.* The body is cinnamon brown and the rounded fins are blue edged with a wide gold border. It spawns in the peat bottom, which should be constantly covered with water. Compared with other species the young fish grow more slowly, attain sexual maturity at a later age, and have a longer life span.

2 Plumed Lyretail or Plumed Aphyosemion

Aphyosemion filamentosum (MEINKEN, 1933)

Syn. *Fundulopanchax filamentosus*

Distribution: southwestern Nigeria. Full length: 5.5 cm. Diet: live foods. Monospecies keeping tank. Breeding tank: of 6- to 10-litre capacity, well covered, with a boiled and rinsed layer of peat on the bottom, diffused lighting, floating plants. Sexual dimorphism: the male is larger, more colourful, the rays of the caudal and anal fins are considerably extended. Sex ratio: 1 male : 3 females. Breeding water: 22–24 °C; pH 6.0–6.5; dCH max. 2°. Eggs: development is discontinuous with an inclination towards intermediary development. Constantly immersed eggs may develop within 4–6 weeks without a diapause. It seems that it is less of a mistake to leave the eggs permanently covered with water than to let the peat with the eggs dry out too much. In moist peat at a temperature of 20 °C development of the eggs takes about three weeks. Feeding of fry: brine shrimp nauplii.

There are numerous local forms with different coloration, markings and shape of the fins. There is a red stripe in the lower part of the caudal fin, but this may be absent in some populations. A local population of *A. filamentosum* with noticeably red fins offered in shops as '*A. ruwenzori*' was imported in 1961.

Cyprinodontidae

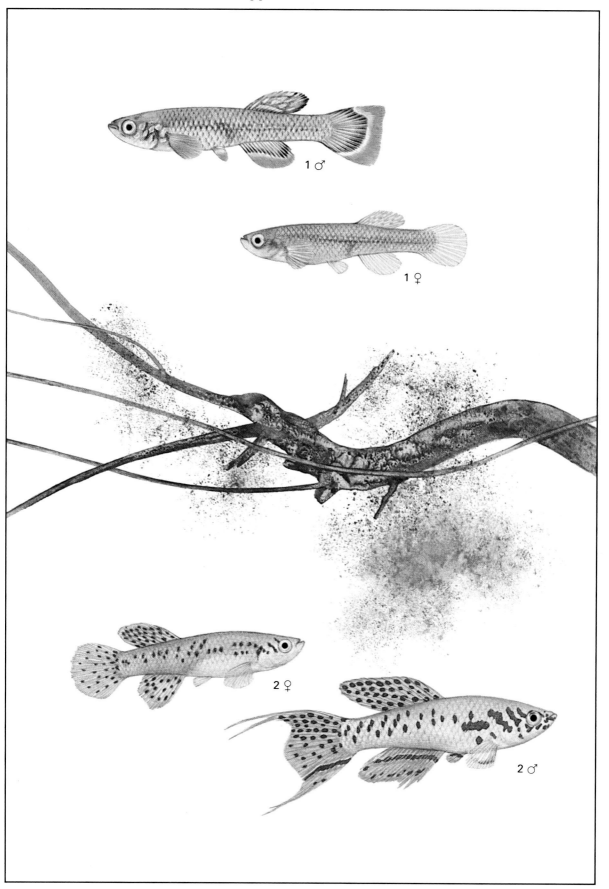

1 Steel-blue Aphyosemion
Aphyosemion gardneri gardneri (BOULENGER, 1911)
Syn. *Fundulus gardneri, Aphyosemion nigerianum, Fundulopanchax gardneri*   Cyprinodontidae

Distribution: relatively widespread – from Nigeria to western Cameroon. Full length: 6 cm. Diet: live foods; may be augmented with artificial foods. Monospecies keeping tank. Breeding tank: of 6- to 10-litre capacity, with layer of peat on the bottom, finely-leaved plants, diffused lighting, well covered. Sexual dimorphism: the male is brightly coloured; the female is smaller, olive-brown, the fins spotted with dark red. Sex ratio: 1 male : 3 females. Water: 22–24 °C; pH 6.5–7.0; dCH max. 2°. Eggs: development is intermediary, incubation period of immersed eggs is 15–20 days. Feeding of fry: brine shrimp nauplii.

A. gardneri forms very variable populations. This was responsible for many mistakes in the scientific description of the individual species.

Officially recognized at present are the subspecies *A. gardneri nigerianum* Clausen, 1963, and *A. gardneri lacustre* Radda, 1974. The two subspecies are from western Cameroon. In the late seventies tooth carp (Cyprinodontidae) breeders came up with hitherto undescribed fish considered to be subspecies or forms of *A. gardneri*. They are distinguished solely according to the locality where they were found, namely: *A. gardneri* 'Akuré' (west Nigeria in the region of Akuré) and *A. gardneri* 'Makurdi' (eastern Nigeria in the region of Makurdi and the nearby neighbouring Benue River). *A. gardneri* interbreeds with *A. australe;* the hybrid offspring are inferior, often with morphological abnormalities – mostly fusion of the dorsal, caudal and anal fins.

2 *Aphyosemion marmoratum* RADDA, 1974
                                                                                            Cyprinodontidae

Distribution: western Cameroon. Full length: 5 cm. Diet: live foods; may be augmented by artificial foods. Monospecies keeping tank. Breeding tank: of 6- to 10-litre capacity with layer of peat on the bottom, finely-leaved plants, diffused lighting, well covered. Sexual dimorphism: the male is brightly coloured, the female is smaller, olive brown. Sex ratio: 1 male : 3 females. Breeding water: 22–24 °C; pH 6.5–7.0; dCH max. 2°. Eggs: development is intermediary. The eggs develop in water as well as in a slightly moist substrate (peat). Incubation period of continuously immersed eggs is 15–20 days (the fry hatch in succession and there are thus great differences in size; the length of incubation depends on the temperature of the water). In a moist substrate the incubation period is longer and when the substrate is covered with water the fry hatch all at once. Feeding of fry: brine shrimp nauplii.

Because the development of the eggs may be interrupted by a diapause, three different methods may be used in breeding these fish: a) plants and a spawning grid are put in the tank; b) a dense tangle of plants is put in the tank; c) a layer of boiled, rinsed peat is put on the bottom of the tank and after the fish have spawned the water above the peat is drawn off leaving only a slightly moist substrate. The hatching fry become free-swimming and take food immediately. They grow rapidly and attain sexual maturity in two to three months.

Cyprinodontidae

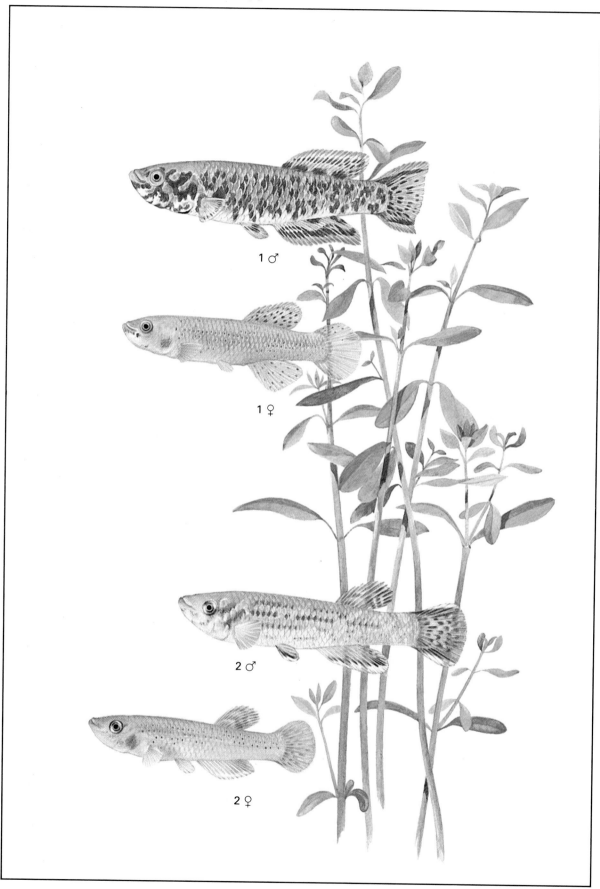

1 ♂

1 ♀

2 ♂

2 ♀

1 Striped Aplocheilus

Aplocheilus lineatus (CUVIER and VALENCIENNES, 1846)

Syn.: *Aplocheilus affinis, A. rubrostigma, A. vittatus, Haplochilus lineatus, H. lineolatus, Panchax lineatus*

Cyprinodontidae

◁
●
Distribution: India, Sri Lanka. Full length: 10 cm. Diet: live foods, including small fish. Mono-species keeping tank. Breeding tank: of 30- to 50-litre capacity with water column about 20 cm high, finely-leaved and floating plants, well covered with glass. Sexual dimorphism: the male is larger, more colourful, with larger dorsal and anal fins, the female has 6–8 conspicuous, dark, transverse bands at the tail end of the body. Sex ratio: 1:1, also a greater number of pairs or even a small shoal with a slight preponderance of males may be put in the tank for spawning. Breeding water: 25 °C; pH 6.5; dCH max. 2°; dGH max. 10°. Eggs: large, sticky, incubation period 11–14 days. Sometimes the development of the eggs is irregular and some of the fry may not hatch until after 30 days. Feeding of fry: nauplii of brine shrimp or *Cyclops*.

The males should be separated from the females for about 14 days before spawning. The breeding fish spawn shortly after they are put in the breeding tank. Spawning generally takes place amidst plants close to the surface. Let the fish spawn for eight days. After this the males and females should again be separated and 14 days later put to spawn again. The female deposits approximately 200 eggs. The rapidly-growing young fish should be sorted according to size as they grow, for otherwise they become cannibalistic.

2 Dwarf Panchax or Green Panchax

Aplocheilus blocki (ARNOLD, 1911)

Syn. *Haplochilus panchax* var. *blockii, Aplocheilus parvus, Panchax panchax* var. *blockii*

Cyprinodontidae

◁
●
Distribution: Coromandel coast region of south-eastern India, Sri Lanka, flat meadows and ditches. Full length: 5 cm. Diet: live foods, chiefly mosquito larvae and insects (fruit fly *Drosophila melanogaster*). Keeping tank: mono-species. Breeding tank: of 30- to 50-litre capacity, with thickets of plants at the surface by the edges of the tank. Sexual dimorphism: the male is more brightly coloured. Sex ratio: the fish are bred in a shoal with a slight preponderance of males. Breeding water: 24–26 °C; pH 7.0–7.5; dCH max. 2°; dGH max. 10°. Eggs: the incubation period depends on the temperature and lasts 12–17 days. Feeding of fry: *Cyclops* or brine shrimp nauplii.

Smallest species of the genus *Aplocheilus*. The fish keep to the middle reaches and upper layers of water. They are peaceable and gregarious. They spawn on plants for several days in succession with the female depositing 10 to 20 eggs daily. The free-swimming fry should be gathered regularly with a catching pipe and transferred to a separate tank with a lower level of water (about 10 cm high). The young fish grow more quickly if sorted according to size. They are susceptible to strong (invasional) attacks by a protozoan of the genus *Oodinium*.

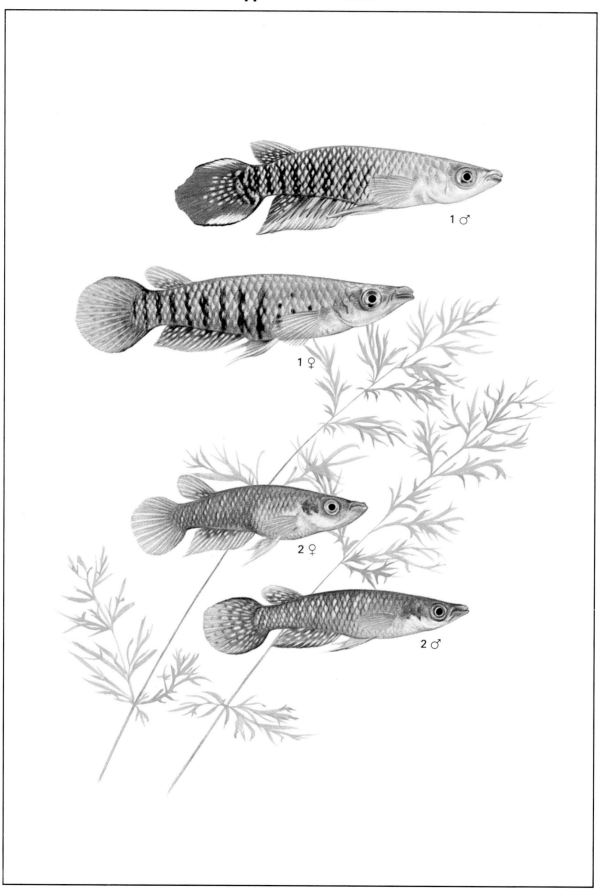

1 ♂

1 ♀

2 ♀

2 ♂

1 White's Pear Fish
Cynolebias whitei Myers, 1942

Distribution: Brazil, region of Rio de Janeiro in periodically dry waters. Full length: male − 8 cm, female − 5.5 cm. Diet: live foods, with occasional artificial foods. Monospecies keeping tank. Breeding tank: of 3- to 6-litre capacity, bottom covered with peat. Sexual dimorphism: the male is colourful, the female has a black spot in the middle of the body on either side. Sex ratio: 1 male : 3 females. Water: 20−24 °C; pH 6.5; dCH max. 2°. Eggs: development is discontinuous and takes 6−20 weeks (it is necessary to inspect the eggs regularly). Feeding of fry: brine shrimp nauplii, after one week finely sifted zooplankton.

The fish spawn in the peat layer. Let them spawn for a week, feeding them generously, mainly on mosquito larvae. After removing the parent fish, carefully siphon off the water and let the surface of the peat dry off slowly (but do not let it dry out completely). Then put the peat into PVC bags and put these in a darkened place at a temperature of 18−20 °C (the temperature of the ambient air may drop as low as 10 °C during the night). At the end of the incubation period pour soft water at a temperature of 16−18 °C over the peat and then gradually raise the temperature to 25 °C. The fry will hatch in one to 24 hours. The process of drying out the peat and pouring water on it may be repeated several times. Ordinary tapwater should gradually be added to the tank as the fry grow. They become sexually mature within a month.

2 Fighting Gaucho
Cynolebias melanotaenia (Regan, 1912)
Syn. *Cynopoecilus melanotaenia, Cynobelias melanotaenia*

Distribution: southeast Brazil and northeastern Uruguay − periodically dry waters. Full length: male − 4.5−5 cm, female 3.5−4 cm. Diet: live foods. Monospecies keeping tank (in view of their marked aggressiveness there should never be more than one male in a tank). Breeding tank: of 30-litre capacity with floating plants and with a weighted bowl filled with a 5 to 10 cm layer of boiled peat on the bottom. The surface of the peat must be 8 to 10 cm below the edge of the bowl for otherwise it is tossed out and scattered round the tank by the fish. Sexual dimorphism: the male is coloured phosphorus-bronze, faintly reddish on the sides and greenish at the base of the dorsal and caudal fin. A broad black band generally extends from the mouth to the end of the caudal fin. The dorsal and caudal fins are broad, the anal fin is likewise reddish. The female is rounder, paler, and the anal fin does not have a reddish tinge. Sex ratio: 1 male : 3 females. Water: 20−24 °C; pH 6.5−7.0; dCH max. 2°. Eggs: ∅ 1 mm, non-adhesive, furnished with fine threads to which small bits of peat adhere making it difficult to find the eggs. Development of eggs: discontinuous, takes 12 weeks. Feeding of fry: brine shrimp nauplii.

The eggs are stored as described for *C. whitei.* At the end of the incubation period water is poured over the peat to a height of 5 to 7 cm above the surface of the substrate. Most of the fry hatch within a short time, the remainder in two to three days. Their growth is very rapid; the first male may be distinguished in 14 days, and within four weeks the young fish reach a length of 2−2.5 cm.

Cyprinodontidae

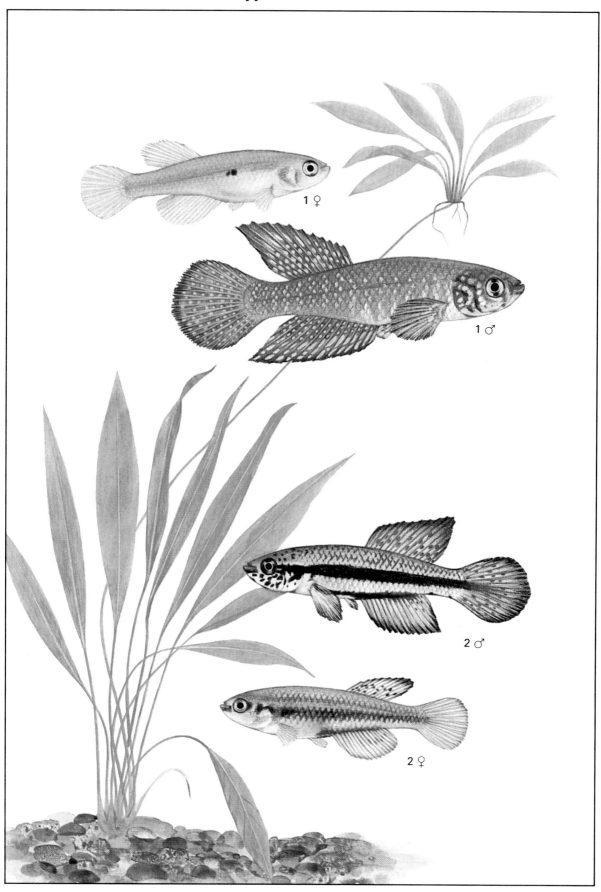

1 *Cynolebias alexandri* CASTELLO and LOPEZ, 1974
Syn. *Haplochilus walkeri, Aphyosemion spurelli, A. litoriseboris*

◁
●

Distribution: Argentina, periodically dry waters. Full length: 9 cm. Diet: live foods. Monospecies keeping tank. Breeding tank: of 10-litre capacity with deep peat-filled dish on the bottom and floating plants on the surface. Sexual dimorphism: the male is colourful, particularly his dorsal and anal fins. Sex ratio: 1 male : 2 females. Water: 24 °C; pH 6.5–7.0; dCH max. 2°. Eggs: development is discontinuous, incubation period 3–4 months. Feeding of fry: brine shrimp nauplii.

Separate the sexes for only a few days before spawning because females separated from males a long time expel the eggs spontaneously without their being fertilized. For spawning to be successful the fish must dig into the soft peat until they are at least half buried in the peat. A week after spawning put the moist, crumbly peat in PVC bags and store at a temperature of 18 to 22 °C. After three months cover the substrate with soft water with a temperature of 18 to 22 °C. Twelve hours later remove the hatched fry, dry the peat again and store it. Repeat this procedure at four-week intervals for a period of nine months. When feeding the fry keep the water level low. The fish are fully grown at the age of six to eight weeks.

2 *Cynolebias heloplites* HUBER, 1981

◁
●

Distribution: northeastern Brazil – long, shallow ponds. Full length: 4 cm in the wild, 7 cm in the aquarium; the male is slightly smaller. Diet: live foods. Monospecies keeping tank. Breeding tank: with capacity of 15 to 50 litres, depending on the number of fish, a deep peat-filled dish on the bottom, and floating plants. Sexual dimorphism: the male is more high-backed, his dorsal and anal fins are broad and pointed, whereas the female's have 3–6 fewer rays and are rounded. The female is brownish with prominent vertical stripes and has 1–3 dark, light-edged spots in the centre of the body. Sex ratio: 1 male : 3–4 females. Water: 20–24 °C; pH 7.0–7.5; dCH < 2°; dGH < 10°. Eggs: development is discontinuous, incubation period 16–23 weeks. Feeding of fry: brine shrimp nauplii.

3 Black-finned Cynolebias or Black-finned Pearl Fish
Cynolebias nigripinnis REGAN, 1912

◁
●

Distribution: Argentina. Full length: 5 cm. Diet: live foods. Monospecies keeping tank. Breeding tank: of 50-litre capacity with a rather deep, peat-filled dish on the bottom and floating plants. Sexual dimorphism: the male is larger, blue-black to black with tiny shimmering green dots, the female is brownish to light grey with marbled pattern. Sex ratio: 1 male : 2–3 females (in a shoal). Water: 22–24 °C; pH 6.5–7.0; dCH max. 2°. Eggs: development is discontinuous, incubation period 6–8 weeks; the fry may hatch even after as long as 5 months. Feeding of fry: brine shrimp nauplii.

In the South American pampas rainy periods (April to October) alternate with dry periods (November to March). In the rainy season depressions fill with rainwater and immediately swarm with a great number of fish fry. These grow fast, become sexually mature within two months, and then spawn. As soon as the rainy season ends the sun dries up the puddles, the adult fish die, and the eggs remain buried in the moist substrate.

Cynolebias bellotti Steindachner 1881 is a similar, somewhat larger species (about 7 cm) originated from La Plata region and south Brazil. The ground colour is greyish-blue to steely blue with whitish shiny spots all over the body. The female is yellowish brown with irregular transverse bands or marbling and often has a dark rounded spot in the middle of the body.

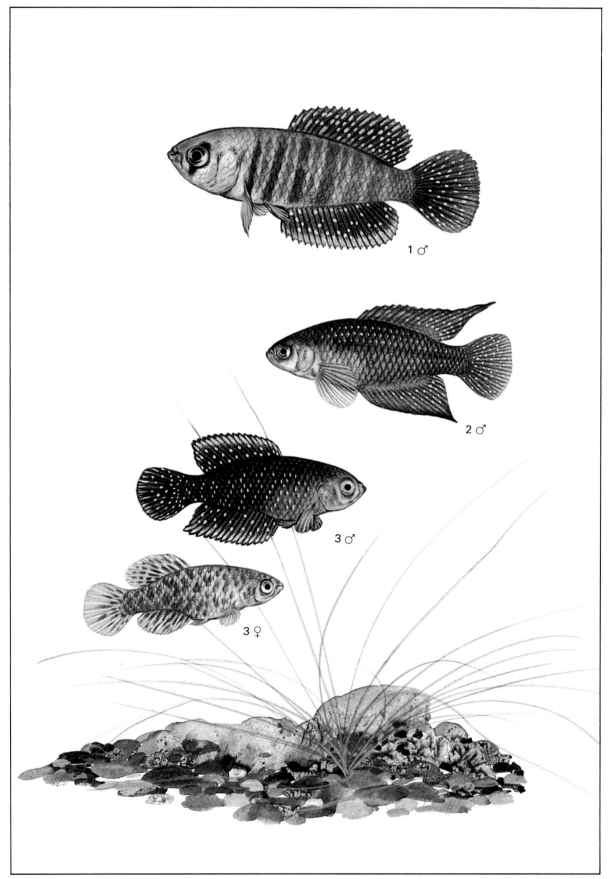

1 ♂

2 ♂

3 ♂

3 ♀

1 Desert Pupfish
Cyprinodon macularius BAIRD and GIRARD, 1853
Syn. *Cyprinodon californiensis*   Cyprinodontidae

Distribution: southern USA to northern Mexico. Full length: 6.5 cm. Diet: live and plant foods. Monospecies keeping tank. Breeding tank: of 10- to 30-litre capacity with spawning grid and Java moss, water column up to 20 cm high. Sexual dimorphism: the male is a glittering pale blue, the female dull brown, spotted. Sex ratio: 1:1. Breeding water: 25 °C; pH 7.5–8.0; dCH 2–3°; dGH 15° or even more (1 teaspoon NaCl for every 10 litres of water). Eggs: incubation period 6–10 days. Feeding of fry: *Cyclops* or extremely fine brine shrimp nauplii.

The males are aggressive and territorial. The fish are in the habit of digging holes in the sand in shallow water and resting there. The males and females should be separated for three days before spawning and generously fed (mosquito larvae, tubifex worms, white worms). Let the breeding fish spawn for about an hour. Adult fish withstand fluctuations in temperature but do not tolerate acidic and soft water.

2 Mexican Killifish
Garmanella pulchra HUBBS, 1936
                                                             Cyprinodontidae

Distribution: Mexico, Yucatán Peninsula, brackish waters round the mouths of rivers. Full length: 4 cm. Diet: live and plant foods. Monospecies keeping tank. Breeding tank: the same as for *C. macularius*. Sexual dimorphism: the male is more colourful. Sex ratio: 1:1. Breeding water: brackish – 7 g NaCl or sea salt for every litre of water; 24 °C; pH 7.5–8.0. Eggs: incubation period 9–10 days. Feeding of fry: *Cyclops* or extremely fine brine shrimp nauplii.

Breeding fish tolerate fluctuations in temperature within a range of 16 to 24 °C. Before spawning the males and females should be separated for several days and fed generously. Let the fish spawn for one or two days. The eggs are transparent at first, later milky. The eleutherembryos rest on the bottom; endogenous nutrition lasts one week. The fry should be reared in a well-lit and algae-covered tank. Fresh water with an addition of NaCl or sea salt is essential for keeping fish in good condition.

3 American Flag Fish
Jordanella floridae GOODE and BEAN, 1879
Syn. *Cyprinodon floridae*   Cyprinodontidae

Distribution: from the coast of Florida to Yucatán, in shallow, slightly salty to brackish waters. Full length: male – 6 cm, female – 4.5 cm. Diet: live and plant foods. Monospecies keeping tank. Breeding tank: of 20- to 50-litre capacity, algae-covered, with spawning grid on the bottom and finely-leaved plants. Sexual dimorphism: the male is more brightly coloured. Sex ratio: 1 male : 3 females. Breeding water: 24 °C; pH 7.0–7.5; dCH 2° (1 teaspoon NaCl for every 2 litres of water). Eggs: glassy, ∅ 0.9–1.0 mm, incubation period 6–14 days. The larvae hatch over a period of several days. Feeding of fry: first three days *Paramecium caudatum,* then *Cyclops* or brine shrimp nauplii and algae.

The males and females should be separated for approximately one week before spawning. Spawning lasts about 20 minutes and takes place both near the bottom and in open water. Each female deposits up to 100 eggs. The parent fish should be taken out immediately after spawning.

Cyprinodontidae

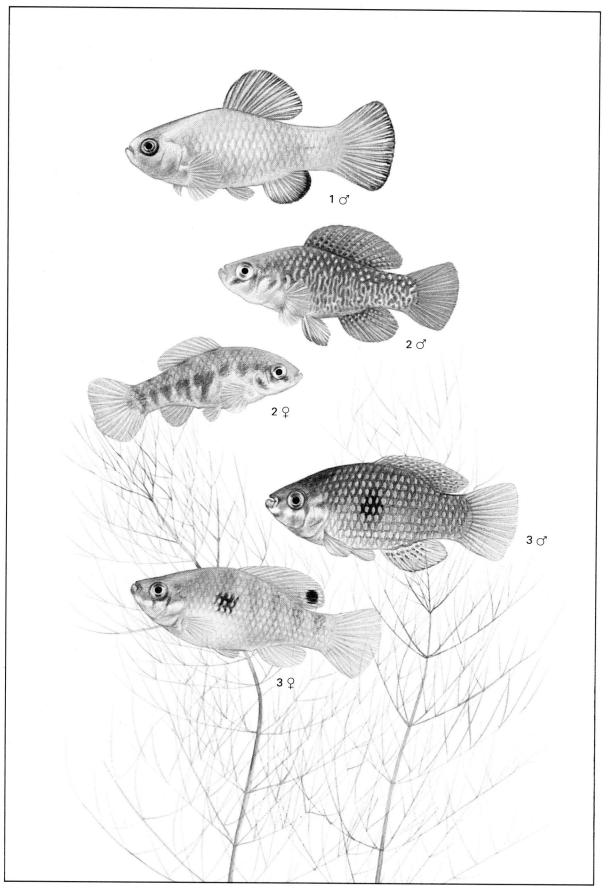

1 ♂

2 ♂

2 ♀

3 ♂

3 ♀

1 Fire-mouth Epiplatys, Red-chinned Panchax or Arnold's Killie
Epiplatys dageti monroviae DAGET and ARNOULD, 1964
Syn. *Epiplatys chaperi*   Cyprinodontidae

◁
●
Distribution: Liberia, savanna along the coast north of the city of Monrovia (the shallow waters of large puddles, ditches and pools with plenty of plants, chiefly water-lilies and bladderwort *(Utricularia).* Full length: 6 cm. Diet: live foods. Monospecies keeping tank. Breeding tank: of 50-litre capacity with dim light, finely-leaved plants. Sexual dimorphism: the male is more brightly coloured and larger. Sex ratio: 1 male : 3–4 females. Breeding water: 24–26 °C; pH 6.5–7.0; dCH max. 2°. Eggs: incubation period 10 days. Feeding of fry: nauplii of brine shrimp or *Cyclops.*

The spawning period lasts for several weeks and the females deposit the eggs successively in plant thickets. The newly-hatched fry are 1.5 mm long and stay near the surface. Remove the fry regularly with a catching pipe or else replace the clumps of plants with new ones once a week, putting the bundles of plants with the eggs in a separate tank. In the case of the second method the fry are in various stages of development and should be sorted and separated according to size, otherwise they become cannibalistic. The young fish grow quickly and at the age of eight weeks their sex begins to become apparent. The males have a red throat and on the sides of the body of both sexes there are generally six, sometimes five or seven, transverse bands. Less well-known is the similar *E. dageti dageti* Poll, 1953, *E. chaperi* (Sauvage, 1882) and *E. chaperi sheljuzhkoi* Poll, 1953.

2 Clown Killie
Epiplatys annulatus (BOULENGER, 1915)
Syn. *Haplochilus annulatus*   Cyprinodontidae

◁
●
Distribution: west Africa from Guinea to the Niger. Full length: 4 cm. Diet: live foods. Monospecies keeping tank. Breeding tank: with capacity of 10 to 50 litres (depending on the number of fish), floating plants interspersed with expanses of open water. Sexual dimorphism: the male is larger, with coloured fins and caudal fin markedly prolonged into a point. Sex ratio: 1 male : 2–3 females, (the basic group for spawning should include at least 20 brood fish). Breeding water: 25 °C; pH 6.5–7.0; dCH max. 2°; dGH max. 10°. (According to E. Roloff the water in the native localities is warmer than 25 °C with pH value of 6.7 and general hardness dGH 5°). Eggs: ∅ 1 mm, furnished with a short stalk, incubation period 8–10 days. Feeding of fry: brine shrimp nauplii.

Adult fish spawn throughout the whole year. The female deposits the eggs among plants and their roots. The fry are generally to be found at the point where the water surface touches the glass. Though nondescript, they are readily identified from above by the metallic glint of the spot on the top of the head. The fry should be caught and taken out regularly with a catching pipe. They immediately take brine shrimp nauplii and their growth is rapid. The fish are variable in colour and the same group may include individual specimens that are differently coloured or striped.

1 – *Epiplatys dageti monroviae*   2 – *Epiplatys chaperi sheljuzhkoi*   3 – *Epiplatys dageti dageti*

1 ♂

1 ♀

2 ♂

2 ♀

1 Guenther's Nothobranch
Nothobranchius guentheri (PFEFFER, 1893)

◁
●
Distribution: coastal lowland region of east Africa – Tanzania and neighbouring island of Zanzibar – in periodically dry waters with sandy to muddy bottom and clear, gently flowing water, also in standing, very murky waters in pools. Full length: 5 cm. Diet: live foods. Monospecies keeping tank with sufficient hiding places. Breeding tank: with capacity of at least 10 litres and layer of peat on the bottom. Sexual dimorphism: the male is brightly coloured, his caudal fin is red with a black edge, the female is grey to brownish. Sex ratio: 1 male : 2–3 females. Water: 22–24 °C; pH 6.5; dCH < 2°; dGH < 10°. Eggs: development is discontinuous, incubation period 10 weeks. Feeding of fry: brine shrimp nauplii.

Mention of this fish appeared as early as 1866 in Playfair's and Günther's 'The Fishes of Zanzibar'. However, the two authors introduced it incorrectly as *N. orthonotus* and, furthermore, as the counterpart of this male, a female that in reality belonged to the species *N. melanospilus*. As early as 1893, however, the German ichthyologist Georg Pfeffer recognized that this was a new species and described it as *N. guentheri*. Today we know that in some localities *N. guentheri* occurs together with the larger species (7 cm) *N. melanospilus* Pfeffer, 1896, the female of which has black spots on the body. The two species do not interbreed, but *N. guentheri* interbreeds with certain closely related species, e. g. *N. palmquisti* – the offspring may be fertile. Eggs should be kept in PVC bags at a temperature of 16 to 18 °C. After 10 weeks soft water should be poured on the peat. Drying up and watering should be repeated at weekly intervals until no further fry hatch. A gold form, named *N. guentheri* 'Gold', was recently bred in captivity.

2 *Nothobranchius rachovi* AHL, 1926
Syn. *Adiniops rachovi*

◁
●
Distribution: coast of Mozambique, locality near the city of Beira, in periodically dry waters of damp savannas. Full length: 5 cm. Diet: live foods. Monospecies keeping tank. Breeding tank: with a capacity of at least 10 litres, layer of peat on the bottom, diffused light. Sexual dimorphism: the male is colourful, the female grey-brown. Sex ratio: 1 male : 3 females. Water: 25 °C; pH 6.5–7.0; dCH max. 2°. Eggs: development is discontinuous, incubation period 20–24 weeks. Feeding of fry: brine shrimp nauplii.

Killifish with discontinuous development are called annual fish. Such fish survive the dry period only in the form of eggs; adult fish die. In the wild they generally live only a few months. The lower temperature recommended by many aquarists may prolong the life of the fish but at the cost of a lowered metabolism that affects their natural behaviour – they are much less lively. *N. rachovi* brood fish should be allowed to spawn for four weeks. After spawning is over put the moist peat with the eggs into PVC bags and store in a dark place at a temperature of 20 to 22 °C. For wetting the peat use soft water with a temperature of 25 °C. The fry hatch within a short time, development lasts three to four weeks.

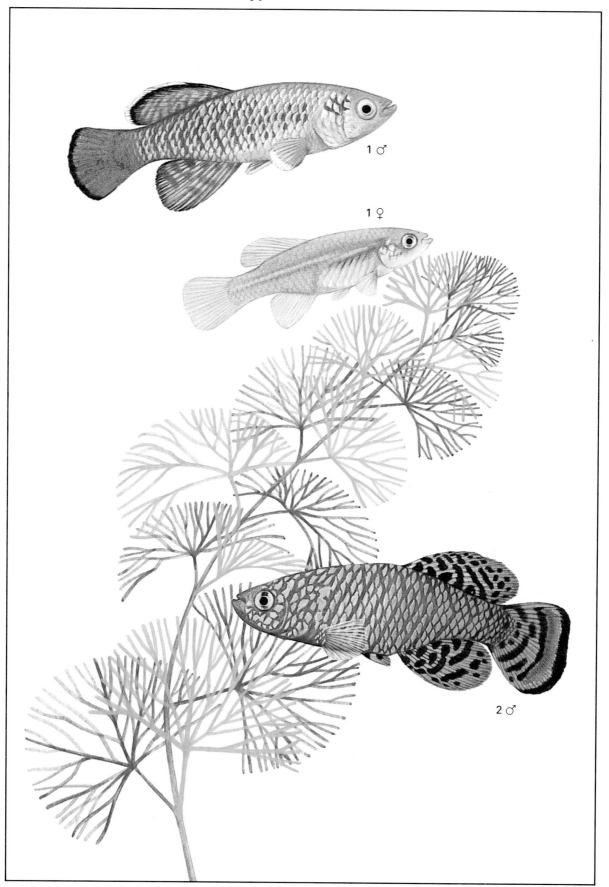

1 ♂

1 ♀

2 ♂

◁

●

Distribution: Somalia, periodically dry waters by the highway from the coastal city of Mogadishu. Full length: 5 cm. Diet: live foods, particularly larvae of mosquitoes and midges. Monospecies keeping tank. Breeding tank: with capacity of 10 litres or more depending on the number of fish, layer of peat on the bottom. Sexual dimorphism: the male is more colourful. Sex ratio: 1 male : 2–3 females. Water: 22–24 °C; pH 7.0–7.5; dCH 2–3°; dGH 10–30° (because of their adaptability the fish spawn and their eggs develop also in much softer water, but keeping the fish constantly in softer water may have undesirable consequences, for in nature this species, unlike other killifish, inhabits very hard water with a dGH value of 36–39°). Eggs: development is discontinuous, incubation period 10–12 weeks? Feeding of fry: brine shrimp nauplii.

This species has not been scientifically described as yet and therefore does not have a valid name. It is currently classed in the 'palmquisti' group together with species found along the coast of east Africa from northeast Tanzania, including the island of Zanzibar, to southern Somalia. These are primarily *Nothobranchius palmquisti* (Loennberg, 1907), *N. guentheri* (Pfeffer, 1893), *N. patrizii* (Vinciguerra, 1927), *N. steinforti* (Wildekamp, 1977), *Nothobranchius* n. sp. 'Kaloleni', and *Nothobranchius* n. sp. 'Kikambala'.

2 **Korthaus's Killie** or **Green Nothobranch**
Nothobranchius korthausae MEINKEN, 1973   Cyprinodontidae

◁

●

Distribution: Mafia Island (Tanzania), in swamps with water flowing through. Full length: 6 cm. Diet: Live foods. Monospecies keeping tank. Breeding tank: with capacity of 10 litres, layer of peat on the bottom, diffused lighting. Sexual dimorphism: the male is more vividly coloured, larger; in the female the eggs are visible in the rear part of the body cavity. Sex ratio: 1 male : 2–3 females. Water: 24–26 °C; pH 7.0; dCH 2° (values of water in native habitats: 26–30 °C; pH 5.8–6.4; dGH max. 3.9°). Eggs: ∅ 1 mm, non-adhesive, with numerous outgrowths by which they become attached to a firm object. Development is discontinuous, not continuous as is often wrongly stated. Incubation period 10–12 weeks. Feeding of fry: brine shrimp nauplii.

The fish inhabit waters that dry up periodically. Do not separate the males from the females because the females deposit eggs even in the absence of a male and in females that are separated from males for a lengthier period the ovaries cease functioning. Let the brood fish spawn for a week. If the eggs are stored at a temperature of 15 °C their development is slightly slowed. The fry become free-swimming and take food shortly after hatching. Like other killifish they are susceptible to a disease caused by a parasitic flagellate of the genus *Oodinium*. This is treated successfully with trypaflavin (dosage according to directions) and by adding a tablespoon NaCl for every 10 litres of water with temperature raised to 30 °C. The flagellate will be eradicated within seven days at the most.

Cyprinodontidae

1 *Nothobranchius* n. sp. 'Kayuni State Farm'

◁
●

Distribution: South Africa – Zambia. Full length: 6 cm. Diet: live foods, particularly larvae of mosquitoes and midges. Monospecies keeping tank. Breeding tank: with a capacity of 10 litres or more, depending on the number of fish, and a layer of peat on the bottom. Sexual dimorphism: the male is more brightly coloured. Sex ratio: 1 male : 2–3 females. Water: 22–24 °C; pH 6.5–7.0; dCH < 2°; dGH < 10°? Eggs: development is discontinuous, incubation period 10–12 weeks? Feeding of fry: brine shrimp nauplii.

Like *Nothobranchius* n. sp. 'Warfa-blue' this species doesn't have a valid name as yet. It is one of the most magnificently coloured members of the genus. The coloration is variable in the intensity of the blue and orange-red hues. Little is known about the members of the genus *Nothobranchius* from Zambia and it is believed that *Nothobranchius* n. sp. 'Kayuni State Farm' is not only a new species but also the only species from Zambia to be kept in aquariums.

2 *Nothobranchius foerschi* WILDEKAMP and BERKENKAMP, 1975

◁
●

Distribution: Tanzania – Selous wild game preserve – shallow puddles with muddy bottom and dense growth of plants that periodically dry up completely. Full length: 5 cm. Diet: live foods. Monospecies keeping tank. Breeding tank: with a capacity of 10 litres or more, depending on the number of fish, and a layer of peat on the bottom. Sexual dimorphism: the male is more brightly coloured, with reticulated pattern and red caudal fin without black edge, the female grey or brown

and smaller. Sex ratio: 1 male : 2–3 females. Water: 18–22 °C; pH 6.5; dCH > 2°; dGH 10°. Eggs: development is discontinuous, incubation of eggs in moist peat lasts 10–12 weeks. Feeding of fry: brine shrimp nauplii.

The name *foerschi* was given to this species in honour of Dr. Foersche of Munich, noted expert and breeder of killifish.

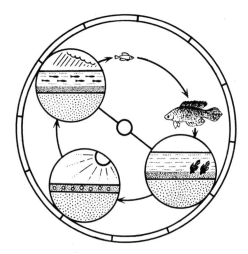

Development of killifish in periodically dry waters

Cyprinodontidae

1 ♂

1 ♀

2 ♂

2 ♀

1 Palmquist's Nothobranch
Nothobranchius palmquisti (LOENNBERG, 1907)
Syn. *Fundulus palmquisti, Adiniops palmquisti*

Cyprinodontidae

Distribution: Africa — periodically dry coastal waters in Tanzania and southern Kenya. Full length: 5 cm. Diet: live foods (particularly black mosquito larvae). Monospecies keeping tank. Breeding tank: with a capacity of 10 litres or more, depending on the number of fish, and a layer of peat on the bottom. Sexual dimorphism: the male is more brightly coloured, with reticulated pattern and red caudal fin without black edge; the female is grey or brown and smaller. Sex ratio: 1 male : 2–3 females. Water: 22–24 °C; pH 6.5; dCH < 2°; dGH < 10°. Eggs: development is discontinuous, incubation period 10–12 weeks. Feeding of fry: brine shrimp nauplii.

This species interbreeds with the closely related *N. guentheri;* the offspring are fertile. The males are aggressive towards one another and continuously chase the females. Individual pairs willingly spawn even in the smallest tank. The eggs are deposited in the soft substrate on the bottom. During the spawning period, which lasts approximately three weeks, the female deposits up to 200 eggs. Put the peat with the eggs in PVC bags and store at a temperature of 16 to 18 °C. Wait at least 10 weeks before pouring water on the eggs. If given suitable food in sufficient quantities the young fish grow very quickly. These are annual fish susceptible to infestation by *Oodinium.*

2 Playfair's Panchax
Pachypanchax playfairi (GÜNTHER, 1866)
Syn. *Haplochilus playfairi, Panchax playfairi*

Cyprinodontidae

Distribution: islands of east Africa — Seychelles, Madagascar and the territory of Tanzania and neighbouring island of Zanzibar. Full length: 10 cm. Diet: live foods, may be augmented by artificial foods. Monospecies keeping tank. Breeding tank: with a capacity of 50 litres or more, depending on the number of fish, plant thickets, well covered. Sexual dimorphism: the male is colourful with scales on the back standing out slightly from the body, the female has a typical black spot on the dorsal fin. Sex ratio: 1 male : 3 females. Breeding water: 22–26 °C; pH 6.5–7.0; dCH max. 1°. Eggs: incubation period 12 days. Feeding of fry: brine shrimp nauplii.

P. playfairi attacks other species of fish and bites their caudal fins, but lives in harmony with members of its own species. During spawning the female deposits the eggs in plant thickets. These should be replaced by new plants every week, and the clumps with the eggs put in a separate tank. The fry grow quickly, reaching a total length of 2 cm in four weeks, at which time it is already possible to identify the sexes. At the age of two months the young fish spawn regularly. They are very fertile and are fully developed at the age of one year. Auxiliary feeding of fruit flies *(Drosophila melanogaster)* promotes their well-being.

Cyprinodontidae

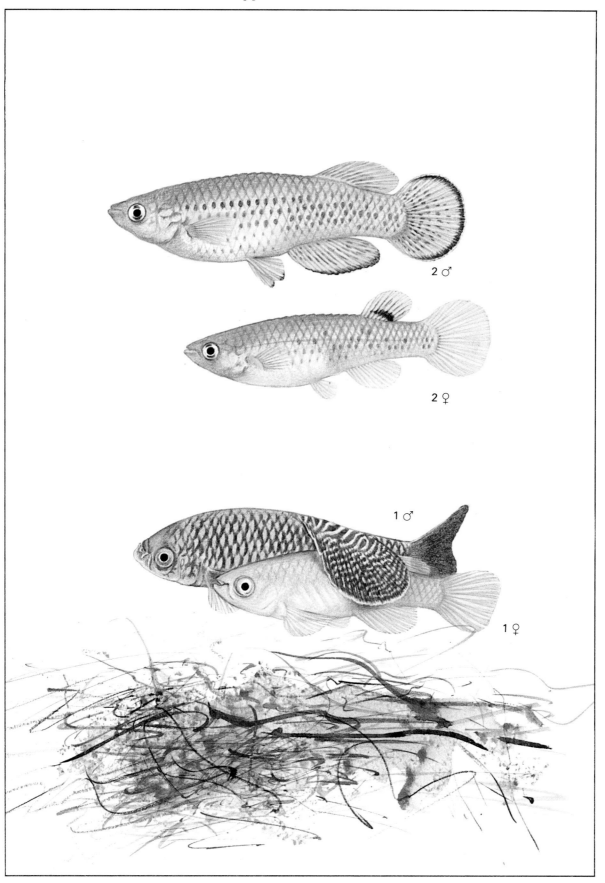

2 ♂

2 ♀

1 ♂

1 ♀

1 Veil Carp
Pterolebias longipinnis (GARMAN, 1895)
Syn. *Rivulus macrurus*

◁
●
Distribution: periodically dry savannas in Brazil, Venezuela, Bolivia and northern Argentina. Full length: 10 cm. Diet: live foods, chiefly mosquito and midge larvae. Monospecies keeping tank. Breeding tank: of 20-litre capacity with layer of peat on the bottom, dim lighting, floating plants, well-covered with glass. Sexual dimorphism: the male is larger, with big, fan-shaped caudal fin and distinct pattern, which is absent in the female. Sex ratio: 1 male : 2 females; Water: 22–24 °C; pH 6.0–6.5; dCH < 2°; dGH < 10°; fresh. Eggs: development is discontinuous, incubation period 70 days. Feeding of fry: finest brine shrimp nauplii.

The fish spawn in the soft bottom (peat). Let them spawn for 14 days, then lightly press the water out of the peat and store the moist peat in PVC bags at a temperature of 20 °C. After 70 days pour water over the peat.

2 Peruvian Longfin
Pterolebias peruensis MYERS, 1954

◁
●
Distribution: the Amazon region in Peru – Loreto (periodically dry waters). Full length: 10 cm. Diet: live foods, chiefly mosquito and midge larvae. Monospecies keeping tank. Breeding tank: with capacity of 50 litres, on the bottom a deep dish with about 10 cm layer of crumbled peat, dim lighting, floating plants. Sexual dimorphism: the male is more strikingly coloured with bigger dorsal and particularly anal and caudal fins. Sex ratio: 1 male : 3–4 females. Water: 22 °C; pH 7.0–7.5; dCH max. 2°; dGH max. 10°. Eggs: development is discontinuous, incubation period 12–13 weeks. Feeding of fry: brine shrimp nauplii.

In the wild the life-span of these fish is eight months at the most, in the aquarium it is somewhat longer. They become sexually mature very quickly – in just three months. The eggs are deposited deep in the bottom substrate. The moist peat with the eggs should be stored at a temperature of 20 °C. After three months pour warm water (20 to 22 °C) over the peat.

3 Blue Lady Minnow
Procatopus nototaenia BOULENGER, 1904

◁
●
Distribution: southern Nigeria and Cameroon – flowing waters in lowland forests near the coast. Full length: 5 cm. Diet: live foods. Monospecies keeping tank. Breeding tank: with capacity of 50–100 litres, dim lighting, floating plants, slightly streaming water. Either put a twisted root (piece of mineralized wood from moors) in the tank or else arrange flat stones to form numerous small cavities and crevices. Sexual dimorphism: the male is larger with sides coloured blue, red dorsal line, and the dorsal, caudal and anal fins coloured yellow to reddish with red spots. The caudal fin is straight. The female has transparent fins and less intense blue sheen, the caudal fin is rounded. Sex ratio: in a shoal with a slight preponderance of females. Breeding water: 22–24 °C; pH 6.5–7.0; dCH max. 1°; dGH max. 10°; fresh. Eggs: ∅ 1.5 mm, yellowish, incubation period 3 weeks. Feeding of fry: brine shrimp nauplii.

Let the fish spawn for about 10 days. Treat the eggs with methylene blue. The fish attain sexual maturity in six months.

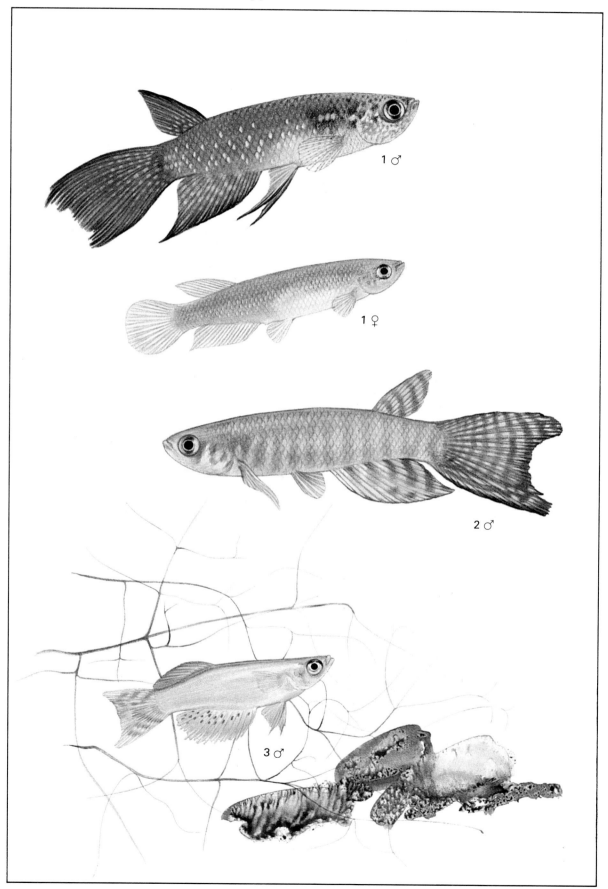

1 ♂

1 ♀

2 ♂

3 ♂

1 Sicklefin Killie or Saberfin
Terranotos dolichopterus (WEITZMAN and WOURMS, 1967)

Syn. *Austrofundulus dolichopterus*

Cyprinodontidae

Distribution: Venezuela, periodically dry puddles in the savannah. Full length: 5 cm. Diet: live foods (tubifex worms, larvae of mosquitoes and midges, fruit flies — *Drosophila melanogaster,* ants are also recommended as additional food but frequent feeding with *Cyclops* and *Daphnia* is advised against). Monospecies keeping tank. Breeding tank: of 20-litre capacity with 5-cm-thick layer of boiled peat on the bottom, well covered. Sexual dimorphism: the male is intensely coloured, his dorsal and anal fins are greatly extended in the shape of a sickle, the female has short fins and is less vividly coloured. Sex ratio: 1 male : 2–3 females. Water: 26 °C; pH 6.0–6.5; dCH < 1°; dGH 2–3°. Eggs: development is discontinuous, incubation period 5–6 months. Feeding of fry: brine shrimp nauplii.

A shy species. The fish like heavily planted tanks but must have plenty of room to swim about. Dim lighting and a dark bottom are the other factors for an optimum environment. When spawning the fish dig into the soft bottom substrate. Let the fish spawn for 14 days. The female deposits up to 400 eggs in one week. After the 14 days are up remove the parent fish and separate the males from the females. Put the moist peat with the eggs into PVC bags and store at a temperature of 22 °C. In five months check on their development with a magnifying lens; the eggs should contain a curled-up embryo. Pour soft water on the peat to a height of about 15 cm. Repeat the process of drying out and wetting several times during the course of a month. As soon as it is possible to identify the sexes rear the young males and females separately. The fish have a maximum lifespan of two years.

2 Venezuelan Killifish
Austrofundulus transilis MYERS, 1932

Cyprinodontidae

Distribution: Orinoco basin in Venezuela — periodically dry waters. Full length: 8 cm. Diet: live foods. Monospecies keeping tank. Breeding tank: with a capacity of 10 to 20 litres, 5 cm thick layer of peat on the bottom, and floating plants on the surface. Sexual dimorphism: the male is more colourful, his caudal fin has a coloured edge, the female is smaller with nondescript colouring. Sex ratio: 1 male : 2 females. Water: 22 °C; pH 6.5–7.0; dCH max. 2°. Eggs: development is discontinuous, Ø 1.5 mm, incubation period 5–6 months. Feeding of fry: brine shrimp nauplii.

Spawning lasts about a week, during which the female deposits up to 500 eggs in the bottom layer. Let the water drain from the peat on a sieve, then spread the peat on a filter paper laid on glass and leave it there for 6 to 12 hours at a temperature of 20 to 22 °C. As soon as the surface dries put the peat in PVC bags, allowing for the entry of air, and store the bags at a temperature of 18 to 20 °C. The peat must not become unduly dry, so sprinkle it with water from the breeding tank every now and then. When the incubation period is up tip the peat out into a smaller tank (of 10-litre capacity) and pour rainwater with a temperature of 18 to 20 °C and pH value of 6.5 to 7.0 onto the peat. The fry may hatch immediately or not until two or several days later. The fish have a maximum lifespan of two years.

1 ♂

2 ♂

Family Poeciliidae

The members of the family Poeciliidae are freshwater live-bearing fish distributed in the southern USA, Central America, West Indies and northern Argentina. Nowadays they are found also outside their native range in warmer regions to which they were introduced. The fish are distinguished by marked differences between the sexes. The males are usually smaller than the females and have a developed external mating organ — the gonopodium (transformed anal fin) — with the aid of which the male projects sperm (spermatophores) into the female's oviducts. The sperm is preserved in the oviducts for a long time so that the female may 'give birth' several times in succession without the presence of a male. Fertilization of the eggs is followed by the development of the embryos in the ovarian follicles, where they obtain nourishment from the yolk. There is no direct connection between the embryos and the body of the female and no nourishing substances pass from the one to the other. That is why in this case we speak of so-called oviviparity (seemingly live-bearing). Fertilized females, apart from a few exceptions, are characterized by a dark pregnancy spot at the rear of the belly and by their plumper bodies. The embryos are enclosed within a thin egg shell which they burst as soon as they are expelled from the mother's body. The newly-born fry are relatively large and greatly developed. Many species are variable in coloration and a great number of species interbreed.

1 Yucatan Sailfin Molly
Poecilia velifera (REGAN, 1914)
Syn. *Mollienesia velifera*   Poeciliidae

Distribution: Mexico, mainly the Yucatán peninsula. Full length: male — 10—15 cm, female — 18 cm. Diet: live, artificial and plant foods. Community tank. Breeding tank: with a capacity of 50 litres for 1 female, 200 litres or more for several females + breeding traps. Sexual dimorphism: the male is more colourful, has a gonopodium, and a dorsal fin that is generally very high. Sex ratio: 1 male : 5 females. Water: 25—28 °C; pH 7.5—8.2; fresh; add 1 tablespoon NaCl for every 10 litres of water. Interval between births: 8 weeks. Feeding of fry: fine live as well as artificial foods, algae.

There are usually 50 to 200 fry to a litter. In aquariums it is recommended to keep young males separate from the females and only a small number of fish in a tank so they have plenty of room. Good specimens, particularly males with a high dorsal fin, may be obtained in spacious, heated, sun-lit pools (Note: if the salinity is gradually increased the fish are capable of living as well as breeding in seawater with a density of 1.024 to 1.028, which corresponds to the environment of the coral sea).

2 *Poecilia velifera* — black form
Poeciliidae

According to some sources it also occurs in the wild. However it was bred and genetically fixed in aquarium conditions. Also a form with lyre-shaped fin was obtained by selective breeding.

3 *Poecilia velifera* — golden form
Poeciliidae

In substance this is an albiniotic form bred and genetically fixed in aquarium conditons.

1 ♂

1 ♀

2 ♂

3 ♂

1 Marbled Molly
Poecilia sphenops CUVIER and VALENCIENNES, 1846
Syn. *Mollienesia sphenops, Gambusia modesta, G. plumbea, Girardinus vandepolli,*
Lembesseia parvianatis, Platypoecilus mentalis, P. spilonotus, P. tropicus, Xiphophorus gillii　　　　Poeciliidae

Distribution: from Mexico to Colombia in fresh as well as brackish waters. Full length: male – 5 cm, female – 7 to 11 cm. Diet: live, artificial and plant foods. Community tank. Breeding tank: with capacity of 10 litres + breeding trap per female. Sexual dimorphism: the male is smaller, more slender, has a gonopodium and his dorsal fin is larger and tinted orange. Sex ratio: 1 male : 5 females. Water: 22–24 °C; pH 7.0–7.5; fresh; add 1 teaspoon NaCl for every 10 litres of water. Interval between births: 4–8 weeks. Feeding of fry: fine live as well as artificial foods, after 14 days also vegetable foods.

Healthy and well-developed breeder fish can be obtained only in roomy tanks with a capacity of at least 200 litres. Lengthy breeding of related fish and uncongenial conditions result in degeneration and stunted growth, particularly in males. The wild form is kept only rarely nowadays, for it is not as colourful as the aquarium-bred fish. Its coloration is extremely variable.

The illustrated form *Poecilia sphenops* 'Black Molly' was bred in the late 1920s in the USA, probably by the breeder Crecenty of New Orleans. In 1930 it was imported from the USA to Europe by the German firm Eimecke in Hamburg. Since that time breeders have developed a great many different forms, e. g. 'Black Yucatán' – an all-black form with high dorsal fin, and 'Mondmolly' – an all-black form with high dorsal fin edged with yellow or red, both developed round 1955 in Miami, Florida, by William Sternk, and an all-red form bred on a Singapore fish farm by Tank Guk Enge. Selectively bred forms are more sensitive and require more warmth than wild specimens.

2 *Poecilia sphenops* – 'Lyre Molly'
　　　　Poeciliidae

The form *Poecilia sphenops* 'Lyre Molly' was bred round 1960 by the Chinese breeder Cheah Yam Menga of Singapore. In the sixties the 'Lyre Molly' was already known to aquarists the world over.

1 ♂

1 ♀

2 ♂

1 Black-bellied Limia or Blue Limia
Poecilia melanogaster GÜNTHER, 1866

Syn. *Limia melanogaster, L. caudofasciata tricolor, L. tricolor*   Poeciliidae

Distribution: Jamaica and Haiti. Full length: male – 4 cm, female – 6.5 cm. Diet: live, artificial and plant foods. Community tank. Breeding tank: with a capacity of at least 100 litres, and a large breeding trap for several females (in commercial breeding). Sexual dimorphism: the male is smaller and has a gonopodium, the female has a big triangular pregnancy spot that is permanent. Sex ratio: 1 male : 5 females. Water: 22–26 °C; pH 6.5–7.5; fresh, half-hard. Live-bearer: intervals between births 6–8 weeks. Feeding of fry: brine shrimp nauplii, finely sifted zooplankton, artificial fry foods.

The fish like a light, partly sunlit tank. The number of young produced by a single female is around 50. In a well planted aquarium containing only this species of fish the pregnant females need not be taken out, but the fry should be removed regularly. The fry measure 10 mm at birth and their growth is rapid. In the case of lengthier interbreeding of closely related individuals and unsuitable diet the fish become smaller in size with each ensuing generation.

2 Hump-backed Limia or Black-barred Limia
Poecilia nigrofasciata (REGAN, 1913)

Syn. *Limia nigrofasciata, L. arnoldi*   Poeciliidae

Distribution: Haiti, in fresh as well as brackish waters. Full length: male – 4.5 cm, female – 7 cm. Diet: live, artificial, and plant foods (soft algal growths). Breeding tank: with capacity of at least 100 litres and large breeding trap. Sexual dimorphism: the male has a gonopodium, in older males the dorsal contour gradually becomes higher until the proportion of body length to height is approximately 2:1. As the body increases in height it becomes narrower in the flanks and the dorsal fin becomes larger, fan-shaped. Sex ratio: 1 male : 5 females. Water: 22–26 °C; pH 7.0–7.5; half-hard, add 1 teaspoon NaCl for every 10 litres of water. Live-bearer: intervals between births 6 weeks. Feeding of fry: brine shrimp nauplii, finely sifted zooplankton.

The fish are sensitive to abrupt changes in their environment – females abort, the young are born dead. For that reason when changing the water replace no more than half. It sometimes also happens that the abdominal cavity of the females is literally filled to bursting with developing embryos. Such females either produce exceedingly large young or else die when the excessively large embryos rupture the abdominal wall. Not even a sudden increase of the water temperature helps. Some breeders believe the excessive fullness of the females is caused by the absence of males who help the timely expulsion of the young by their attempts at mating and butting the bellies of the females with their snouts. That is why in breeding on a larger scale pregnant females are transferred to breeding traps together with males. In well-planted and roomy aquariums, however, it is sufficient to take out only the offspring. A single female produces some 30 young which are relatively large – 10 to 15 mm long. At the age of five months it is possible to identify the sexes.

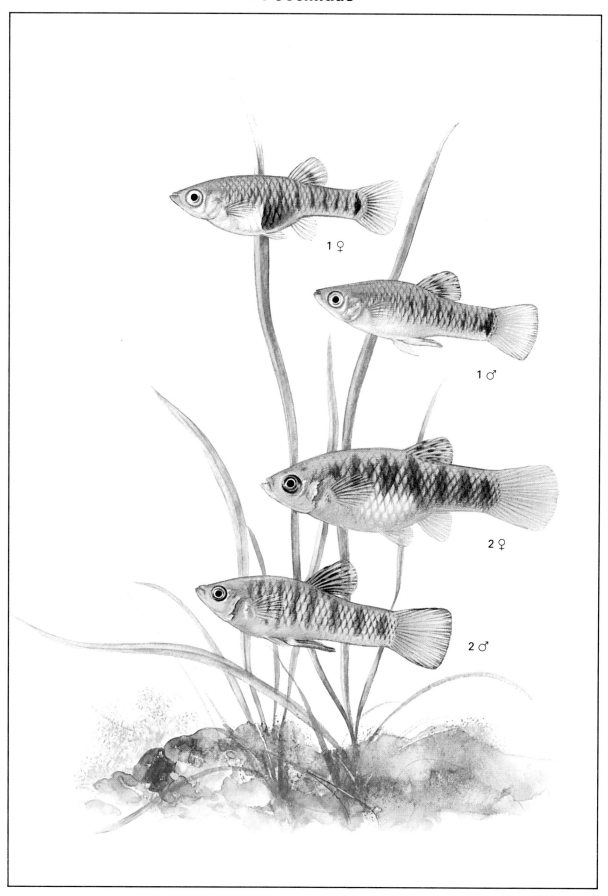

1 ♀

1 ♂

2 ♀

2 ♂

1 Guppy
Poecilia reticulata PETERS, 1859
Syn. *Lebistes reticulatus, L. poecilioides, Acanthocephalus guppii,*
A. reticulatus, Girardinus guppii, G. petersi, G. poeciloides, G. reticulatus,
Haridichthys reticulatus, Heterandria guppyi, Poecilia poeciloides, Poeciloides reticulatus.   Poeciliidae

☐ Distribution: Central America to Brazil (introduced throughout the world and nowadays found in the wild in many warmer regions). Full length: male — 3 cm, female — 5 cm. Diet: live as well as artificial foods, regularly augmented by plant foods. Community tank.

Fish with great variability in coloration. According to eye-witnesses the island populations of Martinique and St. Thomas are exceptionally beautifully coloured and large; on these islands they are found in brackish and sea water. Over the years selective breeding of *P. reticulata* has yielded a great many different forms.

2 *Poecilia reticulata* – cultivated form   Poeciliidae

☐ Full length: male — 6 cm, female — 8 cm. Diet: live and artificial foods, regularly augmented by plant foods. Tank: Monospecies in commercial breeding centres, otherwise community tank. Breeding tank: with capacity of 3 to 10 litres and breeding trap for 1 female. Sexual dimorphism: the male is more brightly coloured and has a gonopodium. Sex ratio: 1 male : 3–4 females. Water: 22–24 °C; pH 7.0–8.0, half-hard to slightly hard, fresh; add 1 teaspoon NaCl for every 10 litres of water. Live-bearer: intervals between births 4–6 weeks; as many as 250 young. Feeding of fry: finely sifted zooplankton, brine shrimp nauplii, after 14 days also occasional vegetable food. Veil-finned forms were first shown in 1954 at the First International Guppy Show in Hanover. They were developed by the 'Guppy King' — German-born American breeder Paul Hahnel of New York (1902–1969).

Essential for successful breeding are healthy, pure strains of brood fish and a basic knowledge of genetics. For the basic breeding group of

1 male : 3–4 females use a tank of 50-litre capacity without any substrate on the bottom but with an efficient mechanical filter and floating plant thickets. Separate spawn-ripe females, putting them either singly in small tanks or singly in small traps suspended in a large tank, or put several females of the same strain together in an adequately large trap. From small tanks pour off fry of the same strain into a large tank with a water level of about 10 cm and raise this level as the young fish grow. One basic rule: never keep fry from several strains together in the same tank. As soon as it is possible to identify the sex of the fry separate the males from the females. The later the males attain sexual maturity the greater is the probability that they will reach the largest possible size. Because the generations follow quickly one upon the other, in time, with constant inbreeding, there are degenerative changes in the fish, particularly a decrease in their size. It is, therefore, advisable to obtain brood fish of the same strain but from different, unrelated groups.

1 ♂

1 ♀

2 ♂

2 ♂

2 ♂

1 Sail-fin Molly
Poecilia latipinna (LE SUEUR, 1821)
Syn. *Mollienesia latipinna*

Poeciliidae

☐ Distribution: Mexico, Texas, Florida, South and North Carolina, Virginia — standing as well as flowing waters by the sea coast, fresh, brackish as well as sea water. The Río Grande and its tributaries on the border between Mexico and the USA is a typical locality. Full length: male — 10 cm, female —12 cm. Diet: live, artificial and plant foods. Community tank, light to sun-flooded with well-filtered water. Breeding tank: of 10-litre capacity with a breeding trap for 1 female; in the case of a larger breeding trap several females may be put inside. Sexual dimorphism: the male is smaller, has a gonopodium, and his dorsal fin is higher as well as wider than the female's. Sex ratio: 1 male : 3—5 females. Water: 24 °C; pH 7.0—8.0; fresh; add 1 tablespoon NaCl for every 10 litres of water or 1 litre sea water for every 50 litres of fresh water. Live-bearer: intervals between births 8—10 weeks. Feeding of fry: brine shrimp nauplii, finely sifted zooplankton, artificial fry foods, algae.

Brood fish as well as young fish are kept in roomy tanks — large, heated and sunlit pools are ideal. A species that is variable in colour, ranging from albinotic to spotted to entirely black. This variability was used by breeders to develop numerous strains: *P. latipinna* — Starburst Molly, gold speckled with red, developed in 1973 by John L. Williams at EKK — Will Tropical Fish Farm, Florida, USA; *P. latipinna* — Balloon Molly, with greatly shortened body, developed in 1975 by Wilson Joe Eng Nam in Singapore. Clean water, low stock density (small number of fish) and ample space are primary conditions for successful breeding. Fry measure up to 12 mm in length; one female produces approximately 100 young.

2 Black-barred Live-bearer
Quintana atrizona (HUBBS, 1934)
Syn. *Eptomaculata lara, Limia eptomaculata lara*

Poeciliidae

☐ Distribution: species endemic to Cuba, found in a small region round Havana and Baracoa. Full length: male — 2 cm, female — 4 cm. Diet: live, artificial and plant foods. Monospecies keeping tank. Breeding tank: of 100-litre capacity, light to sun-flooded, with finely-leaved plants. Sexual dimorphism: the male is smaller, more translucent and has a gonopodium. Sex ratio: 1 : 1 or set up in a shoal with slight preponderance of females. Water: 24—28 °C; pH 7.0—7.5; fresh, well-aerated, clean. Live-bearer: intervals between births 5 weeks. Feeding of fry: brine shrimp nauplii.

Though Cuba has been visited by numerous ichthyological expeditions this species was not described until 1934. The female gives birth to as many as 35 young at intervals of an hour to a day. The young are 6.5 to 7 mm long; they should be taken out and reared in a separate tank. Young fish of varied age may be reared together in the same tank. Their growth is rapid and they are sexually mature at four months.

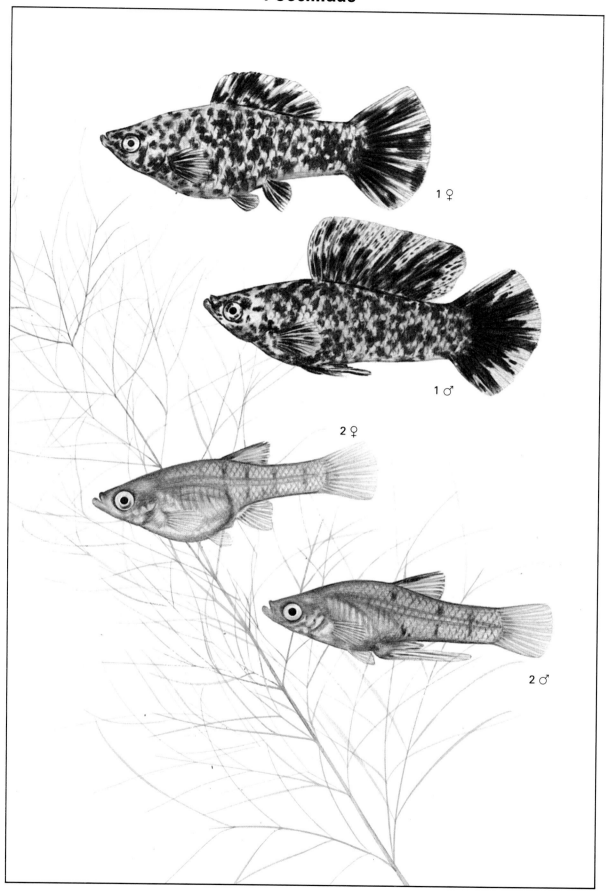

1 ♀

1 ♂

2 ♀

2 ♂

1 Mosquito Fish
Gambusia affinis affinis (BAIRD and GIRARD, 1853)

Syn. *Heterandria affinis, H. patruelis, Gambusia speciosa, G. patruelis, G. humilis,*
G. gracilis, Zygonectes inurus, Z. patruelis, Z. speciosa, Z. brachypterus, Z. gracilis
Poeciliidae

Distribution: Texas is its original home but the present range of this species is not known because it has been so frequently introduced to various localities for mosquito control. *G. a. affinis* has become established, for instance, in Bulgaria in the Ropotamo River and in Hungary in the spa of Hevíz, and in the USSR it occurs in enormous numbers in the warm waste waters of nuclear power plants. Full length: male – 3.5 to 4 cm, female – 6.5 cm. Diet: live as well as artificial foods. Monospecies keeping tank. Breeding tank: of 10-litre capacity with a breeding trap. Sexual dimorphism: the male is smaller, slender and has a long gonopodium. Sex ratio: 1 male : 2–3 females. Water: 20–22 °C; pH 7.0–8.0; fresh; add 1 teaspoon NaCl for every 10 litres of water. Live-bearer: intervals between births 4–6 weeks. Feeding of fry: brine shrimp nauplii, finely sifted zooplankton, artificial fry foods.

A single brood numbers 10 to 80 young. The female pursues and eats the offspring. The young fish grow quickly.

2 Spotted Gambusia or Blue Gambusia
Gambusia punctata (POEY, 1854)
Poeciliidae

Distribution: Cuba. Full length: male – 4 to 4.5 cm, female – 9 cm. Diet: live as well as artificial foods. Monospecies keeping tank. Breeding tank: of 10-litre capacity with breeding trap for 1 female. Sexual dimorphism: the male is smaller and has a gonopodium. Sex ratio: 1 male : 2 females. Water: 20–24 °C; pH 7.0–8.0; fresh, add 1 teaspoon NaCl for every 10 litres of water. Live-bearer: intervals between births 4–6 weeks. Feeding of fry: brine shrimp nauplii, finely sifted zooplankton.

Sometimes breeding presents no difficulties – a single brood numbers 20 to 100 young. At other times there are problems – the females are not fertilized and deposit only a few clear, faintly yellowish eggs. The fry of *G. punctata* are predatory and for that reason should be reared in a tank by themselves. The young fish grow quickly.

This species is not to be confused with the independent species *Gambusia punticulata* Poey, 1854.

3 *Girardinus metallicus* POEY, 1854

Syn. *Girardinus garmani, G. pygmaeus, Heterandria cubensis, H. metallica, Poecilia metallica*
Poeciliidae

Distribution: Cuba, Costa Rica. Full length: male – 5 cm, female – 9 cm. Diet: live as well as artificial foods. Community tank. Breeding tank: of 10-litre capacity with a breeding trap for 1 female. Sexual dimorphism: the male is smaller and has a very long gonopodium terminating in two hooked appendages. Sex ratio: 1 male : 2–3 females. Water: 20–24 °C, pH 7.0–8.0; fresh, add 1 teaspoon NaCl for every 10 litres of water. Live-bearer: intervals between births about 7 weeks. Feeding of fry: brine shrimp nauplii, finely-sifted zooplankton.

Fish variable in coloration. They like a partly sunlit aquarium with algal growths. The female may give birth to as many as 100 young. The young fish grow relatively quickly and are sexually mature at the age of five months. These fish are most attractive if kept by themselves in a large shoal in a tank of at least 100-litre capacity. In such a tank it is not necessary to put the females in a breeding trap, but the fry should be taken out and put in a separate tank. If well fed the adult fish pay no particular attention to the young.

Poeciliidae

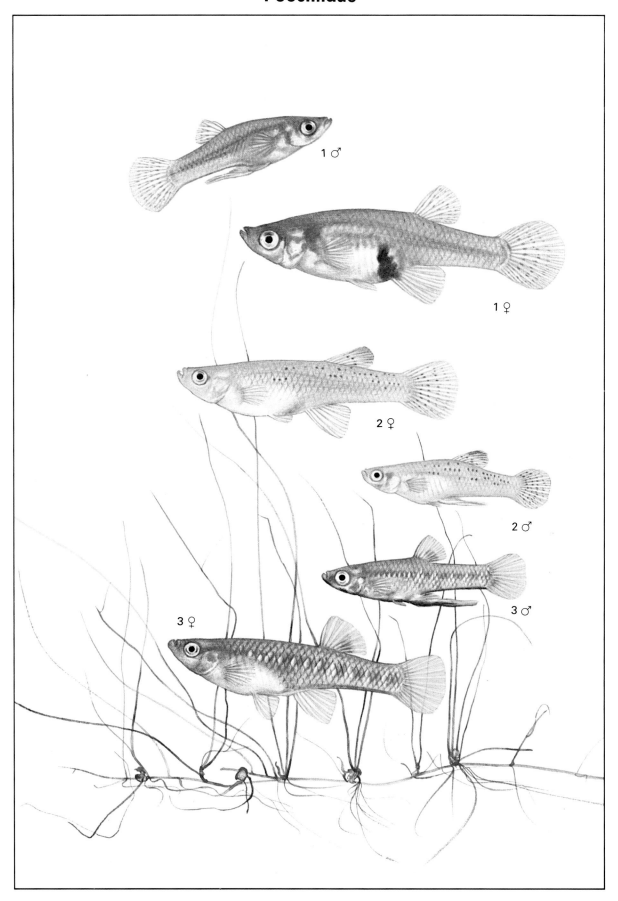

1 Twin-spot Live-bearer
Pseudoxiphophorus bimaculatus (HECKEL, 1846)
Syn. *Xiphophorus bimaculatus, Heterandria bimaculata*
(according to the recent revision of Dr. Rada in 1985)   Poeciliidae

☐
● Distribution: Central and southern Mexico, Guatemala and Honduras, in mountain streams as well as standing waters, including lagoons with brackish water. Full length: male − 6 cm, female − 10 cm. Diet: live foods augmented with artificial and plant foods. Monospecies keeping tank with a capacity of 100 litres or more. Breeding tank: with a capacity of 10 litres and a breeding trap (wire netting with 5 × 5 mm mesh) per 1 female. Sexual dimorphism: the male is smaller, slimmer, has a markedly long gonopodium and the anal fin is coloured faintly orange. Sex ratio: 1 male : 2 females. Water: 20−24 °C; pH 7.0−8.0; 1 teaspoon NaCl may be added for every 10 litres of water. Live-bearer interval between births: 6 weeks. Feeding of fry: brine shrimp nauplii or finely sifted zooplankton.

An aggressive species that attacks even much larger fish, biting their fins. According to the observations of various aquarists the aggressiveness of individual aquarium populations varies. The fish should always be kept in a large shoal. Females produce litters of approximately 100 fry, which are very big (15 mm) and have a black spot at the base of the caudal fin. Their growth is rapid.

2 Midget Live-bearer, Mosquito Fish or Dwarf Top Minnow
Heterandria formosa AGASSIZ, 1853
Syn. *Girardinus formosus, Gambusia formosa, Heterandria omnata,
Hydrargyra formosa, Rivulus ommatus, Zygonectes manni*   Poeciliidae

☐
● Distribution: USA − North Carolina and Florida. Full length: male − 2 cm, female − 3.5 cm. Diet: live (small), artificial as well as plant foods. Monospecies keeping tank. Breeding tank: with a capacity of 10 litres or more (depending on the number of fish), finely-leaved plants, light to sun-flooded. Sexual dimorphism: the male is smaller, more slender, and has a long gonopodium. Sex ratio: 1 male : 3 females. Water: 20−26 °C; pH 7.0−7.5; fresh; add 1 teaspoon NaCl for every 10 litres of water. Interval between births: 4−5 weeks. Feeding of fry: nauplii of brine shrimp or *Cyclops,* may be augmented by fine artificial foods.

These small fish are best kept in a large shoal with other members of the same species. The females give birth to two or three young daily for a period of six to 10 days. The minute fry should be removed from the tank regularly and reared separately in low, well-lit tanks with water column about 10 to 15 cm high. Adult fish do not harass the young.

Poeciliidae

1 ♀

1 ♂

2 ♀

2 ♂

1 Pike Top Minnow
Belonesox belizanus KNER, 1860

Distribution: Central America from southern Mexico to Honduras. Full length: male – 12 cm, female – 20 cm. Diet: live foods, mainly fish. Monospecies keeping tank. Breeding tank: with capacity of 50 litres per 1 female + large breeding trap with 5 × 5 mm mesh. Sexual dimorphism: the male is smaller and has a gonopodium. Sex ratio: 1 male: 2–3 females. Water 24–30 °C; pH 7.0–7.5; fresh; add 1 teaspoon NaCl for every 10 litres of water. Interval between births: 5 weeks. Feeding of fry: zooplankton, chiefly mosquito larvae, later generous amounts of fry of livebearing fish.

In shape and manner of living *B. belizanus* resembles the pike *Esox lucius.* Aquariums should be at least 1 metre long and provided with plenty of hiding places amongst plants.

Breeder males must be big for otherwise they may be attacked and preyed on by the females. Each pregnant female should be kept separately. The fry is expelled from the mother's body very quickly and instinctively seeks a place to hide in the vegetation. A single litter comprises approximately 100 fry, which measure 2 cm. Their 'birth' may take as long as 24 hours. Young fish, particularly from the age of one week, must be generously fed (continuously satiated) for otherwise their number is reduced by cannibalism. For this reason it is also important that there be relatively few specimens in the tank. Young fish grow quickly and attain sexual maturity at the age of six months.

In the Red Data Book *B. belizanus* is on the list of endangered species and is strictly protected.

2 Blue-eyed Live-bearer
Priapella intermedia ALVAREZ, 1952

Distribution: Mexico, in clean flowing waters. Full length: male – 5 cm, female – 7 cm. Diet: live, artificial and plant foods. Monospecies keeping tank. Breeding tank: with a capacity of 100 litres, thickets of plants (the fry are caught and removed). Sexual dimorphism: the male has a gonopodium, his anal fin is coloured lemon-yellow. Sex ratio: 1 male : 2 females. Water: 20–22 °C; pH 6.5–7.5; fresh, filtered, oxygen-rich, streaming water provided by circulating filters. Interval between births: 5–6 weeks. Feeding of fry: brine shrimp nauplii, finely sifted *Cyclops.*

Typical of these fish are the vivid blue eyes. The fish should be kept in a large shoal. They are a sensitive species susceptible to disease in an environment that is not congenial. The fish are particularly fond of congregating near the surface in streaming water. They are affected by stressful situations, particularly by sudden changes in the environment, disturbing influences, and the like. The fry are not pursued by the adult fish. They should be reared in separate tanks with a sufficiently large surface area and water column 10 to 15 cm high. The females are not very productive, producing some 30 fry at one birth. Pregnancy in the female is imperceptible, the body is only slightly enlarged. Sudden changes in the temperature and chemical composition of the water cause the females to abort. Young fish grow quickly and at the age of five months begin to show signs of sexual maturation.

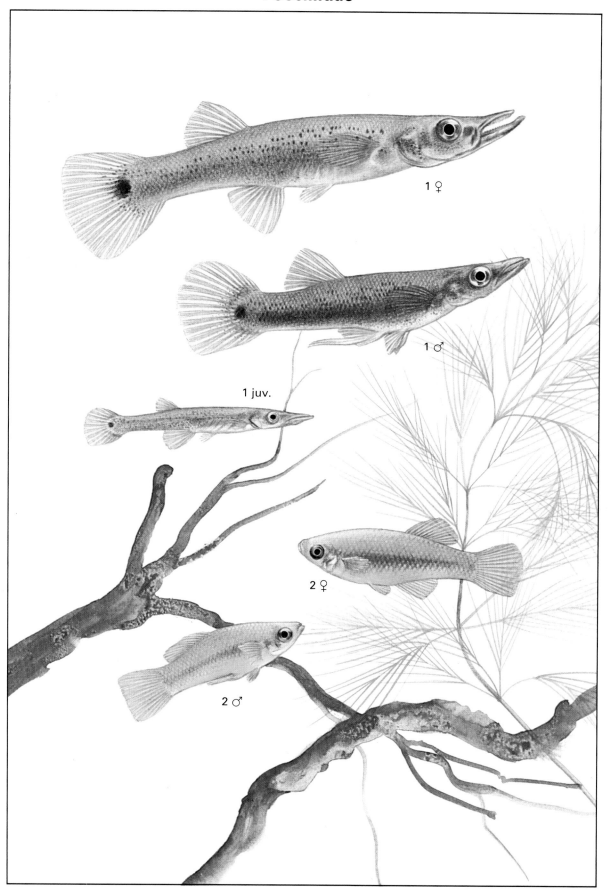

1 ♀

1 ♂

1 juv.

2 ♀

2 ♂

1 Caudo
Phalloceros caudomaculatus reticulatus (HENSEL, 1868)
Syn. *Girardinus januarius reticulatus, G. reticulata* Poeciliidae

Distribution: central Brazil, Paraguay, Argentina, Uruguay. Full length: male − 4 cm, female − 7 cm. Diet: live as well as artificial foods, augmented by plant foods. Monospecies keeping tank, well-planted. Breeding tank: of 6-litre capacity with breeding trap for 1 female (in large tanks and large breeding traps it is possible to put several dozen females). Sexual dimorphism: the male is smaller and has a long gonopodium. Sex ratio: 1 male : 3 females. Water: 16−20 °C; pH 7.0−8.0; fresh; add 1 teaspoon NaCl for every 10 litres of water, of 1 litre sea water for every 50 litres of fresh water. Live-bearer: intervals between births 4−6 weeks. Feeding of fry: brine shrimp nauplii, finely sifted zooplankton.

Though the fry are not pursued by the female it is best to remove them regularly (unless use is made of a breeding trap) and raise them in a separate tank. Currently this species is differentiated into two subspecies: *P. caudomaculatus auratus* (Hensel, 1868), and *P. caudomaculatus reticulatus* (Hensel, 1868). There is also the variety *P. caudomaculatus reticulatus* var. *auratus* from Brazil. The basic colour is yellow to golden yellow. The body and fins are mottled with irregular black, brown and white spots.

2 Merry Widow
Phallichthys amates amates (MILLER, 1907)
Syn. *Poecilia amates, Poeciliopsis amates* Poeciliidae

Distribution: Central America − Guatemala to Panama. Full length: male − 6 cm, female − 10 cm. Diet: live as well as artificial foods. Monospecies keeping tank. Breeding tank: of 10-litre capacity with breeding trap. Sexual dimorphism: the male is smaller and has a long gonopodium, which in many specimens extends to the base of the caudal fin. Sex ratio: 1 male : 3 females. Water: 20−25 °C; pH 7.0−7.5; add 1 teaspoon NaCl for every 10 litres of water. Live-bearer: intervals between births 6 weeks. Feeding of fry: brine shrimp nauplii, finely sifted zooplankton.

Timid and peaceful fish. Keep them in a small shoal in a well-planted tank with a capacity of at least 100 litres. The adult fish take no notice of the fry and, if you don't use a breeding trap, remove the fry regularly with a catching pipe. A single litter numbers about 50 young, which grow slowly. Males attain sexual maturity at four to six months, females at the age of a year (occasionally even earlier).

The genus *Phallichthys* was established by C. L. Hubbs in 1924. It includes three species: *P. tico, P. fairweatheri* and *P. amates. P. amates* is differentiated into two subspecies: *P. amates amates* (Miller, 1907) and *P. amates pittieri* (Meek, 1912). *P. amates pittieri* is found in Panama and Costa Rica and is probably distributed also in the region of the West Indies. The females of *P. amates pittieri* are more fertile, one litter numbering as many as 100 young.

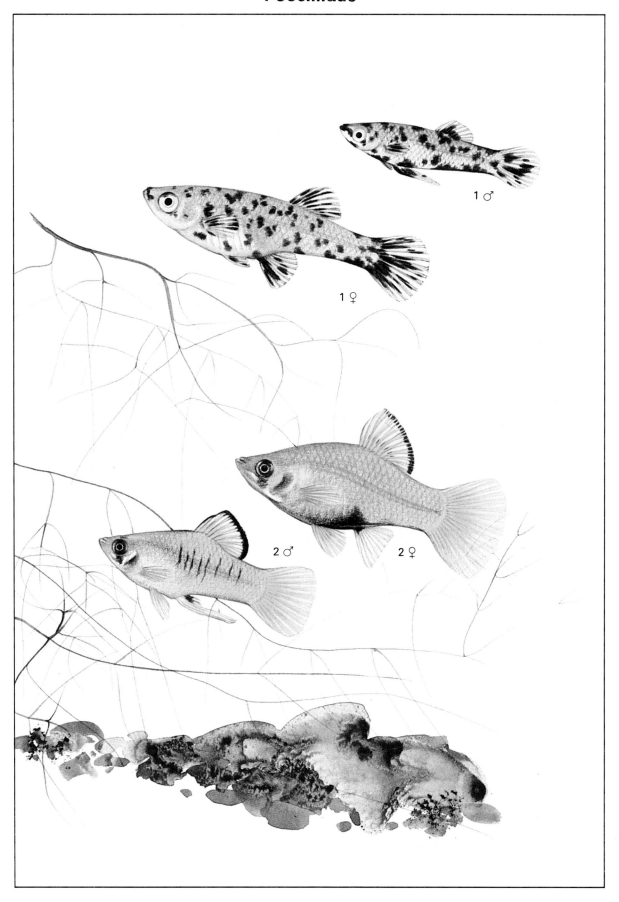

1 ♂

1 ♀

2 ♂

2 ♀

1 Swordtail
Xiphophorus helleri helleri (HECKEL, 1848)
Syn. *Mollienesia helleri, Xiphophorus jalapae, X. rachovi*

☐ Distribution: Central America from Mexico to Costa Rica. Full length: male − 10 cm, female
◑ − 12 cm. Diet: live, artificial and plant foods. Community tank. Breeding tank: with capacity of 10 litres per 1 female + a breeding trap. Sexual dimorphism: the male has a gonopodium, his caudal fin is extended into a 'sword'. Sex ratio: 1 male : 5 females. Water: 20−25 °C; pH 7.0−7.5; fresh; add 1 teaspoon NaCl for every 10 litres of water. Live-bearer: interval between births 4−6 weeks. Feeding of fry: fine live and artificial foods, after 14 days plant food (strained spinach).

The number of fry in one litter may be anywhere between several dozen to 200 or more. The fry should be reared in large, low tanks with water column 10 to 15 cm high. In commercial breeding use is made of large breeding traps holding several dozen females. It is important to reduce the number of fish in the tank in time, and provide a continuous supply of fresh water (through-flow tanks), and intensive feeding three to four times a day. From the end of June/July till the beginning of September the young fish may be kept in garden pools. They tolerate a temporary drop in temperature to as low as 15 °C.

Sexual transformation in *X. helleri* has been described many times − older females that have produced several litters may be transformed into males; however reverse transformation of male into female has not been known to occur.

Besides the nominate form of this popular live-bearer, which through selective breeding has yielded many forms varying in shape and coloration. The following subspecies have been described: *X. helleri guentheri* Jordan and Evermann, 1896, from Guatemala, Honduras and Mexico, *X. helleri strigatus* Regan, 1907, from Mexico, and *X. helleri alvarezi* Rosen, 1960, likewise from Mexico. Mutual cross-breeding of the subspecies as well as pure strains is undesirable.

2 *Xiphophorus helleri* − Simpson Swordtail

☐ Developed in 1960 by Thomas Simpson in the USA (California). This form is currently bred in
◑ a whole range of colour strains.

3 *Xiphophorus helleri* − Tuxedo Swordtail

☐ Developed and exported in 1956 from Sri Lanka. The colour of the original wild stock is green or
◑ red. Red-and-black forms have a tendency to develop tumours, which may be kept in check by eliminating specimens with large amounts of black when selecting fish for breeding.

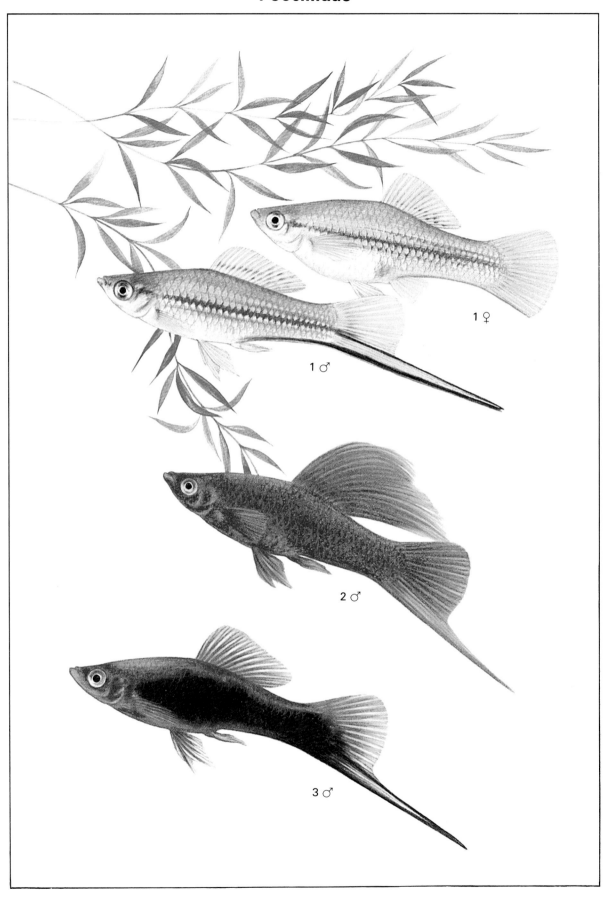

1 *Xiphophorus helleri* – Red Swordtail

This form comes in various shades of red – from brick red to mahogany red; particularly prized are strains coloured a deep velvety red, without any iridescence or white belly, called Velvet Red.

2 *Xiphophorus helleri* – 'Sunset' Swordtail

Developed at Florida fish farms and exported from there.

3 *Xiphophorus helleri* – Black Lyre-fin and Veil-fin Swordtails

The basic black form with classic shape of caudal fin, likewise known as the 'Hamburg' Swordtail, was developed in 1912 by W. Hoffman in Germany. The body is black, the scales have a blue, green or opalescent sheen, the fins are transparent to yellowish. The fish reach a considerable length (20 cm) and often do not attain sexual maturity until the second year. They require more warmth than other colour forms. When selecting breeder fish eliminate specimens with an accumulation of black in the fins which causes the fins to decay.

In 1962 O. Adams developed in Florida the first lyre form of *X. helleri* – coloured red. Nowadays lyre swordtails are bred in a whole range of colours. The males of the lyre form are fertile but because of their exceedingly long gonopodiums are unable to fertilize a female. For this reason lyre-form females are often cross-bred with 'ordinary' males. The offspring of such matings, however, include a large percentage of specimens without the lyre-shaped caudal fin. Artificial insemination is necessary for producing pure offspring. The black veil-fin form with red fins was developed in 1963 in Hawaii by the breeders E. and L. Nishida. It was further developed in Florida under the name 'Nishida High-fin helleri'.

The following aids are used in the artificial insemination of the lyre forms: a preparative microscope, microscopic slides with a well, a 'Pasteur' pipette – narrow glass tube 0.5 mm in diameter with rubber suction cap, tissue paper, and a physiological solution (a 0.6 per cent solution of NaCl). After removing the male from the tank and calming him down (this is done by covering the eyes), place him on a square of moistened tissue paper and cover him with another square of moist tissue paper, leaving the hind end of the body including the gonopodium exposed. Place a microscopic slide with two drops of the physiological solution under the gonopodium. Then using forceps turn the gonopodium in the clockwise direction several times. Pressing lightly with the thumb and forefinger stroke the belly from the front end towards the base of the gonopodium thereby expelling spermatophores into the physiological solution. The female is calmed in the same manner. After having done so place the female on the table of the microscope belly side up. Then take up the physiological solution containing the spermatophores with the pipette and carefully insert the end of the pipette into the sexual opening of the female (no more than 2 mm at the most). This completes the process of artificial insemination. The spermatophores of one male may be used to fertilize several females.

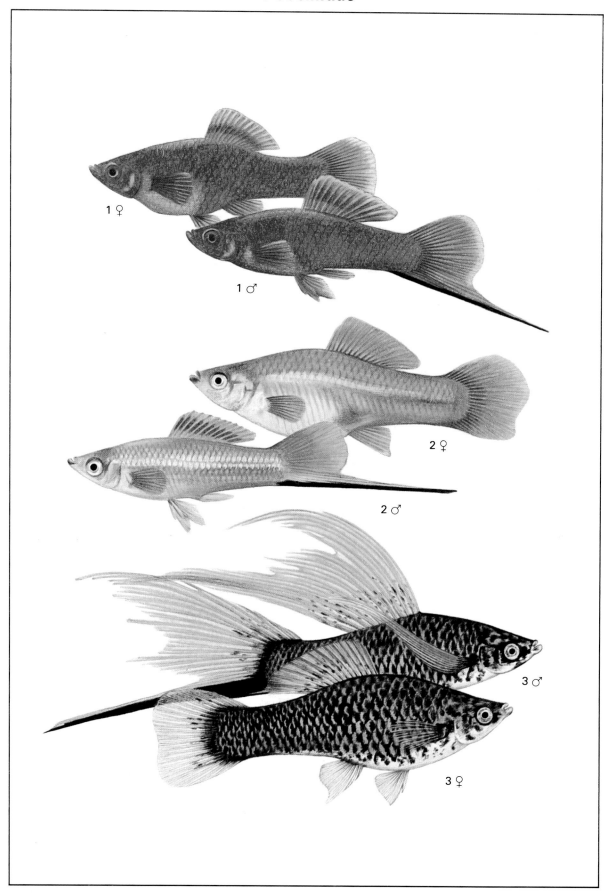

Platy
Xiphophorus maculatus (GÜNTHER, 1866)
Syn. *Platypoecilus maculatus, P. nigra, P. pulchra, P. rubra, Poecilia maculata* Poeciliidae

Distribution: Atlantic coast of Mexico, Guatemala and Honduras. Full length: male – 3.5 cm, female – 6 cm. Diet: live, artificial and plant foods. Community tank. Breeding tank: with capacity of 3 to 10 litres + breeding trap per 1 female. Sexual dimorphism: the male is slimmer, smaller, and has a gonopodium. Sex ratio: 1 male : 3 females. Water: 20–25 °C; pH 7.0–7.5; you may add 1 teaspoon NaCl for every 10 litres of water. Interval between births: 22–25 days. Feeding of fry: fine live as well as artificial foods.

A species with variable coloration even in the wild. The number of fry produced by a single female is between 30 and 100. This species readily and prolifically cross-breeds with *Xiphophorus helleri;* the male hybrid offspring have only a short sword extension. A great number of other hybrids have been developed by crossings with *Heterandria formosa, Poecilia nigrofasciata, P. reticulata, P. sphenops, P. velifera* and *Xiphophorus variatus.*

1 *Xiphophorus maculatus* – 'Coral Platy'
Poeciliidae

A popular deep red cultivated form with whitish-blue iridescence in the ventral and anal fins and also partly in the caudal fin. It is not known where it was developed.

2 *Xiphophorus maculatus* – 'Wagtail Platy'
Poeciliidae

The body colour is grey, yellow or red. This is one of the first genetically stabilized selectively-bred forms. The black colour has been genetically fixed with such success that it can be considered a dominant characteristic. Responsible for this is the American geneticist Dr.

Myron Gordon (1900–1959) who engaged in research of malignant tumours. He performed extensive experiments on live-bearers and published numerous works answering a great number of questions about selection and heredity in these fish.

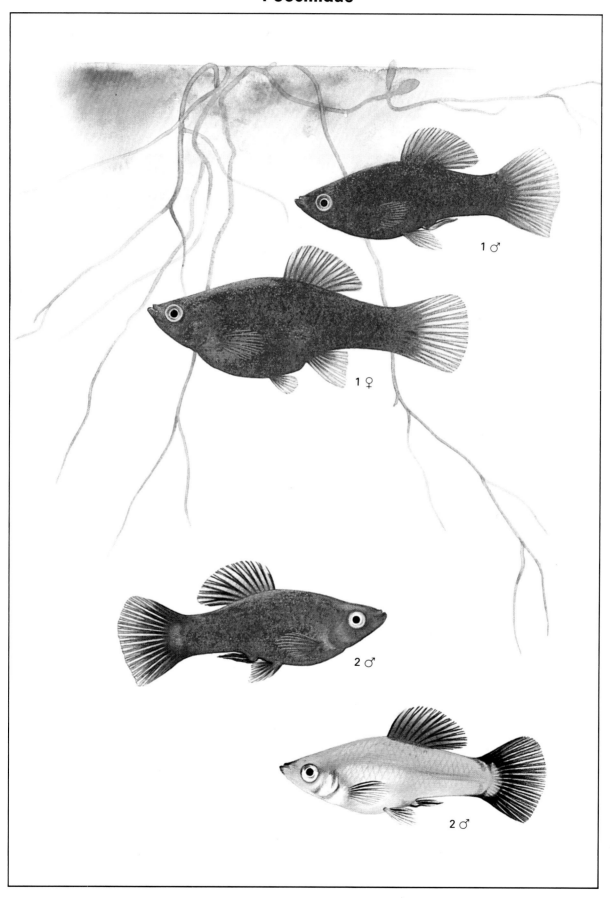

1 ♂

1 ♀

2 ♂

2 ♂

1 *Xiphophorus maculatus* – Simpson Platy

☐
◑ This platy is a long-established aquarium fish. There are a number of colour forms – the red-black tuxedo (in various shades of red), yellow-black tuxedo, green-black tuxedo, and the wagtail with black dorsal and caudal fins. Some populations, particularly specimens with an excessive accumulation of black pigments (melanophores) in the skin, tend to develop tumorous growths followed by disintegration of the dorsal or caudal fin. For that reason such specimens should be removed and discarded.

2 *X. helleri* x *X. variatus* – Papagai Platy
Poeciliidae

☐
◑ The high-finned Papagai Platy is very similar to the Simpson Platy. It was developed by the American breeder Bill Hearin in 1963 by crossing a male *X. helleri* 'Simpson' and female *X. variatus* and is also known under the names of Topsail, Delta, Hi-Fin, etc. Despite the marked morphological similarity to the Simpson Platy, however, it is a cross-breed of the two aforesaid species which have nothing in common with *X. maculatus.*

3 *Xiphophorus maculatus* – Spitz Platy
Poeciliidae

☐
◑ The Spitz Platy was apparently developed in GDR or FRG in the late sixties or early seventies. A similar form, called the Pinsel Platy with the centre of the caudal fin extended in the shape of a fan, appeared in Hamburg in 1969. Over the years aquarists have succeeded in developing these fish in various colours. The shape of the caudal fin, however, exhibits marked variability; apparently neither of the two forms is genetically fixed so far.

Poeciliidae

1 ♂

1 ♂

1 ♀

3 ♂

2 ♂

1 Montezuma Swordtail

Xiphophorus cortezi ROSEN, 1960

Syn. *Xiphophorus montezumae cortezi*

Distribution: southern Mexico, Yucatán, rivers Axtla, Panaco, Montezuma and Salto de Agua. Full length: male – 5.5 cm, female – 6.5 cm. Diet: live, artificial and plant foods. Community tank. Breeding tank: of 10-litre capacity with breeding trap for 1 female. Sexual dimorphism: the male is smaller than the female and has a short gonopodium and short sword. Sex ratio: 1 male : 5 females. Water: 20–25 °C; pH 7.0–7.5; fresh; you may add 1 teaspoon NaCl for every 10 litres of water. Live-bearer: intervals between births 4–6 weeks. Feeding of fry: brine shrimp nauplii, finely sifted zooplankton, artificial fry foods.

A species that is rarely kept in the aquarium. In nature it is found in swiftly flowing waters. It is recommended that the temperature of the water in the aquarium be no higher than 25 °C. This fish species generally has fewer young than *X. helleri* – 20 to 60 in number. The sexes may be identified as early as six to eight weeks after birth. According to some aquarists fish kept in aquariums lose the intense coloration they have in the wild. They readily interbreed with other species of *Xiphophorus*. There is also a sub-species: *X. montezumae montezumae*.

2 Variegated Platy

Xiphophorus variatus (MEEK, 1904)

Syn. *Platypoecilus variatus, P. maculatus dorsalis, P. variegatus*

Distribution: eastern Mexico, Rio Grande, Conchos, Salado, Panuco, Axtla, Papaloapan and other rivers. Full length: male – 5.5 cm, female – 7 cm. Diet: live, artificial and plant foods. Community tank. Breeding tank: of 6- to 10-litre capacity with breeding trap for 1 female. Sexual dimorphism: the male is more brightly coloured and has a gonopodium. Sex ratio: 1 male : 5 females. Water: 19–24 °C; pH 7.0–7.5; half hard, fresh. Live-bearer: intervals between births 4–5 weeks. Feeding of fry: brine shrimp nauplii, finely-sifted zooplankton, artificial fry foods.

Young males bear a dark spot resembling a pregnancy mark on the flanks; this becomes paler and acquires a blue-green hue in older males. The females are very prolific – a single litter may number as many as 200 young. During the summer months the fish may be kept outdoors in a garden pool.

X. variatus has many colour forms: albinotic, red, tuxedo, gold-marigold, gold-tuxedo, marigold-tuxedo, gold wagtail, marigold-wagtail, black, etc. In many of these colour forms breeders have developed a high dorsal fin (high-finned varieties) and in others a coudal fin extended into a point or in the shape of a brush.

3 *Xiphophorus variatus* 'MARIGOLD PLATY'

This is the product of hybridization between *X. variatus* x *X. maculatus, X. variatus* x *X. helleri* and the further crossing of hybrids over a period of many years so that the name *X. variatus* is purely symbolic. It is a hybrid whose origin must be sought only in aquarium tanks.

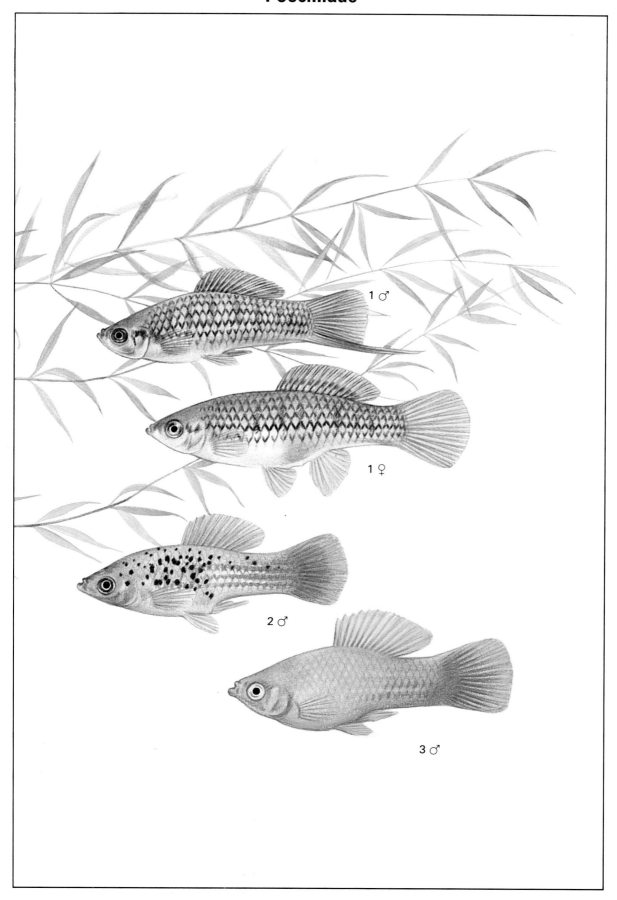

1 ♂

1 ♀

2 ♂

3 ♂

Family Goodeidae

The members of this family inhabit the water courses of the Mexican plateau, both slow-flowing waters as well as white waters with stony bottoms. The biotopes of the various species are practically all in populated areas with polluted water courses so that many are in danger of extinction.

The males have a copulating organ called a spermatopodium formed by the first rays of the anal fin which are joined together and separated from the hind end of the fin by a notch. Unlike the live-bearers of the Poeciliidae family the female must be inseminated anew for each litter. The embryos develop from eggs that have a relatively meagre yolk and take their nourishment from the mother's body. The nutrients are passed to the embryos via twisting rope-like organs (*trophotaeniae*), from the lining of the ovary (so-called ovarian placentation).

1 Butterfly Goodeid
Ameca splendens MILLER and FITZSIMONS, 1971

Distribution: Mexico. Full length: 10 cm. Diet: live, artificial and plant foods. Community tank. Breeding tank: for large-scale breeding a large aquarium with a capacity of 100 litres or more and a breeding trap for several females, otherwise a tank of 10-litre capacity for 1 female. Sexual dimorphism: the male has a bigger, dark-coloured dorsal fin, caudal fin edged yellow and black, anal fin likewise edged yellow and black and transformed into a spermatopodium; the sides of the body bear very dark, glittering scales. The female is more plainly coloured. Sex ratio: 1:1 or with a slight preponderance of males — in a larger group. Water: 22–25 °C; pH 7.0–8.0; fresh water that has been allowed to stand; add 1 teaspoon NaCl for every 10 litres of water (the fish are sensitive to sudden changes in the chemical composition of the water). Live-bearer: intervals between births 6–8 weeks. Feeding of fry: brine shrimp nauplii, finely sifted zooplankton, after a week supplemented by strained spinach.

There are usually 10 to 40 young to a litter. They are not pursued to any great degree by the adult fish.

2 Red-tailed Goodeid
Xenotoca eiseni RUTTER, 1896
Syn. *Characodon variatus, C. ferrugineus*

Distribution: Mexico — Río Grande de Santiago and tributaries round the city of Tepic. Full length: 10 cm. Diet: live as well as artificial foods, augmented by plant foods. Monospecies keeping tank with capacity of at least 100 litres. Breeding tank: of 10-litre capacity with breeding trap for 1 female. Sexual dimorphism: the male has a spermatopodium and the tail is coloured orange to the base of the caudal fin, in the female it is coloured light brown. Older males have a greatly arched dorsal and ventral contour. Sex ratio: 1 male : 2 females in a group. Water: 22–24 °C; pH 7.0–8.0; fresh; add 1 teaspoon NaCl for every 10 litres of water. Live-bearer: intervals between births 6–8 weeks. Feeding of fry: brine shrimp nauplii, finely sifted zooplankton.

X. eiseni is a threatened species listed in the Red Data Book. It is inadvisable to keep it together with other fish, for it attacks them and bites their fins.

In the females the area round the genital opening becomes swollen shortly before the birth of the offspring. There are 20 to 60 young to a litter and they are about 12 mm long.

Goodeidae

1 ♀

1 ♂

2 ♂

2 ♀

Typical of the members of this family (except for a single species – *Elassoma evergladei*) are the dorsal fins, the first of which is low with hard rays and the second higher with soft rays; the two are generally joined. The family includes North American fish inhabiting waters east of the Rocky Mountains. They dwell in clear waters with thick vegetation. All species hunt live foods. Their number includes fish that spawn in sand (psammophilic fish). The eggs are the colour of sand and become coated with grains of sand and hence invisible (natural protection of eggs). The vivid colouring of the young fish fades with advancing age. During the spawning period it is the female that is usually more intensely coloured.

1 Pygmy Sunfish
Elassoma evergladei JORDAN, 1884   Centrarchidae

Distribution: USA: North Carolina to southern Florida. Full length: 3.5 cm. Diet: small live foods. Monospecies keeping tank. Breeding tank: with capacity of at least 10 litres, finely-leaved plants. Sexual dimorphism: the male is dark to black with metallic glints on the scales, the dorsal and anal fin are relatively large; the female is plainer and fuller in the body. Sex ratio: 1:1 (may also spawn in groups). Breeding water: 18–20 °C; pH 7.0; dCH max. 2°. Eggs: incubation period 2–3 days. Feeding of fry: *Cyclops* and newly-hatched brine shrimp nauplii.

The fish may be wintered at a temperature falling as low as 8 °C and they can in summer tolerate temperatures of up to 30 °C. The female deposits about 60 eggs, mostly among plants. Adult fish take no notice of either the eggs or the fry and several generations of young fish generally reach maturity in their company. In commercial breeding, however, the breeder fish should be set up in pairs in 10-litre aquariums and moved to other, new tanks once a week. The fry should be poured off into a larger nursery tank. Young fish may be put outdoors in garden pools from April till September.

2 Black-banded Sunfish
Enneacanthus chaetodon (BAIRD, 1854)
Syn. *Pomotis chaetodon, Bryttus chaetodon, Apomotis chaetodon, Mesogonistius chaetodon*   Centrarchidae

Distribution: USA – New York, Maryland, New Jersey. Full length: 10 cm. Diet: live foods. Monospecies keeping tank. Breeding tank: of at least 50-litre capacity, light to sun-flooded, with 3–5 cm-thick layer of gravel on the bottom. Sexual dimorphism: imperceptible; during the spawning period the female has intensely dark markings. Sex ratio: 1:1. Breeding water: 18–20 °C; pH 7.0; dCH max. 2°. Eggs: glassy, faintly yellowish, incubation period 5 days. Feeding of fry: *Cyclops* or brine shrimp nauplii.

The fish live in environments with considerable variations in temperature during the course of the year. That is why they should be wintered at temperatures only slightly above freezing point (4 °C). At low temperatures they fall into a lethargic torpor and do not take food. In spring, as soon as the temperature rises above 14 °C, the males dig pits in the bottom and the females' dark markings become more conspicuous. At 18 °C the pairs spawn in the prepared pits. The female deposits up to 500 eggs which become coated with grains of sand and, thereby, invisible. The eggs are watched over by the male. The female should be removed from the tank after spawning and when the fry become free-swimming so should the male. Young fish thrive in sunlit tanks and grow rapidly if provided with sufficient live foods. Bigger fry may be put in an outdoor pool in summer. Keeping the fish in warm water during the year is not good for them.

1 ♂

1 ♀

2

1 Common Sunfish or Pumpkinseed Sunfish
Lepomis gibbosus LINNAEUS, 1758
Syn. *Perca gibbosa, Eupomotis aureus, E. gibbosus, Pomotis gibbosus,*
P. ravenelli, P. vulgaris, Sparus aureus

Centrarchidae

Distribution: USA — deeper rivers and large lakes in Florida and southern Texas. Introduced into Europe, where it causes damage to the eggs and fry of commercial fish. Full length: 20 cm. Diet: live foods. Monospecies keeping tank. Breeding tank: with capacity of at least 200 litres and gravel bottom. Sexual dimorphism: imperceptible; the male has a colourful spawning dress, the female is fuller in the body. Sex ratio: 1:1. Breeding water: 18—20 °C; pH 7.0—7.5; dCH 2°. Eggs: incubation period 5 days. Feeding of fry: *Cyclops* or brine shrimp nauplii.

During the spawning period the male digs a pit 30 cm in diameter in the gravel bottom with his caudal fin and vigorously defends the spawning site. The act of mating is preceded by a striking display. The female expels up to 1,000 eggs into the pit. She should be taken out of the tank after spawning and when the fry become free-swimming so should the male. Breeder fish kept in warm water throughout the year do not spawn. 12 °C is the optimum temperature in winter. The fish will survive the winter in a garden pool even at a temperature slightly above freezing.

Family Centropomidae

The members of this family are distributed in Africa, Asia and Australia. They are characterized by having two dorsal fins, the first with only hard spiny rays. The ventral fins are underneath the pectoral fins. Numerous species are glassily transparent. Many large fish are inhabitants of the sea, others live in the rivers and lakes of central Africa. Only a few small freshwater species are suitable for the aquarium.

2 Red-finned (Indian) Glassfish
Chanda ranga (HAMILTON-BUCHANAN, 1822)
Syn. *Ambassis lala, A. ranga, Chanda lala, Pseudambassis lala*

Centropomidae

Distribution: India, Burma, Thailand — fresh and brackish waters. Full length: 8 cm. Diet: live foods, primarily zooplankton. Monospecies keeping tank. Breeding tank: with a capacity of at least 20 litres, finely-leaved plants. Sexual dimorphism: the male is more colourful. Sex ratio: 1:1. Breeding water: 24—28 °C; pH 7.0—7.5; dCH 2°. Eggs: small, glassy, incubation period 20—24 hrs. Feeding of fry: difficult; only the smallest *Cyclops* nauplii, after five days brine shrimp nauplii.

The fish spawn among finely-leaved plants and are very prolific. Breeding is difficult in that the fry will take only the finest nauplii of specific species of *Cyclops*. They refuse rotatoria, infusoria and other substitute food and die of hunger. This critical period lasts five days. Besides this the fish are often attacked by the flagellate *Piscinoodinium pillularis*. Treatment is difficult because they are sensitive to changes in the chemical composition of the water. That is why most fish in Europe's aquariums are from Thailand and only a negligible percentage are aquarium-bred.

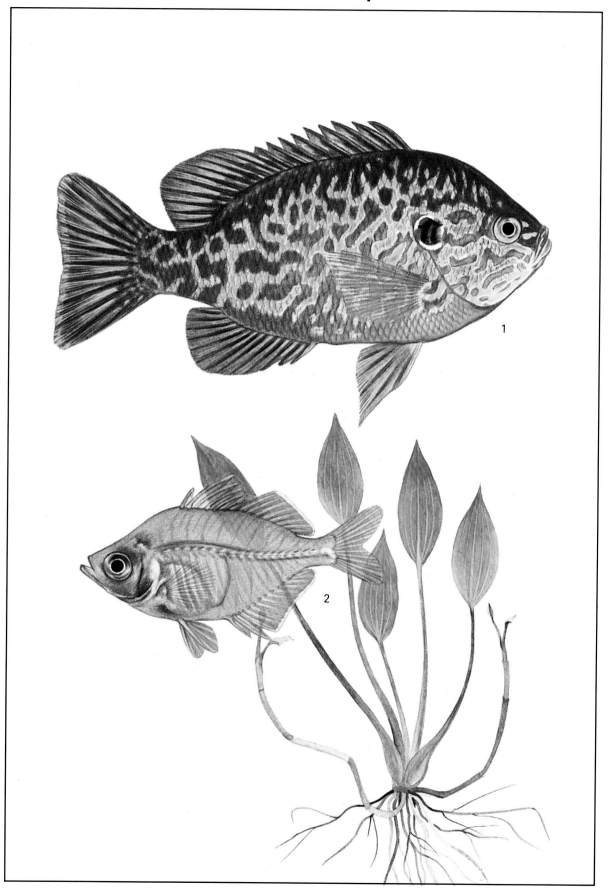

Family Monodactylidae

This family comprises only one genus: *Monodactylus* Lacépéde, 1802. The fish are found on the west coast of Africa (*M. sebae*) and on all the coasts of the three continents bordering the Indian Ocean (*M. argenteus* (Linnaeus, 1758)) and *M. falciformis* Lacépéde, 1802. All three species dwell in shallow waters near the coast, when young in the mouths of rivers, when grown in salt and brackish water. They are fast and enduring swimmers, characterized by their high body which is strongly compressed laterally.

1 Sebae Silverfish

Monodactylus sebae (CUVIER and VALENCIENNES, 1846)
Syn. *Psettus sebae*   Monodactylidae

Distribution: coast of west Africa. Full length: 20 cm. Diet: live foods, augmented by artificial and vegetable foods. Monospecies keeping tank. Breeding tank: of 500- to 1,000-litre capacity with sandy bottom covered with aquatic plants and with plenty of room to swim about. Sexual dimorphism: monomorphic fish. Spawn-ripe females have a fuller belly. Sex ratio: set up the fish in a shoal. Breeding water: fresh; 26–27 °C; pH 7.5–8.0; half-hard to hard; add non-iodized kitchen salt (NaCl) – 1 teaspoon for every 4 litres of water. Eggs: pelagic, ⌀ 0.6–0.9 mm, incubation period 24 hrs./26 °C. Feeding of fry: not entirely solved as yet. The fry are capable of catching only infusoria; when this is fed to them a large percentage die of hunger nevertheless. It seems that only the Japanese ichthyologist H. Azuma has succeeded in breeding these fish in captivity – in the early seventies.

M. sebae attains sexual maturity at the age of 2 years. In nature it dwells in open waters and, therefore, the manner of spawning is the kind typical of pelagic fish: a large number of eggs and sperm are expelled within a few seconds into open water. The eggs, and later the larvae, become part of the plankton. The larvae are extremely small.

2 Common Fingerfish

Monodactylus argenteus (LINNAEUS, 1758)
Syn. *Chaetodon argenteus, Acanthopodus argenteus, Centogaster rhombeus, Centropodus rhombeus, Monodactylus rhombeus, Psettus argenteus, P. rhombeus, Scomber rhombeus*   Monodactylidae

Distribution: the coasts of Africa, Asia and Australia bordering the Indian Ocean, shallow sea and brackish coastal waters. Young fish dwell in the mouths of rivers. Full length: 23 cm. Diet: smaller live foods. Monospecies keeping tank with capacity of 500 litres or more, sandy-rocky bottom and room for swimming about. Breeding tank: same as keeping tank. Sexual dimorphism: monomorphic fish. Keep the fish in a shoal. Water: fresh; 26 °C; pH 7.5–8.0; half-hard to hard, later brackish to sea water with density of 1.020–1.023; the fish must be gradually conditioned to the change. Nothing is known about the reproduction of this species, which apparently will be the same as for *M. sebae*.

The first dorsal and anal fin rays are greatly extended and covered with scales. The fish are timid and readily take fright. As they grow older the young fish lose their black and gold colouring.

Monodactylidae

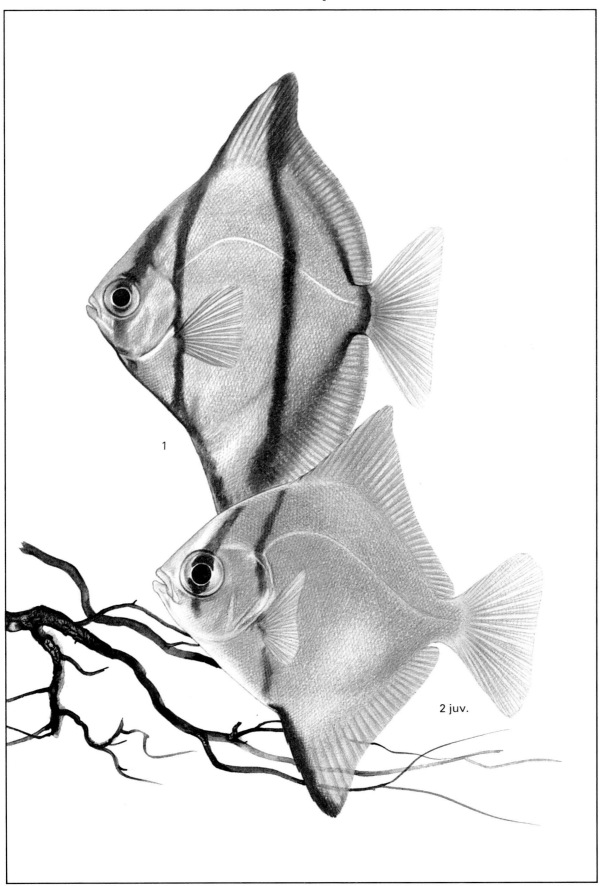

1

2 juv.

Family Scatophagidae

These are fish of high body build, strongly compressed laterally, and nearly disc-shaped. Adult fish inhabit the coastal waters of the Indian Ocean, young fish are found at the mouths of large rivers.

The body is covered with small, comb-shaped scales extending into the dorsal and caudal fins. In young specimens it is protected by bony plates on the head and back. The mouth is small and equipped with small teeth arranged in rows. There are four known species belonging to a single genus – *Scatophagus*. Distinguishing between them is difficult; their coloration is extremely variable.

1 Argus or Scat
Scatophagus argus (LINNAEUS, 1766)
Syn. *Chaetodon argus, Ch. astromaculatus, Ch. pairatalis, Cacodoxus argus, Ephippus argus, Sargus maculatus, Scatophagus macronotus, S. ornatus*

Scatophagidae

Distribution: Indonesia and the Philippines, coastal zone and reefs. Full length: 30 cm. Diet: all digestible foods, including aquatic plants, boiled rice, oat flakes, etc. Monospecies keeping tank, roomy, equipped with efficient filters. Sexual dimorphism: monomorphic fish. Water: fresh, 20–28 °C; pH 7.5–8.5, gradually add sea salt; adult fish should be kept in sea water with density of up to 1.020–1.023 (they are sensitive to higher concentrations of nitrites). When buying these fish check on the chemical composition of the water in the dealer's tank and adjust the water in the new tank accordingly. No particulars are known about the reproduction of these fish.

Peaceful school fish feeding in the wild on excrement and waste matter. The embryo passes through the metamorphosis; the characteristic features of the larval stadia *Tholichthys* – large head with a long bony armour and a spine on both sides of the neck. There are many questions concerning the colour form *'rubrifrons'* (1a).

Family Toxotidae

This family contains only the single genus *Toxotes* with five known species found in fresh, brackish and sea water near the coast – Red Sea, India, Sri Lanka to southeast, Asia, New Guinea and northern Australia.

2 Archer Fish
Toxotes jaculatrix (PALLAS, 1766)
Syn. *Sciaena jaculatrix, Labrus jaculatrix, Toxotex jaculator*

Toxotidae

Distribution: southern coast of the entire Asian continent to northern Australia, in sea, brackish as well as fresh waters near the coast. Full length: 24 cm. Diet: live foods, chiefly insects, insect larvae, and small fish. Monospecies keeping tank with capacity of at least 500 litres, shallow, with large water surface. Sexual dimorphism: unknown. The fish should be of the same size and kept in a larger shoal. Breeding water: 26–30 °C; pH 7.0–8.5; rather hard; add 1 tablespoon sea salt or NaCl for every 10 litres of water. So far this species has not been bred in captivity.

The fish take food mostly from the surface. A peculiar characteristic is their ability to shoot down a resting insect from a distance of up to 150 cm by spitting a thin stream of water with great violence. This is made possible by a groove in the upper jaw to which the tongue is pressed to form a tube, through which water is ejected from the mouth under pressure by the contraction of the gill covers.

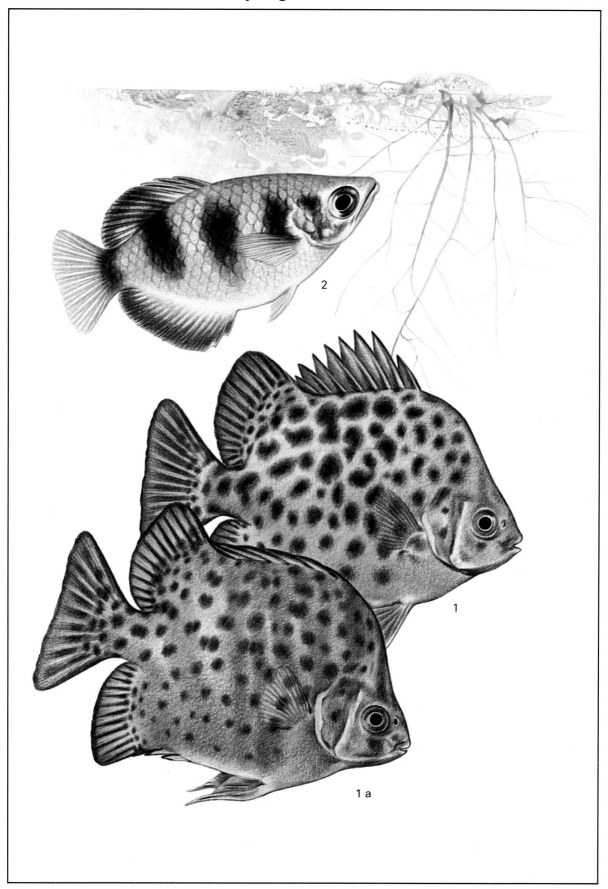

Family Nandidae

Most of the species belonging to this ancient family are already extinct. The remaining species are distributed in South America, Africa and southeast Asia. All are predators. The jaws can be extended far forward and the fish are capable of swallowing prey three-quarters of their own length. The strongly compressed body and marbled pattern, or the ability to create the impression of dead leaves drifting in the water not only protects them from natural enemies, but also enables them to come close to their prey undetected. The first part of the dorsal fin with hard spines is connected with the second part of the dorsal fin with branching rays.

1 Schomburgk's Leaf Fish
Polycentrus schomburgki MÜLLER and TROSCHEL, 1848
Syn. *Polycentrus tricolor*

Nandidae

Distribution: Guyana, Venezuela, Trinidad. Full length: 10 cm. Diet: more robust live foods, chiefly fish. Monospecies keeping tank. Breeding tank: with capacity of 100 litres, broad-leaved plants and sufficient cavities. Sexual dimorphism: the male is bigger, during the spawning period he becomes velvety black, the hind end of the dorsal, anal and caudal fins is also black. The female is more cloudily coloured, during the spawning period she turns a very light hue and is fuller in the body. Sex ratio: 1:1. Breeding water: 28 °C; pH 7.0; dCH 2°; dGH max. 20°. Eggs: small, yellowish, incubation period 3 days. Feeding of fry: brine shrimp nauplii, later sifted zooplankton.

The fish spawn in cavities or on the underside of leaves, also on roots and stones. The female deposits 300 to 600 eggs. Spawning takes place at night and lasts two to five hours. Remove the female after spawning. The newly-hatched fry hang from a thread at the spawning site. Endogenous nutrition lasts five days and as soon as it is over remove the male from the tank. Feed the fry three to four times a day.

2 Leaf Fish
Monocirrhus polyacanthus HECKEL, 1840
Syn. *Monocirrhus mimophyllus*

Nandidae

Distribution: Amazon region, Peru, Guyana – in slow-flowing and standing waters. Full length: 10 cm. Diet: live foods, chiefly small fish. Monospecies keeping tank. Breeding tank: of 100-litre capacity, generously planted, containing retreats and supplied with diffused lighting. Sexual dimorphism: monomorphic fish. Sex ratio: 1:1. Breeding water: 25–28 °C; pH 6.0–6.5; dCH 0°; dGH < 10°. Eggs: ∅ 1.2 mm, anchored to the substrate by a long stalk, incubation period 60 hrs./28 °C. Feeding of fry: brine shrimp nauplii, sifted zooplankton.

Predatory fish, consuming large amounts of food. Poor swimmer. It is aided in its pursuit of prey by its mimicry – in shape and coloration it resembles a dead leaf. The body is of high build, strongly compressed laterally, egg-shaped. The head is drawn out into a point, the jaws can be extended far forward. The female deposits up to 300 eggs on a previously cleaned object. They are cared for by the male. Feeding mosquito larvae promotes the growth of young fish.

Nandidae

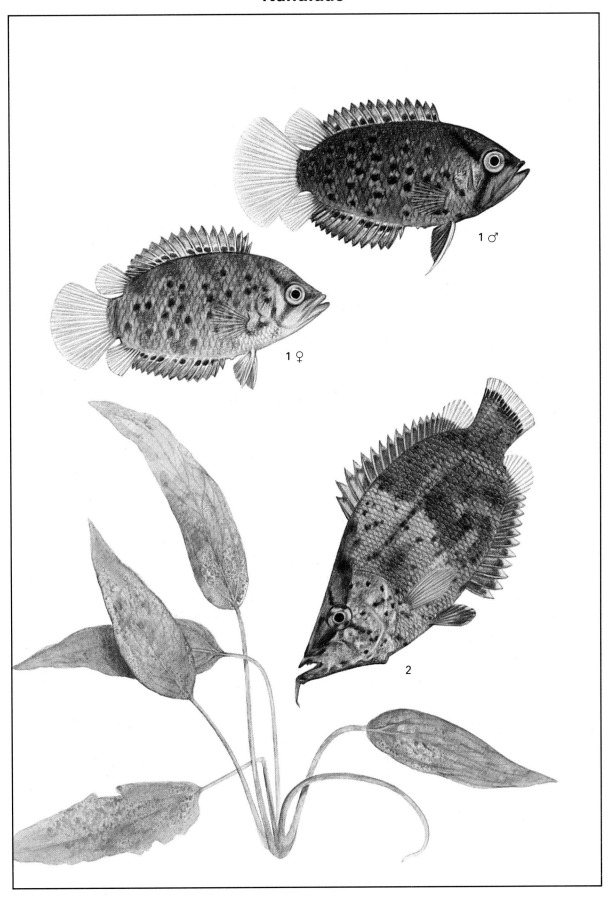

1 ♂

1 ♀

2

Family Badidae

This family comprises only one genus: *Badis,* with only a single species: *Badis badis* (monotypic family and monotypic genus). Originally this species was classed in the Nandidae family, but on the basis of the works of Barlow and Barlow, Liem and Wickler, it was put in a separate family. This decision was supported by a great many different characteristics. *B. badis* has been differentiated into three subspecies: *B. badis badis, B. badis burmanicus* Ahl, 1936, and *B. badis siamensis* Klauzewitz, 1957.

1 Badis
Badis badis (HAMILTON–BUCHANAN, 1822)
Syn. *Labrus badis, Badis buchanani*   Badidae

◁
●
Distribution: standing waters in India. Full length: 8 cm. Diet: live foods. Monospecies keeping tank. Breeding tank: with capacity of 10 litres per pair, notched flowerpot and several plants on the bottom. Sexual dimorphism: the male has a metallic sheen with many colour variations (he changes colour rapidly) and larger fins. Older males are slightly bow-shaped with convex back and concave belly region. The female is smaller, considerably plainer in colour and has a conspicuously convex belly. Sex ratio: 1:1. Breeding water: 26 °C; pH 6.5; dCH < 1°. Eggs: clear, sticky, ∅ 0.8 mm, incubation period 48 hrs. Feeding of fry: brine shrimp nauplii.

Most males seek a spawning site in a cavity, some dig shallow pits in the bottom substrate. They defend their spawning sites. The females are very prolific, though the opposite is sometimes stated in the literature – a young female measuring only 2.5 cm in length can deposit 200 or more eggs. Remove the female after spawning. The male watches over the eggs, but his presence is not necessary. The fry switch over to exogenous nutrition after one week. They remain near the bottom and are inactive. Except for the black spots on the head and tail section they are transparent and thus readily escape notice.

2 Burmese Badis
Badis badis burmanicus AHL, 1936   Badidae

◁
●
Distribution: Burma – streams. Full length: 7 cm. Care and breeding of this brownish-red, dark-spotted subspecies will apparently be the same as for *Badis badis.* It is only rarely kept in aquariums.

1

2

More than 900 species of this family are distributed in South and Central America, some 700 are found in Africa and Madagascar, and only three species originate from Asia. Many African lake cichlids are endemic species not found elsewhere. In the wild cichlids inhabit mostly coastal waters where they have their fixed territories which they defend against intruders. The eggs are laid close beside each other on stones or leaves, in sand or in cavities.

Both partners (or at least one) have a strong parental instinct; they care for the eggs and later also the fry. Some species even care for the eggs and fry in the mouth (mouth-brooders).

The body structure varies greatly in the various species because the fish had to adapt to varied environments during the course of evolution. The hard-rayed and soft-rayed parts of the dorsal fin are fused together; the anal and dorsal fins are often greatly elongated in the males. The lateral line usually stops in the middle of the body.

1 Dolphin Cichlid
Aequidens itanyi PUYO, 1943

Cichlidae

Distribution: French Guiana, lower reaches of the Itany River and its tributaries. Full length: 15 cm (male). Diet: mainly robust live foods, may be augmented by granulated foods. Monospecies keeping tank (in a mixed aquarium only with cichlids of like characteristics). Breeding tank: of 200-litre capacity with flat stones and hiding possibilities on the bottom. Sexual dimorphism: the male is larger, his dorsal and anal fins are drawn out into a point. Sex ratio: 1:1. Breeding water: 24–28 °C; pH 6.0–7.0; dCH max. 2°. Eggs: whitish, incubation period 42–56 hrs. Feeding of fry: nauplii of brine shrimp or *Cyclops*.

The fish spawn in open water on the bottom on flat stones which they have previously cleaned. The female deposits 400 to 500 eggs; she has a very thick ovipositor. The fish are aggressive during spawning. Both partners care for the eggs and fry. It is recommended to let a greater number of young fish grow up together so pairs can mate according to preference when they become sexually mature.

2 Golden Cichlid
Aequidens awani HASEMAN, 1911

Cichlidae

Distribution: eastern Bolivia and western Mato Grosso – Río Guaporé. Full length: 20 cm. Diet: more robust live foods. Monospecies keeping tank (or together with cichlids of like characteristics). Breeding tank: with capacity of 200 litres or more, flat stones and sufficient hiding places on the bottom. Sexual dimorphism: the dorsal fin of the female has 1 to 2 light spots edged with luminescent green in the middle of the base. Sex ratio: 1:1. Breeding water: 25–28 °C; pH 6.5–7.0; dCH max. 2°; dGH max. 10°. Eggs: incubation period? Feeding of fry: brine shrimp nauplii.

This species is only rarely kept in aquariums. It is a peaceful fish; specimens kept singly do not thrive and are shy. Paired fish spawn in open water either on flat stones or in pits dug in the sand. Both partners care for the eggs and fry. A clean tank and fresh water promote the good health and well-being of the fish.

1

2

1 Blue Acara or Blue-spot Cichlid
Aequidens pulcher (GILL, 1858)
Syn. *Cichlasoma pulchrum, Aequidens latifrons*

Distribution: Trinidad, northern Venezuela, Colombia, Panama. Full length: 20 cm. Diet: live foods, may be augmented with artificial foods. Monospecies keeping tank. Breeding tank: with capacity of 100 litres per pair, large flat stones on the bottom (lithophilous fish). Sexual dimorphism: extremely slight; the male's dorsal and anal fin are drawn out longer in an arc round the caudal fin, the female has smaller fins and a more intense spawning coloration — the transverse bands on the sides turn black. Sex ratio: 1:1. Breeding water: 24 °C; pH 6.5–7.0; dCH max. 2°. Eggs: yellowish, incubation period 2–3 days/24–26 °C. Feeding of fry: *Cyclops* or brine shrimp nauplii.

The female deposits approximately 500 relatively large eggs on a flat stone. Both parents take turns tending the eggs, fanning them with their pectoral fins so that they are kept in a constant current of fresh, aerated water. If the bottom of the tank is covered with gravel they scoop out depressions in it and transfer the newly-hatched fry to these pits; if there is no gravel they move the fry to various parts of the tank. After five days the fry begin exogenous nutrition and their growth is rapid. After 14 days they may be given finely sifted zooplankton. As soon as the young fish reach a length of 1 cm the parent fish may be taken out of the tank. Sexual maturity is attained when they are about 7 cm long.

2 Red-breasted Cichlid
Aequidens dorsiger (HECKEL, 1840)
Syn. *Acara dorsigera, A. flavilabrus, Astronotus dorsigerus*

Distribution: Paraguay River — locality: Villa María and Puerto Suarez in Bolivia's border region. Full length: 12 cm. Diet: live foods, may be augmented by artificial foods. Monospecies keeping tank. Breeding tank: with capacity of 50 litres per pair; put flat stones and flower pots with bottoms knocked out inside. Sexual dimorphism: the male is more colourful and larger, with dorsal and anal fin drawn out longer. Sex ratio: 1:1. Breeding water: 25–28 °C; pH 6.5–7.0; dCH max. 2°; dGH max. 10°; fresh (through-flow tank). Eggs: minute, glassy, incubation period 40-48 hrs., depending on the temperature. Feeding of fry; brine shrimp nauplii.

This species differs from the similar *A. curviceps* in coloration, particularly during the spawning period. The Brazilian name *'Acara Bobo'*, meaning 'stupid cichlid' refers to the fact that it is easily caught in the hand. These are peaceful, timid fish, but become aggressive during the spawning period. They are also monogamous and very attentive in their care of the eggs and fry. The female deposits up to 1,000 eggs. When the fry hatch the parent fish move them to depressions scooped-out in the bottom. They begin exogenous nutrition in four days. These fish are susceptible to various diseases. A greater concentration of nitrites causes exophthalmy (protruding eyes) followed by blindness. Fresh water and cleanliness are preventative measures.

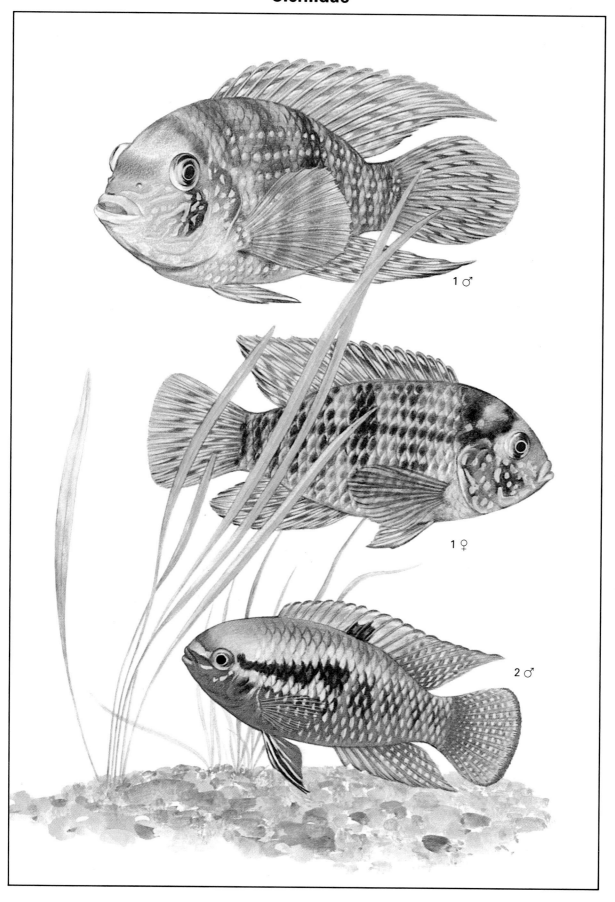

1 ♂

1 ♀

2 ♂

1 Keyhole Cichlid or Maroni Cichlid

Aequidens maronii (STEINDACHNER, 1882)

Syn. *Acara maroni*

Cichlidae

Distribution: Guyana. Full length: male – 10 cm, female slightly smaller. Diet: live foods, may be augmented by artificial foods. Monospecies keeping tank. Breeding tank: with capacity of 50–100 litres per pair; put flat stones and flowerpots with bottoms knocked out inside. Sexual dimorphism: very slight, the dorsal and anal fins of the male are longer. Sex ratio: 1:1. Breeding water: 24–28 °C; pH 6.5–7.0; dCH max. 2°. Eggs: incubation period 5 days. Feeding of fry: first week brine shrimp nauplii, later sifted zooplankton, from the third week chopped tubifex worms.

Peaceable, timid fish. They spawn on flat stones, preferably in places that are not exposed. The female deposits up to 400 eggs. The fish are monogamous and tend their fry for a long time. As soon as the young fish reach a length of 1 cm they may be moved to a separate tank. If generously fed live foods their growth is rapid. Sudden fright causes the fish to change their colours.

2 Spotted Cichlid

Aequidens curviceps (AHL, 1924)

Syn. *Acara curviceps*

Cichlidae

Distribution: Amazon basin, quite sheltered spots with a slight current. Full length: male – 9 cm, female – 7 cm. Diet: live foods. Monospecies keeping tank. Breeding tank: with capacity of 50 litres per pair; put flat stones and flowerpots with bottoms knocked out inside. Sexual dimorphism: the male is more colourful and bigger, and his dorsal and anal fins are more pointed. Sex ratio: 1:1. Breeding water: 25–28 °C; pH 6.5–7.0; dCH max. 2°, dGH 6°, continuously fresh (through-flow tank). Eggs: incubation period 4 days. Feeding of fry: brine shrimp nauplii.

Generally peaceful fish, but aggressive during the spawning period. They are monogamous and are very attentive in their care of the eggs and fry. Young pairs, however, generally eat the first batches of eggs. A fully developed female deposits up to 1,000 eggs on a flat stone. In the absence of a male two females may spawn together, as often happens in numerous other species of cichlids – a case of substitute, infertile spawning. The fish are susceptible to diseases, being particularly sensitive to nitrites, which combine with the haemoglobin in the fish's blood, causing listlessness often accompanied by exophthalmy (protruding eyes) and ensuing blindness. Prevention of the disease consists chiefly in providing the fish with fresh water and a healthy environment.

1 ♀

1 ♂

2 ♂

2 ♀

1 Agassiz' Dwarf Cichlid
Apistogramma agassizi (STEINDACHNER, 1875)
Syn. *Biotodoma agassizi, Geophagus agassizi, Mesops agassizi*

Cichlidae

◁
●
Distribution: flowing sections of the Amazon River and its southern tributaries in Bolivia and Brazil, upper reaches of the Paraná and Paraguay Rivers. Full length: 8 cm. Diet: live foods. Monospecies keeping tank (in a mixed aquarium only with small species of cichlids). Breeding tank: with capacity of 50 litres per pair, sufficient hiding places and cavities, diffused light. Sexual dimorphism: the male is larger and more colourful, his dorsal and anal fins are bigger, the caudal fin drawn out into a point and coloured. Sex ratio: 1:1. Breeding water: 26–28 °C; pH 6.5; dCH max. 1°. Eggs: oval, cherry-coloured, incubation period 3 days/28 °C. Feeding of fry: brine shrimp nauplii.

The fish change colour as well as markings under various conditions, a characteristic typical of all species of the genus *Apistogramma.* The females of various species are similar and easily confused. The female deposits up to 300 eggs on the sides of cavities. Some females eat the eggs, usually 24 hours after spawning. The reasons for this may be unsuitable water, disturbances in the environment, a too young female, or simply the female's inclination to do so. The eggs may be transferred to separate 3-litre tanks and further care and rearing may take place without the presence of the parent fish. Young fish grow slowly even when generously fed.

2 Reitzig's Dwarf Cichlid or Yellow Dwarf Cichlid
Apistogramma reitzigi AHL, 1939

Cichlidae

◁
●
Distribution: middle reaches of the Paraguay River. Full length: male – 7 cm, female – 5 cm. Diet: live foods. Monospecies (or monogeneric) keeping tank. Breeding tank: with capacity of 50 litres per pair, sufficient hiding places and cavities, diffused light. Sexual dimorphism: the male is larger, his caudal and anal fins bigger. Sex ratio: 1:1. Breeding water: 24–26 °C; pH 6.5; dGH < 1°; dCH < 10°; filtered through peat. Eggs: relatively large, oval, cherry-coloured, incubation period 5 days. Feeding of fry: brine shrimp nauplii.

There are doubts about the validity of the specific name. The name *reitzigi* was given to it by Ahl in honour of the Berlin importer Reitzig.

The predominant colour of the fish is yellow. Several distinct, dark, transverse and longitudinal streaks appear when the fish are excited; these vary according to the given situation – e.g. when the fish is at rest, suddenly startled, threatening another fish, displaying, or watching over the fry. The female deposits 100 to 150 eggs on the sides of the cavity. The eggs and fry are cared for by the female, so the male may be removed after spawning. If necessary the eggs may be incubated without the presence of the female. The growth of the young fish is slow.

1 ♂

1 ♀

2 ♀

2 ♂

1 Borelli's Dwarf Cichlid
Apistogramma borelli (REGAN, 1906)
Syn. *Heterogramma borelli, Apistogramma ritenze, A. reitzigi*

Cichlidae

◁ Distribution: Brazil – rivers in the territory of Mato Grosso. Full length: male – 8 cm, female – 5 cm. Diet: live foods. Keeping tank: monospecies or monogeneric. Breeding tank: with capacity of 50 litres per pair, sufficient refuges and cavities, diffused lighting. Sexual dimorphism: the male is larger with larger dorsal, caudal and anal fins. Sex ratio: 1:1. Breeding water: 26 °C; pH 6.5; dCH < 1°; filtered through peat. Eggs: oval, cherry-red, incubation period three days. Feeding of fry: brine shrimp nauplii.

The predominant basic colour of the fish is yellow; several dark transverse stripes and longitudinal bands appear when the fish are ex-

cited; these change according to the given situation: e.g. when they are calm, suddenly frightened, threatening, displaying, or watching over the batch of eggs. *A. borelli* requires a peaceful environment and temperature that does not fall below 24 °C. The female deposits 50 to 100 eggs on the side of a cavity. After spawning the female chases the male away and takes over the care of the eggs and later the fry. The eggs may be incubated without the female. If the fish spawn in water that is not suitable the eggs must be transferred within half an hour into breeding water. The eggs may be scraped off the substrate with a brush.

2 *Apistogramma kleei* MEINKEN, 1964

Cichlidae

○ Distribution: Brazil, northern Amazon basin. Full length: male – 8.5 cm, the female is smaller. ● Diet: live foods, may be augmented by artificial foods. Keeping tank: monospecies or monogeneric. Breeding tank: with capacity of 50 litres per pair, sufficient refuges and cavities, diffused lighting. Sexual dimorphism: the male is larger, more colourful, darker, and rusty-brown towards the upper side; his fins are greatly developed, particularly the dorsal fin with extended first rays. The female is greyish-yellow, the coloration of the longitudinal band changing in intensity according to her mood – it may also disappear altogether, being replaced by a black spot in the centre of the body. This is typical of the females of other species of *Apistogramma* as well and they may be easily confused when examined only superficially. Sex ratio: 1:1. Breeding water: 26 °C; pH 6.5; dCH < 1°, filtered

through peat. Eggs: oval, cherry-red, incubation period 80 hours. Feeding of fry: brine shrimp nauplii in small amounts several times daily.

The name was given this species by Meinken in honour of the American Albert J. Klee who gave him the fish for the purpose of determining its identity. A monogamous species; the females attach the eggs to the tops of cavities. The larvae begin exogenous nutrition five days after hatching. The fish attain sexual maturity at the age of six months.

A. kleei can be easily confused with the species *A. sweglesi* Meinken, 1961. They differ in the number of hard rays in the dorsal fin (*A. kleei* has 15, *A. sweglesi* 16). According to Kullander *A. kleei, A. klauzewitz* and *A. sweglesi* are the synonyms of the species *A. bitaeniata* Pellegrin, 1936.

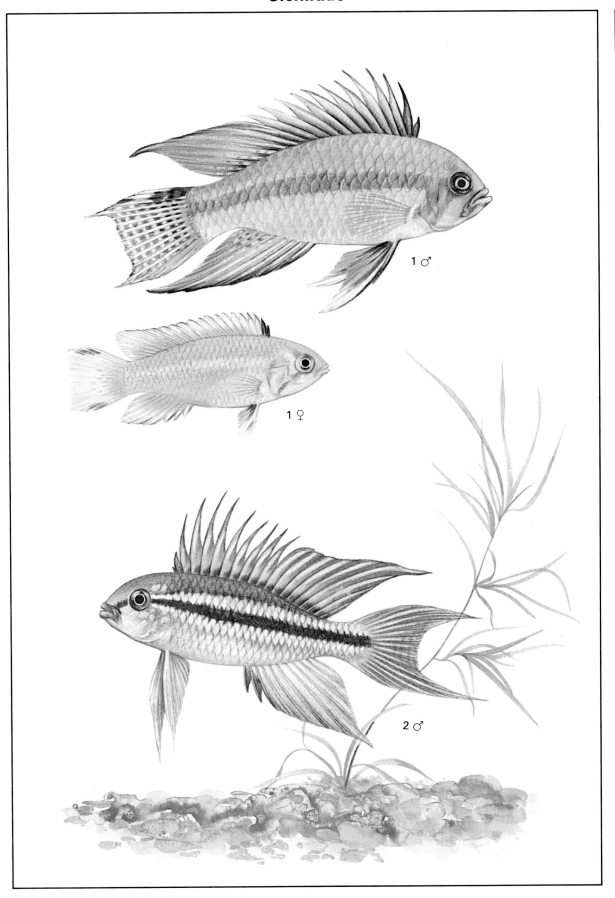

1 ♂

1 ♀

2 ♂

1 Oscar Cichlid, Peacock Cichlid or Velvet Cichlid

Astronotus ocellatus (CUVIER, 1829)

Syn. *Acara ocellatus, Acara crassipinnis, Cychla rubroocellata, Hygrogonus ocellatus, Lobotes ocellatus*

◁

●

Distribution: South America: Amazon, Negro, Paraná and Paraguay rivers. Full length: 35 cm. Diet: live foods (fish, snails, earthworms, pieces of fish, beef and poultry). Monospecies keeping tank. Breeding tank: with capacity of 300–500 litres per pair, flat stones on the bottom. Sexual dimorphism: very slight, (monomorphous fish). Sex ratio: 1:1. Breeding water: 24–28 °C; pH 6.5–7.0; dCH < 2°; fresh. Eggs: barrel-shaped, 2 × 1.5 mm, dingy white, incubation period 3 days. Feeding of fry: brine shrimp nauplii, finely sifted zooplankton, after five days finely chopped tubifex worms.

Brood pairs are best selected from young fish reared together from a size of 3 to 4 cm. As soon as they mature sexually (when they attain a length of about 12 cm) they begin to pair of their own accord, cleaning stones together and driving off other fish. Each such pair should be put in a separate tank. *A. ocellatus* is a lithophilous fish (fond of stones). Sexual maturation of the brood fish is promoted by feeding them young molluscs of the genus *Ampullaria* (apple snails) with shell less than 2 cm in diameter. Young females deposit about 300 eggs, older females as many as 2,000. Newly-hatched fry are not very developed and have a large yolk sac. The period of endogenous nutrition lasts five days. If the parent fish show a tendency towards cannibalism (possible with young pairs, limited space) the stone with the eggs should be moved to a separate tank. If the eggs are located on the bottom or some other fixed object suck them up with a small hose about 10 mm in diameter. They should be treated with methylene blue. The fry, coloured black and white, grow very quickly.

2 *Astronotus ocellatus* – 'Red Oscar', red form

◁

●

When the 'Red Oscar' first appeared on the market it not only created a sensation but also raised numerous conjectures as to its origin. Many believed it was a new species. These conjectures were put to rest by Dr. H. R. Axelrod in an article he wrote for the *Tropical Fish Hobbyist* magazine in 1970, in which he states that Red Oscars were developed as early as 1966 by Charoen Pattabougs, a Bangkok (Thailand) breeder, who, by lengthy selective breeding, genetically fixed this form so that the offspring of brood fish are 100 per cent red. Because the manner of reproduction and fecundity are the same as in the wild form, Red Oscars are propagated on a large scale on Thai fish farms and imported to the USA and Europe in large numbers.

1

1 juv.

2

1 Emerald Cichlid
Cichlasoma temporale (GÜNTHER, 1862)
Syn. *Cichlasoma hellabrunni, C. crassum*

◁
●
Distribution: Amazon basin, Guyana. Full length: 30 cm. Diet: more robust live foods. Monospecies keeping tank. Breeding tank: with capacity of 500 litres, flat stones on the bottom. Sexual dimorphism: monomorphic fish; older males have more extended dorsal and anal fins, a protruding pad of fat on the forehead and brighter colours during the spawning period. Sex ratio: 1:1. Breeding water: 24–28 °C; pH 6.5–7.0; dCH max. 2°. Eggs: incubation period? Feeding of fry: brine shrimp nauplii, finely sifted zooplankton.

A quiet, peaceable species. The brood fish spawn in open water on a firm object. Both partners watch over the eggs and fry. The young fish grow slowly.

According to W. Staeck, who acknowledges the nomenclature in the heading, *C. arnoldi* Ahl, 1936 and *C. coryphaenoides* (Heckel, 1840) are closely related to this species. According to H. J. Mayland *C. temporale* is a synonym for *C. coryphaenoides;* on the other hand he considers *C. hellabrunni* Ladiges, 1942 and *C. crassum* (Steindachner, 1875) to be separate, individual species.

2 *Cichlasoma citrinellum* (GÜNTHER, 1864)
Syn. *Astronotus basilaris, A. citrinellus, Heros basilaris, H. citrinellus, Cichlasoma basilare, C. granadense*

◁
●
Distribution: Central America, throughout a large territory in lakes with differing chemical compositions, namely Lake Nicaragua, Managua, Xiloa, Apoyo, Apoyeque, Masaya, Yoya and Tiscapa. Full length: up to 30 cm. Diet: more robust live foods and granulated foods. Monospecies keeping tank. Breeding tank: with capacity of 500 litres or more, flat stones, hiding places, and 5 to 10 cm layer of sand on the bottom. Sexual dimorphism: older males have a protruding pad of fat on the forehead, females have a more pointed head and are usually smaller. Sex ratio: 1:1. Breeding water: 24–26 °C; pH 6.5–7.5; dCH max. 2°; dGH 10°; small deviations in the chemical composition of the water do not matter. Eggs: ∅ 1 mm, light brown, transparent, incubation period 65 hrs./25 °C. Feeding of fry: brine shrimp nauplii, later sifted zooplankton and chopped tubifex worms in generous amounts.

Because the various lake localities are distributed over a relatively large territory the fish from the separate localities are variously coloured: they may be yellowish white, lemon white, yellowish orange, as well as dark grey with stripes – similar to the juvenile coloration. They begin to acquire the yellow colouring when they are 10 cm long. Adult fish are very aggressive, even towards unripe females. It is, therefore, recommended to keep the sexes separate, always one specimen to a tank. When the female is spawn-ripe introduce the male into her tank, not vice versa. It is necessary to keep an eye on the spawning pair. The eggs are deposited on a firm object in open water. Both partners watch over the fry. The female transfers the newly-hatched fry to one of the previously prepared pits. In about five days the fry become free-swimming. It is recommended to remove the parent fish after 10 days.

1

2 ♀

2 ♂

1 Chanchito Cichlid or Chameleon Cichlid
Cichlasoma facetum (JENYNS, 1842)

Syn. *Acara faceta, Astronotus facetus, A. acaroides, A. autochthon, A. oblongus,*
Cichlasoma oblongum, C. facetus, Heros acaroides, H. facetus, H. autochthon,
H. oblongus, H. jenynsii, Chromis facetus, Ch. oblonga

Cichlidae

Distribution: southern Brazil, Paraguay, northern Argentina, Uruguay – standing and slow-flowing waters. Full length: 30 cm. Diet: live foods, particularly small fish and earthworms, may be augmented by artificial foods. Monospecies keeping tank. Breeding tank: with capacity of 300 litres or more per pair, about 5 cm layer of sand on the bottom, sufficient refuges amongst stones or flowerpots with bottom knocked out. Sexual dimorphism: monomorphous fish; during the spawning period the male's colours become more intense, his genital papilla is pointed and extends hindward at an angle, the female's genital papilla is rounded and extends straight downward. Sex ratio: 1:1. Breeding water: 25–27 °C; pH 6.5–7.0; dCH max. 2°. Eggs: incubation period 3 days. Feeding of fry: nauplii of brine shrimp or *Cyclops*. First propagated in 1894 at the Matte breeding centre in Lankwitz.

One of the first cichlids known to aquarists, now no longer kept in aquariums. Very tame in captivity. The fish do a great deal of digging in the bottom substrate. The female deposits 300 to 1,000 eggs on a firm object that has been cleaned beforehand. When they hatch the fry are transferred to scooped-out depressions close to the spawning site. Parental care lasts six to eight weeks.

2 Texas Cichlid
Cichlasoma cyanoguttatum (BAIRD and GIRARD, 1854)

Syn. *Herichthys cyanoguttatus, Heros cyanoguttatus, H. temporalis, Neetroplus carpinitis*

Cichlidae

Distribution: northeastern Mexico and Texas. Full length: 30 cm. Diet: live and artificial foods. Monospecies keeping tank. Breeding tank: with capacity of 200 litres or more, bottom covered with a layer of coarse gravel and with several heavy flat stones arranged to form a cavity into which it is possible to see well. Sexual dimorphism: extremely slight; older males have protruding pads of fat on the forehead. A species with extremely variable coloration. Sex ratio: 1:1. Breeding water: 24–26 °C; pH 7.0; dCH < 2°. The temperature of the water is an important factor in incubation – at temperatures below 24 °C and above 30 °C there is a sharp increase in the mortality of the eggs. Eggs: incubation period 58 hours. Feeding of fry: brine shrimp nauplii, finely sifted zooplankton.

The fish are already sexually mature and spawn when they are 10 cm long. The best pairs of brood fish are those in a school of young fish that choose their mates. Some pairs eat their fry. In the wild *C. cyanoguttatum* has two spawning periods a year – during the rainy season. Spawning is triggered by a drop in atmospheric pressure and temperature. Spawning generally takes place in the morning. The female deposits up to 600 eggs on a firm, previously cleaned object. If the object with the eggs is removed from the tank the parent fish will often spawn again. Both parents take care of the fry. The newly-hatched fry are transferred by the parents to previously scooped-out pits. The fry are quite big when they become free-swiming.

1 Cutter's Cichlid
Cichlasoma spilurum (GÜNTHER, 1862)

Syn. *Heros spilurus, Cichlasoma cutteri*

Distribution: Guatemala. Full length: male — 12 cm, female — 8 cm. Diet: live foods, augmented by granulated and vegetable foods. Monospecies keeping tank. Breeding tank: with capacity of 200 litres per pair and flat stones, retreats and closed hiding caves on the bottom. Sexual dimorphism: imperceptible; the male may be larger and his dorsal and anal fins more drawn out. Older males have a protruding pad of fat on the forehead, ripe females are fuller. Sex ratio: 1:1. Breeding water: 26—27 °C; pH 6.5—7.0; dCH max. 2° (this species tolerates deviations in the chemical composition of the water). Eggs: incubation period 3 days. Feeding of fry: nauplii of brine shrimp or *Cyclops*..

Monogamous and relatively peaceable fish. For spawning they seek a spot in the open, very occasionally also in a cavity. The female deposits approximately 300 eggs on a solid object. If there is a layer of loose material on the bottom of the tank the female transfers the larvae from the breeding site to a previously scooped-out pit. The parent fish care for and guide the fry. *C. spilurum* interbreeds with *C. nigrofasciatum*. The hybrid offspring show a closer resemblance to *C. spilurum* and are markedly aggressive.

2 Sajica or T-bar Convict
Cichlasoma sajica BUSSING, 1974

Distribution: Costa Rica; Sierpe, Terraba, Esquinas, Jicote, Palo Seco and Rincón rivers. Full length: male — 10 cm, female — 7 cm. Diet: live foods, may be augmented by granulated foods. Monospecies keeping tank. Breeding tank: with capacity of 100 litres per pair, on the bottom a 5 to 10 cm layer of sand with open expanses, flat stones and hiding cavities. Sexual dimorphism: the male is larger, older males have a vaulted forehead contour, longer dorsal and anal fins drawn out into a point and tipped with black and a reddish caudal fin. In the female these fins are yellowish. Sex ratio: 1:1. Breeding water: 24—26 °C; pH 6.5—7.0; dCH max. 2°; dGH 10°. Eggs: minute, white to brown transparent (cryptic coloration), incubation period 3 days. Feeding of fry: nauplii of brine shrimp and *Cyclops*.

For spawning the fish seek a spot in the open or in a cavity. The parent fish care for the eggs as well as the fry, transferring the newly-hatched fry from the breeding site to a previously-dug pit. The fry become free-swimming in six to seven days. They are often afflicted by constitutional dropsy, which causes disorders in absorbing the yolk sac. Such fry are incapable of developing and die. Young fish are sensitive to changes in the chemical composition of the water, which results in the stunted growth of part of the population and sometimes even death. That is why great care is recommended when transferring young fish from one tank to another by gradually conditioning them to their new environment.

Cichlidae

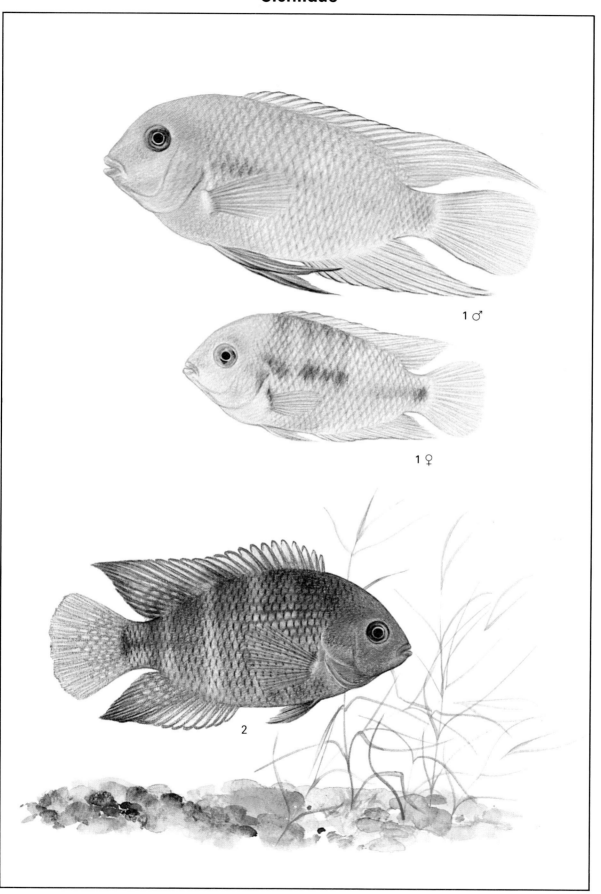

1 ♂

1 ♀

2

1 Three-spot Cichlid
Cichlasoma trimaculatum (GÜNTHER, 1869)
Syn. *Astronotus trimaculatus, Cichlasoma cajali, C. centrale, C. gordonsmithi, C. mojarra*   Cichlidae

Distribution: Mexico, Guatemala, San Salvador and northwestern Honduras. Full length: 30 cm. Diet: more robust live foods, may be augmented by granulated foods. Monospecies keeping tank (in a mixed aquarium only together with fish of the same size and characteristics). Breeding tank: with capacity of 200–500 litres, sufficient hiding places on the bottom (notched flower-pots, etc). Sexual dimorphism: the male is more brightly coloured. Sex ratio: 1:1. Breeding water: 26 °C; pH 6.5–7.0; dCH max. 2°. Eggs: brownish transparent, oval, $\emptyset$ *c.* 1.5 mm; incu-bation period 72 hrs. Feeding of fry: brine shrimp nauplii, finely sifted zooplankton.

Aggressive and territorial fish. They spawn on flat stones, generally in a quiet and covered place. The average number of eggs is about 100. Remove the male immediately after spawning; he may be put in with another ripe female. The eggs may be taken out and incubated separately. The fry become free-swimming in five days and their growth is rapid.

2 *Cichlasoma labiatum* (GÜNTHER, 1864)
Syn. *Amphilophus froebelii, Curraichthys dorsatum, C. erythraeum; C. labiatum, Astronotus erythraeus, A. lobochilus, A. labiatus, Heros erythraeus, H. labiatum, H. lobochilus, H. trimaculatus, Cichlasoma dorsatum, C. erythraeum, C. lobochilus*   Cichlidae

Distribution: Nicaragua, in the lake of the same name and in Lake Managua. Full length: 20 cm. Diet: more robust live foods, may be augmented by artificial foods. Monospecies keeping tank. Breeding tank: with capacity of 200 litres per pair, flat stones, sufficient hiding places. Sexual dimorphism: imperceptible; older males may have swollen lips and they are a lighter colour. Sex ratio: 1:1. Breeding water: 26 °C; pH 6.5–7.0; dCH max. 2°; dGH max. 10°. Eggs: brownish transparent, oval, longer axis *c.* 2 mm long. Feeding of fry: brine shrimp nauplii.

Territorial and aggressive fish, which may be yellowish, reddish, spotted or faintly striped, depending on their age and origin. This species is very similar to *C. citrinellum,* which has identical juvenile coloration up to the age of one year.

Several days before spawning both partners display to one another and clean a firm object. The actual spawning takes place in open water and lasts several hours. The female deposits an average of 250 eggs which are watched over by her while the male stands guard by the spawning site. She transfers the newly-hatched fry to a hiding place or pit, moving them frequently to another hiding place during their five-day development. After this take out the male because he tends to become a disturbing element and is continuously chased away by the female. The young fish grow quickly.

1 ♂

1 ♀

2 ♀

2 ♂

1 Zebra Cichlid or Convict Cichlid
Cichlasoma nigrofasciatum (GÜNTHER, 1869)
Syn. *Heros nigrofasciatus, Astronotus nigrofasciatum*

☐ ● Distribution: Guatemala – in the lakes Atitlan and Amatillan. Full length: 15 cm. Diet: robust live foods, augmented by plant and artificial foods. Monospecies keeping tank. Breeding tank: with capacity of 100 litres per pair; put flat stones and flowerpots with bottom knocked out inside. Sexual dimorphism: the male has a long-drawn-out dorsal and anal fin, the female is smaller with the hind part of the belly coloured bronze. Sex ratio 1:1. Breeding water: 24 °C; pH 6.5–7.0; dCH max. 2°. Eggs: incubation period 3 days. Feeding of fry: nauplii of brine shrimp or *Cyclops*, later finely sifted zooplankton.

An aggressive and intolerant species distinguished by intensive parental care of both eggs and fry. The fish continuously dig up and rebuild the tank bottom. They are fond of seeking out hiding places. The eggs are tended mostly by the female while the male stands guard. On hatching the fry are transferred by the parents to a previously-dug pit in the gravel amidst stones. There are several such pits in various parts of the tank and the fry are moved from one to another. The parent fish may remain with their offspring a long time – until they begin to exhibit interest in further spawning. If provided with sufficient food the young fish's growth is rapid and regular. *C. nigrofasciatum* interbreeds with *C. spilurum;* the hybrid offspring are fertile.

2 *Cichlasoma nigrofasciatum* – xanthistic (gold) form

☐ ● Selectively bred and genetically fixed in Czechoslovakia in 1966. Interbreeds with *C. spilurum.* The first generation of hybrids is very aggressive, the second is generally incapable of life, the larvae dying shortly before they become free-swimming.

3 Firemouth Cichlid
Cichlasoma meeki (BRIND, 1918)
Syn. *Thorichthys helleri meeki*

○ ● Distribution: Guatemala, Mexico – Yucatán peninsula. Full length: 15 cm. Diet: live foods, augmented by granulated foods. Monospecies keeping tank. Breeding tank: with capacity of 100 litres or more per pair, refuges and flat stones on the bottom. Sexual dimorphism: the male is larger, his dorsal and anal fins are drawn out into a point, and the throat and belly are a vivid purple. Sex ratio: 1:1. Breeding water: 24 °C; pH 7.0–7.5; dCH 2°; fresh, filtered. Eggs: incubation period 48 hrs. Feeding of fry: nauplii of brine shrimp or *Cyclops*.

A territorial and monogamous fish. The female deposits 500 or more eggs on a solid object, providing them and later the fry with intensive care for a long time. A pH of less than 6.0 and an increased concentration of nitrites endanger the health of the fish and may be responsible for a relatively large number of deaths without evident cause. For rearing large numbers of young fish aquariums with water flowing through are ideal.

1 ♂

1 ♀

2

3 ♀

3 ♂

1 Salvin's Cichlid
Cichlasoma salvini (GÜNTHER, 1862)
Syn. *Heros salvini, H. triagramma, Astronotus salvini*

Distribution: southern Mexico, Guatemala and Belize. Full length: 15 cm. Diet: live as well as artificial foods, augmented by plant foods. Monospecies keeping tank. Breeding tank: with capacity of 200 litres per pair, flat stones and drainage pipes on the bottom. Sexual dimorphism: the male has longer fins and brighter colours. Sex ratio: 1:1. Breeding water: 24 °C; pH 7.0–7.5; dCH 2°. Eggs: incubation period 48 hrs. Feeding of fry: nauplii of brine shrimp or *Cyclops*.

A bellicose and vicious species that takes intensive care of the eggs and fry. The fish spawn in open water on a stone they have cleaned beforehand (lithophilic fish). The female deposits up to 500 eggs. In 1907 Miller reported that he caught several specimens in a sulphur river near mountain springs where the water reached a temperature of 32 °C.

2 Eight-banded Cichlid
Cichlasoma octofasciatum (REGAN, 1903)
Syn. *Cichlasoma biocellatum, C. hedricki, Heros octofasciatus*

Distribution: southern Mexico, Yucatán, Guatemala and Belize. Full length: 20 cm. Diet: more robust live foods, augmented by plant foods. Monospecies keeping tank. Breeding tank: with capacity of 200 litres per pair, gravel bottom and flat stones. Sexual dimorphism: the dorsal fin of the male is drawn out into a point, the female is smaller, her dorsal fin is rounded, and she is more vividly coloured. Sex ratio: 1:1. Breeding water: 24–28 °C; pH 6.5–7.0; dCH max. 2°. Eggs: incubation period four days. Feeding of fry: nauplii of brine shrimp or *Cyclops*.

A bellicose species that roots in the bottom. The female deposits up to 800 eggs. The parents care for the eggs and fry. The young fish have a typical juvenile coloration.

3 Banded Cichlid
Cichlasoma severum (HECKEL, 1840)
Syn. *Acara spuria, Astronotus (Heros) severus, A. (Cichlasoma) severus,*
A. (Heros) efasciatus, Heros coryphaeus, H. modestus, H. severus, H. spurius,
H. efasciatus, Centrarchus notatus, Chromys appendiculata,
Ch. fasciata, Uaru centrarchoides

Distribution: rivers of the Amazon basin. Full length: 20 cm. Diet: live foods, may be augmented by artificial foods. Monospecies keeping tank (or mixed aquarium together with large and peaceful species of fish). Breeding tank: with capacity of 200 litres per pair, flat stones on the bottom. Sexual dimorphism: imperceptible; the male is more vividly coloured, his dorsal and anal fins are more drawn out than the female's, his head is patterned with a sprinkling of reddish brown dots and wavy lines, which are absent in the female. Sex ratio: 1:1. Breeding water: 25–28 °C; pH 6.0–6.5; dCH max. 1°. Eggs: incubation period 48 hrs. Feeding of fry: nauplii of brine shrimp or *Cyclops*.

Territorial and aggressive fish during the spawning period, otherwise quiet and peaceful. The female deposits 1,000 or more eggs on a firm object on the bottom. The parent fish care for the eggs and fry. A xanthistic gold form 'Gold Severum' has been bred in recent years.

Cichlidae

1 Red-headed Cichlid
Cichlasoma synspilum Hubbs, 1935
Syn. *Cichlasoma hicklingi* (in the opinion of some authorities it is possible that
C. synspilum is a synonym for the previously described species *C. melanurum*)

Cichlidae

Distribution: rivers of Central America from the basin of Río Usumacinta in Guatemala to the coastal rivers of Belize. Full length: 30 cm. Diet: live, artificial and plant foods; the fish are fond of earthworms. Monospecies keeping tank. Breeding tank: with capacity of at least 500 litres, on the bottom a 5-cm-layer of sand and flat stones arranged to form cavities, or notched flowerpots. Sexual dimorphism: imperceptible; the male has more red colour on the head, older males have pads of fat on the head. Sex ratio: 1:1. Breeding water: 22–30 °C; pH 7.0–7.5; dCH 2°; dGH 10–15°; fresh. Eggs: dark beige, oval, longitudinal axis 2 mm long, incubation period 4 days/25 °C. Feeding of fry: brine shrimp nauplii, finely sifted zooplankton, artificial fry foods.

C. synspilum is very similar to *C. maculicauda*. The fish are very aggressive towards others of the same species. They spawn in large pits dug-out in the bottom or on a firm object in a retreat. Sometimes the parent fish eat the eggs from the first few spawnings, but later they may take excellent care of the offspring. The female watches over the eggs, the male guards the area round the spawning site. The female deposits 200 to 800 eggs. Newly-hatched fry are 6 mm long and switch over to exogenous nutrition in five days. Their growth is rapid. Parental care ends after four weeks. Young fish transferred to another tank try to jump out in the new and strange environment, so either lower the water level or cover the tank with glass. Sexual maturity is attained when they are 8 cm long, but full coloration not until they are several years old.

2 Blackbelt Cichlid
Cichlasoma maculicauda Regan, 1905
Syn. *Chuco manana, Cichlasoma manana, C. nigritum*

Cichlidae

Distribution: Atlantic coast of Central America, from Guatemala to Panama. Calm, shallow waters by the coast; the fish often migrate into brackish waters. Full length: 25–30 cm. Diet: live, artificial and plant foods (the fish are fond of earthworms). Monospecies keeping tank. Breeding tank: with capacity of at least 500 litres, on the bottom about 5 cm layer of semi-coarse sand and a few flat stones. Sexual dimorphism: imperceptible; the male is usually more robust, larger, has more red on the head and throat, and slightly longer fins. Sex ratio: 1:1. Breeding water: 22–30 °C; pH 7.0–7.5; dCH 2°; dGH 10–15°; filtered through activated coal, fresh (replace half of the water once a week). Eggs: olive-grey, oval, longitudinal axis 2 mm long, incubation period 3 days/26 °C. Feeding of fry:

brine shrimp nauplii, finely sifted zooplankton, and artificial fry foods.

Adult fish are very aggressive towards others of the same species. From a shoal of maturing fish successively remove the most aggressive individuals – these are usually males. Prior to spawning the fish dig out holes but spawn on a firm object. The task of caring for the eggs is generally taken on by the female with the male guarding the area round the spawning site. The female deposits 300 to 1,000 eggs. Endogenous nutrition lasts four days. Brood care ends after five weeks. The young fish grow quickly; they become sexually mature on reaching a length of 10 cm.

1 Checkerboard Lyretail
Crenicara filamentosa LADIGES, 1959

○ Distribution: middle Amazon, very shallow, acidic waters with a large concentration of humic
◑ substances. Full length: male − 9 cm, female − 6 cm. Diet: live foods. Community tank, together with small tetras. Breeding tank: with capacity of 100 litres per pair, generously planted, and with flat stones on the bottom. Sexual dimorphism: pronounced; the male is bigger, more vividly coloured, his caudal fin is prolonged in the shape of a lyre, the dorsal, caudal and anal fins are coloured black, red and

blue; the female has transparent fins. Sex ratio: 1:1. Breeding water: 26−28 °C; pH 5.5; dCH 0°; dGH max. 8°; filtered through peat. Eggs: yellowish, incubation period three days. Feeding of fry: brine shrimp nauplii.

The female deposits up to 120 eggs on flat stones or leaves. Remove the male after spawning is over. The fish are sensitive to changes in the chemical composition of the water.

2 Ring-tailed Pike Cichlid
Crenicichla saxatilis (LINNAEUS, 1758)
Syn. *Sparus saxatilis, S. rufescens, Perca saxatilis, Cichla saxatilis, Cychla rutilans, Sparus pavoninus, Crenicichla argynnis, C. frenata, C. labrina, C. proteus, C. proteus* var. *argynnis, C. albopunctatus saxatilis, C. saxatilis* var. *semicincta, C. vaillanti*

◁ Distribution: Venezuela − Orinoco basin, Guyana, Trinidad and Brazil. Full length: 35−40 cm.
● Diet: live foods, mainly fish, including flesh of seafish. Monospecies keeping tank. Breeding tank: with capacity of at least 200 litres per pair, rocky bottom, cavities, overhangs. Sexual dimorphism: visible only at the age of 18 months; the male is larger, the underside of his belly is faintly tinged with pink, the sides of the body are sprinkled densely and irregularly with gold nacreous glints, and his anal fin is bigger. The female is coloured delicate pastel hues without gold glints, and with the belly coloured pink to

deep pink. Sex ratio: 1:1. Breeding water: 25 °C; pH 5.5; dCH < 1°; dGH < 10°. Eggs: oval, 1×3 mm, white to yellow, incubation period six days. Feeding of fry: sifted zooplankton.

The female deposits up to 2,000 eggs on the roofs of cavities. These are cared for mainly by the female, while the male guards the territory. The newly-hatched fry have a large yolk sac and hang by threads from a firm object. They become free-swimming on the sixth day after hatching and are led about by both parents.

3 Pike Cichlid
Crenicichla lepidota HECKEL, 1840
Syn. *Crenicichla saxatilis* var. *lepidota* (often confused with *C. saxatilis*)

◁ Distribution: South America − from northern Brazil to northern Argentina. Full length: 20 cm.
● Diet: keeping tank and breeding tank are the same as for *C. saxatilis*. Sexual dimorphism: very slight; only in the spawning dress are the males more colourful. Sex ratio: 1:1. Breeding water: 24−28 °C; pH 5.5−6.0; dCH max. 2°; dGH max. 10°. Eggs: incubation period 6 days. Feeding of fry: brine shrimp nauplii, finely sifted zooplankton, later chopped tubifex worms.

The female deposits several hundred yellowish eggs on the roof of cavities and rock overhangs. The eggs and fry are cared for by both parents. The young fish grow quickly and should be separated from the parent fish after three weeks.

1 ♂

2 ♂

3 ♂

1 *Geophagus steindachneri* REGAN, 1912
Syn. *Geophagus hondae, G. magdalenae, G. pellegrini*

Distribution: Colombia, upper Magdalena River and its tributaries. Full length: 25 cm. Diet: live as well as artificial foods, variegated as much as possible. Community tank, but only together with larger species of peaceful cichlids – capacity of at least 500 litres. Breeding tank: with capacity of 300 litres per pair. Cover the bottom with a 5 cm layer of fine sand on which are laid flat stones and a large notched flowerpot which will serve as a hiding place for the pair. Sexual dimorphism: older males have the dorsal and anal fins extended and a prominent reddish-brown pad of fat on the head; the genital papillae appear about 10 days before spawning, in the female they do not show until a few hours before spawning. Sex ratio: 1:1. Breeding water: 26–28 °C; pH 6.5–7.0; dCH max. 2°. Eggs: development in the mouth of the female lasts 17–20 days. Feeding of fry: brine shrimp nauplii. In view of the large size of the aquarium it is recommended to put the food for the fry into the tank through a glass tube close by the female (then the food is not unduly scattered).

Apart from the spawning period these are peaceable fish. The female deposits about 50 yellow eggs on a flat stone. As soon as all the eggs are laid she takes them up in her mouth (sometimes she takes them up in succession as they are laid). Remove the male immediately after spawning (after about an hour). It is said that *G. steindachneri* is the only South American species of cichlid that takes the eggs into the mouth immediately. The female takes no food while she is caring for the eggs and fry in her mouth. After three weeks remove the female from the tank containing the young fish and put her in again with the male. The young fish grow quickly.

2 Earth-eater or Demon Fish
Geophagus jurupari HECKEL, 1840
Syn. *Geophagus leucostictus, G. mapiritensis, G. pappaterra, Satanoperca pappaterra, S. jurupari, S. leucosticta, S. macrolepis*

Distribution: Brazil, Guyana. Full length: 25 cm. Diet: live as well as artificial foods. Community tank, see also *G. steindachneri.* Breeding tank: same as for *G. steindachneri.* Sexual dimorphism: imperceptible, the male is slimmer, his genital papilla is pointed, the female's is short and blunt. Sex ratio: 1:1. Breeding water: 28 °C; pH 6.5–7.0; dCH max. 2°. Eggs: development in the mouth lasts 10 days. Feeding of fry: see *G. steindachneri.* First breeding: 1936, H. Härtel – Dresden.

Young fish keep together in small groups, from whose number they later select their partners. Paired fish should be separated for further breeding. The female deposits 150 to 400 eggs on a flat stone. Both partners take care of the spawning site. Twenty-four hours after spawning both take the eggs into their mouths. They do not have a throat sac – the eggs rest on the jaws. In 10 days the fry leave their parents' mouths, returning there, however, when danger threatens and also for the night. After four weeks the young are too large to fit into the mouth, but continue to be cared for by the parents for another four weeks, after which time the parent fish should be transferred to a separate tank.

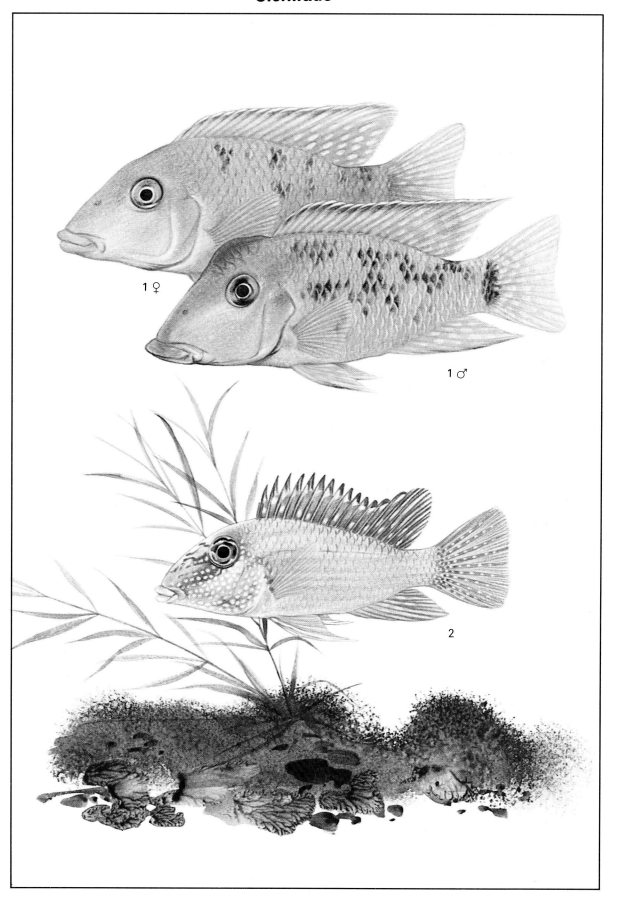

1 ♀

1 ♂

2

1 Surinam Geophagus

Geophagus surinamensis (BLOCH, 1791)

Syn. *Sparus surinamensis, Chromis proxima, Satanoperca proxima, Geophagus altifrons, G. megasema*

Cichlidae

Distribution: South America, Guyana, Surinam, French Guiana, northern Brazil to the Amazon – standing to slowly-flowing waters with sandy or stony bottom. Full length: 30 cm. Diet: live as well as artificial foods. Monospecies keeping tank (or mixed aquarium together with peaceable species of cichlids or catfish). Breeding tank: with capacity of 300–500 litres per pair, fine-grained sand and flat stones on the bottom. Sexual dimorphism: very slight; the female is more silvery. Sex ratio: 1:1. Breeding water: 25–28 °C; pH 7.0; dCH < 2°. Eggs: incubation period 3 days. Feeding of fry: nauplii of brine shrimp or *Cyclops* placed close beside the fry or the parent fish.

During the spawning period the fish are territorial and aggressive. The best pairs are ones that mate according to preference, having selected their partner from amongst a school of young fish. The fish spawn on flat stones, sometimes also on plant roots or in dug-out pits. The female deposits up to 300 eggs. In two days both partners start taking the eggs into their mouths, doing so with increasing frequency as the time of hatching draws near, until just before or immediately after hatching, the whole brood remains in the mouths of the parent fish throughout the ensuing development. Further care is similar to that of *G. jurupari.*

2 Paraguay Mouthbrooder

Gymnogeophagus balzani (PERUGIN, 1891)

Syn. *Satanoperca balzanii, Geophagus duodecimspinosum, G. balzani, Gymnogeophagus cyanopterus*

Cichlidae

Distribution: Paraguay, Paraná River. Full length: 20 cm. Diet: live foods, may be augmented by artificial foods. Community tank, only together with peaceful species of cichlids. Breeding tank: with capacity of 200–300 litres per pair, and hiding places and flat stones on the bottom. Sexual dimorphism: in older males the dorsal and anal fins are elongated and there is a big pad of fat on the upper part of the large head; there is a group of green iridescent scales behind the gill covers of the males. Sex ratio: 1:1. Breeding water: 25–28 °C; pH 7.0; dCH < 2°. Eggs: the fry hatch in 25 hrs., development in the mouth of the female lasts 8–10 days. Feeding of fry: nauplii of brine shrimp or *Cyclops.*

Peaceful fish. The best pairs are ones that mate according to preference, selecting their partners from amongst a school of young fish. The female deposits up to 500 eggs on a firm object. Remove the males after spawning. The female watches over the eggs and after 24 hours, or sometimes not till three days later, she takes the eggs or the newly-hatched fry into her mouth. The fry leave the mother's mouth after 10 days, at which time they measure 5 to 6 mm. Their growth is rapid and in four weeks they reach a length of 2 cm; the female may be taken out of the tank.

1

2 ♂

2 ♀

1 Golden-eyed Dwarf Cichlid
Nannacara anomala REGAN, 1905
Syn. *Acara punctulata*

Distribution: West Guyana. Full length: male – 9 cm, female – 5 cm. Diet: live foods. Community tank. Breeding tank: with capacity of 50 litres per pair, floating plants on the surface, hiding places (cavities), flat stones on the bottom. Sexual dimorphism: the male's dorsal and anal fins are larger and prolonged into a point. Sex ratio: 1:1. Breeding water: 24–26 °C; pH 6.5–7.0; dCH max. 2°. Eggs: incubation period three days. Feeding of fry: brine shrimp or *Cyclops* nauplii.

The female deposits the eggs in a cavity in a concealed corner of the aquarium or on a stone. Remove the male after spawning, for the female is often aggressive towards her partner. The newly-hatched fry are transferred by the female to pits in the sand or to other hiding places on the bottom. The fry switch over to exogenous nutrition on the fifth to seventh day. The eggs may be sucked up with a tube or transferred together with the object on which they are laid to a nursery tank. It is also possible to wait till the fry hatch and then suck them up and transfer them along with the female. In most instances the female resumes her care of the fry after such a move. Females have been known to care for the young of another female along with those of their own brood. The brood care instinct is so strong that if she loses her young the female may even gather about her a cluster of *Daphnia*. It is recommended to leave the female with the fry as long as possible. The period between individual spawnings is thus prolonged, the females have time to regain strength and the production of eggs at the next spawning is greater.

2 Ramirez's Dwarf Cichlid or Butterfly Dwarf Cichlid
Papiliochromis ramirezi (MYERS et HARRY, 1948)
Syn. *Apistogramma ramirezi, Microgeophagus ramirezi*

Distribution: western Venezuela, Colombia, western Brazil, Bolivia. Full length: male – 10 cm, female – 7 cm. Diet: live foods. Community tank. Breeding tank: with capacity of 50 litres per pair, diffused light, hiding places and flat stones on the bottom. Sexual dimorphism: the female has a fuller and redder belly and the second ray of the dorsal fin, unlike that of the male, is only a little extended. Sex ratio: 1:1. Breeding water: 24–26 °C; pH 6.5–7.0; dCH < 1°; dGH < 10°. Eggs: greyish-yellow, $\varnothing$ *c.* 1 mm, incubation period 4 days. Feeding of fry: brine shrimp or *Cyclops* nauplii.

A monogamous species; the parent fish care for the eggs and the fry. The eggs can be transferred to a nursery tank, as the presence of the parent fish is not necessary. The fish are lithophilic – the female deposits 300 to 400 eggs on a firm object. Endogenous nutrition lasts eight days. The young fish grow slowly. A xanthistic (gold) form of this species has been bred and genetically fixed in captivity. Both the wild and the xanthistic form are susceptible to various infections and diseases. The fish have a short life span of about two years.

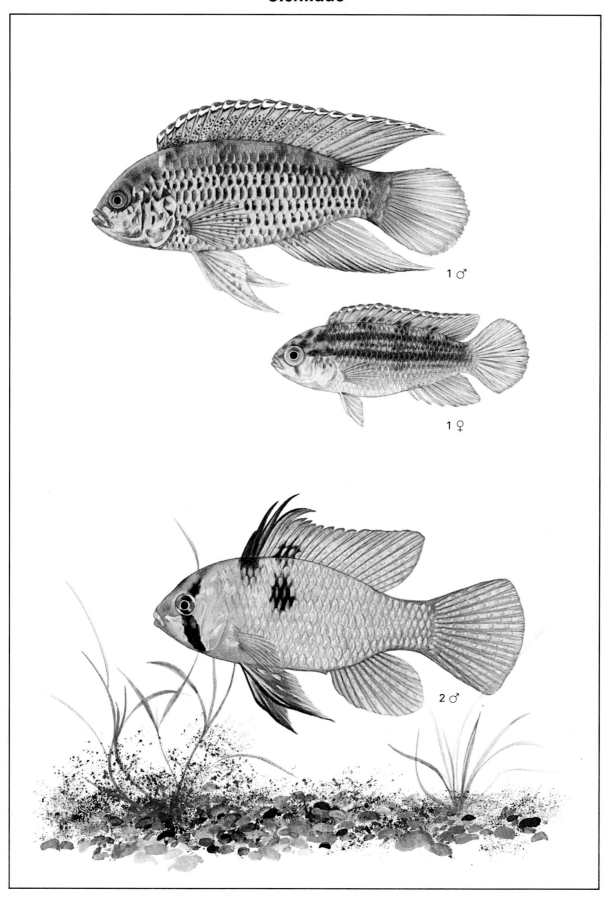

1 ♂

1 ♀

2 ♂

1 Long-finned Angelfish
Pterophyllum altum PELLEGRIN, 1903

◁

●

Distribution: South America – only in the upper Orinoco in Venezuela. Full length: 15–18 cm. Diet: small live foods, including fish fry. Monospecies keeping tank. Breeding tank: with capacity of at least 500 litres, heavily planted in places, and with firm vertical surfaces or broadleaved plants. Sexual dimorphism: monomorphic fish. Sex ratio: 1:1; set up breeder fish in a small shoal. Water: 26–30 °C; pH 6.5–7.0; dCH < 2°; dGH < 10° (hypothetical data for the development of the eggs, for it seems the species has not yet been bred).

Peaceful, quiet fish but easily startled. According to H. Mayland this may be mitigated by putting the fish in a sufficiently roomy tank where there is regular traffic (people regularly passing by), so the fish will become conditioned. The fish live in a school the same as the related species *P. scalare* and *P. dumerili.* In 1967 Dr. L. P. Schultz revised the genus *Pterophyllum*, on which occasion he considered classifying *P. altum* as a subspecies of *P. scalare,* but in the end decided *P. altum* is a separate species. At that time he could not anticipate that later Dr. H. R. Axelrod would discover in the Negro River a scalare that seemed to be an intermediate form between *P. scalare* and *P. altum,* not only by the number of rays in the dorsal and anal fins but also in general appearance. From H. Mayland's considerations it follows that what was previously given as a characteristic of identification (i.e. the shape of the head typical of *P. altum*) suddenly turns up also in the specimen discovered by Axelrod, even though its fins differ from those of *P. altum.* A similar head contour appears also in some aquarium-bred *P. scalare* specimens, which casts even greater doubt on the opinion that this is a typical characteristic of identification of the species *P. altum.* The matter of the nomenclatorial classification of *P. altum* will probably not be made absolutely certain for the time being.

In all the three hitherto known species of *Pterophyllum* there is a black cross bar passing through the eye. *P. altum* has a second, brownish or greyish bar extending round the whole body just behind the gill covers, and behind this a third cross bar coloured black like the first. This bar pattern is absent in the other two species. Furthermore, the extreme vertical extension of the dorsal and anal fins is typical of *P. altum.*

1 Angel Fish
Pterophyllum scalare (LICHTENSTEIN, 1823)
Syn. *Platax scalaris, Zeus scalaris, Pterophyllum eimekei*

Distribution: Brazil – the Amazon, Tapajós and their tributaries. Full length: 15 cm; full height: 26 cm. Diet: live foods, including fry of live-bearing fish. Community tank: high, with capacity of 200 litres or more. Breeding tank: high, with capacity of 150 litres per pair, upright or slanting pieces of slate or glass panes and large-leaved plants of the genus *Echinodorus*. Sexual dimorphism: very slight; older males have a larger head with small pad of fat. Sex ratio: 1:1. Breeding water: 26–28 °C; pH 6.5–7.0; dCH max. 2°. Eggs: yellowish, translucent, incubation period 48 hrs. Feeding of fry: brine shrimp or *Cyclops* nauplii.

There are two local strains of the wild form, one bigger than the other. The smaller strain was described in 1928 by Ahl as *Pterophyllum eimekei*. In 1967 this was revised by L. D. Schultz and *P. eimekei* was cancelled as a separate independent species.

Before selecting paired fish for breeding keep a large group of young fish together until they attain sexual maturity. When they have selected a mate paired fish separate from the group and spawning begins. Keeping each pair in a separate tank, if this can be done, is ideal. The fish spawn on an upright or slanting object. The parents watch over and care for the eggs but only very occasionally do they care for the fry. It is recommended to transfer the eggs to a separate tank either with the object on which they are resting (leaf, piece of slate or glass) or scrape them off into a small-meshed sieve with a brush. Treat the eggs with methylene blue, maintain a constant temperature of 26 °C and provide abundant aeration. The newly-hatched fry are suspended in clusters from leaves or other objects by filaments. They switch over to exogenous nutrition after one week and their growth is rapid. Fresh water, sufficient live foods and a roomy aquarium are factors that promote the growth of the young fish.

2 *Pterophyllum scalare* – veil-finned form

The veil-finned form was developed and genetically fixed in aquarium-raised fish, apparently in the USA.

3 *Pterophyllum scalare* – bicoloured form

The bicoloured form was developed and genetically fixed in aquarium-raised fish, according to some reports in Sweden.

Cichlidae

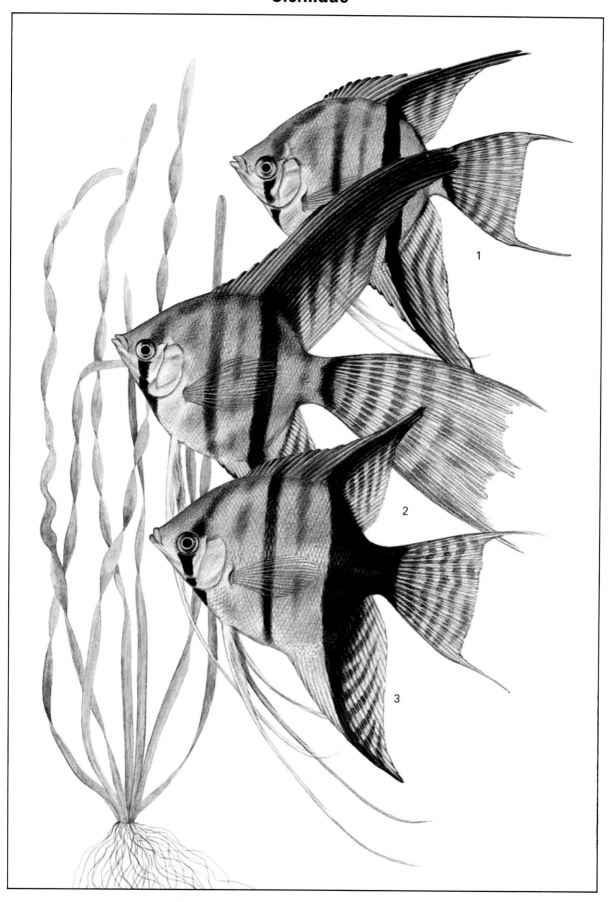

1 *Pterophyllum scalare* – xanthistic (gold) form

Cichlidae

◁ This form was developed independently by two separate breeders in 1969–1970. One was Peter ● Wong of Hong Kong and the other Carl Naja of Milwaukee, USA. The fish bred by the latter are more colourful.

2 *Pterophyllum scalare* – xanthistic (gold) veil-finned form

Cichlidae

◁ The gold veil-finned form was genetically fixed by further selective breeding.
●

3 *Pterophyllum scalare* – dusky form

Cichlidae

◁ The dusky form was bred and genetically fixed in the aquarium, apparently in the forties or even ● earlier.

4 *Pterophyllum scalare* – dusky veil-finned form

Cichlidae

◁ The genetically-fixed dusky veil-finned form was developed by further selective breeding. Selec- ● tive breeding of the duskiest specimens has also yielded pure black forms.

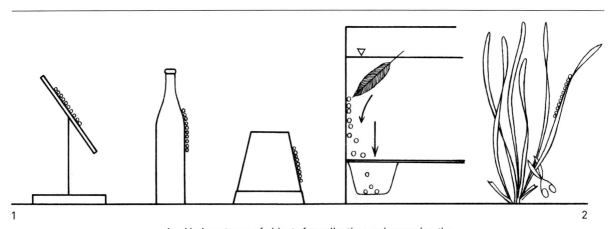

1 – Various types of objects for collecting and removing the spawn of angelfish.
2 – Two methods of transferring eggs to a separate tank

1 *Pterophyllum scalare* – marbled form

The first marbled scalare appeared in 1965 among the fish being bred by the American breeder Bud Goddard, but he did not succeed in making this a genetically fixed trait and it disappeared. In 1969–1970, however, success crowned the efforts of another American breeder – Charles Ash of California – who thus became the first to make this a genetically fixed form.

2 *Pterophyllum scalare* – marbled veil-finned form

Further selective breeding, apparently again in the USA, produced a marbled veil-finned form that was genetically fixed.

Because of the species' ability to produce colour mutations, particularly in the make-up and pattern of the cross bars, scalare breeders continued to try and develop further new forms. Thus it was that in the early seventies the Gulf Fish Farm in Florida developed the genetically fixed 'spirit form' (a). This was followed soon after by another new strain of unknown origin – the 'zebra' (b) – in four different forms: normal, dusky, short-finned and veil-finned. Derived apparently from the 'zebra' is another new form – the 'leopard' (c), widespread in the USSR.

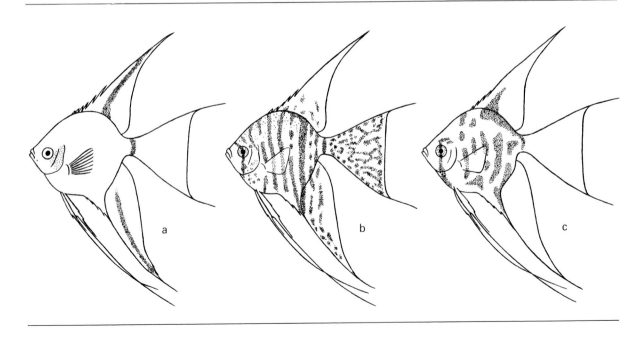

Cichlidae

1 *Pterophyllum scalare* – black form

Cichlidae

◁

◑

This form was developed from the dusky form by the American breeder James Ellis of California, who showed the fish for the first time in the early fifties at the aquatic exhibition in Los Angeles.

2 *Pterophyllum scalare* – black veil-finned form

Cichlidae

◁

◑

Further selective breeding produced the genetically fixed, black veil-finned form. Compared with the other forms both black strains are more sensitive, more warmth-loving, and the growth of the young fish is slower.

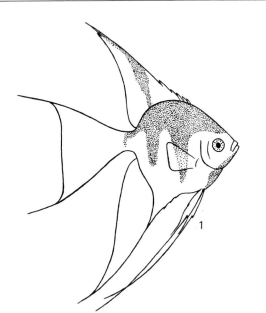
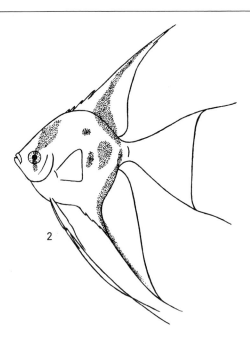

The continual interbreeding of aquarium fish produces chance mutations that may be attractive and interesting (1, 2) and thus represent a challenge for further selective breeding.

1 Real Discus Fish or Pompadour Fish
Symphysodon discus HECKEL, 1840 Cichlidae

Distribution: Brazil – middle Amazon (Manaus, Teffé), Río Negro and Xingu River. Full length: 20 cm. Diet: live foods, augmented by artificial and plant foods. Monospecies keeping tank. Breeding tank: with capacity of 200–300 litres per pair, water level at least 50 cm, dim lighting, drainage pipes placed in a slanting position on the bottom, and undisturbed environment. Sexual dimorphism: monomorphic fish. Sex ratio: 1:1. Breeding water: 30 °C; pH 6.5; dCH 0°; dGH < 8°. Eggs: incubation period 50–62 hrs. Feeding of fry: skin secretion of the parents, then brine shrimp nauplii.

For many decades these fish were a rarity in the aquarium. Not until the sixties were they first bred with success. According to the revision of the genus *Symphysodon* by Dr. L. P. Schultz in 1960 we now differentiate the Real Discus (*S. discus*), Blue Discus (*S. aequifasciatus haraldi*) and Brown Discus (*S. aequifasciatus axelrodi*). Care and rearing is the same for all forms, but more difficult in the case of *S. discus.*

The nominate form *Symphysodon aequifasciatus aequifasciatus* Pellegrin, 1903, with two subspecies *S. a. haraldi* and *S. a. axelrodi* is the second and last species native to the upper reaches of the Amazon and Putumayo Rivers. The basic colour is brownish with nine transversal bands and longitudinal blue-green shiny 'waves' all over the body including the head and fins.

2 Blue Discus
Symphysodon aequifasciatus haraldi L. P. SCHULTZ, 1960 Cichlidae

Distribution: middle Amazon where the river is called Solimoes. Full length: 20 cm. Other requirements the same as for *S. discus.*

Breeders throughout the world have developed many colour forms of Blue Discus. The handsomest are the ones named Royal Blue, Turkis Discus, and Wattley's Turkis-Discus. In the red forms it is necessary, according to Mayland, to distinguish between true red fish from specimens coloured red as a result of the food they eat e.g. the red-coloured eggs of krill.

3 Brown Discus
Symphysodon aequifasciatus axelrodi L. P. SCHULTZ, 1960 Cichlidae

Distribution: Amazon River and its water system from Manacapur (west of Manaus) to the mouth of the river, Orinoco River and its water system. Full length: 20 cm. Other requirements the same as for *S. discus.*

Paired fish spawn on the slanting or vertical surface of a firm object. The newly-hatched fry hang from short threads. Five days after hatching the fry begin swimming and attach themselves to the sides of their parents' bodies. The partners take turns in 'carrying' the young. At this time the skin of the parent fish produces a secretion that is the fry's first food. After feeding on the secretion for several days the fry begin to hunt food actively by themselves. The difficulty in breeding is that many pairs eat the eggs or fry or the skin of the parent fish does not produce a secretion and the fry die of hunger. In the USA breeders worked out a successful but laborious method of rearing the fry during the critical period before they begin actively hunting food by themselves. Pieces of plexiglass shaped like fish (serving as mock parents) are coated with a yolk emulsion. The emulsion must be fresh, applied anew at each feeding, and given to the fry at regular intervals throughout the day. Also the tank must be kept absolutely clean (fresh water all the time). Some breeders, however, are of the opinion that fry raised in this manner have problems producing their own secretion as adults.

1 Uaru
Uaru amphiacanthoides HECKEL, 1840
Syn. *Acara amphiacanthoides, Pomotis fasciatus, Uaru imperialis, U. obscurus*   Cichlidae

Distribution: South America – the Amazon and waters of Guyana. Full length: 30 cm. Diet: live and plant foods; the live foods should be varied e.g. mosquito larvae, earthworms, pieces of beef heart, large *Daphnia.* Of the plant foods the fish take lettuce, finely grated carrots, duckweed and bits of pear or apple. They also nibble wood from moors (the sawdust helps in the digestion of food). Monospecies keeping tank provided with efficient filters and aeration. Breeding tank: with capacity of 300 litres or more, at least 100 cm long. On the bottom place pieces of slate at a slant, mineralized wood from moors, and a layer of dark gravel. The light should be muted. Sexual dimorphism: minute (monomorphic fish; the sexes can be identified only a few days before spawning when the genital papillae emerge – the male's is pointed, the female's blunt). Sex ratio: 1:1. Breeding water: 30 °C; pH 5.8–6.0; dCH 0°; dGH 6°; fresh, filtered through peat. Eggs: small, amber yellow, incubation period 48 hrs/30 °C. Feeding of fry: for 5 days the newly-hatched fry feed on a secretion produced by the skin of the parent fish, later they take brine shrimp nauplii.

School fish occurring together with fish of the genus *Symphysodon* in the wild. It is recommended to keep them in a rather small group (four to six fish). The group has a social hierarchy, the dominant position being held by a strong male, followed by his mate and then the other fish. During the spawning period, however, weaker pairs defend their territory even against fish higher up in the social order. Prior to spawning mated pairs separate from the group and seek a hidden, shaded spot for the act. They spawn on a slanting object (slate), digging a pit about 30 cm in diameter at its base. Spawning lasts about two hours during which time the female deposits some 150 eggs. On hatching the fry remain two days in the pit and a further three days close by the pit, feeding only on the secretion produced by the skin on the parents' back and dorsal fins. On the sixth day the fry leave the spawning site in a group, accompanied by the parents. Feeding on the skin secretion gradually tapers off as the fry take increasingly more food from their surroundings. The young fish grow quickly, increasing in length from 5 mm on hatching to 1 cm in a single week. They have a typical juvenile coloration (see illustration).

1

1 juv.

1 Rainbow Cichlid
Herotilapia multispinosa (GÜNTHER, 1869)
Syn. *Heros multispinosus, Cichlasoma multispinosa*

Cichlidae

Distribution: Panama, Nicaragua, to Lake Managua. Full length: 13 cm. Diet: live as well as artificial foods. Monospecies keeping tank. Breeding tank: with capacity of 100 litres per pair, flat stones on the bottom or large-leaved plants. Sexual dimorphism: the male's dorsal and anal fins are longer, extended into a point, the female is fuller in the body and has shorter, intense black ventral fins. Sex ratio: 1:1. Breeding water: 27 °C; pH 6.0–7.0; dCH max. 2°. Eggs: ∅ c. 1 mm, dingy yellowish (the colour of the eggs may change with diet); incubation period 24 hrs. Feeding of fry: brine shrimp or *Cyclops* nauplii.

Very prolific fish; the female deposits up to 1,000 eggs on a firm object on the bottom of the tank or directly on the glass bottom, as well as on the leaves of plants. When the fry hatch the parents continually move them. The fry often hang by thin filaments in a dense thicket of plants close to the surface. After four days they become free-swimming, measure 5 mm in length, and the gland with remnant of the filament is still apparent behind the head. Both partners care for the fry; during this time they both turn black. The young fish grow quickly; in 14 days they reach a length of 1 cm and can be separated from the parents. The temperature of the water may be gradually lowered to 22 °C.

2 *Julidochromis dickfeldi* STAECK, 1975

Cichlidae

Distribution: southeastern part of Lake Tanganyika, north of Sumbu National Park (Zambia) – an endemic species. Shallow stony and rocky littoral zone to depths of 3 metres. The fish constantly assemble near hiding places in rocks. Full length: 11 cm. Diet: live as well as artificial foods. Monospecies keeping tank. Breeding tank: with capacity of 60–100 litres per pair, sufficient vertical crevices and cavities. Sexual dimorphism: monomorphic fish; during the spawning period the genital papilla of the males is thicker. Sex ratio: 1:1. Breeding water: 25–28 °C; pH 7.5–8.0; dCH 2–3°; fresh. Eggs: incubation period 60 hrs/28 °C. Feeding of fry: brine shrimp nauplii.

Fish aggressive towards others of the same species. Only the partner and offspring are tolerated within the fish's territory. Weaker fish are killed in cramped quarters. Disturbances in the environment cause quarrels between partners. The brood fish spawn in brief cycles, with the female laying about 10 eggs each time on the roof of the cavity. Later, fry in various stages of development may be found at the spawning site in the immediate vicinity of the cavity. In the aquarium, according to Staeck, the fish form groups of three, consisting of the parent fish and a young fish, accepted by the parents as a partner. This, of course, is abnormal behaviour in aquarium conditions.

The most closely related species are *Julidochromis ornatus* and *J. transcriptus*.

1 ♀

1 ♂

2

1 Marlier's Julie

Julidochromis marlieri POLL, 1956 Cichlidae

○
●

Distribution: A species endemic to Lake Tanganyika, rocky littoral zone at the northwestern tip of the lake. Full length: 15 cm. Diet: live as well as artificial foods. Monospecies keeping tank. Breeding tank: with capacity of 100–200 litres per pair and on the bottom mounds of stones with sufficient cavities or flowerpots with knocked-out bottoms. Sexual dimorphism: inconspicuous – the fully developed male has a pad of fat on the forehead and is usually smaller than the female; the male's genital papilla is pointed, the female's blunt. Sex ratio: 1:1. Breeding water: 24–26 °C; pH 7.5–8.0; dCH 2°; dGH 12°; fresh, clean, well filtered. Eggs: incubation period 3 days? Feeding of fry: brine shrimp nauplii, later sifted zooplankton.

Territorial and quarrelsome fish, particularly towards others of the same species. They are monogamous and spawn in cavities. The female deposits up to 300 eggs. The young fish exhibit strong ties to the spawning site, remaining a long time in the crevices of the respective cavity. Breeders have succeeded in obtaining sterile hybrids from *J. marlieri* × *J. ornatus* that show a slight resemblance to *J. transcriptus*. *J. regani* Poll, 1942, is a closely related species. Fish whose bodily appearance gives the impression of an intermediate form between *J. marlieri* and *J. regani* are found in the Kigoma region of Tanzania.

2 Masked Julidochromis

Julidochromis transcriptus MATTHES, 1959 Cichlidae

○
●

Distribution: A species endemic to Africa's Lake Tanganyika – rocky shores. Full length: 7 cm (smallest member of the genus). Diet: live as well as artificial foods. Monospecies keeping tank. Breeding tank: with capacity of 50 to 100 litres per pair, and mounds of stones with sufficient cavities and hiding possibilities on the bottom. Sexual dimorphism: very slight (monomorphic fish); the genital papilla of the male is longer, the female may be larger than the male and fuller. Sex ratio: 1:1. Breeding water: 24–26 °C; pH 7.5–8.0; dCH 2°; dGH 12°; fresh,

clean, filtered. Eggs: incubation period 3 days? Feeding of fry: brine shrimp nauplii, later sifted zooplankton.

The fish's coloration is similar to that of *J. marlieri,* but the profile of the head is different and the line of the forehead is straight, without a pad of fat. The fish are aggressive towards other members of the same species. The female is not very productive, depositing only several dozen eggs. The young fish stay a long time in the vicinity of the spawning site.

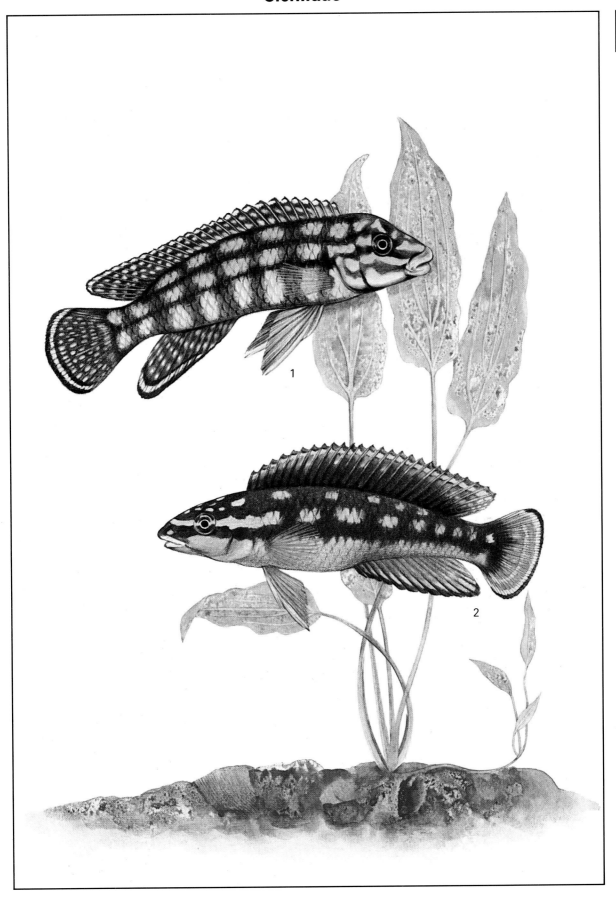

1 Convict Julidochromis
Julidochromis regani POLL, 1942

○
●
Distribution: A species endemic to Africa's Lake Tanganyika. Full length: 30 cm. Diet: live as well as artificial foods. Monospecies keeping tank. Breeding tank: with capacity of 100−200 litres per pair and mounds of stones with sufficient cavities and crevices. Sexual dimorphism: minute (the female is usually larger). The female's papilla is shorter and wider. Fish put in a glass container may be observed through the bottom. It is possible to identify the sexes by this means when they reach a length of 4 cm. Sex ratio: 1:1. Breeding water: 25 °C; pH 7.0−8.0; hard to half-hard, e.g. dCH 4°, dGH 14° or dCH 2°, dGH 10°. The water may be treated with sodium bicarbonate ($NaHCO_3$), add ordinary kitchen salt − 1 tablespoon for every 20 litres of water. Filter the water through active coal. Eggs: incubation period 3 days. Feeding of fry: brine shrimp nauplii.

Spawning of mated pairs is irregular. Spawning is easiest in the case of pairs that have selected their mates according to preference from amongst a group of young fish. Spawning takes place in retreats between stones or in dug-out holes beneath stones. The female deposits up to 300 eggs on the roof or sides of the cavity. The fish may visit several cavities during the act of spawning. Endogenous nutrition lasts five days. The fry stay close to the firm walls of the hiding place for a long time. Not till they reach a length of 2 cm are they chased away from the spawning site by the parent fish. In a shoal of fish there exists a definite social order respected by all its members. Weaker fish indicate their lower position in the hierarchy by peculiar movements of the fins. In tanks with little room and insufficient hiding places the fish may kill one another.

2 Julie
Julidochromis ornatus BOULENGER, 1898

○
●
Distribution: A species endemic to Africa's Lake Tanganyika, in rocky shoreline zones. Full length: 8 cm. Diet: live as well as artificial foods. Monospecies keeping tank. Breeding tank: with capacity of 50−100 litres per pair, and mounds of stones with sufficient cavities on the bottom. Sexual dimorphism: imperceptible; the female is slightly smaller. Sex ratio: 1:1. Breeding water: 26−28 °C; pH 7.0−8.0; dCH 2°; dGH 12°; fresh, clean, well filtered. Eggs: incubation period 48 hrs. Feeding of fry: brine shrimp nauplii, later sifted zooplankton.

Adult fish are territorial and pair for life. The males are usually more aggressive than the females. A peculiar form of behaviour (wriggling and showing the belly) was observed in females whereby they warded off the attack of the males. The female deposits 20 to 50 eggs on the roof of cavities. Spawning is inconspicuous, concealed. The eggs are laid singly or in clusters in various parts of the cavity. The fry hatch in succession; they are anchored to the substrate by a sticky filament and are transferred from place to place by the parents. In seven days the fry switch over to exogenous nutrition. The parents care for the fry until the next spawning, but even then they do not attack their offspring. The young fish's growth is regular but slow. Sexual maturity is attained at eight months. Brood fish spawn every three to four weeks.

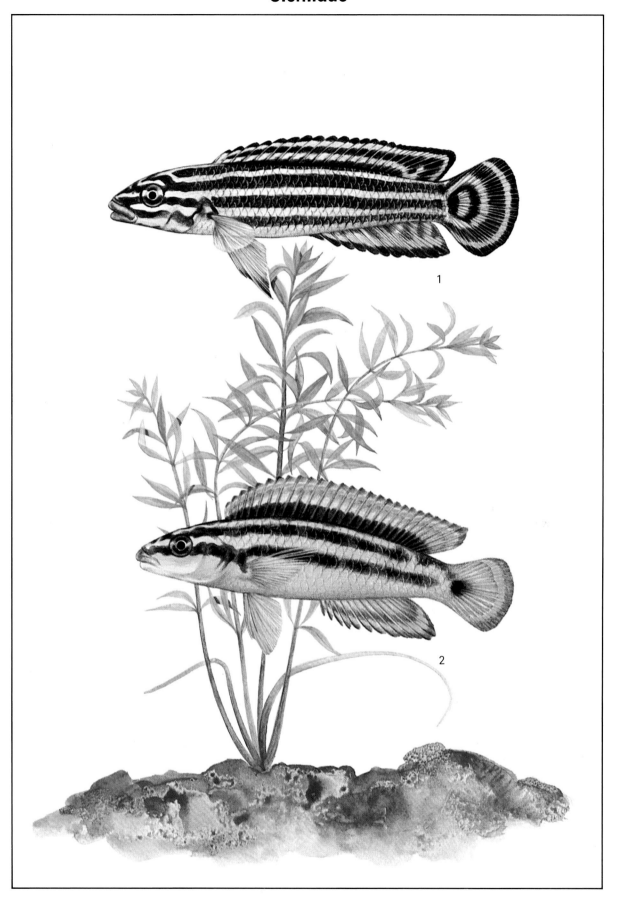

1 African Peacock

Aulonocara nyassae REGAN, 1921

Cichlidae

Distribution: A species endemic to Lake Malawi. The range of the orange-blue form is limited to the middle of the eastern shore. The fish dwell in the intermediate zone between sandy and rocky bottoms but also in definitely rocky localities with caves. Full length: 18 cm; specimens kept in aquariums are mostly smaller. Diet: more robust live foods; may be augmented by artificial foods. Monospecies keeping tank, or a mixed aquarium together with endemic cichlids of similar characteristics. Breeding tank: of 200-litre capacity with sufficient hiding possibilities (drainage pipes) on the bottom. Sexual dimorphism: dichromatism; the male is blue, the female brown. Sex ratio: 1 male : 2−3 females. Breeding water: 26−28 °C; pH 7.5−8.0; dCH 2°; dGH 10−15°. Eggs: incubation period in the mouth of the female? Feeding of fry: brine shrimp nauplii, finely sifted zooplankton.

There are several local forms which do not have a reddish area behind the gill covers; the colour red, however, is present in the centre of each scale and in the caudal fin. Similar mouthbrooders from Lake Malawi coloured all blue or all yellow or blue with a yellow belly are also imported under the same name. These fish have not been scientifically described as yet and therefore it is impossible to say whether this is merely a colour form or a separate species.

The fish are very aggressive towards other members of the same species; the males do battle for the females and display prior to spawning. The female deposits about 60 eggs, which she cares for in her mouth.

2 Guenther's Cichlid

Chromidotilapia guentheri (SAUVAGE, 1882)

Syn. *Hernichromis guentheri, H. tersquamatus, H. voltae, Pelmatochromis guentheri, P. pellegrini, P. boulengeri*

Cichlidae

Distribution: West Africa − from Sierra Leone to Gabon, in coastal rivers and lagoons within the tidal zone, in fresh as well as brackish waters. Full length: 20 cm. Diet: live foods. Monospecies keeping tank. Breeding tank: with capacity of 100 litres per pair and flat stones on the bottom. Sexual dimorphism: the female is much more brightly coloured and smaller. Sex ratio: 1:1. Breeding water: 26 °C; pH 7.0−7.5; dCH 2°. Eggs: development in the mouth of the male lasts 12 days. Feeding of fry: brine shrimp or finely sifted zooplankton.

Lithophilic fish; before spawning the male cleans a firm object (a stone in open water), the female displays to the male and then deposits the eggs, which the male fertilizes at brief intervals. The female deposits approximately

100 eggs either one on top of the other, or spread out one beside the other. The eggs are joined by cobweb-fine filaments which makes it easier for the male to pick up several at a time. Spawning lasts about 20 minutes. As soon as it is completed the male immediately collects the eggs. The female, which becomes aggressive, should be taken out of the tank. The male does not take food. In 12 days the fry, measuring 5 mm in length, leave his mouth but continue to return there occasionally for another two to five days. Passive care of the fry by the male lasts four weeks.

In 1898 Boulenger described the species *Chromidotilapia (Pelmatochromis) kingsleyae,* which, according to Meinken, is very closely related to, if not the same as, *C. guentheri.*

1

2 ♂

2 ♀

1 *Limnochromis auritus* (BOULENGER, 1901)

Syn. *Pelmatochromis auritus*

○
●

Distribution: A species endemic to Lake Tanganyika – in parts distant from the shore at depths of 5 to 125 metres with a relatively constant temperature throughout the year. Full length: 19 cm. Diet: live as well as artificial foods, primarily zooplankton; continual feeding with tubifex worms is inadvisable. Monospecies keeping tank. Breeding tank: with capacity of 500 litres per pair, hiding places, dim lighting. Sexual dimorphism: monomorphic fish. Sex ratio: 1:1. Breeding water: 26 °C; pH 7.5–8.5; dCH 2°–4°. Eggs: period of development in the mouth of the female? Feeding of fry: brine shrimp nauplii.

Shy and peaceable fish. Breeding is difficult. Their behaviour is quite different from that of other African mouthbrooders. Before spawning the brood fish dig vigorously in the bottom. The female deposits a large number of minute eggs (purportedly 400 or even more); sometimes there are so many that the female is unable to take them all up in her mouth and the remainder are collected by the male. The male's brood instinct, however, is not as developed and he may eat the eggs. According to a number of aquarists the male does not attack the female but shares the task of caring for the fry by taking them from her mouth into his. Because the fish dwell at greater depths with a constant temperature they are more sensitive to fluctuations in temperature than species that dwell in more shallow waters by the shoreline.

2 **Striped Goby Cichlid**

Eretmodus cyanostictus BOULENGER, 1899

☐
●

Distribution: A species endemic to Lake Tanganyika, where it occurs sporadically in the shallow waters of the stony to rocky littoral zone of the whole lake to depths of 1.5 metres. It is a bottom-dwelling fish that tends to move by jumping rather than swimming and continually stays close to hiding places. Full length: 8 cm. Diet: live foods, augmented by plant foods (algae). Monospecies keeping tank (or mixed aquarium together with only a small number of other fish – less aggressive species of the shoreline zone of Lake Tanganyika). Breeding tank: with capacity of 200 litres per pair, stony bottom with crevices and cavities. Sexual dimorphism: very slight; the male is larger with slightly extended ventral fins; his dorsal and anal fins may be longer. Sex ratio: 1:1. Breeding water: 26–28 °C; pH 7.5–9.0; dCH 3° (or more), dGH 10–20°; fresh, oxygen-rich, filtered through active coal. Eggs: oval, 5 mm long, incubation period in the mouth of the female *c.* 12 days, in the mouth of the male a further 12 days. Feeding of fry: brine shrimp nauplii, finely sifted zooplankton.

There are a great number of local colour forms (populations) in the various parts of the lake's extensive shoreline. The fish are quarrelsome towards other members of the same species; individual pairs as well as individual specimens defend large territories. Breeding in captivity is difficult and has been achieved only occasionally. Brood care in the case of these mouthbrooders is unusual in that both partners share the task of caring for the eggs and fry. The fish spawn on a firm object that has been previously cleaned. The female deposits 20 to 25 eggs which she takes up into her mouth. On about the twelfth day, accompanied by an interesting ritual, the male takes the embryos into his mouth for a further 12 days when their development is completed. For this reason under no circumstances should the parent fish be separated.

Cichlidae

1 Livingstoni

Haplochromis livingstonii (GÜNTHER, 1893)

Syn. *Hemichromis livingstonii*

○
●
Distribution: A species endemic to Africa's Lake Malawi (Nyasa) — primarily the localities Masimbe and Likoma Island. Full length: 20 cm. Diet: live foods (earthworms, tubifex worms, larvae of aquatic insects, beef, fish), which may be augmented also with occasional granulated foods. Keeping tank: monospecies with capacity of 500 litres or more, sufficient cavities and hiding possibilities. Breeding tank: with capacity of 200 litres per pair. Sexual dimorphism: the dominant male has large dorsal and anal fins extended into a point and is a bluish hue, chiefly about the head. Young fish, females and males lower in the social order or in a state of sudden fright have the same coloration — the body is coloured beige, spotted with dark brown. Sex ratio: 1:1 under the following conditions, otherwise 1 male : 3—4 females. Breeding water: 25—27 °C; pH 7.0—7.5; dCH 3°; fresh. Add 1 teaspoon sodium chloride for every 10 litres of water + 1 teaspoon sodium bicarbonate for every 50 litres of water. Eggs: yellowish white to yellow, pear-shaped, 3 × 4 mm. Development in the mouth of the female lasts 25 days. Feeding of fry: minute, sifted zooplankton, brine shrimp nauplii.

The males allow only 'ripe' females that are willing to spawn into their large territories. Towards other members of their own kind as well as towards other fish they are very aggressive. In cramped quarters the dominant male will even thrash weaker males and females with unripe eggs to death. A means of preventing harm due to the male's aggressiveness is to partition the tank with a transparent pane of glass positioned so as to leave a gap of about 10 mm at the bottom. The male remains in one compartment, the female in the other; spawning and fertilization of the eggs takes place at the gap. As soon as the female is depleted lower the pane to the bottom to prevent the free-swimming fry from getting through to the male. While keeping constant watch the glass partition may be removed for a while and the female allowed to join the male. If the female is 'ripe' the pair will spawn within a short time. Afterwards they should be separated again. The female releases and incubates in her mouth about 50 to 100 eggs. When they leave her mouth the fry are 1 cm long and fully capable of fending for themselves. The following day the fry may be taken out and put into a separate tank. Their growth is rapid. Young fish attain sexual maturity at the age of a year.

Spawning 'merry-go-round' of mouthbrooders

Cichlidae

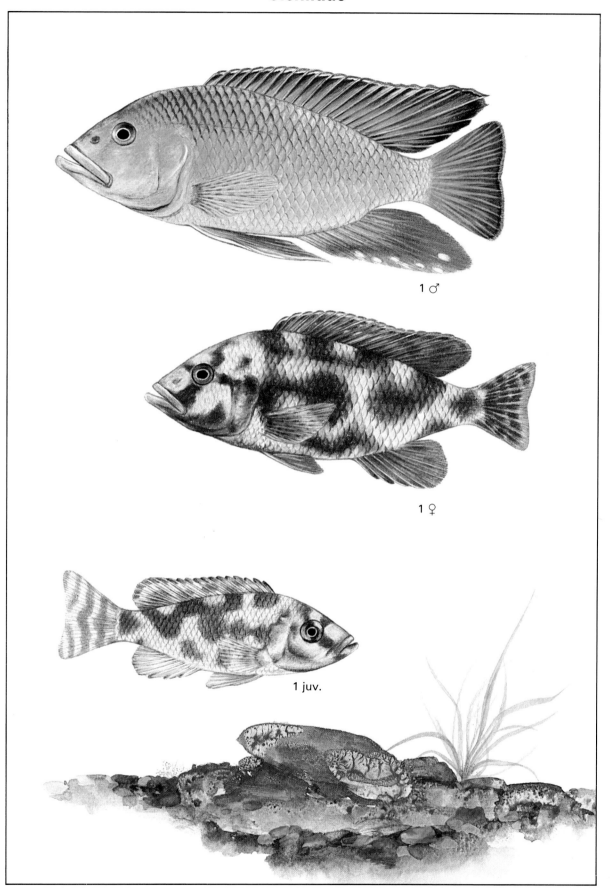

1 ♂

1 ♀

1 juv.

1 *Haplochromis euchilus* TREWAVAS, 1935

Distribution: A species endemic to Lake Malawi, between rocky and sandy zones. Full length: male − 30 cm, female − 20 cm. Diet: live as well as artificial foods, augmented by plant foods, chiefly algae. Monospecies keeping tank. Breeding tank: with capacity of 300−500 litres, 5 cm layer of sand and hiding places, e.g. drainage pipes, on the bottom. Sexual dimorphism: conspicuous; the male is larger and a shimmering blue, the female yellow with two longitudinal bands on the sides. Sex ratio: 1 male : 4 females. Breeding water: 26 °C; pH 7.5−8.5; dCH max. 3°; dGH 10−15°. Eggs: ∅ 3−4 mm, whitish-yellow; development in the mouth of the female lasts 18−21 days. Feeding of fry: brine shrimp nauplii, sifted zooplankton.

Peaceful fish (is not territorial); a very specialized species of mouthbrooder with greatly developed lips, apparently furnished with sensory cells. In all probability the lips serve to locate food by sense of touch − benthic organisms hidden in algal growths. The lips become larger with advancing age. The fish take also large pieces of food. They seek a spawning site on a firm object (flat stones in the middle of the aquarium) but they have also been observed to spawn in previously dug pits. During each spawning the female deposits strings of four or five eggs; 100 to 150 altogether. When she is depleted the female must be separated from the other fish. As soon as the fry leave her mouth her presence is no longer necessary.

2 *Haplochromis labrosus* (TREWAVAS, 1935)
Syn. *Melanochromis labrosus*

Distribution: A species endemic to Lake Malawi. Full length: 13−14 cm. Diet: live foods, augmented by artificial and plant foods (algae). Monospecies keeping tank (or mixed aquarium with African cichlids of similar characteristics). Breeding tank: with capacity of 200−300 litres for one group of brood fish and drainage pipes on the bottom. Sexual dimorphism: the male has more gold between the dark transverse bands, gold on the gill covers and along the edges of the unpaired fins, and small, orange 'egg-like' spots on the anal fin. The female is brownish or reddish-brown and may have spots on the anal fin. Sex ratio: 1 male : 3−4 females. Breeding water: 26 °C; pH 7.5−8.0; dCH 2−3°. Eggs: development in the mouth of the female lasts about 22 days. Feeding of fry: brine shrimp nauplii, finely sifted zooplankton.

Aggressive fish, particularly towards other members of the same species. Greatly swollen lips are characteristic of this mouthbrooder too. Such lips are likewise found in other species of fish, e.g. *Haplochromis chilotes* from Lake Victoria, *H. euchilus* and *H. lobochilus* from Lake Malawi, and *Lobochilotes labiatus* from Lake Tanganyika.

Depleted females should be put into separate tanks. However, it is recommended to wait a few days after spawning before taking them out thereby reducing the danger that they will spit out or swallow the eggs. The fry are brownish, finely striped, and entirely self-sufficient. As soon as they leave the mouth of the female her presence is no longer necessary.

Cichlidae

1 ♂

1 juv.

2

1 Morii, Blue Lumphead
Cyrtocara moorii (BOULENGER, 1902)
Syn. *Haplochromis moorii, Tropheus moorii*

Cichlidae

Distribution: A species endemic to Africa's Lake Malawi, where it is found in sandy shoreline zones, generally at depths of more than 5 metres. Full length: 25 cm. Diet: live as well as artificial foods, augmented by plant foods (detritus and algae). Monospecies keeping tank (may be kept together with members of the genus *Lethrinops* and with the species *Haplochromis rostratus* in tanks with capacity of 500 litres or more). Very low stock density. Breeding tank: of 500-litre capacity with sufficient refuges amongst stones at the back of the tank, sand and ample room to swim about in the front part of the tank. Sexual dimorphism: minute; the male may have a larger pad of fat on the head, but this is not a reliable means of identification. Sex ratio: 1 male : 3–4 females. Breeding water: 25–26 °C; pH 7.2–7.8; dCH 2–3°; dGH 10–18°; filtered through active coal. Eggs: yellow; the fry hatch in the mouth of the female on the sixth or seventh day and leave the mouth for the first time on the nineteenth or twentieth day. Feeding of fry: brine shrimp nauplii.

Peaceful, timid mouthbrooders. The males defend their territories. The number of eggs is between 20 and 90. The depleted female should be separated from the other fish by a glass partition with the minimum of handling. The fry are 8 mm long when they leave the female's mouth. Their coloration changes during growth. The fish are not entirely blue until the age of four months.

2 *Haplochromis polystigma* REGAN, 1921

Cichlidae

Distribution: A species endemic to Lake Malawi. Full length: 24 cm. Diet: live foods (small fish, earthworms), may be augmented by granulated foods. Monospecies keeping tank. Breeding tank: of 500-litre capacity with hiding possibilities (drainage pipes). Sexual dimorphism: indistinct; the dominant male has a blue-green sheen, red and orange spots (inconspicuous in other males) that are brightly luminous, and prominent 'egg-like' spots in the anal fin. The female is more plainly coloured and the 'egg-like' spots are not as prominent. Sex ratio: 1 male : 3–4 females. Breeding water: 25–27 °C; pH 7.0–8.0; dCH 3°; fresh. The addition of sodium chloride (1 tablespoon for every 10 litres of water) and sodium bicarbonate (1 tablespoon for every 100 litres of water) promotes the fish's well-being. Eggs: development in the mouth of the female lasts about 21 days. Feeding of fry: brine shrimp nauplii or finely sifted zooplankton.

Aggressive fish, particularly towards others of the same species; weaker males and unripe females may be killed. *H. polystigma* is a predator that actively hunts small fish. The female deposits approximately 20 eggs. Depleted females should be separated from the other fish. The fry should be reared only with others of their own kind. The fish live in a shoal throughout the whole period of their development, i.e. for seven or eight months. This species is very similar in coloration and markings to *H. linni* Burgess and H. Axelrod, 1975.

1

2

1 Electric Blue Hap
Haplochromis sp.

Commercial name: *'Haplochromis ahli', 'H. jacksoni'*

Distribution: A species endemic to Lake Malawi – found in all parts of the lake in the rocky shoreline zone, but is rare. Full length: 10–12 cm; in aquariums reaches a length of 16 cm. Diet: live foods; is fond of catching fish. Monospecies keeping tank with capacity of 500 litres and sufficient hiding possibilities among stones. Breeding tank: same as keeping tank. Sexual dimorphism: the male is blue, the female brownish (both sexes may have 'egg-like' spots). So far it is not known if this species has been bred in captivity but it may be assumed that breeding, including water requirements, is the same as for other *Haplochromis* species that are endemic to Lake Malawi.

Shy fish, quarrelsome towards members of the same species, particularly in cramped quarters. The commercial name for this fish is the valid scientific name of another species – *H. jacksoni* Iles, 1960 (Mayland, H. J.: Grosse Aquarienpraxis III., p. 194). This gives rise to much confusion, increased by the fact that both are little known endemic Lake Malawi species.

H. jacksoni Iles, 1960 is much bigger (18–20 cm), high-backed and has a relatively small head. Young fish, weaker males and females are silvery-grey and have two dark spots. The unpaired fins are marked with red spots. *H. jacksoni* likewise differs from the illustrated mouthbrooder in diet: it feeds chiefly on zooplankton.

2 Venustus
Haplochromis venustus BOULENGER, 1908
Syn. *Cyrtocara venustus, C. venusta, Haplochromis simulans*

Distribution: A species endemic to Lake Malawi – sandy shoreline zone. Full length: 26 cm. Diet: live foods (favourites are gastropods, small fish, and earthworms), may be augmented by artificial foods. Monospecies keeping tank. Breeding tank: of 500-litre capacity with drainage pipes on the bottom. Sexual dimorphism: the male is more colourful and larger. Sex ratio: 1 male : 3–4 females. Breeding water: 26 °C; pH 7.0–8.0; dCH 2–3°; fresh – change 1/3 of the water weekly. Eggs: yellow-brown, 3 mm long; development in the mouth of the female lasts 21 days. Feeding of fry: brine shrimp nauplii, sifted zooplankton, may be augmented by artificial fry foods (minute granules).

Fish aggressive towards others of the same species. During spawning they swim slowly around in circles as do other members of the genus. If there is a substrate on the bottom of the tank the male digs a pit in it and tries to attract a ripe female there. The female deposits about 120 eggs during spawning. When depleted she must be put in a separate tank and not be disturbed (see the similar *H. livingstonii*). If she is not handled with care and is disturbed in any way the female may spit the fry out of her mouth. When the fry leave the mouth they are 10 mm long and fully developed. They are cared for by the female for a further 10 days; she takes them up in her mouth for the night and whenever danger threatens. On the tenth day (or even earlier) separate the fry from the female.

Cichlidae

1

2

1 Malawian Eye-biter

Haplochromis compressiceps (BOULENGER, 1908)

Syn. *Paratilapia compressiceps*

◁

●

Distribution: A species endemic to Lake Malawi, sandy shoreline zone overgrown with reeds and eel grass (aquatic plants of the genus *Vallisneria*). Full length: 25 cm. Diet: live foods, mainly fish (it is predatory). Monospecies keeping tank. Breeding tank: of 300- to 500-litre capacity, light, with plants, best of all eel grass. Sexual dimorphism: the male is green or a shimmering blue with faintly reddish fins (depending on the locality); the female is silvery. Sex ratio: 1 male : 3–4 females. Breeding water: 25–27 °C; pH 7.0–8.0; dCH 2–3°. Eggs: development in the mouth of the female lasts three weeks. Feeding of fry: brine shrimp nauplii, finely sifted zooplankton.

Typical of these variably-coloured fish is the strongly laterally compressed body and large pointed head. The head comprises 40 per cent of the total body length. The mouth is deeply cleft with greatly protruding lower jaw. The fish lie in wait for prey in a slanting position head downward. They swallow smaller fish whole, tail first. Their coloration and body shape facilitate hunting for food amidst growths of reeds and aquatic plants and at the same time serve to protect them from such natural enemies as fish-eating birds. A characteristic occasionally ascribed to this species, i.e. that the fish bite out the eyes of other fish, is rather unlikely, even though such a thing may sometimes happen – this, of course, is true not only of *H. compressiceps* but of a great many other fish as well.

2 Burton's Nigerian Mouthbreeder

Astatotilapia burtoni (GÜNTHER, 1893)

Syn. *Chromis burtoni, Haplochromis burtoni*

◁

●

Distribution: Africa's Lake Tanganyika and its tributaries, Lake Kivu. Full length: 12 cm. Diet: live foods, may be augmented with granulated foods. Monospecies keeping tank. Breeding tank: with capacity of 200 litres or more, sufficient hiding possibilities (drainage pipes) on the bottom. Sexual dimorphism: the male is larger, his dorsal, ventral and anal fins are bigger, there are 5–7 black-edged orange spots on the anal fin; the female is less colourful, the spots on the anal fin are less prominent and fewer in number. Sex ratio: 1 male : 3 females. Breeding water: 25–27 °C; pH 7.0–8.0; dCH 2°. Eggs: development in the mouth of the female lasts 15–20 days. Feeding of fry: brine shrimp nauplii or finely sifted zooplankton.

When she is depleted the female leaves the spawning site, holding the eggs in her mouth, and seeks a place to hide. When they have completed their development the fry continue to return to her mouth for a few days longer during the night and when danger threatens. This instinct is so strong that the fry will even attempt to enter the mouth of a mock fish that has been put in the aquarium. The female should be separated from the fry after three or four days. Some young females spawn on reaching a length of just 4 cm.

Günther named the species *burtoni* in honour of R. Burton, who, together with Spek, discovered Lake Tanganyika in 1858.

1 ♂

2 ♀

2 ♂

1 Banded Jewel Fish
Hemichromis fasciatus PETERS, 1857
Syn. *Chromichthys elongatus, Hemichromis auritus, H. desguezi, H. leiguardi*

Distribution: West Africa — from the Senegal River to Lake Turkana (Lake Rudolf) in the east; forest and savanna waters, turbid waters rich in sediment; the fish also enter river mouths with brackish water. They are not found in fast-flowing waters and the open waters of lakes. Full length: 25 cm. Diet: more robust live foods, larvae of aquatic insects, earthworms, live fish. Monospecies keeping tank. Breeding tank: with capacity of at least 200 litres per pair, layer of medium-grained gravel, flat stones, cavities and other hiding possibilities on the bottom. Sexual dimorphism: imperceptible; the female may be smaller, fuller, and during spawning darker. Sex ratio: 1:1. Breeding water: 24—26 °C; pH 7.0—7.5; dCH max. 2°; dGH 10—12° (species adaptable to changes in the chemical composition of the water); add 1 tablespoon sea salt (or NaCl) for every 50 litres of water. Eggs: incubation period three to five days. Feeding of fry: brine shrimp nauplii, later sifted zooplankton.

The fish are anti-social and bite one another. Apart from the spawning period it is recommended to separate the male from the female by a glass pane. As soon as the female's genital papilla becomes enlarged the two may be allowed to join. The female deposits up to 1,000 eggs on a flat stone that has been only haphazardly cleaned. She watches over the eggs while the male guards the territory. On hatching the fry are transferred to pits that have been previously dug out in the gravel. The parents care for the fry until they reach a length of 3 cm. Young males attain sexual maturity when they are 10 cm long, females when they are 7 cm long.

2 Jewel Fish
Hemichromis bimaculatus GILL, 1862
Syn. *Hemichromis letoumeuii, H. rolandi, H. saharae*

Distribution: northwest and central Africa, to the south and east to Zaire. The various localities are in flowing as well as standing waters and also in coastal lagoons with brackish water. Full length: 15 cm. Diet: live foods, augmented by granulated foods. Monospecies keeping tank. Breeding tank: with capacity of 200 litres per pair and flat stones on the bottom (lithophilic fish). Sexual dimorphism: during the spawning period the female is a vivid red, the male tends to be brownish red. Sex ratio: 1:1. Breeding water: 24 °C; pH 7.0—7.5; dCH 2°. Eggs: yellowish, incubation period 3—5 days. Feeding of fry: brine shrimp or *Cyclops* nauplii.

Specimens caught directly in the wild, in their native waters, are redder, particularly the form from Mali, imported in 1960. The fish are territorial and quarrelsome. The female deposits up to 500 eggs on a firm object that has been carefully cleaned beforehand. Both parents take care of the eggs and fry. The young fish grow quickly. They should be removed when the parent fish prepare to spawn again. After six months the young fish measure 7 cm and are sexually mature.

1

2 ♀

2 ♂

Distribution: A species endemic to Lake Tanganyika, rocky shoreline zone. Full length: 15 cm. Diet: live as well as artificial foods, augmented by plant foods. Monospecies keeping tank. Breeding tank: with capacity of 200 litres per pair, and sufficient hiding possibilities (cavities). Sexual dimorphism: imperceptible: the male may have dark fins and his dorsal, ventral and anal fins may be longer than the female's. Sex ratio: 1:1. Breeding water: 25−28 °C; pH 7.5−8.0; dCH 2−3°. Eggs: minute, white, incubation period 48 hrs. Feeding of fry: brine shrimp nauplii.

An aggressive species. The fish are not very willing to spawn. One spawning may produce 400 to 700 fry. The free-swimming fry are not led about by the parent fish. The similar *Cyphotilapia frontosa* and *Lamprologus sexfasciatus* differ from the illustrated species by having six bands across the body whereas *L. tretocephalus* has only five.

2 Lemon Cichlid
Lamprologus leleupi leleupi POLL, 1956   Cichlidae

Distribution: A species endemic to Africa's Lake Tanganyika, the northwestern section, Luhanga and the eastern shore. Full length: 10 cm. Diet: live foods, may be augmented by artificial foods. Monospiecies keeping tank. Breeding tank: with stony bottom and sufficient hiding possibilities. Sexual dimorphism: imperceptible; the male is bigger with slightly larger fins and more aggressive, older males have a slight protuberance on the forehead. The most conspicuous difference is in the length of the genital papillae. Sex ratio: 1:1. Breeding water: 22−26 °C; pH 7.0−7.5; rather hard to hard, e.g. dCH 7°, dGH 21°, but also dCH 2°, dGH 10°, fresh. Eggs: ∅ 1.5 mm, white with yellowish tinge, incubation period 3 days. Feeding of fry: brine shrimp nauplii.

Before spawning the paired fish display by opening their mouths and dig pits in the sand close to the spawning site. The female deposits the eggs on the previously cleaned, dark, vertical sides of a cavity, often one on top of another, so that the clutch forms a grape-like cluster. There are some 200 altogether. The eggs and fry are cared for by the female, the male guards the site. During this period of caring for the brood the female turns a darker hue. Three days after laying the eggs the female sucks the embryos out of the egg case and transfers them to the prepared pits. (Some young females may eat the embryos during this process.) The embryos are 5 mm long and have a large yolk sac. The female successively moves them to various places. The fry become free swimming after nine days, at which time they are 7 mm long and switch over to exogenous nutrition. Remove the young fish before the next spawning but leave the parent fish in the same tank.

Cichlidae

1

2

1 Tetracanthus

Lamprologus tetracanthus BOULENGER, 1899

Syn. *Lamprologus brevianalis, L. marginatus*

Distribution: a species endemic to Lake Tanganyika — sandy-stony biotopes from the upper layers of water to depths of 10 metres. Full length: 20 cm. Diet: live foods, chiefly molluscs, small fish and larvae of aquatic insects. Monospecies keeping tank. Breeding tank: with capacity of 200—300 litres per pair and drainage pipes on the bottom. Sexual dimorphism: monomorphic fish. Sex ratio: 1:1. Breeding water: 26 °C; pH 7.5—8.0; dCH 2—3°. Eggs: whitish, incubation period 3 days. Feeding of fry: brine shrimp nauplii.

Paired fish spawn in a cavity. The female deposits some 500 eggs on the sides of the cavity. The parent fish care for the eggs as well as the fry. After one week the fry switch over to exogenous nutrition. As soon as the parent fish prepare to spawn again the fry must be removed.

2 Compressed Cichlid

Lamprologus compressiceps BOULENGER, 1898

Distribution: a species endemic to Lake Tanganyika — rocky shoreline zones. Full length: 15 cm. Diet: live foods (larvae of aquatic insects, small fish). Monospecies keeping tank — roomy. Breeding tank: with capacity of 200—300 litres per pair, sufficient caves and crevices. Sexual dimorphism: monomorphic fish. Water: 24—26 °C; pH 7.0—7.5; dCH 2—3°. There are no reports about the breeding of this species in the aquarium.

Two forms have been imported: a) the northern form, which has the body and fins tinted ochre with six dark, double cross bars on the sides, and b) the southern form which has the sides coloured whitish beige and crossed by more than six bars, two of which are behind the eyes and converge at the bottom of the gill cover (see illustration). Both forms are high-backed and strongly compressed laterally. The species is solitary and pays no attention to larger fish.

3 Lyretail Lamprologus

Lamprologus brichardi POLL, 1974

Syn. *Lamprologus savoryi elongatus*

Distribution: a very abundant species endemic to Lake Tanganyika. Full length: 10 cm. Diet: live foods (zooplankton, brine shrimp). Monospecies keeping tank (1 pair to a tank). Breeding tank: with capacity of 50—100 litres for 1 pair, on the bottom piles of flat stones providing sufficient cavities and crannies. Sexual dimorphism: older males have a small pad of fat on the forehead. Sex ratio: 1:1. Breeding water: 25 °C; pH 7.0—8.0; dCH 2—4°; fresh, filtered. Eggs: ∅ 1 mm, deep dark red with whitish end, incubation period 3 days. Feeding of fry: brine shrimp nauplii.

The brood pair does not tolerate larger fish in the vicinity. The female deposits approximately 200 eggs on the roof of a cavity. Six days after hatching the fry switch over to exogenous nutrition. It often happens that the parent fish will spawn again while still leading the fry about, thereupon giving intensive care to two and even three generations simultaneously. The young fish grow slowly. They are choosy as to food and do not eat much. When they are about nine months old it is necessary to keep careful watch and separate those that have paired off. Fish reaching sexual maturity kill one another.

Cichlidae

1

2

3

1 Red-top Cichlid
Labeotropheus trewavasae FRYER, 1956

☐
● Distribution: A species endemic to Africa's Lake Tanganyika, rocky shoreline. Full length: 12 cm. Diet: live as well as artificial foods, augmented by plant foods. Monospecies keeping tank (or a mixed aquarium with mouthbrooders of like characteristics). Breeding tank: of 200-litre capacity with drainage pipes on the bottom. Sexual dimorphism: the male is blue, but may also be streaked, his dorsal fin rust-coloured to orange-red, the anal fin with several prominent yellow spots; the female is slightly smaller, greyish or yellowish brown, but may also be variously spotted. Sex ratio: 1 male : 3–4 females. Breeding water: 26 °C; pH 7.5–8.0; dCH 2–4°. Eggs: development in the mouth of the female lasts 20 days. Feeding of fry: brine shrimp nauplii, finely sifted zooplankton.

L. trewavasae is closely related to *L. fuelleborni*. Both mouthbrooders are found in the same localities. *L. trewavasae* is slightly slimmer. The Red-top Cichlid is confined to a stony bottom and does not travel over areas of a different character (sandy, muddy) which leads to the isolation of populations and consequently to the occurrence of many colour forms. Keeping the fish together with other mouthbrooders of like characteristics mitigates their innate aggressiveness. Depleted females (which may be identified by the enlarged throat sac) should be transferred – each to a separate tank together with the drainage pipe (the female may also be taken out carefully with a net). As soon as the young fish leave her mouth remove the female from the tank.

2 *Labeotropheus trewavasae* – other forms

☐
● This species occurs in a great variety of colour forms in various localities. This variability generally occurs in females, which may be grey, yellow, orange or streaked. The males are mostly blue. Males in the north of the lake have a red dorsal fin and a red glint in the caudal and anal fins. The systematic classification of the yellow form, found on the eastern shore of the lake and known on the market as *'Labeotropheus pernostus'*, is so far unclear.

3 Fuelleborn's Cichlid
Labeotropheus fuelleborni AHL, 1927
Syn. *Labeotropheus curvirostris*

☐
● Distribution: A species endemic to Africa's Lake Malawi, gravelly and rocky shorelines. Full length: 15 cm. Diet: live as well as artificial foods, augmented by plant foods. Monospecies keeping tank (or mixed aquarium together with mouthbrooders of like characteristics). Breeding tank: with capacity of 200 litres for 1 group of brood fish and drainage pipes on the bottom. Sexual dimorphism: the male is an intense blue with prominent transverse stripes, his colouring is variable; the female is smaller and a dingy greyish-violet. Sex ratio: 1 male : 3–4 females. Breeding water: 26 °C; pH 7.5–8.0; dCH 2–4°. Eggs: development in the mouth of the female

lasts 19–20 days. Feeding of fry: brine shrimp nauplii and finely sifted zooplankton, chopped tubifex worms.

When they leave the mother's mouth the young fish are 1 cm long, fully developed, and selfsufficient. During the period of incubation of the eggs each female should be kept in a separate tank. An aquarium of 14-litre capacity provided with a drainage pipe and good aeration and placed in an undisturbed spot is sufficient for the purpose. The young fish grow quickly.

1 ♂

1 ♀

2 ♂

3 ♂

1 Dimidiatus

Nanochromis dimidiatus (PELLEGRIN, 1900)

Syn. *Pelmatochromis dimidiatus*

Distribution: Central Africa — Ubangi River — tributary of the Congo (Zaire). Full length: male — 8 cm, female — 7 cm. Diet: live foods, may be augmented by artificial foods (Do not overfeed brood fish. It is recommended to let them go hungry for a whole week on occasion and then feed them generously again). Monospecies keeping tank. Breeding tank: with capacity of 50—100 litres per pair, a 3 cm layer of sand on the bottom and cavities formed by stones, flowerpots or coconut shells. Sexual dimorphism: the male is larger, his dorsal and anal fins are longer. The female is more colourful, her dorsal fin bears a band with a pearly glint. She has a black spot in the hind third of the dorsal fin, and her belly is coloured lilac-red. Sex ratio: 1:1. Breeding water: 26—28 °C; pH 6.5; dCH max. 1°; dGH max. 10°; filtered through peat or with an addition of peat extract. Eggs: incubation period 40—50 hrs. (depending on the temperature of the water). Feeding of fry: brine shrimp or *Cyclops* nauplii.

The fish spawn in cavities. The female deposits approximately 60 eggs. Endogenous nutrition lasts four to six days. The parents care for the eggs and fry.

2 Blue Cichlid

Nanochromis nudiceps (BOULENGER, 1899)

Syn. *Pseudoplesiops nudiceps* (according to some sources *Nanochromis nudiceps* is a synonym for *N. parilius* Roberts and Stewart, 1976).

Distribution: water system of the Congo River (Zaire), also Stanley Pool (Pool Malebo). Full length: male — 8 cm, female — 6 cm. Diet: live foods, may be augmented by artificial foods (Do not overfeed brood fish.) Monospecies keeping tank. Breeding tank: with capacity of 50 litres per pair, a 3 cm layer of sand on the bottom, inverted flowerpots with notched rim. Sexual dimorphism: the male is bigger with larger dorsal and anal fins, the female's belly is a more vivid emerald green and rounded when she is spawn-ripe. Sex ratio: 1:1. Breeding water: 26—28 °C; pH 6.5; dCH max. 1°; dGH max. 10°; filtered through peat or with an addition of peat extract. Eggs: yellow, anchored to the substrate by thin filaments; incubation period 40—50 hrs. depending on the temperature of the water. Feeding of fry: brine shrimp or *Cyclops* nauplii.

Quarrelsome fish leading a hidden existence. Spawning takes place in cavities which the fish clean carefully beforehand, carrying the sand out to the front of the entrance. The female deposits up to 200 eggs on the roof of the cavity and cares for them by herself; she does not allow the male inside. The fry leave the cavity after eight to ten days but are led back by the female for the night while the male conceals himself in the vicinity. Young fish grow quickly and at the age of five weeks are 3 cm long.

Cichlidae

1 ♂

1 ♀

2 ♂

1 Johanni
Melanochromis johanni (ECCLES, 1973)
Syn. *Pseudotropheus johanni,* commercial name: *'P. daviesi'*

☐ ● Distribution: a species endemic to Lake Malawi, southeastern shore and Likoma Island – stony and rocky shores. Full length: 10 cm. Diet: live foods, augmented by artificial and plant foods. Monospecies keeping tank (or mixed aquarium together with mouthbrooders of like characteristics). Breeding tank: of 200-litre capacity with drainage pipes on the bottom. Sexual dimorphism: dichromatism – the male is dark blue to black with vivid blue bands and small 'egg-like' spots in the anal fin, the female is orange-yellow. Sex ratio: 1 male : 3–4 females. Breeding water: 26–27 °C; pH 7.5–8.0; dCH 2–3°, fresh. Eggs: large, development in the mouth of the female lasts 22–26 days. Feeding of fry: brine shrimp nauplii, finely sifted zooplankton.

M. johanni is an aggressive species, even the females are bellicose towards one another. The number of eggs laid by the female is approximately 15. As soon as the fry leave the mother's mouth they are fully self-sufficient and the female may be removed. Keep such females in separate tanks and feed them generously and often.

2 Rusty Cichlid
Melanochromis brevis TREWAVAS, 1935
Syn. *Iodotropheus sprengerae*

☐ ● Distribution: a species endemic to Lake Malawi, rocky localities Nkudzi and Monkey Bay. Full length: 12 cm. Diet: live as well as artificial foods, regularly augmented by vegetable foods. Monospecies keeping tank. Breeding tank: of 200-litre capacity with stony bottom and sufficient hiding places (drainage pipes, notched flowerpots). Sexual dimorphism: the male is a vivid brown with dark blue glints and with vivid orange spots on the anal fin. Sex ratio: 1 male : 3 females. Breeding water: 26 °C; pH 7.5–8.5; dCH 2–4°. Eggs: development in the mouth of the female lasts 17 days. Feeding of fry: brine shrimp nauplii, finely sifted zooplankton.

It seems that the taxonomy of this species is not yet definitive. According to Mayland the fish are caught and imported only rarely – it is believed they dwell in the deeper layers of water. Care and rearing is the same as for other species of African mouthbrooders.

1 ♂

2 ♂

1 Nyasa Golden Cichlid
Melanochromis auratus (BOULENGER, 1897)
Syn. *Tilapia aurata, Pseudotropheus auratus*

Cichlidae

Distribution: a species endemic to Lake Malawi. Full length: male – 11 cm, female – 9 cm. Diet: live as well as artificial foods, augmented by plant foods. Monospecies keeping tank (or a mixed aquarium with mouthbrooders of like characteristics). Breeding tank: of 200-litre capacity with suitably arranged drainage pipes on the bottom. Sexual dimorphism: dichromatism – the male is velvety black with white longitudinal bands, the female is yellow with dark bands. Sex ratio: 1 male : 3–4 females. Breeding water: 26 °C; pH 7.5–8.0; dCH 2–4°; fresh, filtered. Eggs: incubation in the mouth of the female lasts 22–26 days. Feeding of fry: brine shrimp nauplii or finely sifted zooplankton.

Spawned-out females may be identified by the enlarged throat sac on the underside of the mouth. Transfer each female carefully together with the drainage pipe to a separate tank of about 20-litre capacity. The individual tanks must be placed in a quiet, undisturbed spot and provided with diffused light and aeration. The fry leave the mother's mouth when they are 1 cm long, at which time they are fully self-sufficient and fully coloured. They no longer stay by the female for any length of time and instinctively look about for a hiding place. The female may therefore be removed. First of all grasp the female lightly in the palm of the hand, turn her head downward and with a blunt rod lightly press on the lower jaw until the mouth is opened. If there are still any remaining fry inside the female will spit them out (this applies to other mouthbrooders as well). The litter usually consists of about 40 young; their growth is regular and rapid.

2 *Pseudotropheus joanjohnsonae* (JOHNSON, 1974)
Syn. *Labidochromis joanjohnsonae, Melanochromis exasperatus?*
Commercial name: *'Labidochromis caeruelus likomae'* – apparently a name for several species.

Cichlidae

Distribution: A species endemic to Lake Malawi – Likoma Island, upper layers of the water in the rocky shoreline zone. Full length: 10 cm. Diet: live foods, augmented by artificial and plant foods. Monospecies keeping tank. Breeding tank: with capacity of 200 litres or more, drainage pipes on the bottom. Sexual dimorphism: dichromatism; the male is blue, the female is a pale blue-green with longitudinal rows of gold-ochre spots and a shimmering spot on the hind edge of the gill covers (young fish have a similar coloration). Sex ratio: 1 male : 3 females. Breeding water: 26–28 °C; pH 7.5–8.5; dCH 2–3°; fresh. Eggs: development in the mouth of the female lasts 20–24 days. Feeding of fry: brine shrimp nauplii or finely-sifted zooplankton.

A territorial and aggressive mouthbrooder. The female deposits approximately 20 eggs. At the age of 14 days young fish have the juvenile coloration with a red belly.

When describing this fish in 1974 Johnson classed it in the genus *Labidochromis*. Oliver is of the opinion that it is the species *L. fryeri,* but in 1976 Burgess described it as *Melanochromis exasperatus,* all of which made the systematic classification of this species a matter of confusion. In 1976 A. D. Stoch revised the species and classed it in the genus *Pseudotropheus,* supporting his decision, among other things, by the characteristics of the teeth.

1 ♂

1 ♀

2 ♂

2 ♀

1 *Pseudotropheus socolofi* JOHNSON, 1974

Commercial name: *Pseudotropheus* sp. *'pindani'*

Cichlidae

☐
●

Distribution: A species endemic to Lake Malawi, rocky shore round the islands of Likoma and Chisumula, also the eastern shore of the lake in Mozambique. Full length: 12 cm; the female is slightly smaller. Diet: live and plant foods, may be augmented by artificial foods. Monospecies or monogeneric keeping tank. Breeding tank: with capacity of 200 litres for a group of brood fish and sufficient hiding possibilities. Sexual dimorphism: evident only in older fish; the male is strikingly blue, his anal fin is longer and marked with orange 'egg-like' spots. Sex ratio: 1 male : 3–4 females. Breeding water: 24–28 °C; pH 7.5–8.0; dCH 2–3°; dGH 10–15°. Eggs: development in the mouth of the female lasts 21 days. Feeding of fry: brine shrimp nauplii, finely sifted zooplankton.

An aggressive and territorial mouthbrooder. Its aggressiveness is mitigated if it is kept together with mouthbrooders of similar characteristics, on condition that the tank is sufficiently roomy and provides numerous hiding places. A depleted female is readily identified by the enlarged throat sac. Each female should be put in a separate tank. The fry are self-sufficient as soon as they leave the female's mouth and her presence is no longer necessary. After a short while the fry seek out hiding places of their own rather than the mouth of the female. Young fish are slender, older specimens high-backed. Young fish attain sexual maturity when they reach a length of 8 cm.

2 *Melanochromis crabro* RIBBINK and LEWIS, 1982

Commercial name: *Pseudotropheus* sp. *'chameleo'*

Cichlidae

☐
●

Distribution: a species endemic to Lake Malawi, shoreline waters of Likoma Island. Full length: 15 cm. Diet: more robust live foods, augmented by plant and granulated foods. Monospecies keeping tank (or mixed aquarium with mouthbrooders of like characteristics). Breeding tank: with capacity of 200–300 litres for a breeding group, and drainage pipes on the bottom. Sexual dimorphism: the male is larger, with one or more 'egg-like' spots on the anal fin (these may, however, be absent), his anal fin is bigger and drawn out into a point. Sex ratio: 1 male : 3–4 females (basic breeding group). Breeding water: 24–28 °C; pH 7.5–8.0; dCH max. 4°, fresh. Eggs: development in the mouth of the female lasts 20–21 days. Feeding of fry: brine shrimp nauplii, finely sifted zooplankton.

The fish are extremely aggressive towards members of their own species as well as members of other species. The female deposits 20 to 50 eggs, which she picks up in her mouth as soon as they are fertilized. After spawning she retreats to a secluded spot. If she is transferred to another tank after spawning, when she is returned to the breeding tank she may be thrashed to death as an alien fish (this also applies to a great many other species of endemic Africa mouthbrooders). It is, therefore, better to wait until nearly the end of incubation before transferring the females. Some females take food during the incubation period. The fish were named *'chameleo'* because of their ability to change colour quickly. The scientific name given in the heading is probably not definitive.

Cichlidae

1 *Pseudotropheus lombardoi* Burges, 1977

Commercial name: *'Pseudotropheus liliancinius'*

Distribution: A species endemic to Africa's Lake Malawi (Nyasa), steep rocky shoreline of the Mbenji Islands. Full length: 12 cm (the wild form is generally smaller). Diet: more robust live and plant foods, may be augmented by artificial flaked and granulated foods. Community tank (together with African Lake Cichlids), with capacity of 500 litres or more. Breeding tank: with capacity of 200 litres for one group of brood fish and sufficient hiding places on the bottom, e.g. drainage pipes. Sexual dimorphism: sexual dichromatism; the male is yellow with 'egg-like' spots on the anal fin, the female is pale blue with blue-black transverse stripes and does not have the 'egg-like' spots in the anal fin; very occasionally the female may be coloured a dingy yellowish brown. Sex ratio: 1 male : 2–3 females (basic breeding group). Breeding water: 24–28 °C; pH 7.5–8.0; dCH 2°; dGH 10–15°. Eggs: development in the mouth of the female lasts four weeks. Feeding of fry: brine shrimp nauplii, finely sifted zooplankton.

P. lombardoi is very aggressive, both towards members of the same species and to other fish. The males lay claim to large territories. Keeping the fish together with other mouthbrooders of like size and characteristics mitigates their natural aggressiveness. The coloration of young fish is similar to that of the female. Differentiation of coloration according to sex begins when they reach a length of 4 cm: the males become paler and gradually turn grey to yellow with the transverse stripes still visible; the females, on the other hand, are bluish, including the fins, and the anal fin is always without the 'egg-like' spot. Sexual dimorphism in *P. lombardoi* may be viewed as a classic example. The female and young fish show a slight resemblance to *Cynotilapia afra* (Günther, 1893), which reaches a total length of 10 cm. Morphologically *Pseudotropheus lombardoi* is similar to *P. zebra* (Boulenger, 1899).

The specific name was given to the fish in honour of John Lombard, American importer of fish.

1 ♂

1 ♀

1 juv.

1 Nyasa Blue Cichlid
Pseudotropheus zebra (BOULENGER, 1899)
Syn. *Tilapia zebra*

Distribution: A species endemic to Africa's Lake Malawi, rocky shores. Full length: 12 cm. Diet: live, artificial and plant foods. Monospecies keeping tank (or mixed aquarium with like species of mouthbrooders). Breeding tank: with capacity of 200 litres or more, depending on the number of fish, and drainage pipes on the bottom. Sexual dimorphism: the male is more robust, his ventral and anal fins are bigger, and there are prominent yellow spots in the anal fin; in the female these spots are inconspicuous or completely absent. Sex ratio: 1 male : 3—4 females. Breeding water: 26 °C; pH 7.5—8.5; dCH 2—4°; fresh. Eggs: $\emptyset$ 4 mm, development in the mouth of the female lasts 21 days. Feeding of fry: brine shrimp nauplii, finely sifted zooplankton.

P. zebra (BB-blue-black form, Fig. 1) with vivid black and blue bands is one of the longest-known of the MBUNA group of mouth-brooders, i.e. fish bound to rocky lake biotopes.

They are territorial and aggressive fish. Like other mouthbrooders they swim slowly round in circles during spawning. A single female deposits an average of 25 to 35 eggs, 60 at the most. When they leave the mouth of the female the fry are 1 cm long and fully self-sufficient.

2 *Pseudotropheus* sp. aff. *zebra*

The abbreviation aff. (from the Latin word *affinis* meaning related) is used in the case of a group of individuals that are morphologically different from known species but exhibit a very close kinship to one such species and where it is impossible to establish with certainty a new species for the given individuals. It is also used as an expression of doubt about membership of a certain species.

The individual populations of these fish are polymorphic, having various shapes, sizes as well as colouring. Various coloration occurs in both males and females (see, for example, the form shown in Fig. 2b). On the one hand there are local populations resulting from the permanent isolation of nearby localities due to the insurmountable natural boundary formed by the zones of sand where tributaries flow into the lake, and on the other hand there are mutations, sudden changes of hereditary traits that occur in wild forms as well as in aquarium-raised fish. This is the reason for the great problems in the systematic classification of these mouth-brooders. The confusion is multiplied by the import of red, blue, as well as mottled forms from the wild that are likewise named *Pseudotropheus zebra*, even though in all probability they are different, closely related species.

Fig. 2a shows the mottled form called OB — Orange Blossom — in which the male is light blue, the female dark blue, and both are marked with dark spots. Fig. 2c shows the blue form called B — blue, in which both sexes are blue.

In the opinion of breeders there is no need to fear that the separate forms will interbreed. Nevertheless this may happen, even though not every form will spawn with every other form. A greater willingness to spawn is exhibited by the males, not the females. Hybrids that have been successfully bred so far are fertile.

1 ♂

2 a ♂

2 b ♂

2 c ♂

1 *Pseudotropheus* sp. aff. *zebra* – form TB – Tangerine Blue

☐
●
One of the forms of this polymorphic species marked by pronounced sexual dichromatism that becomes evident shortly after the fry hatch from the eggs: the male is blue, the female yellow to reddish orange.

2 *Pseudotropheus tropheops* REGAN, 1921

☐
●
Distribution: A species endemic to Lake Malawi – rocky shoreline. Full length: 15 cm (20 cm). Diet: live foods augmented by granulated and plant foods. Monospecies keeping tank (or mixed aquarium together with endemic mouth-brooders of like characteristics). Breeding tank: with capacity of 500 litres for one breeding group, and drainage pipes on the bottom (sufficient hiding places are essential). Sexual dimorphism: dichromatism: the male is grey-blue, the female may be golden-yellow, ochre-yellow patterned with yellow-white spots (one spot on each scale), brownish yellow with dark-edged scales (reticulated pattern), mottled with red-blue markings and black spots, etc. The males have one or more 'egg-like' spots on the anal fin, the females are smaller. Sex ratio: 1 male: 3–4 females; basic breeding group. Breeding water: 26–27 °C; pH 7.0–8.5; dCH 2°; dGH max. 10°; fresh. Eggs: incubation in the mouth of the female lasts 21 days? Feeding of fry: brine shrimp nauplii or finely-sifted zooplankton.

An aggressive, territorial and anti-social fish. One of the largest species of the genus. The female deposits about 40 eggs. A polymorphic species of varied colouring, size and anatomical-morphological characteristics, all of which cause difficulties in terms of the clear-cut systematic classification of this fish.

In 1935 the British ichthyologist Dr. E. Trewavas divided this species into two sub-species: *P. tropheops tropheops* Regan, 1921 and *P. tropheops gracilior* Trewavas, 1935. *P. tropheops gracilior* is slightly slimmer, as revealed by its name (*gracilis* is the Latin word meaning slender).

Duel of males – pushing mouth against mouth

Cichlidae

1 ♀

2 ♂

2 ♀

1 Slender Pseudotropheus
Pseudotropheus elongatus FRYER, 1956

☐
●
Distribution: A species endemic to Lake Malawi, rocky zones with algal growths. Full length: 13 cm. Diet: live and artificial granulated foods augmented by plant foods. Spacious mono-species keeping tank. Breeding tank: with capacity of 200–300 litres for one breeding group and sufficient hiding possibilities on the bottom (drainage pipes). Sexual dimorphism: the male is bigger, more vividly coloured, with yellow, black-edged egg-like spots in the anal fin. Sex ratio: 1 male : 5–6 females. Breeding water: 24–28 °C; pH 7.5–8.0; dCH max. 4°; dGH up to 18°; fresh. Eggs: development in the mouth of the female lasts 18–22 days. Feeding of fry: brine shrimp nauplii or finely-sifted zooplankton.

Fish with variable colouring, either white and blue or cobalt blue, depending on the geographical origin. Both the male and female have a remarkably elongated body. They are very aggressive towards members of the same species as well as towards other fish. The male allows only spawn-ripe females to enter his territory. The fish spawn in the typical 'merry-go-round' manner of mouthbrooders (swimming round and round slowly). The female deposits up to 40 eggs. Depleted females should be removed and each put in a separate tank. During the development of the eggs and embryos the female does not take food. As soon as the fry leave the mouth of the female she may be taken out of the tank. Spawned-out females should be kept separate for about 14 days and generously fed.

2 *Petrochromis trewavasae* POLL, 1948

☐
●
Distribution: A species endemic to Lake Tanganyika – found only on the southwestern shore of the border territory of Zambia and Zaire, in shallow waters above a rocky bottom with algal growths. Full length: 16–18 cm. Diet: live and plant foods (algae, strained spinach), may be augmented by granulated foods. Monospecies keeping tank. Breeding tank: with capacity of 500 litres for one breeding group and drainage pipes on the bottom arranged so as to provide cavities and crevices into which it is possible to see. Sexual dimorphism: the male has large, orange egg-like spots in the anal fin, the female's body is spotted white. Sex ratio: 1 male : 3–4 females. Breeding water: 27 °C; pH 7.0–8.5; dCH 2°; dGH 10°; fresh. Eggs: exceptionally large, development in the mouth of the female lasts 4 weeks. Feeding of fry: finely sifted zooplankton, regularly augmented by plant foods.

Very aggressive fish, particularly towards other members of the same species. Lives mostly near a hiding place; it is rarely seen in open water. During the spawning period the body and fins are pitch black and the belly is a shimmering yellow-green. Young fish are covered with light spots; they resemble the females. The dorsal, anal and caudal fins are extended and pointed. The forked caudal fin differentiates this species from the other members of the genus. It is a species that rasps algal growths off the substrate with its brush-like teeth. The female deposits 10 to 12 eggs and does not take any food during the period of their development. The young fish are 2 cm long when they leave the mouth of the female.

1

2 ♀

1 Dwarf Egyptian Mouthbrooder

Pseudocrenilabrus multicolor (HILGENDORF, 1903)

Syn. *Paratilapia multicolor, Haplochromis multicolor, Hemihaplochromis multicolor*

Cichlidae

Distribution: Northeast Africa to Tanzania. Full length: 8 cm. Diet: live foods, may be augmented by granulated foods. Monospecies keeping tank. Breeding tank: of 50- to 100-litre capacity with a flat stone and appropriately arranged drainage pipes on the bottom. Sexual dimorphism: the male is more colourful, the tip of the anal fin is an intense red. Sex ratio: 1 male : 3–4 females. Breeding water: 22–26 °C; pH 7.0–7.5; dCH 2°. Eggs: orange, development in the mouth of the female lasts 10–12 days. Feeding of fry: brine shrimp or *Cyclops* nauplii.

The male digs a pit in the sand where spawning is to take place, but will also be content with a firm substrate. The female's throat sac is so wide that it can hold as many as 100 eggs and is so distended that it is practically transparent and it is possible to see the maturing embryos. After spawning the female takes cover in a hiding place. Each depleted female should be put in a separate tank by herself (this applies to all species of mouthbrooders). When they leave the female's mouth the fry are 6 mm long and fully developed. They continue to return to her mouth for a few days longer, after which the female may be taken out.

2 South African Mouthbrooder

Pseudocrenilabrus philander dispersus (TREWAVAS, 1936)

Syn. *Haplochromis moffati, H. philander dispersus, Tilapia philander, Hemihaplochromis philander dispersus.* (In the late sixties it appeared on the market under the commercial name *'Haplochromis kirawira'*).

Cichlidae

Distribution: South Africa – Namibia, Zimbabwe, Mozambique, Angola, southern Zaire. Full length: 11 cm. Diet: live foods, may be augmented by granulated foods. Monospecies keeping tank. Breeding tank: of 50- to 100-litre capacity with a flat stone and drainage pipes on the bottom. Sexual dimorphism: the male is more colourful, bigger, and has a typical bright red spot on the anal fin. Sex ratio: 1 male : 3–4 females. Breeding water: 22–26 °C; pH 7.0–7.5; dCH 2°; fresh. Eggs: yellow, ∅ 2 mm, development in the mouth of the female lasts 12 days. Feeding of fry: brine shrimp or *Cyclops* nauplii.

P. philander dispersus is found in rivers and lakes. As a result of its numerous and differing habitats it occurs in a number of local forms, differing in size as well as colouring. Spawning takes place by swimming in a circle slowly round and round as do other mouthbrooders in a so-called 'merry-go-round'. The mature female deposits and takes up into her throat sac as many as 150 eggs. After spawning she swims off into a secluded spot, usually inside a drainage pipe. During the period of incubating the eggs in the mouth the female does not take food and grows thin. On leaving the female's mouth the fry are 7 mm long and self-sufficient, but their growth is slow.

Cichlidae

1 Thomas's Dwarf Cichlid

Pelmatochromis thomasi (BOULENGER, 1915)

Syn. *Paratilapia thomasi*

Distribution: West Africa, Sierra Leone, Kenema, southeastern Guinea and western Liberia. Full length: 10 cm (male). Diet: live foods, may be augmented by granulated foods. Monospecies keeping tank. Breeding tank: with capacity of 50–100 litres per pair, put flat stones on the bottom (lithophilic fish) and arrange hiding places. Sexual dimorphism: imperceptible; the male is bigger, his dorsal and anal fins are extended, the ventral fins rimmed blue to black along the leading edge. Sex ratio: 1:1. Breeding water: 24–28 °C; pH 6.5–7.5; dCH 2°; dGH max. 15°. Eggs: faintly grey-green, incubation period 48 hrs/28 °C. Feeding of fry: brine shrimp or *Cyclops* nauplii.

The female deposits more than 500 eggs on a flat stone that has been cleaned beforehand. Development of the embryos is speeded up by a higher temperature. Endogenous nutrition lasts three days. Both parents take intensive care of the eggs and fry. Rearing the young fish is easy.

In body shape *Pelmatochromis thomasi* resembles *Papiliochromis ramirezi.* It is capable of changing rapidly colour. Adult males may be grey-green with a shimmering blue spot on each scale. Three dark spots, one on the gill cover, another in the middle of the body and a third at the base of the tail, complement the body colouring. These spots may change in an instant into transverse bars with further spots appearing on the body at the same time. In all there are six bars across the body and a seventh that crosses the eye obliquely.

1 ♂

1 ♀

1 Eye-spot Cichlid
Pelvicachromis subocellatus (GÜNTHER, 1871)
Syn. *Hemichromis subocellatus, Pelmatochromis subocellatus*

○
● Distribution: coastal territory of West Africa from Libreville (Gabon) to the mouth of the Congo (Zaire), also in brackish waters. Full length: male − 10 cm, female smaller. Diet: live foods, may be augmented by artificial foods. Monospecies keeping tank. Breeding tank: with capacity of 100 litres per pair and sufficient hiding possibilities (cavities) on the bottom. Sexual dimorphism: the dorsal and anal fins of the male end in points, the female is smaller, fuller, more colourful, the belly is rounded. During the spawning period the front and rear section of the female's body is black, the belly reddish-violet. Sex ratio: 1:1. Breeding water: 24−26 °C; pH 6.5; dCH max. 2°; dGH 8−12°. Eggs: incubation period 3 days. Feeding of fry: brine shrimp or *Cyclops* nauplii.

Paired fish seek a spawning site in a cavity. The female deposits 60 to 200 eggs. If the bottom of the aquarium is covered with gravel the female transfers the fry to dug-out pits. The parents care for the eggs and fry and the young fish may, therefore, be left with the parent fish until they prepare to spawn again. Mild fish of variable coloration. Similar, larger fish that have not been scientifically described yet are found in southern Nigeria.

2 Niger Cichlid
Pelvicachromis pulcher (BOULENGER, 1901)
Syn. *Pelmatochromis pulcher* (the name *Pelmatochromis kribensis* that is also used was assigned by Boulenger to the species *Pelvicachromis taeniatus*).

○
● Distribution: southern Nigeria, the Niger delta. The fish are also found in brackish waters. Full length: male − 10 cm, female somewhat smaller. Diet: live foods augmented by artificial foods. Monospecies keeping tank. Breeding tank: with capacity of 50−100 litres per pair, medium-coarse gravel and sufficient cavities on the bottom. Sexual dimorphism: the dorsal and anal fins of the male are more pointed (the female's are rounded) and the rays of his caudal fin are prolonged. The female is usually more colourful. Sex ratio: 1:1. Breeding water: 24−26 °C; pH 6.5−7.0; dCH max. 2°; dGH 8−10°. Eggs: ∅ 2 mm, incubation period three days. Feeding of fry: brine shrimp or *Cyclops* nauplii.

Territorial, monogamous fish, relatively compatible. The male seeks a spawning site in a cavity, where he tries to attract a ripe female. The two then jointly clean the inside top part of the cave where the female later deposits 200 to 300 eggs. The female cares for the eggs while the male guards the boundary of the territory. The fry switch over to exogenous nutrition after one week. Leave them with the parent fish until the latter prepare to spawn again. This enables the female to ripen fully before the next spawning.

Cichlidae

1 ♂

1 ♀

2 ♂

2 ♀

1 Roloff's Kribensis
Pelvicachromis roloffi (THYS, 1968)

◁
●
Distribution: West Africa − Liberia, Sierra Leone and Guinea. Full length: male − 8.5 cm, female − 6 cm. Diet: live foods. Monospecies keeping tank. Breeding tank: with capacity of 50 litres per pair, gravel and sufficient hiding possibilities on the bottom. Sexual dimorphism: in the spawning period the male has a prominent violet spot on the sides and black ventral fins. Sex ratio: 1:1. Breeding water: 25−28 °C; dCH 2°; dGH 8°; fresh. Eggs: incubation period 3 days. Feeding of fry: brine shrimp nauplii.

Most fish have a row of spots along the base of the dorsal fin and several scattered spots in the caudal fin. These spots are very variable and are not a means of identifying the sex.

Spawning of a ripe pair may be triggered by a partial exchange of water and slight raising of the temperature. The fish spawn in cavities, the female watches over the eggs and newly-hatched fry, while the male guards the area round the spawning site.

2 Banded Cichlid
Pelvicachromis taeniatus (BOULENGER, 1901)

Syn. *Pelmatochromis taeniatus, P. klugei, P. kribensis,*
P. kribensis klugei, P. kribensis var. *callipterum*

◁
●
Distribution: West Africa − southern Nigeria and Cameroon. Full length: male − 9 cm, female − 7 cm. Diet: live foods. Monospecies keeping tank. Breeding tank: with capacity of 50 litres per pair and sufficient hiding places. Sexual dimorphism: the male is more colourful, particularly in the caudal fin, the female is fuller and has a vivid wine-red spot covering the belly. Sex ratio: 1:1. Breeding water: 25−28 °C; pH 6.5−7.5; dCH 2°; dGH 8°; fresh. Eggs: incubation period 3 days. Feeding of fry: brine shrimp nauplii.

P. taeniatus occurs in a number of local, differently coloured forms, e.g. 'Lobe', 'Kienke', 'Nigeria'. Linke also classified the colour forms 'Muyuka' and 'Moliwe' in the species *P. taeniatus*. The form 'Lobe' is the one according to which Boulenger described the species

P. taeniatus. The form 'Kienke' was described by Boulenger in 1911 as *Pelmatochromis kribensis,* which was later used for other species, mainly for the one whose valid name is *Pelvicachromis pulcher.* The form 'Nigeria' was wrongly described in 1960 by Meinken as *Pelmatochromis klugei.* Despite the fact that the first three forms differ in coloration the Belgian ichthyologist Thys van den Andeanerde recognized that they belong to a single species − *P. taeniatus.* The native waters of the aforesaid forms are clear and clean and differ markedly in pH values. The 'Lobe' and 'Kienke' forms dwell in soft water with a pH value of 5.5 to 6.5, the 'Muyuka' and 'Moliwe' forms dwell in much harder water with pH value of 7.7 to 7.9. The individual forms are named after a local river or village in the place of their occurrence. Care and breeding of *P. taeniatus* is the same as for *P. pulcher.*

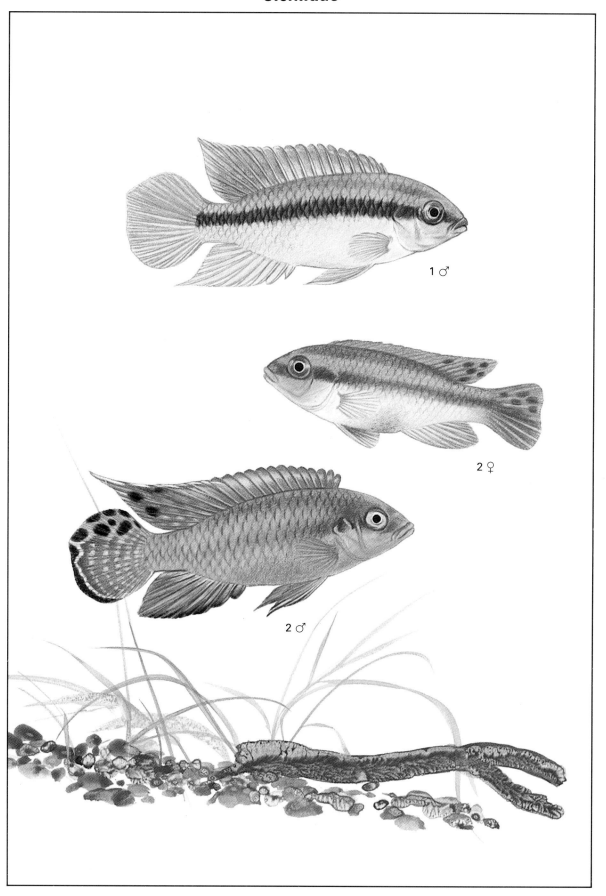

1 ♂

2 ♀

2 ♂

1 Mozambique Mouthbrooder

Oreochromis mossambicus (PETERS, 1852)
Syn. *Chromis mossambicus, Ch. dumerili, Tilapia mossambica, T. natalensis*

Cichlidae

Distribution: East Africa is the original home of this species – from the Nile to the Natal province in the south (RSA). It is an important fish found in fresh as well as brackish waters. Having been introduced to other warm regions it is currently found also in Java, Borneo, Sumatra, the Celebes, Philippines, Thailand, South Korea and elsewhere. Full length: 40 cm (the fish are already sexually mature when only 10 cm long). Diet: live, artificial and plant foods. Monospecies keeping tank. Breeding tank: with capacity of 200–500 litres per pair, a 20 cm layer of fine sand and scattered stones on the bottom. Sexual dimorphism: during the spawning period the male is deep black, the female grey-green. Sex ratio: 1:1. Breeding water: 24–26 °C; pH 7.0–7.5; dCH max. 2° (this species is very adaptable as to the composition of the water). Eggs: development in the mouth of the female lasts four weeks. Feeding of fry: brine shrimp nauplii, finely sifted zooplankton, augmented by vegetable foods.

An aggressive fish towards other members of the same species. The dominant male in the social hierarchy is intensely coloured. The fish defend their territories only during the spawning period. The male digs pits up to 25 cm across in the sand. It was observed that young males capable of spawning assemble in a colony (as many as eight to one square metre) and dig their spawning pits in the same spot. The female deposits several hundred eggs in the pit, but simultaneously gathers them up into her mouth together with the milt. During their development in the mouth the female does not take food and grows thin. The free-swimming fry return to the female's mouth at dusk and when danger threatens, but gradually this instinct disappears and the young become fully independent.

2 African Blockhead

Steatocranus casuarius POLL, 1939
Syn. *Steatocranus elongatus*

Cichlidae

Distribution: Africa – Congo River (Zaire) between the cities of Kinshasa and Matadi, peaceful stretches in rapidly-flowing sections of the river. Full length: male – 12 cm, female – 8 cm. Diet: live as well as artificial foods. Monospecies keeping tank. Breeding tank: with capacity of 200 litres per pair and sufficient caves and cavities on the bottom. Sexual dimorphism: the most striking characteristic of the male is the large pad of fat on the forehead, which increases in size with age; his dorsal and anal fins are more extended. Sex ratio: 1:1. Breeding water: 26–28 °C; pH 6.5–7.0; dCH max. 2°; dGH 10–15° (the fish tolerate deviations from the given values). Eggs: ∅ 2.5–2.8 mm, incubation period 24 hrs. Feeding of fry: brine shrimp nauplii, later finely-sifted zooplankton.

Monogamous fish, quarrelsome and aggressive towards others of the same species during the spawning period. Paired fish select a spawning site in a cavity where the female deposits approximately 150 eggs. The author observed that both parents devotedly care for the eggs and fry (according to Mayland the eggs and larvae are cared for by the female; endogenous nutrition lasts 14 days after which the fry become free-swimming and the female's brood instinct disappears). The fish are adapted to life in rapidly-flowing waters; their gas bladder is greatly reduced and that is why their movements are jerky. They are unable to swim in open water for long period of time.

Cichlidae

1 ♂

2 ♂

2 ♀

1 Dolphin Cichlid or Five-spot African Cichlid

Thysia ansorgei (BOULENGER, 1901)

Syn. *Tilapia maculifer, Pelmatochromis maculifer, P. arnoldi, P. ansorgii, P. ansorgei*

Cichlidae

Distribution: from southern Nigeria to the Ivory Coast. Full length: 13 cm. Diet: live foods, may be augmented by artificial foods. Monospecies keeping tank. Breeding tank: with capacity of 100 litres per pair, flat stones, notched flowerpots, and thin layer of gravel on the bottom. Sexual dimorphism: during the spawning period the female is more intensely coloured than the male, her belly and anal fin are red with a prominent white spot by the anal opening, her throat is also whitish. Sex ratio: 1:1. Breeding water: 25 °C; pH 7.0; dCH max. 2°. Eggs: incubation period 48 hrs. Feeding of fry: nauplii of brine shrimp or *Cyclops.*

This species occurs in two colour forms: a) the ochre-yellow form (illustrated) − the dorsal and caudal fins are edged with white, the male has a white spot on the lower part of the gill cover; b) the silvery form − the white edge on the dorsal and caudal fins is absent, the male has blue markings with a red to gold iridescent sheen round the first black spot.

The female deposits about 500 eggs, generally on the slanting, flat surface of a stone; sometimes the pair spawns in a cavity. When the fry hatch the female transfers them to relatively large pits in the bottom substrate; it is advisable to remove the male. The fry become free-swimming six days after hatching and in four weeks attain a length of 1 cm, at which time the female may also be taken out of the tank.

2 Maria's Tilapia

Tilapia mariae BOULENGER, 1899

Syn. *Tilapia dubia, T. meeki, T. (Pelmatolapia) mariae*

Cichlidae

Distribution: Nigeria, Niger River and round Lagos. Full length: 15 cm. Diet: live and plant foods, may be augmented by artificial foods. Monospecies keeping tank. Breeding tank: with capacity of 100−200 litres per pair and stony bottom. Sexual dimorphism: imperceptible; the male has the caudal fin prominently edged with white. Sex ratio: 1:1. Breeding water: 26 °C; pH 7.0−7.5; dCH max. 3°. Eggs: oval, 2 mm long (longitudinal axis), dingy greyish yellow tinged with olive, incubation period 48 hrs. Feeding of fry: brine shrimp or *Cyclops* nauplii.

Aggressive, bellicose and territorial fish. Individuals of lower standing in the social order have prominent transverse stripes. The fish are fond of feeding on aquatic plants. The brood fish spawn on a firm object near the bottom, the female deposits about 400 eggs (the maximum stated by authorities is 2,000). The eggs and fry are cared for by the female; the male should be removed. After 48 hours the female begins sucking the larvae out of the egg cases and transferring them to previously prepared holes, virtually pressing the larvae into cracks between larger stones. The larvae have a large yolk sac. During the five days of their development the female limits her care to guarding the hole. The fry are a pale hue with faint pigmentation and measure 5 mm. They grow very quickly and in 10 days the female may also be removed. In three weeks the young fish have a total length of 15 mm and the typical juvenile coloration. The parent fish can spawn at two-week intervals.

1 ♂

1 ♀

2 ♂

2 juv.

Distribution: A species endemic to Africa's Lake Tanganyika, where it occurs in two separate, isolated localities. One is on the eastern (Tanzania) shore of the lake between Kigoma-Ujiji and the mouth of the Malagarasi River, the other is on the opposite shore in Zaire near Bemba. Full length: 12 cm (max. 14 cm). Diet: live foods, chiefly zooplankton and the larvae of aquatic insects, augmented by plant foods. Monospecies keeping tank. Breeding tank: with capacity of 200 litres or more and drainage pipes on the bottom. Sexual dimorphism: monomorphic fish; older males have longer ventral fins, may be bigger, and of higher build. Sex ratio: 1 male : 6 females. Breeding water: 24–27 °C; pH 7.5–8.5; dCH 2–3° (or even more); dGH 10° (or even more); fresh, filtered. Eggs: $\varnothing$ 6–7 mm, development in the mouth of the female lasts 25 days/26 °C (± 3 days depending on the temperature). The embryos hatch in the mouth of the female a week after spawning; they have a large yolk sac. A week later they begin to show signs of pigmentation. At 18 days the fry still have a relatively large yolk sac but if they are removed from the mouth of the female they begin to show interest in food. Feeding of fry: brine shrimp nauplii or finely-sifted zooplankton.

A very aggressive fish towards others of the same species. There are several colour forms. Unlike the related *T. moorei, T. duboisi* is a solitary fish that dwells at greater depths. Adult fish are generally found at depths of 5 to 15 metres. The fish spawn on stones; some males attempt to clean the substrate on which they spawn. The female deposits a maximum of 25 eggs and does not take food the entire time the eggs and fry are in her mouth. When the fry leave the female's mouth they are 12 to 14 mm long and fully self-sufficient, but the female nevertheless cares for them a few days longer. The fry have an attractive juvenile coloration – at 14 days they are velvety black and the body is covered with luminous white dots. Sexual maturity is attained at 14 to 16 months.

1 juv.

1

1 Blunt-headed Cichlid
Tropheus moorei BOULENGER, 1898
Syn. *Tropheus annectens*

Distribution: A species endemic to Africa's Lake Tanganyika. Full length: 15 cm. Diet: live and plant foods. Monospecies keeping tank. Breeding tank: with capacity of 200 litres or more and drainage pipes on the bottom. Sexual dimorphism: monomorphic fish. Sex ratio: 1 male : 3 females. Breeding water: 25−28 °C; pH 7.5−8.5; dCH 2−4 °C; fresh, filtered. Eggs: ∅ 7 mm, development in the mouth of the female lasts 42 days/25 °C. Feeding of fry: brine shrimp nauplii, finely-sifted zooplankton.

Aggressive and territorial fish. During spawning the female lays 7 to 17 eggs which she picks up in her mouth. When spawning is completed she retires to a secluded place. Depleted females should be put in separate tanks. During the incubation period the female takes food. On leaving the mouth the fry are 12 to 14 mm long, fully self-sufficient, and have the typical juvenile coloration. The female cares for the fry for about one week. The juvenile coloration disappears at the age of five to eight months and sexual maturity is attained after one year.

Spawning takes place in open water, where the female also collects the eggs. It is interesting to note that before spawning the fish clean stones and prepare holes even though neither are ever used. In some authors' opinion this behaviour represents an unfinished evolutionary process involving the residual behaviour of ancestors spawning on a firm substrate.

2 *Tropheus moorei* − other forms
Commercial names: Orange II., Gelb-rote, Kigoma, Kaiser

Tropheus moorei forms local ecotypes in circumscribed populations that do not intermingle. According to Scheurmann the count is 18 forms. They differ primarily in colouring, which may be black, blue-black, olive green, variously striped, orange, yellow-red, yellow, brown, rainbow-coloured, etc. These colour forms were successively discovered and introduced as separate varieties of the species. The form with lyre-shaped tail fin known as 'Wimpel-Moorii' was reclassified by Glen Axelrod as a separate species − *Tropheus polli* G. Axelrod, 1977.

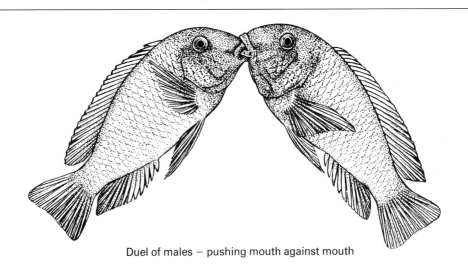

Duel of males − pushing mouth against mouth

2 a

2 b

2 c

1

1 Orange Chromide
Etroplus maculatus (BLOCH, 1795)
Syn. *Chaetodon maculatus, Ch. kakaitsel, Etroplus coruchi, Glyphisodon kakaitsel* Cichlidae

☐
●
Distribution: southern India and Sri Lanka along the coast, in fresh and brackish waters. Full length: male 8 cm, female slightly smaller. Diet: live foods, augmented by plant foods. Monospecies keeping tank. Breeding tank: with capacity of 100 litres per pair; arrange flat stones and notched flowerpots on the bottom (layer of gravel, hiding places, cavities). Sexual dimorphism: imperceptible; the female is more cloudily coloured and does not have any red in the edges of the fins. Sex ratio: 1:1. Breeding water: 26–28 °C; pH 7.5; dCH 2°; dGH 10–15°; add 1 teaspoon NaCl or sea salt for every 10 litres of water (unsuitable chemical composition of the water causes the fry to die). Eggs: furnished with a short stalk, incubation period four days. Feeding of fry: brine shrimp nauplii.

Peaceful, monogamous fish. They spawn on uncovered stones, on their level as well as upright surfaces. The female lays 200 to 300 eggs, one beside the other. On hatching the fry are transferred to pits excavated in the bottom substrate. Both partners care for the eggs for a long time and later also the fry, the male chiefly guarding the territory. The fry are typically coloured yellow-black. Occasionally they feed on the mucous secretion produced by the parent fish. For the first 14 days filter the water through active charcoal and check on the pH values. Then you can replace a quarter of the water with fresh water, and later a third to a half. The fish are sensitive to chemicals.

2 *Etroplus maculatus* – gold form
Cichlidae

☐
●
A xanthistic form developed in aquarium conditions. Care and breeding are the same as for the wild form.

3 Striped Chromide
Etroplus suratensis (BLOCH, 1790)
Syn. *Chaetodon suratensis, Ch. caris, Etroplus meleagris* Cichlidae

☐
●
Distribution: India, Sri Lanka – open sea and mouths of rivers; prefers brackish water, is not found in fresh water. Full length: 40 cm. Diet: more robust live foods, beef and fish meat, shrimp meat, frozen brine shrimp, augmented by vegetable foods. Monospecies keeping tank with a capacity of 500 litres. Breeding tank: with capacity of at least 200 litres, bottom without plants, rocky (eg travertine), efficient filter with active charcoal. Sexual dimorphism: monomorphic fish. Sex ratio: 1:1. Breeding water: 24 °C; pH 7.5–8.0; add 3 tablespoons sea salt for every 10 litres of water; salinity may be increased up to a density of 1.022. Eggs: incubation period 48 hrs. Feeding of fry: brine shrimp nauplii, augmented by fine plant foods.

Species of the genus *Etroplus* are an intermediate group between fresh and salt water fish. Anatomic, ethologic and ecologic indices phylogenetically class the genus *Etroplus* in the family Cichlidae.

The fish spawn on the open bottom. The female deposits 200 to 300 eggs. The parent fish care for the eggs and fry, which become free-swimming six days after hatching.

Family Anabantidae

The Anabantidae family formerly included all labyrinth fish, i.e. fish with a developed accessory respiratory organ called the labyrinth. The labyrinth organ is a cavity located above the gill arches, inside which are numerous lamellae that increase the surface area covered with epithelium rich in blood capillaries. In the capillaries the blood absorbs oxygen from the atmosphere which the fish take in by gulping air at the surface. On the basis of Liem's 1963 works the family now includes only three African genera: *Anabas*, *Ctenopoma* and *Sandelia*. Outside the breeding period the temperature for these fish may be 2 to 3 °C lower than the values given in the text.

1 Kingsley's Ctenopoma
Ctenopoma kingsleyae GÜNTHER, 1896

Anabantidae

Distribution: central and west Africa from Zaire to Gambia — flowing waters. Full length: 20 cm. Diet: live as well as artificial foods augmented by plant foods. Monospecies keeping tank. Breeding tank: with capacity of 100—200 litres per pair, plant thickets, and calm water surface without bubbled aeration. Sexual dimorphism: imperceptible. Sex ratio: 1:1. Breeding water: 25 °C; pH 6.5—7.0; dCH max. 2°; Eggs: contain droplets of oil, rise to the surface; incubation period 24—48 hrs. Feeding of fry: brine shrimp nauplii.

A relatively peaceful species. Apart from the spawning period the fish may be kept together with other fish of the same size. They like to nibble fine aquatic plants. During the mating games and spawning they make smacking and whimpering sounds and release bubles from the gill slits. The male is aggressive towards the female and often tears her fins. The female is exceptionally prolific: according to Ostermöller's observations the female deposits as many as 20,000 eggs. Spawning takes place near the surface; the male does not build a bubble nest. The eggs should be collected and transferred to a separate tank with low water level. The fry become free-swimming in four or five days. Their growth is rapid but uneven. At six months the young fish are about 5 cm long and grow more slowly. During the growth period gradually decrease the number of fish in the tank and separate them according to size. Replace two-thirds of the water with fresh water weekly.

2 Peacock-eye Bush Fish, Sharp-nosed or Marbled Climbing Perch
Ctenopoma oxyrhynchus (BOULENGER, 1902)
Syn. *Anabas oxyrhynchus*

Anabantidae

Distribution: Zaire — Pool Malebo (Stanley Pool). Full length: 10 cm. Diet: live foods, may also be augmented by granulated foods. Monospecies keeping tank. Breeding tank: with capacity of 50 litres per pair, sufficient plants, dim lighting, calm water surface without bubbled aeration. Sexual dimorphism: extremely slight; the dorsal and anal fins of the male are slightly extended into a point, the female is paler in colour and fuller in the body. Sex ratio: 1:1. Breeding water: 28—30 °C; pH 6.5—7.0; dCH max. 2°. Eggs: minute, rich in oil, float on the surface, incubation period 3—4 days. Feeding of fry: brine shrimp nauplii.

A relatively peaceful fish. The male does not build a nest, the eggs float freely on the water surface. Collect them with a catching pipe and transfer to a separate tank with low water level. Free-swimming fry are light-shy. Young fish have a different juvenile coloration. Sexual maturity is attained only after a number of years. The fish are good jumpers and therefore the tank must be well covered with glass.

Anabantidae

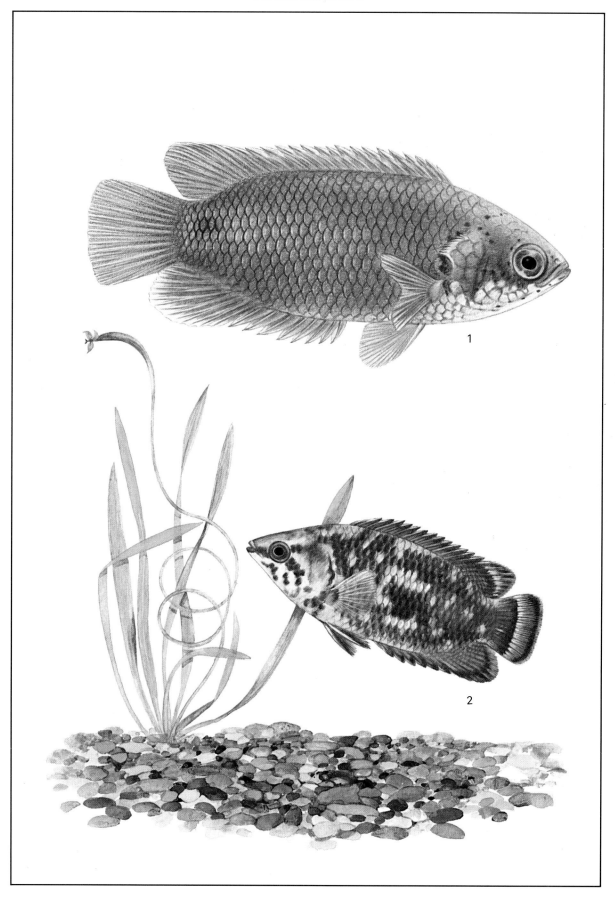

1 Banded Bush Fish
Ctenopoma fasciolatum (BOULENGER, 1899)
Syn. *Anabas fasciolatus, A. fasciatus*

◻
●
Distribution: Zaire – Pool Malebo (Stanley Pool), area round Kinshasa. Full length: 8 cm. Diet: more robust live foods, including small fish, plus granulated and plant foods. Monospecies keeping tank. Breeding tank: with capacity of 50 litres per pair, light diffused through floating plants, calm water surface without bubbled aeration. Sexual dimorphism: the male is more colourful, his dorsal and anal fins are prolonged but the differences between the sexes are extremely slight. Sex ratio: 1:1. Breeding water: 26–28 °C; pH 6.5–7.0; dCH max. 1. Eggs: glassily transparent, ∅ 0.5 mm, incubation period 36–40 hrs. Feeding of fry: brine shrimp nauplii.

Hardy and aggressive fish. They like a well-planted tank with plenty of room for swimming. During the spawning period the fish change various colours. The male builds a nest at the surface in a part of the tank that has less light. The nest is composed of large bubbles; it may be small and high, or thin, broad and haphazard. The fish spawn frequently. The eggs are rich in oil and rise to the surface. Using a large catching pipe take up the whole nest with the eggs and transfer it to a nursery tank with soft light and low water level. The glassily transparent fry become free-swimming four or five days after hatching. The young fish grow slowly.

2 Bullseye Ctenopoma or Chocolate Bushfish
Ctenopoma ocellatum PELLEGRIN, 1899
Syn. *Anabas ocellatus, A. weeksii, Ctenopoma acutirostrae, C. denticulatum, C. petherici* (not Günther)

Anabantidae

○
◑
Distribution: Zaire, Pool Malebo (Stanley Pool) and Boyoma Falls (Stanley Falls), Kasai province. Full length: 10 cm. Diet: live foods, including small fish, may be augmented by artificial foods. Community tank, but only with fish of similar size; sufficient plants and hiding possibilities, diffused lighting. Breeding tank: same as keeping tank with calm water surface. Sexual dimorphism: imperceptible; the spot at the base of the caudal fin is darker in the male, the female

is more high-backed. Sex ratio: 1:1. Water: 24–28 °C; pH 6.5–7.0; dCH max. 2°, filtered through peat. The species has not yet been bred in captivity.

Fish kept singly are shy. In a large tank with subdued lighting and in the company of other fish of the same size they are less timid. They do not like strongly circulating water.

Anabantidae

1 Leopard Bush Fish
Ctenopoma acutirostre (PELLEGRIN, 1899)

Anabantidae

◁ ● Distribution: middle and lower reaches of the Zaire (Congo) River. Full length: 15 cm. Diet: more robust live foods, chiefly small fish. Monospecies keeping tank. Breeding tank: with capacity of 100 litres per pair, hiding places, diffused light. Sexual dimorphism: the male has a patch of spines on the body, the female has small spots on the fins. Sex ratio: 1:1. Water: 23–26 °C; pH 6.5–7.0; dCH max. 2°. The species has not yet been bred in captivity.

The fish become active at twilight and their activity peaks in the night hours. They resemble a dead leaf, lie in wait in plant thickets for their prey and then seize it with remarkable swiftness. Young fish are very slow to mature (it is said that it may take several years for them to attain sexual maturity).

2 *Ctenopoma ansorgei* (BOULENGER, 1912)
Syn. *Anabas ansorgii*

Anabantidae

◁ ● Distribution: tropical west Africa in the Chiloango River region in Angola. Full length: 8 cm. Diet: more robust live foods. Monospecies keeping tank. Breeding tank: with capacity of 50 litres per pair, hiding possibilities, plant thickets, diffused lighting. Sexual dimorphism: sexually mature males are slightly bigger and more colourful. Sex ratio: 1:1. Breeding water: 24 °C; pH 6.0–6.5; dCH max. 1°, plus peat extract or filtered through peat. Calm water surface without bubbled aeration. Eggs: rich in oil, they float on the surface, incubation period 24 hrs. Feeding of fry: brine shrimp nauplii.

Twilight fish. They spawn at night after several hours of displaying by the male. The male builds a nest of large bubbles and bits of plants. Unlike other species of labyrinth fish the female is never belly-side up but remains in normal position during spawning. She deposits approximately 400 eggs. As soon as the fry hatch transfer them with the nest to a separate tank. Three days after hatching the fry switch over to exogenous nutrition.

3 Climbing Perch
Anabas testudineus (BLOCH, 1795)
Syn. *Amphiprion scausor, A. testudineus, Anabas elongatus, A. macrocephalus, A. microcephalus, A. oligolepis, A. scandens, A. spinosus, A. trifoliatus, A. variegatus, Antias testudineus, Cojus cobujius, Lutjanus scandens, L. testudo, Perca scandens, Sparus testudineus*

Anabantidae

▢ ● Distribution: Pakistan, India, Sri Lanka, southern China, Taiwan, Philippines, Malay Peninsula, Indonesia, fresh as well as brackish waters. Full length: 20 cm. Diet: live and plant foods, may be augmented by artificial foods. Monospecies keeping tank. Breeding tank: with capacity of 200 litres or more, flat, well covered, height of water column 30 cm, sufficient hiding possibilities amidst plants, diffused lighting, calm water surface. Sexual dimorphism: imperceptible; the anal fin of the male is more extended. Sex ratio: 1:1. Breeding water: 24–30 °C; pH 6.5–7.5; dCH max. 2°; dGH 10°. Eggs: rise to the surface, incubation period 24 hrs. Feeding of fry: *Paramecium caudatum, Cyclops* and brine shrimp nauplii.

The fish tolerate temperature fluctuations between 15 and 30 °C. In the wild they bury themselves in the mud during the dry season. They are able to move on dry land by means of the spiny gill covers and by pushing off with the tail. The male does not build a nest and the parent fish do not care for the eggs after spawning.

Family Belontiidae

This family was established in 1963 by Liem. It includes African fish closely related to perches from which they differ by possessing a labyrinth. The labyrinth organ probably developed as an adaptation to life in tropical waters that are often muddy and very poor in oxygen. However, gill-breathing is not sufficient for labyrinth fish even in oxygen-rich waters. If they were unable to surface they would die. The dorsal and anal fins are furnished with spines. The males of many species are territorial and aggressive. The males of some species build bubble nests, other males keep the eggs and fry in their mouths.

1 Siamese Fighting Fish
Betta splendens REGAN, 1909
Syn. *Betta trifasciata* (not Bleeker), *Betta pugnax, Betta rubra* (not Perugia)　　　　　Belontiidae

Distribution: Thailand, Kampuchea, Vietnam, Malaysia − shallow, sun-warmed waters. Full length: 6 cm. Diet: live foods (chiefly tubifex worms and larvae of mosquitoes and midges), may be augmented by the cooked eggs of coldwater fish or scrapped beef. Monospecies keeping tank. Breeding tank: with capacity of 3−6 litres, calm water surface without bubbled aeration, floating plants on the surface, moist air above the surface. Sexual dimorphism: the fins of the male (except the ventral fins) are longer than those of the female and under certain conditions are capable of attaining extreme lengths and shapes. Sex ratio: 1:1. Breeding water: 26−30 °C; pH 7.0; dCH max. 2°. Eggs: ∅ 0.8 mm, they sink to the bottom, incubation period 30 hrs. Feeding of fry: brine shrimp nauplii, later chopped tubifex worms.

Before spawning and when building the nest the males are aggressive and may thrash the females to death. That is why plant thickets are so important for they provide the female with a place to hide. Weaker males, on the other hand, are attacked by the females and spawning does not take place. Such males should be eliminated from further breeding. The male builds a bubble nest on the surface. It was found that the bubbles contain bacteriostatic substances and substances that have a beneficial effect on the chemical composition of the water in the vicinity of the eggs, which usually number several hundred. During spawning the pair gather the eggs and press them into the bubble nest. As soon as spawning is over remove the female and when the fry become free-swimming the male also. Carefully take out most of the plants and lower the water level to 5 cm. The intensive metabolism of the growing young fish necessitates frequent cleaning of the tank and regular water replacement. Their growth is very rapid. Some specimens attain sexual maturity at the age of five weeks, but the best breeding results are achieved with a brood fish five or six months old. (*B. splendens* is a short-lived species). The ability of the male's fins to grow to various lengths has been put to good use by breeders. When they are sexually mature the males are put in separate jars placed one beside the other. Regular cleaning of the jars and clean, fresh water are essential for successful results. The best males are selected for further breeding. The females are reared together.

1 ♀

1 ♂

1 ♀

1 ♂

1 Emerald Betta
Betta smaragdina LADIGES, 1972 Belontiidae

◁
●
Distribution: northeastern Thailand. Full length: 7 cm. Diet: live foods. Monospecies keeping tank. Breeding tank: with capacity of 6–10 litres, floating plants, calm water surface without bubbled aeration. Sexual dimorphism: the male has longer ventral fins, the female has several prominent bands across the body during spawning. Sex ratio: 1:1. Breeding water: 28 °C; pH 7.0; dCH max. 2°. Eggs: incubation period 24–26 hrs. Feeding of fry: brine shrimp nauplii.

Care and breeding the same as for *B. splendens,* the only difference being that the males may be kept together, for these are peaceful fish. The male builds a bubble nest on the surface. The fry of separate pairs less than a week apart in age may be poured into a larger flat tank with water column 5 to 10 cm high. Add water as they grow. Separate the young fish according to size (their growth is uneven).

2 Big Mouthbrooding Betta
Betta pugnax (CANTOR, 1850)
Syn. *Betta brederi, Macropodus pugnax* Belontiidae

◁
●
Distribution: Malaysia, Indonesia, Kampuchea, occurs in flowing waters. Full length: 10 cm. Diet: live foods. Monospecies keeping tank (in pairs). Breeding tank: with capacity of 50 litres per pair, sufficient hiding possibilities amidst plants, diffused lighting. To provide clean and flowing water it is recommended to install a forced-circulation filter. Sexual dimorphism: the male is more intensely coloured and has longer fins. Sex ratio: 1:1. Breeding water: 26–28 °C; pH 6.5–7.0; dCH < 2°; dGH max. 10°. Eggs: incubation period in the mouth of the male 12–26 days; the development of the embryos is irregular. As the fry successively fill their gas bladders they are left free swimming outside the male's mouth. Feeding of fry: brine shrimp nauplii.

In flowing water the fish cannot build bubble nests. That is perhaps why, in the process of evolution, this species resolved the problem of incubation by having the eggs cared for in the mouth of the male. During the separate acts of mating the eggs fall into the arched anal fin of the male, are taken from there by the female, and spat out again in front of the male immediately after. This is repeated a number of times until the male has all the eggs (approximately 50) in his mouth. As soon as the fry leave the male's mouth they are fully self-sufficient and his task is completed. Rearing the young fish is simple. A similar manner of spawning is exhibited by *Betta anabatoides* Bleeker, 1850, *B. foerschi* Vierke, 1979, *B. taeniata* Regan, 1909, *B. picta* (Cuvier and Valenciennes, 1846), *B. macrostoma* Regan, 1909 and *B. unimaculata* (Popta, 1905).

1 ♂

1 ♀

2 ♂

2 ♀

1 Peacock Betta
Betta macrostoma REGAN, 1910

Belontiidae

Distribution: Borneo, state of Brunei, the rocky, white-water mountain river Sungai Mendaram (locality Kampong Labi — pools beneath waterfalls). Temperature of the air 37 °C; temperature of the water 24 °C; pH 4.3, very soft water. Full length: 10 cm. Diet: live foods, chiefly flies and fruit flies *(Drosophila melanogaster),* mosquito larvae, pieces of earthworms. Monospecies keeping tank: well covered. Breeding tank: with capacity of 50 litres per pair and plant thickets. Sexual dimorphism: the male is more colourful. Sex ratio: 1:1. Breeding water: 24 °C; pH 5.0−6.0; dCH < 1°; dGH < 10°. Eggs: incubation in the mouth of the male lasts 8−10 days. Feeding of fry: brine shrimp nauplii.

In 1910 C. Tate Regan described this species according to a single specimen. What impressed him when he was describing the fish was its big mouth and hence his choice of the Latin name *macrostoma.* For several decades after, however, there were no further reports of this species until 1980, when *B. macrostoma* was discovered anew by Mrs. Sharon Eden of Brunei, who was the first aquarist in the world to observe these fish spawning. Displaying and spawning is similar to that of *B. splendens,* but the male does not build a nest because he incubates the eggs in the mouth. The female helps him find the eggs on the bottom and literally spits them into his open mouth. The male cares for the eggs and embryos in his mouth for 8 to 10 days. One of the difficulties in breeding these fish is that the males sometimes swallow the eggs or embryos. The males defend their territories and are very aggressive towards one another. Sexually mature males must, therefore, be kept in separate tanks. Females and the longitudinally striped young fish are tolerated within his territory by the male. It is believed that the male's territorial aggressiveness has more to do with his hunting grounds than with his spawning grounds. The fish are extremely voracious but one must be careful not to overfeed them. Flying insects are a favourite food. They are very good jumpers and are prone to various parasitic and infectious diseases.

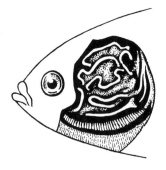

Schema of labyrinth organ

1 ♀

1 ♂

1 Peaceful Betta or Crescent Betta
Betta imbellis LADIGES, 1975

◁
●
Distribution: Malaysia, area round the city of Kuala Lumpur. Full length: up to 5 cm. Diet: live foods. Monospecies keeping tank. Breeding tank: with capacity of 3−6 litres, floating plants on the surface, calm surface without bubbled aeration. Sexual dimorphism: the male is more colourful, his fins are larger. Sex ratio: 1:1. Breeding water: 26−28 °C; pH 7.0; dCH max. 2°. Eggs: ∅ 1 mm, they sink to the bottom; incubation period 32 hrs. Feeding of fry: brine shrimp nauplii.

This species inhabits the same territory as *B. splendens* but is found in different localities. The male builds a bubble nest. The female deposits approximately 200 eggs. Remove the female after spawning is over, and the male

when the fry become free-swimming. The young fish grow relatively slowly. Brood fish spawn frequently and throughout the year. They are sociable towards members of the same species. In appearance *B. imbellis* resembles *B. smaragdina,* with which it also interbreeds, but the hybrid offspring are not viable. On the other hand the hybrid offspring of *B. imbellis* and *B. splendens* are not only viable but also fertile. As fish of the species *B. imbellis* are only kept in aquariums for a short time, the result is long-term. and repeated inbreeding. Because they are short-lived (a year is the average life span) the generations follow in rapid succession, and aquarium-raised specimens are delicate and sickly. The same problem of multiple inbreeding is also encountered in breeding *B. splendens.*

2 One-spot Betta
Betta unimaculata (POPTA, 1905)
Syn. *Parophiocephalus unimaculatus, Betta ocellata*

◁
●
Distribution: Northeastern Borneo, Kretam Kechil River, irrigation ditches and forest streams. In streams the individual biotopes are in pools separated by a swift current and waterfalls. These obstacles must be overcome by the fish on their migration to the isolated pools. Full length: male − 11 cm, female − 9 cm. Diet: more robust live foods (robust zooplankton, larvae of aquatic insects, fruit flies − *Drosophila melanogaster,* small crickets, small earthworms, etc.). Monospecies keeping tank. Breeding tank: with capacity of 50 litres per pair, bottom provided with hiding possibilities amidst plants and in cavities. Sexual dimorphism: the male is darker on the back with bright glittering green markings, the female is a vivid brown. Sex ratio: 1:1. Breeding water: 23−28 °C; pH 7.0; dCH max. 2°; dGH max. 10°; fresh. Eggs: ∅ 1 mm, white,

development in the mouth of the male lasts 11 days. Feeding of fry: brine shrimp nauplii.

The fish are excellent jumpers and therefore the tank must be well covered with glass. Replace about a third of the water with fresh water once a week. 'Ripe' females have a conspicuously rounded belly. Feeding with mosquito larvae (black larvae) promotes the maturation of the eggs. Spawning usually takes place in the evening. After spawning, which lasts two or three hours, the male, whose throat sac is very full, retreats to a secluded spot. As soon as the fry leave the male's mouth they are fully self-sufficient and immediately take food. Remove the parent fish and lower the water level to 3 to 5 cm.

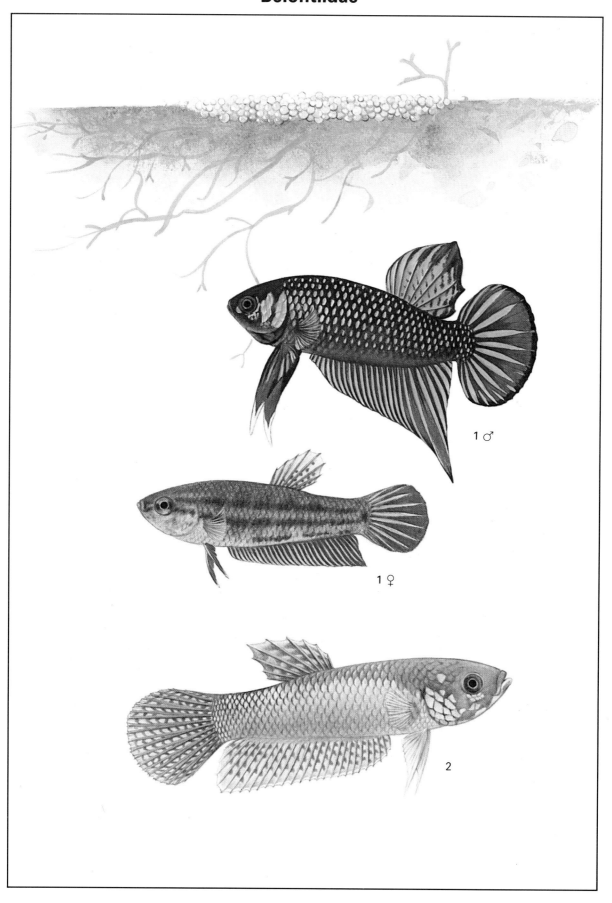

1 ♂

1 ♀

2

1 Java Combtail
Belontia hasselti (CUVIER and VALENCIENNES, 1831)

Syn. *Polyacanthus einthoveni, P. hasselti, P. helfrichi, P. kuhli, P. olivaceus*

Distribution: Java, Sumatra, Borneo, Malay Peninsula, in clean, slowly-flowing waters. Full length: 20 cm. Diet: primarily live foods but also artificial foods. Community tank (together with species of like characteristics). Breeding tank: of 100-litre capacity, light to sun-drenched, with thickets of aquatic and floating plants, and calm water surface without bubbled aeration. Sexual dimorphism: imperceptible; during the spawning period the female does not have the reticulated pattern in the scales and after spawning she is a pale 'washed-out' colour. Sex ratio: 1:1 (the pair will not spawn in the presence of other fish). Breeding water: 26–30 °C; pH 6.5–7.0; dCH max. 2°. Eggs: incubation period 24–48 hrs. Feeding of fry: first week on infusoria *(Paramecium caudatum)* monoculture, *Cyclops,* later brine shrimp nauplii.

Although the males may build a loose bubble nest, they generally do not do so and the eggs are scattered freely on the water surface. After spawning is over remove the female. The fry switch over to exogenous nutrition three days after hatching. At this time remove the male also and lower the water level to 10 to 15 cm. Take care that the temperature of the air above the surface is the same as the temperature of the water (this applies to all species of labyrinth fish). Separating the large number of fry according to size, reducing the number of fish in the tank and fresh water promote the growth of the young fish.

2 Comb Tail or Comb-tail Paradise Fish
Belontia signata (GÜNTHER, 1861)

Syn. *Polyacanthus signatus*

Distribution: Sri Lanka, Sumatra, Borneo, Java. Full length: 13 cm. Diet: live foods (small larvae of aquatic insects, small fish fry, small earthworms, etc.). Monospecies keeping tank. Breeding tank: with capacity of 50 litres per pair, floating plants, and calm water surface without bubbled aeration. Sexual dimorphism: the male is more robust, a deeper red, and the rays of the caudal fin are extended in the shape of a comb and are longer than those of the female. Sex ratio: 1:1. Breeding water: 24–26 °C; pH 6.5–7.0; dCH max. 2°. Eggs: ∅ 1.2 mm, rich in oil, rise to the surface, incubation period 48 hrs. Feeding of fry: nauplii of brine shrimp or *Cyclops,* later chopped tubifex worms.

The parent fish vigorously defend their spawning site. The prominently dark-pigmented fry switch over to exogenous nutrition five days after spawning; their growth is rapid. A typical characteristic of the juvenile coloration is the black spot at the base of the caudal fin.

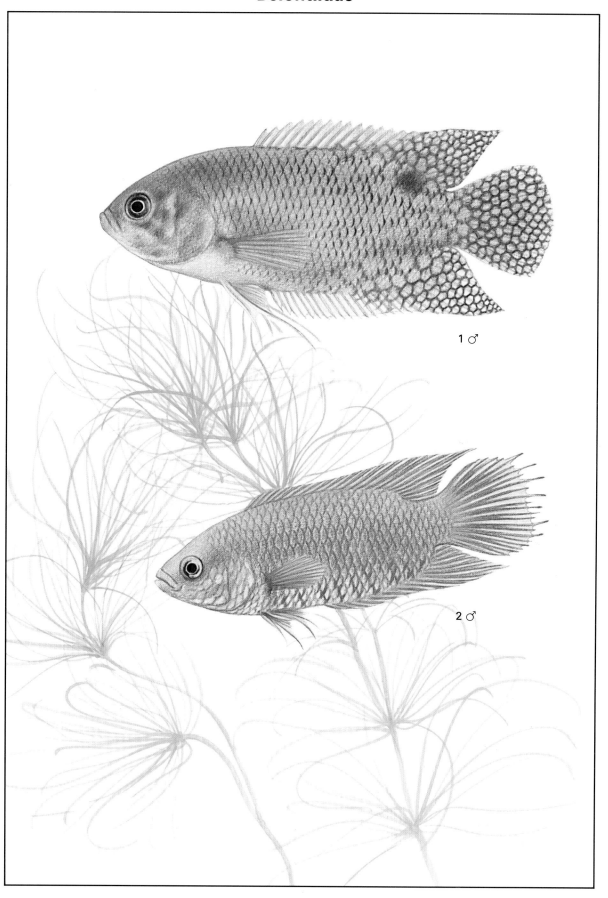

1 ♂

2 ♂

1 Dwarf Gourami
Colisa lalia (HAMILTON—BUCHANAN, 1822)
Syn. *Colisa unicolor, Trichopodus lalius, Trichopsis lalius, Trichogaster unicolor, T. lalius*   Belontiidae

Distribution: India — the Ganges, Jumna and Brahmaputra river regions, Borneo — Baram River. Full length: 5 cm. Diet: live foods, chiefly tubifex worms, may be augmented by artificial foods. Community tank. Breeding tank: with capacity of 3—5 litres per pair, floating plants on the surface, and a calm water surface without bubbled aeration. Sexual dimorphism: the male is brightly coloured and larger. Sex ratio; 1:1. Breeding water: 26—28 °C; pH 6.5—7.0; dCH max. 2°. Eggs: minute, rich in oil, rise to the surface, incubation period 24 hrs. Feeding of fry: first 10 days on infusoria *(Paramecium caudatum)* monoculture, then brine shrimp nauplii.

The male builds a bubble nest on the surface, strengthening it with bits of plants. The female is very prolific. The male picks up the eggs scattered on the water surface and puts them in the nest. Remove the female after spawning and the male when the fry become free-swimming. Lower the water level to 5 cm. The growth of the young fish is uneven and relatively slow. After several days pour the fry from a greater number of brood pairs into a larger tank with large water surface and low water level (5 cm). Both young and adult fish are susceptible to infectious and parasitic diseases.

2 *Colisa lalia* 'Sunset'   Belontiidae

In 1979 males of an interesting colour mutation appeared in the greenhouses of West German wholesale establishments under the commercial designation 'Red Lalius'. They created a sensation in the aquaristic world not only by their interesting coloration but also their high price. Later the American specialist press brought out the first report about the origin of this fish. *Colisa lalia* 'Sunset' had been bred in secret and for a long time together with other novelties by the breeder Tan Guk Eng at the fish farm in Singapore. Singapore newspapers wrote that Sunset Laliuses worth US $ 32,000 had been stolen from this farm. The fish were then offered for sale under the name *C. 'gukengi'* and males of the smaller and similarly coloured *C. chuna* were also passed off as such. For commercial reasons only males were imported to Europe at first; these were spawned with females of the wild form with varying success. Nowadays females are imported from Singapore as well. There is also a blue form of *C. lalia*.

Belontiidae

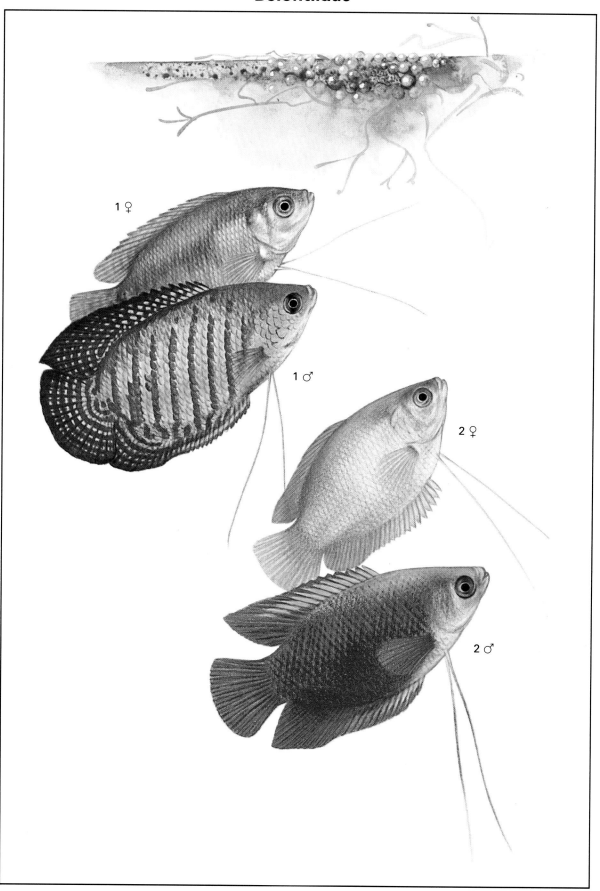

1 ♀

1 ♂

2 ♀

2 ♂

1 Honey Gourami
Colisa chuna (HAMILTON–BUCHANAN, 1822)
Syn. *Trichopodus chuna, T. sota, Chuna kolisha, Trichogaster chuna, T. sota*   Belontiidae

Distribution: northeast India – Assam, Bangladesh. Full length: 5 cm. Diet: live foods, may be augmented by artificial foods. Community tank. Breeding tank: with capacity of 10 litres per pair, height of water column 6–8 cm, floating plants, calm water surface without bubbled aeration. Sexual dimorphism: the male is intensely brownish red, the female fuller in the body and coloured grey-brown with a brown band extending from the eye to the base of the caudal fin. Sex ratio: 1:1. Breeding water: 28–30 °C; pH 7.0; dCH max. 2°. Eggs: they contain a large oil droplet and rise to the surface, incubation period 12 hrs/30 °C. Feeding of fry: first 10 days *Paramecium caudatum,* later brine shrimp nauplii.

Some males do not build a nest, others build one before or during spawning. The males transfer the eggs from one place to another until the fry begin to swim freely. At the age of three to six weeks the fry are particularly sensitive; that is the period when the labyrinth develops. Their growth is uneven.

2 Giant Gourami, Striped or Banded Gourami
Colisa fasciata (BLOCH and SCHNEIDER, 1801)
Syn. *Trichogaster fasciatus, Trichopodus colisa, T. bejeus, T. cotra, Colisa vulgaris, C. bejeus, C. cotra, C. ponticeriana, Polyacanthus fasciatus*   Belontiidae

Distribution: India – Assam, Bangladesh, Burma, Thailand, Malay Peninsula. Full length: 10 cm. Diet: live as well as artificial foods. Community tank. Breeding tank: with capacity of 50 litres per pair, floating plants and surface without bubbled aeration. Sexual dimorphism: the male is more colourful, his dorsal and anal fins are extended into a point at the hind end. Sex ratio: 1:1. Breeding water: 28 °C; pH 6.5–7.0; dCH max. 2°. Eggs: rise to the surface, incubation period 24 hrs. Feeding of fry: first four days *Paramecium caudatum,* then brine shrimp nauplii.

The males are territorial, they fight amongst themselves, and build large bubble nests. The female deposits up to 800 eggs during spawning. The fry should be reared in a tank with a water level of 3 to 5 cm. During growth separate the young fish according to size and add water.

3 Thick-lipped Gourami
Colisa labiosa (DAY, 1878)
Syn. *Trichogaster labiosus*   Belontiidae

Distribution: Burma, Thailand, Laos. Full length: 12 cm. Diet: live as well as artificial foods. Community tank. Breeding tank: same as for *C. fasciata.* Sexual dimorphism: the male's dorsal fin is extended into a point, the tip of his anal fin is blue, the female's red. Sex ratio: 1:1. Breeding water, incubation period and feeding of fry the same as for *C. fasciata.*

Breeding is the same as for *C. fasciata.* The male builds a large flat bubble nest which holds together only if the water surface is calm and the air above it moist. That is why the tank should not be provided with aeration and should be covered with glass (this applies to all labyrinth fish that build bubble nests). In the case of aquarium-raised specimens of *C. labiosa* and *C. fasciata* it is practically impossible to tell them apart because the populations of the two species are multiply interbred.

There is now a golden form of *C. labiosa.*

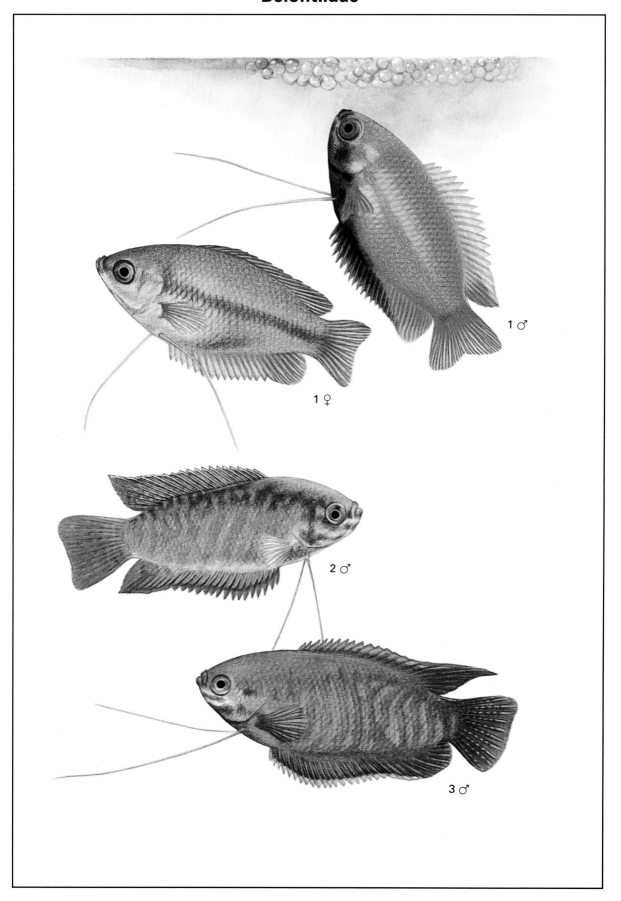

1 ♂

1 ♀

2 ♂

3 ♂

1 Paradise Fish
Macropodus opercularis (LINNAEUS, 1758)
Syn. *Labrus opercularis, Polyacanthus opercularis, Platypodus gurca,*
Macropodus viridi-auratus, M. concolor, M. filamentosus,
M. venustus, M. opercularis var. *viridi-auratus*

Distribution: Korea, China, South Vietnam, Taiwan, Ryukyn Island, Malay Peninsula (shallow waters and rice paddies). Full length: 9 cm. Diet: live foods, chiefly tubifex worms, insect larvae, small fry of live-bearing fish, may be augmented by granulated foods, beef, etc. Monospecies keeping tank. Breeding tank: with capacity of 20–50 litres per pair, floating plants on the surface, and calm water surface without bubbled aeration. Sexual dimorphism: the male is more robust, his unpaired fins are extended into points. Sex ratio: 1:1. Breeding water: 20–24 °C; pH 7.0; dCH max. 2°. Eggs: ⌀ 1 mm, incubation period 36 hrs/24 °C, 24 hrs/28 °C. Feeding of fry: brine shrimp or *Cyclops* nauplii.

Hardy fish, always aggressive during the spawning period. Fish put in outdoor garden pools survive even autumn frosts. The male builds a bubble nest where he spawns with a single female – on a rare occasion with several females. If spawning takes place in a large tank wait until the fry hatch and then take up the whole nest with a large catching pipe and transfer it to a nursery tank with low water level (about 5 cm). As the fry grow gradually add more water and separate them according to size. When selecting brood fish, those with sufficient red or blue colouring are recommended. The Paradise Fish is used in aquariums to control gastropods and planarians.

2 *Macropodus opercularis* – albinotic form

The albinotic form was bred and genetically fixed in aquarium conditions.

3 Black Paradise Fish
Macropodus concolor AHL, 1937
Syn. *Macropodus opercularis concolor*

Distribution: southern China, Vietnam, Malaysia. Full length: male – 12 cm, female – 8 cm. Diet: live foods. Community tank (with fish of like characteristics). Breeding water: with capacity of 50–100 litres per pair, calm water surface with floating plants. Sexual dimorphism: the male has longer dorsal and anal fins, the rays of his caudal fin are greatly drawn out; the rays of the red ventral fins are also drawn out; the dorsal and caudal fins have a white edge with blue glitter. Sex ratio: 1:1. Breeding water: 22–30 °C; pH 7.0–7.5; dCH max. 2°. Eggs: incubation period 36 hrs/24 °C, 24 hrs/28 °C. Feeding of fry: brine shrimp or *Cyclops* nauplii.

For a long time this fish was classified as an ambiguous species, primarily because when first describing it the author did not know its geographical origin. Originally Ahl classified it as a subspecies of *M. opercularis*. Crosses between *M. opercularis* and *M. concolor* yield fertile hybrid offspring. The hybrids are unattractively coloured, gather round flowing water and jump out of the tank all at the same time. Cross-breeding the two species is not recommended.

Belontiidae

1 ♂

1 ♀

2 ♂

3 ♂

1 Malpulutta

Malpulutta kretseri DERANIYAGALA, 1937

◁
●
Distribution: Sri Lanka. Full length: male − 7−9 cm, female − 4−5 cm. Diet: live foods. Monospecies keeping tank. Breeding tank: with capacity of 30−50 litres, sufficient broad-leaved plants *(Cryptocoryne)* and hiding possibilities, low water level (20−30 cm), without bubbled aeration. Sexual dimorphism: the male is larger, his unpaired fins longer. Sex ratio: 1:1. Breeding water: 25−27 °C; pH 6.5−7.0; dCH < 2°. Eggs: incubation period 45 hrs. Feeding of fry: newly-hatched brine shrimp nauplii.

In their native habitats the fish spawn during the dry season. The male builds a small underwater bubble nest usually near the surface on the underside of horizontally spreading leaves. For spawning the fish require an undisturbed environment and diffused light penetrating through floating plants. They are very shy. The male builds the bubble nest several days before spawning. The eggs sink to the bottom and are picked up and taken to the nest by both parents. The number of eggs is approximately 100. Because the fish are so shy the female is not removed after spawning, on condition that there are sufficient hiding places for her to conceal herself from the male, who is aggressive. Six days after spawning the fry switch over to exogenous nutrition; they are fewer in number because the male usually eats part of the spawn. When the fry become free-swimming remove the parent fish, take out the plants, and lower the water level to 3 to 4 cm.

2 Licorice Gourami

Parosphromenus deissneri (BLEEKER, 1859)

Syn. *Osphronemus deissneri*

◁
●
Distribution: Southeast Asia − Sumatra, Malay Peninsula, apparently also Singapore, slowly to swiftly-flowing waters; a rarely encountered species. Full length: 7.5 cm. Diet: small live foods. Monospecies keeping tank. Breeding tank: of 50-litre capacity with floating plants on the surface and cavities on the bottom (drainage pipe, flowerpot with knocked-out bottom). Sexual dimorphism: the male is more brightly coloured, particularly in his spawning dress. Sex ratio: 1:1. Breeding water: 27 °C; pH 5.0−6.0; dCH < 1°; dGH < 10°; filtered through peat. Eggs: large, whitish, incubation period 45 hrs. Feeding of fry: first three days on infusoria *(Paramecium caudatum)* monoculture or rotatoria, later extremely fine, newly-hatched brine shrimp nauplii.

Breeding the fish in the aquarium is difficult. An undisturbed environment and feeding of black mosquito larvae are factors that promote maturation of the eggs and spawning of the fish. The act of spawning is preceded by a striking display on the part of the male and an apparent mating during which the female does not release eggs. The actual spawning lasts about an hour. The female deposits approximately 50 eggs, which are picked up and attached to the roof of a cavity. After spawning is over remove the female. Endogenous nutrition from the large yolk sac lasts a week. Some males eat part of the fry during their development and it is, therefore, recommended to remove the male 90 hours after spawning. At this time pronounced pigmentation appears on the fry. Start feeding the fry at a water level of about 5 cm, gradually adding small amounts of water as they grow and slowly conditioning them to changes in the chemical composition of the water. The growth of the young fish is slow.

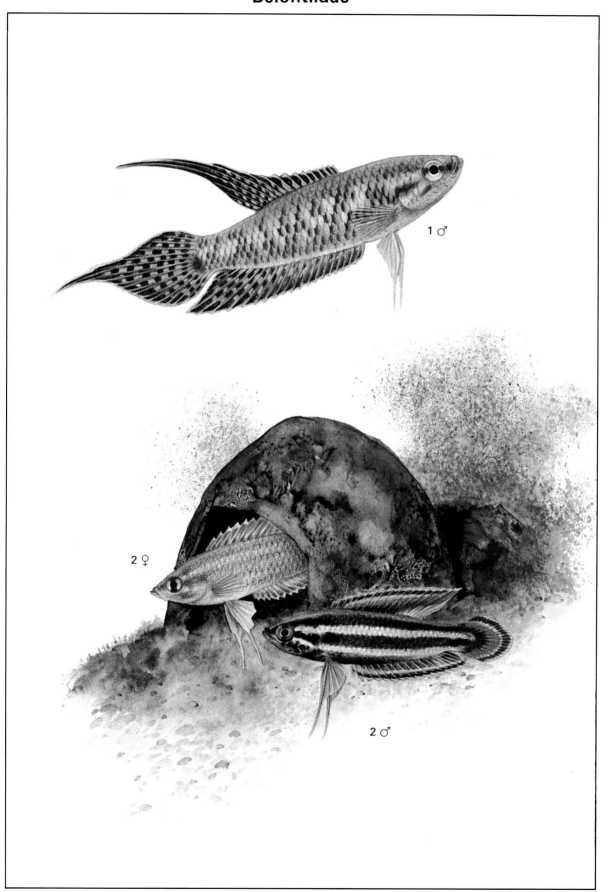

1 ♂

2 ♀

2 ♂

1 Spike-tail Paradise Fish
Pseudosphromenus cupanus cupanus (CUVIER and VALENCIENNES, 1831)
Syn. *Polyacanthus cupanus, Macropodus cupanus*   Belontiidae

◁
●
Distribution: India, Sri Lanka to southeast Asia, standing or slowly-flowing waters, ditches and wet lands. Full length: 8 cm. Diet: live foods. Monospecies keeping tank (only with smaller, peaceful species of fish). Breeding tank: of 20- to 50-litre capacity, light to sun-drenched, without bubbled aeration, surface sparsely covered with floating plants, height of water column *c.* 20 cm. Mineralized wood may be suspended on the wall of the tank with quarter to half of its length submerged; there should be hollowed or flat (not convex) areas on the submerged end. Lay a flowerpot on its side on the bottom. Sexual dimorphism: very slight apart from the spawning period; the male's dorsal fin is usually more pointed, and he is more colourful, with black the predominating colour;

the female is almost entirely black. Sex ratio: 1:1. Breeding water: 26 °C; pH 7.0; dCH max. 2°. Eggs: incubation period 36–42 hrs. Feeding of fry: *Paramecium caudatum, Cyclops* or brine shrimp nauplii.

Fish variable in coloration. The reason for this is the extensive range of this species. Paired fish generally spawn in a cavity. If there is no suitable cavity available in the tank the male builds a bubble nest on the surface beside a large leaf or directly underneath the leaf. The female deposits 20 to 50 eggs. After spawning is over remove the female and when the fry become free-swimming (about three days after hatching) the male also. Lower the water level to 5 cm. The young fish have a typical juvenile spot at the tail end of the body.

2 *Pseudosphromenus cupanus dayi* (KÖHLER, 1909)
Syn. *Polyacanthus dayi, P. cupanus* var. *dayi, Macropodus dayi, M. cupanus dayi*   Belontiidae

◁
●
Distribution: Southeast Asia (Burma to Vietnam), India and Pakistan, ditches and wet lands. Full length: 8 cm. Diet: live foods. Monospecies keeping tank. Breeding tank: of 20- to 50-litre capacity, without bubbled aeration, with diffused light and with floating plants. Place an overturned flowerpot on the bottom. Sexual dimorphism: the dorsal and anal fins of the male have longer rays, the central rays of the caudal fin are likewise drawn-out. Sex ratio: 1:1. Breeding water: 26–30 °C; pH 6.5–7.5; dCH max. 2°. Eggs: incubation period 30 hrs. Feeding of fry:

Paramecium caudatum, Cyclops nauplii, after three to four days brine shrimp nauplii.

Males sometimes build a bubble nest at the surface but prefer to spawn in a cavity. The eggs and newly-hatched fry are generally cared for by the male, occasionally also by the female. When the fry become free-swimming remove the parent fish and lower the water level to 5 to 10 cm. Fresh water promotes the growth of young fish.

1 ♂

2 ♂

2 ♀

1 Blue Gourami or Three-spot Gourami
Trichogaster trichopterus (PALLAS, 1777)
Syn. *Labrus trichopterus, Osphromenus trichopterus* var. *koelreuteri,*
O. saigonensis, O. siamensis, O. trichopterus, Trichopodus trichopterus,
Trichopterus trichopterus, T. sepat, T. cantoris, T. siamensis   Belontiidae

Distribution: Malaysia, Thailand, Burma, Vietnam, the Greater Sunda Islands. Full length: 15 cm. Diet: live as well as artificial foods. Community tank. Breeding tank: with capacity of 50–100 litres per pair, floating plants on the surface, water surface calm, without bubbled aeration. Sexual dimorphism: the male is more robust, his dorsal fin is extended into a point. Sex ratio: 1:1. Breeding water: 24–26 °C; pH 7.0; dCH max. 2°. Eggs: rich in oil, rise to the surface, incubation period 24 hrs. Feeding of fry: newly-hatched brine shrimp nauplii.

In the company of other fish (even members of the same species) the brood fish are generally unwilling to spawn. The male builds a relatively haphazard, spreading nest on the surface. A very prolific fish; the female deposits up to 4,000 eggs during spawning. After spawning is over remove the female and as soon as the fry begin leaving the nest the male also. When feeding the fry lower the water level to about 10 cm. Feed them three to four times a day and during the first week one more time at night under faint illumination. Add water as the fish grow; because of their rapid metabolism do so frequently, replacing 50 to 70 per cent of the water with fresh water. The growth of the young fish is very uneven and they should be separated according to size during this period.

2 *Trichogaster trichopterus sumatranus* LADIGES, 1933
(There is doubt about the use of this name;
it may be regarded as a blue form of *T. trichopterus*).   Belontiidae

Distribution: Sumatra. Full length: 15 cm. Diet: live as well as artificial foods. Community tank. Breeding tank: same as for *T. trichopterus*

Care and breeding the same as for *T. trichopterus*.

3 *Trichogaster trichopterus* 'Cosby'
                                                                            Belontiidae

A cultivated form developed by the American breeder Cosby, apparently before the Second World War. It was derived from *T. trichopterus sumatranus.*

Belontiidae

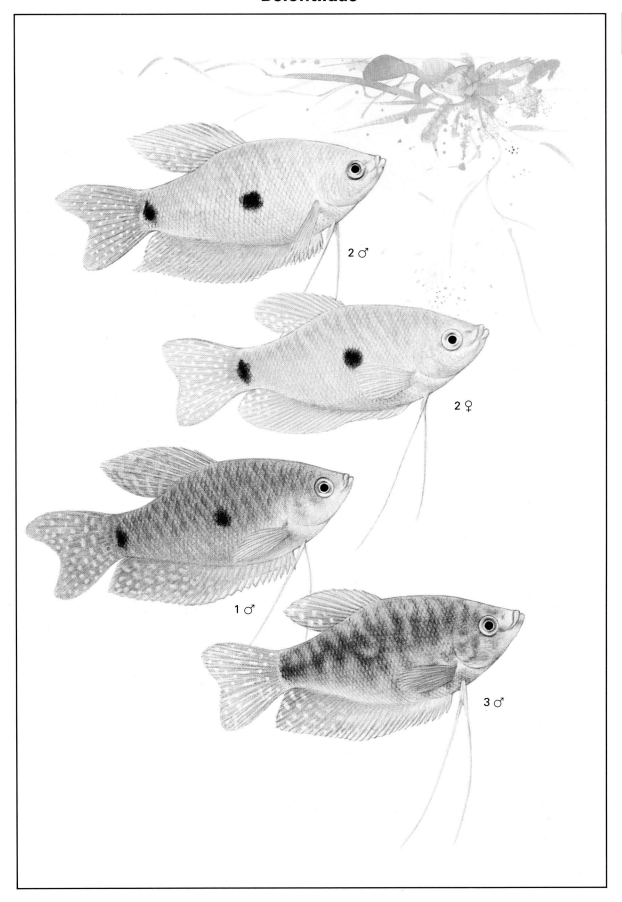

1 *Trichogaster trichopterus* – gold form

Cultivated form. Its total length is slightly less than that of *T. trichopterus* and *T. trichopterus sumatranus.* It is derived from *T. trichopterus* 'Cosby'. The gold, xanthistic form was developed in the GDR in 1971. According to reports it was produced by accident during the spawning of *T. trichopterus* 'Cosby' in a garden pool in summer. That same year (1971) it was exported to the USA. It is genetically fixed. Sexual dimorphism: the male is more robust than the female and his dorsal fin is drawn-out into a point.

2 *Trichogaster trichopterus* – silver form

During the selective breeding of the gold form occasional silver specimens appeared among the gold. The silver form, however, is not firmly genetically fixed so far. Sexual dimorphism: the same as in the wild and 'gold' form.

All forms of *T. trichopterus* are very prolific. Spawning as well as hatching of the fry from the eggs is not difficult. Problems in breeding set in only when the fry become free-swimming – firstly because of their great number and secondly because of their uneven growth. The young fish must be separated according to size as they grow and the population density gradually decrease. If the fish are not separated according to size then cannibalistic tendencies emerge (this is evidenced by the exceedingly rapid growth of individual specimens). The rate of growth is determined not only by the amount of food, but indirectly also by the density of the population. An excessive number of young fish apparently triggers the formation and secretion of substances capable of destroying weaker individuals in the early stages of life and later of retarding growth. The functioning of this mechanism in nature ensures the survival of the population – albeit in limited numbers – until more favourable conditons are restored.

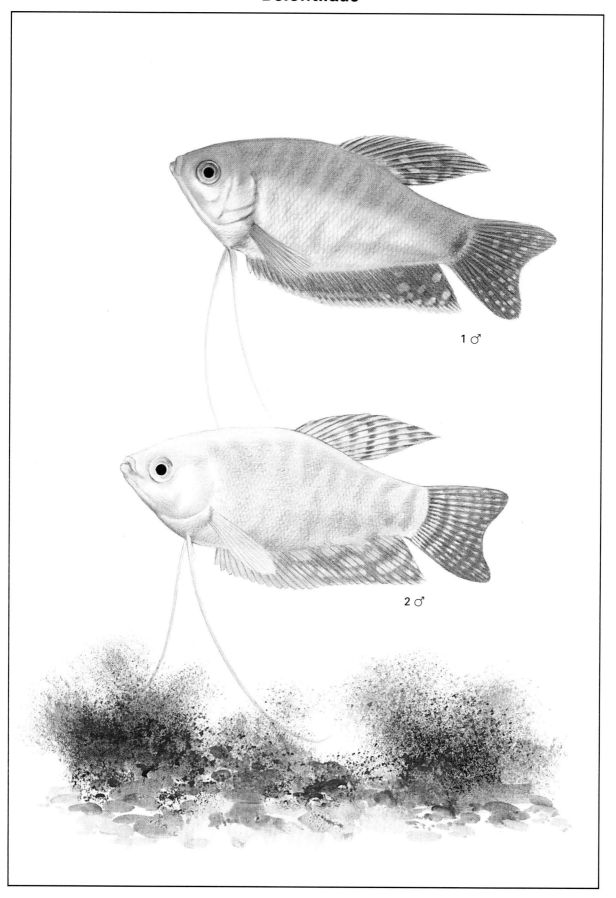

1 ♂

2 ♂

1 Silver Gourami or Moonlight Gourami

Trichogaster microlepis (GÜNTHER, 1861)

Syn. *Osphromenus microlepis, Trichopsis microlepis, Trichopodus microlepis, Trichopus microlepis, T. parvipinnis, Deschauenseeia chryseus*

Distribution: Thailand and Cambodia, in standing and slowly-flowing waters. Full length: 18 cm. Diet: live as well as artificial foods. Community tank. Breeding tank: with capacity of 50–100 litres per pair, thickets of rooting and floating plants, calm water surface without bubbled aeration. Sexual dimorphism: the male has the anal fin edged with orange and orange to red-coloured ventral fin threads; the female's are yellowish. Sex ratio: 1:1. Breeding water: 26–30 °C; pH 6.5–7.0; dCH max. 2°. Eggs: incubation period 24 hrs. Feeding of fry: first 3–5 days on infusoria *(Paramecium caudatum)* monoculture, then *Cyclops* or brine shrimp nauplii.

Peaceful and timid fish. The male builds a bubble nest strengthened by tattered aquatic plants. The female is very prolific, depositing approximately 5,000 eggs during spawning. After spawning is over remove the female and when the fry become free-swimming the male also. The water level should be low when first feeding the fry, and then gradually raised as the young fish grow. The young fish should likewise be separated according to size as they grow (their growth is uneven) and their number thinned, for too dense a population slows their growth.

2 Snake-skinned Gourami

Trichogaster pectoralis (REGAN, 1910)

Syn. *Trichopodus pectoralis, Osphromenus trichopterus* var. *catoris*

Distribution: Kampuchea, Thailand (in the north and south of Thailand it was artificially introduced into the wild), Malay Peninsula, in shallow flowing waters as well as in the wet lands of rice paddies. Full length: 20 cm. Diet: live as well as artificial foods. Community tank. Breeding tank: with capacity of 100 litres per pair, floating plants on the surface, water surface calm, without bubbled aeration. Sexual dimorphism: the male's dorsal fin is drawn out into a point and the edge of his anal fin and the ventral fin threads are coloured orange-red; the female's are coloured yellow. Sex ratio: 1:1. Breeding water: 26–30 °C; pH 6.5–7.0; dCH max. 2°. Eggs: incubation period 24 hrs. Feeding of fry: first three days on infusoria *(Paramecium caudatum)* monoculture, then *Cyclops* or brine shrimp nauplii.

These are peaceful and prolific fish. They feel safer in well-planted tanks. *T. pectoralis* is the largest species of the genus *Trichogaster* (in Thailand it is a popular food fish). It take its specific name from the extraordinarily long pectoral fins, which in adult specimens may be longer than the head. Higher temperatures increase the activity of the fish and 24 °C appears to be the lower limit. The male builds a bubble nest and cares for the eggs and newly-hatched fry; in some males, however, this instinct is absent. After spawning is over remove the female, and after the fry begin to swim freely the male also. Lower the water level to 10 cm. During growth separate the young fish according to size. The density of the young fish population should not be too great.

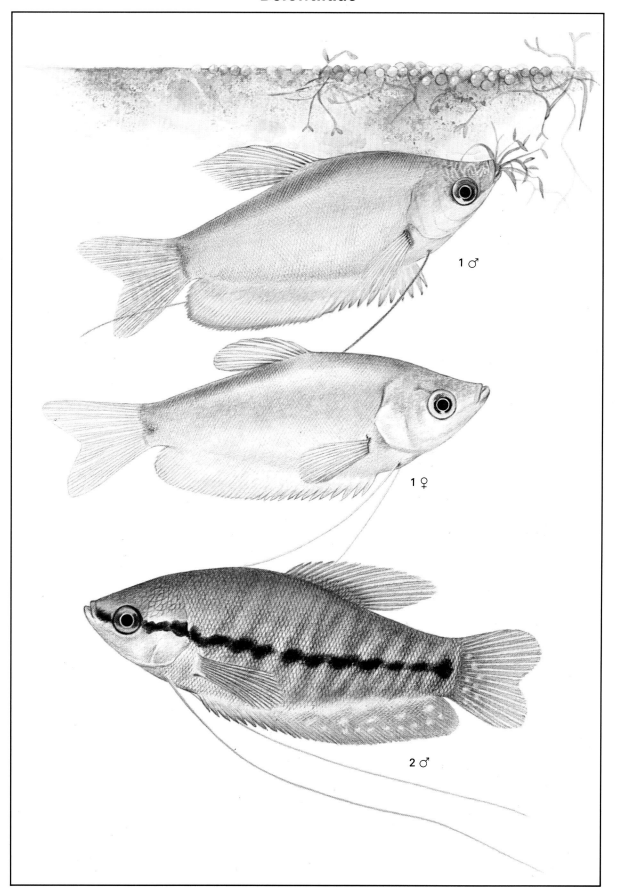

1 ♂

1 ♀

2 ♂

1 Pearl Gourami or Mosaic Gourami
Trichogaster leeri (BLEEKER, 1852)
Syn. *Trichopodus leeri, Osphromenus trichopterus, Trichopus leeri*   Belontiidae

Distribution: Thailand, Malay Peninsula, Sumatra, Borneo. Full length: 11 cm. Diet: live as well as artificial foods. Community tank. Breeding tank: with capacity of 50 litres per pair, floating plants, diffused light, calm water surface without bubbled aeration. Sexual dimorphism: the male has a blood-red belly, long dorsal fin drawn out into a point, and a more strongly developed anal fin with rays extended in the shape of threads that form a fringe. Sex ratio: 1:1. Breeding water: 25–28 °C; pH 7.0; dCH max. 2°. Eggs: rich in oil, rise towards the surface; incubation period 24 hrs. Feeding of fry: first 4–5 days *Paramecium caudatum,* then *Cyclops* or the finest, newly-hatched brine shrimp nauplii.

A readily startled, warmth-loving fish. Before or during spawning the male generally builds a large bubble nest. Sometimes, however, he does not have time to build a nest because the fully-ripe female literally forces him to spawn without delay. In such a case the male builds the nest after the fry hatch or doesn't build one at all and the eggs float freely on the surface. After spawning is over remove the female and when the fry become free-swimming the male also. When feeding the large number of fry lower the water level to 10 cm. Feed them three to four times a day and during the first week once more at night under faint illumination. During growth it is necessary to separate the young fish according to size and decrease their population density. Their growth is slow.

2 Chocolate Gourami
Sphaerichthys osphromenoides CANESTRINI, 1860
Syn. *Osphromenus malayanus, O. nonatus*   Belontiidae

Distribution: Malay Peninsula, Sumatra by the city of Djambi. Full length: 5 cm. Diet: live foods. Monospecies keeping tank. Breeding tank: of 50-litre capacity with thickets of aquatic plants, diffused light, height of water column *c.* 20 cm. Sexual dimorphism: very slight; the male is slimmer, his anal and caudal fins are edged with soft yellow. Sex ratio: 1:1. Breeding water: 28–30 °C; pH 6.0; dCH 1°; dGH 10°; filtered through peat. Eggs: whitish, opaque, Ø *c.* 1.5 mm, incubation period in the mouth of the parent fish 14 days (?) Feeding of fry: brine shrimp nauplii.

Breeding is difficult. There are only isolated reports of successful breeding and these are contradictory. Some state that incubation of the eggs takes place in the throat sac of the female, others that it takes place in the throat sac of the male. The males often build a bubble nest even though it will not be needed (apparently an evolutionary leftover). The eggs number several dozen to as many as 150. The fry leave the mouth of the female (male) after 14 days and are about 7 mm long. This rare species of fish will require numerous further observations with precise conclusions.

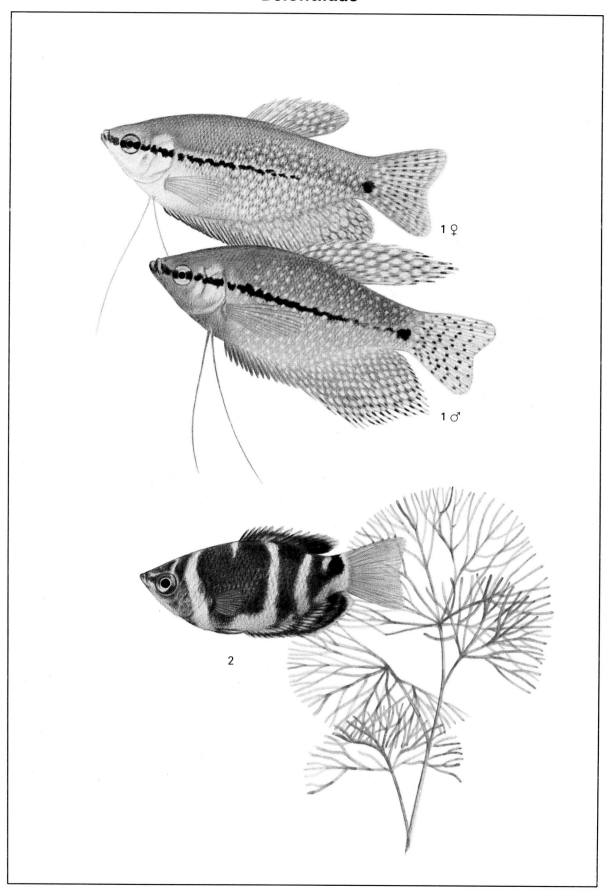

1 ♀

1 ♂

2

1 Croaking Dwarf Gourami

Trichopsis pumilus (ARNOLD, 1936)

Syn. *Ctenops pumilus*

Distribution: Vietnam, Thailand, Sumatra. Full length: 3.5 cm. Diet: live as well as artificial foods. Monospecies keeping tank. Breeding tank: with capacity of 3–6 litres per pair, calm water surface and floating plants. Sexual dimorphism: the male is more colourful and has longer fins. Sex ratio: 1:1. Breeding water: 25–28 °C; pH 7.0; dCH max. 2°. Eggs: incubation period 36 hrs. Feeding of fry: first 10 days on infusoria *(Paramecium caudatum)* monoculture, rotatoria, the finest *Cyclops* nauplii, then brine shrimp nauplii.

The male builds a small bubble nest under the leaf of an aquatic plant in the middle layers of the water. During the courtship display and spawning the males emit a faint droning sound. It is believed that the sounds are produced in the paired labyrinth cavities when air bubbles are released. The bubble nest is watched over by the male. The fry hang by threads from the nest after hatching; these shrink and are absorbed as the fry develop. The number of eggs is between 50 and 100. After spawning is over remove the female, and when the fry become free-swimming the male also. The water level should be lowered to 5 cm when feeding the minute fry.

2 Croaking Gourami

Trichopsis vittatus (CUVIER and VALENCIENNES, 1831)

Syn. *Osphromenus vittatus, O. striatus, Trichopus striatus, Ctenops nobilis* (not McCleland), *C. vittatus, Trichopsis harrisi, T. striata, T. schalleri*

Distribution: Thailand, Kampuchea, South Vietnam, Malay Peninsula and the Greater Sunda Islands. Full length: 7 cm. Diet: live foods. Monospecies keeping tank. Breeding tank: of 50-litre capacity with height of water column *c.* 15 cm, floating plants on the surface and without bubbled aeration. Sexual dimorphism: the male is more vividly coloured and his anal fin is extended into a point. Sex ratio: 1:1. Breeding water: 26–30 °C; pH 6.5–7.0; dCH max. 2°. Eggs: incubation period 48 hrs/27 °C. Feeding of fry: *Paramecium caudatum,* finest *Cyclops* nauplii, rotatoria, after 4–5 days brine shrimp nauplii.

In the separate localities of its widespread range this species occurs in variously coloured populations, often classed as independent species (e.g. *T. schalleri* classified as a separate species until recently). It was successfully bred in captivity for the first time in 1903. The male builds a bubble nest, the female deposits 100 to 200 eggs. Like *T. pumilus* the males emit a droning sound during the courtship display and spawning. As soon as spawning is over remove the female, and two days after the fry hatch the male also. Lower the water level to 5 cm. The young fish grow rapidly if regularly provided with suitable food.

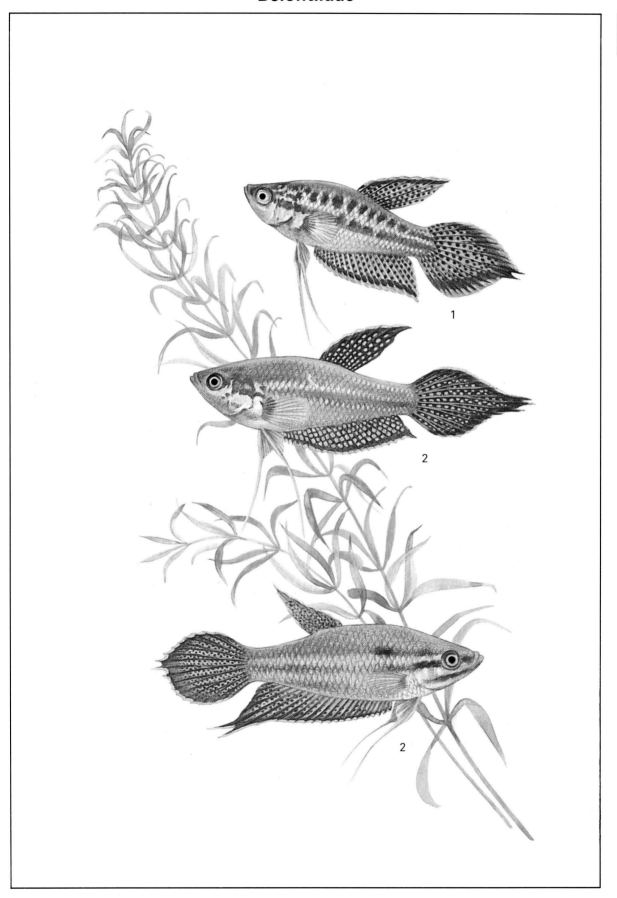

1

2

2

Family Helostomatidae

This family has only one, highly specialized, species which differs from the other labyrinth fish by a number of characteristics described by Liem in 1963. A prominent characteristic is the shape of the ventral fins, which are never modified into threads, and the location of the dorsal fin, which inserts in line with the base of the pectoral fins.

Various authors are of the opinion that in its native waters *Helostoma temmincki* feeds on planktonic organisms which it sifts out directly from the water through the gills.

1 Kissing Gourami
Helostoma temmincki CUVIER and VALENCIENNES, 1831
Syn. *Holostoma oligacanthum, H. servus, H. tambakhan, Helostoma rudolfi*   Helostomatidae

☐ Distribution: Thailand – Lake Bung Borapet – green form (according to Riehl and Baensch), other authors also include the Malay archipelago. Standing water. Full length: 30 cm; according to H. M. Smith's 1945 report a length of 56 cm may be occasionally attained in its native habitat. Diet: live as well as artificial foods, regularly augmented by plant foods, also rolled oats. Community tank. Breeding tank: of at least 200-litre capacity, flat, with plant thickets at the surface. Sexual dimorphism: invisible; the posterior end of the dorsal and anal fins with branching rays is sharp-cornered in the male and rounded in the female. The female is broader in the back. Sex ratio: 1:1. Breeding water: 24–26 °C; pH 7.0; dCH max. 2°; Eggs: very sticky, rise to the surface; incubation period 50 hrs. Feeding of fry: *Paramecium caudatum,* fine artificial fry foods, later brine shrimp nauplii.

The males wage harmless, often lengthy jousts during which they pucker up their thick lips and push against each other with what may be called a kiss. It is from this behaviour that the fish gets its name. *H. temmincki* is a peaceful species that grazes off algal growths. Besides this the fish also feed on nanoplankton (the finest planktonic organisms) by sifting them out of the water with their gills. The male does not build a bubble nest. The female is the more active partner in spawning and may deposit up to 5,000 eggs. Spawning takes place in the bottom layers of water; the eggs rise and adhere to plants or float on the surface. The parent fish do not care for the eggs and fry and should therefore be removed after spawning is over. The fry switch over to exogenous nutrition on the fifth day.

2 *Helostoma temmincki* – pink form   Helostomatidae

☐ Flesh-coloured fish. According to Riehl and Baensch they occur in the wild in Java. According to other authorities this is a cultivated form, but with no statement as to its origin. Breeding is the same as for the previous green form.

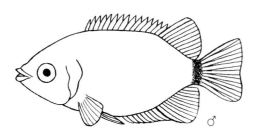
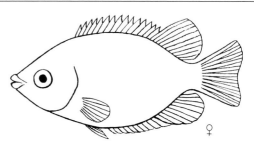

Helostomatidae

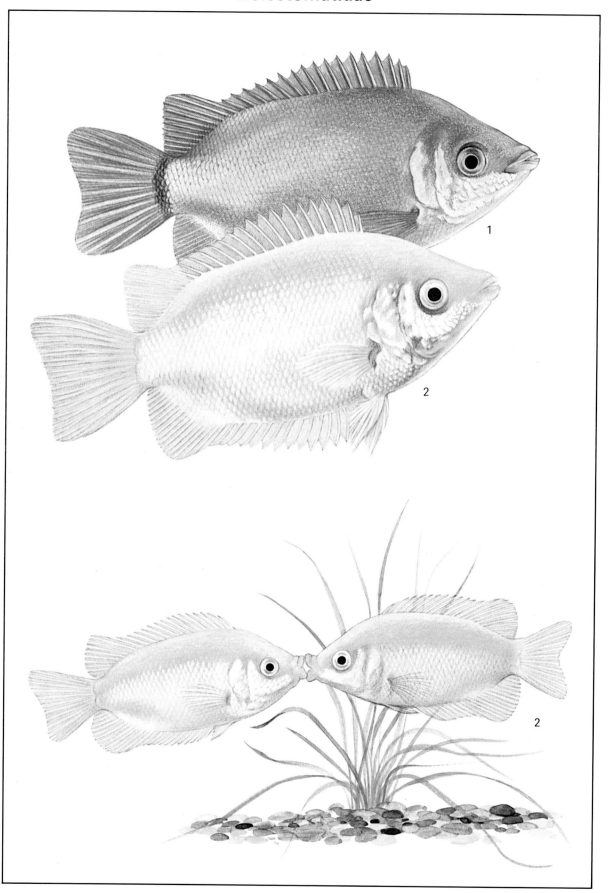

This family is monotypical with only one genus – *Osphronemus* – and a single species – *Osphronemus gorami* Lacépéde, 1802. In 1963 Liem gave reasons in his work for the Osphronemidae being a separate family differing by many characteristics from the Belontiidae.

1 Giant Gourami

Osphronemus gorami LACÉPEDE, **1802**
Syn. *Osphronemus olfax, O. notatus, O. satyrus, O. gourami*

Osphronemidae

☐
●

Distribution: found throughout a large part of southeast Asia, probably spread by man, for it is a highly prized commercial fish (food fish). Full length: 60 cm. Diet: live and plant foods, including rolled oats. Monospecies keeping tank with capacity of more than 1,000 litres (pool), shallow with large water surface and floating plants. Breeding tank: same as keeping tank. Sexual dimorphism: the dorsal and anal fins of the male are more pointed. Sex ratio: 1:1. Breeding water: 24–26 °C; pH 6.5–7.5; dCH max. 2°. Eggs: $\emptyset$ 2.7–2.9 mm, float on the surface, incubation period 24 hrs. Feeding of fry: brine shrimp nauplii, then finely sifted zooplankton, and later chopped tubifex worms.

Young fish are brownish with a few darker cross bands. Older specimens have a bulging forehead with a pad of fat. The fish withstand low temperatures. The male builds a cone-shaped bubble nest on the surface strengthened with bits of plants. The female deposits more than 1,000 eggs in the nest during spawning. The eggs and newly-hatched fry are cared for by the male. The young fish grow quickly and in their second year are up to 30 cm long. Older fish are solitary.

1 juv.

1

Family Gobiidae

Most species dwell in shallow waters in the surf zone of warm seas but some live in brackish waters in river mouths or migrate occasionally to fresh water. The ventral fins are generally grown together, partially or entirely, and form a sucking plate with the aid of which the fish are able to stick onto objects or which, with the pectoral fins, aids the fish in moving on the bottom. There are two dorsal fins: the first has only hard spines, the second soft branching rays. The caudal fin is rounded.

1 Bumblebee Fish
Brachygobius xanthozona (BLEEKER, 1849)
Syn. *Gobius xanthozona, Thaigobiella sua*

Gobiidae

Distribution: Thailand, South Vietnam, Malay Peninsula, and the Greater Sunda Islands – in fresh and brackish water. Full length: 4 cm. Diet: live foods. Monospecies keeping tank. Breeding tank: with capacity of 20 litres, cavities and overhangs on the bottom. Sexual dimorphism: imperceptible. Sex ratio: 1:1. Breeding water: 26–30 °C; pH 7.0–8.5; dCH max. 4°; dGH 20–30 °; add 1 tablespoon NaCl for every 10 litres of water and filter through activated char-coal. Eggs: whitish, tear-drop shaped, $\emptyset$ 1 mm, incubation period 5–6 days. Feeding of fry: difficult; rotatoria, finest *Cyclops* and brine shrimp nauplii.

The female deposits 100 to 150 eggs on the roof of a cavity. The spawning site is cared for by the male. The newly-hatched fry do not have a yolk sac and take food right away.

Family Eleotridae

These are bottom-dwelling fish generally found in the seas, in shallow waters near the coast, as well as in brackish waters; only a very few species inhabit fresh waters. The ventral fins, unlike those of the related Gobiidae family, are always separate. There are two dorsal fins, the first of which has hard spines and the second soft branching rays only. The caudal fin is rounded.

2 Spotted Sleeper
Dormitator maculatus (BLOCH, 1785)
Syn. *Sciaena maculata, Dormitator gundlaichi, D. lineatus, D. microphthalmus, Eleotris latifrons, E. megiloides, E. omocyaneus, E. quadriquama, E. sima*

Eleotridae

Distribution: Atlantic coast – from Carolina (USA) through Mexico to Brazil – found mostly in the sea and in brackish water, may also go for a short while into fresh water. Full length: 30–60 cm. Diet: live foods. Monospecies keeping tank. Breeding tank: with capacity of at least 100 litres, layer of fine sand, sufficient roots and flat stones on the bottom, and good filtration through activated coal. Sexual dimorphism: the male is more darkly coloured, more densely spotted, the ripe female is very full in the body. Sex ratio: 1 male : 3–4 females. Breeding water: 25 °C; brackish or sea water, well aerated. Eggs: minute, incubation period 25–26 hrs. Feeding of fry: brine shrimp nauplii.

The fish are incapable of adapting to fresh water. They are lithophilic – both the male and female first clean a firm object (stone) on which the female then deposits the eggs in rows. The individual batches of eggs may be transferred to separate tanks.

Family Mastacembelidae

The members of this family are bottom-dwelling fish of very elongated build resembling an eel. It is thought that they live in fresh and brackish waters in southeast Asia and Africa. The dorsal and anal fins with branching rays form an edge, which generally connects with the caudal fin at the hind part. On the fore part of the back in front of the dorsal fin it develops into many single erectile spines. The head is pointed, equipped with a projecting beak-like snout that serves as a taste organ. These are twilight fish that are active at night. They inhabit mostly shoreline littoral zones.

1 Spiny Eel
Macrognathus aculeatus (BLOCH, 1788)
Syn. *Macrognathus maculatus*   Mastacembelidae

◁ ● Distribution: Thailand, Sumatra, Java, Borneo, the Molucca Islands, in fresh and brackish waters. Full length: 35 cm. Diet: live foods – worms, larvae, minute fish fry. Monospecies keeping tank. Breeding tank: of 200- to 300-litre capacity, without sand, with streaming water provided by a forced circulation filter and ferns of the genus *Bolbitis* or *Microsorium* placed close to the stream of water. Sexual dimorphism: imperceptible. Sex ratio: 2 males : 1 female. Breeding water: 26–28 °C; pH 7.0–7.5; dCH < 2°; dGH 8°. Eggs: sticky, clear, $\varnothing$ c. 1 mm, incubation period 24 hrs. Feeding of fry: brine shrimp nauplii. First breeding in captivity: 1981, USSR – M. Likhachev and the Kochetov brothers.

The fish attain sexual maturity when they reach a length of 20 cm. Success in spawning has so far been achieved only by hypophysation with carp hypophysis. Before spawning the fish swim together above the bottom, the males at the sides, the females in the centre. The actual act of spawning takes place in shaded parts of the tank close by streaming water. The entire spawning lasts several hours. The female deposits 2,000 to 2,500 eggs. Transfer the aquatic plants with the eggs sticking to them to a separate tank. Six days after hatching the fry switch over to exogenous nutrition.

2 Half-banded Spiny Eel
Mastacembelus circumcinctus HORA, 1924
Mastacembelidae

◁ ● Distribution: southeast Thailand. Full length: 16 cm. Diet: live foods. Monospecies keeping tank. Breeding tank: of 100- to 200-litre capacity with spawning grid. Arrange pieces of a flowerpot on the grid so as to leave a narrow space (form a low cavity) between the piece of crockery and the grid; provide strong aeration or filtration. Dim lighting. Sexual dimorphism: the female is much fuller during the spawning period. Sex ratio: 1:1, or 2 males : 1 female. Breeding water: 26–28 °C; pH 7.0–7.5; dCH max. 2°; dGH 8°. Eggs: incubation period 6 days. Feeding of fry: brine shrimp nauplii. First breeding in captivity: 1981, USSR – M. Likhachev and the Kochetov brothers.

In this case, too, spawning in captivity took place only after hypophysation of ripe brood fish. The fish spawned in a cavity. Because the fry are eagerly devoured by the parent fish they should be protected by a spawning grid. The female deposits approximately 400 eggs. The fry become free-swimming and hunt food a few hours after hatching. Their growth is slow.

1 Spotted Fire Eel
Mastacembelus erythrotaenia BLEEKER, 1850
Syn. *Macrognathus erythrotaenia*

◁
●
Distribution: Thailand, Burma, Sumatra, Borneo. Full length: 100 cm. Diet: live foods, mainly earthworms, larvae of aquatic insects and small fish; if none of these is available then strips of beef heart. Monospecies keeping tank with layer of sand on the bottom (the sand must not be sharp), sufficient hiding places − drainage pipes, notched flowerpots, etc., diffused lighting (floating plants), and efficient filter. The aquarium should be spacious and covered with glass. Sexual dimorphism: apparent only in mature specimens; the female is fuller in the body. Water: 24−28 °C; dCH 2−3°; dGH as much as 15°; add 1−2 teaspoons sea salt or sodium chloride for every 10 litres of water. The species has not yet been bred in captivity.

The fish are very aggressive towards members of their own species. They should therefore be kept only in a small group and in the largest of tanks or a pool. Because they burrow in the bottom substrate the sand must not be sharp. *M. erythrotaenia* is a delicate species sensitive particularly to wounds and to invasional attack by ectoparasites.

2 White-spotted Spiny Eel
Mastacembelus armatus GÜNTHER, 1861
Syn. *Macrognathus armatus*

◁
●
Distribution: India, Sri Lanka, southern China, Sumatra. Full length: 75 cm. Diet: live foods − worms, larvae of aquatic insects, chiefly midge larvae, and small fish. Monospecies keeping tank with capacity of 1,000 litres or more, not too high, and well covered − otherwise the fish jump out. On the bottom a 10 cm layer of fine gravel, hiding places and caves, or notched flowerpots or drainage pipes. Diffused lighting. Sexual dimorphism: imperceptible; only during the spawning period is the female markedly fuller. Sex ratio: 1:1. Water: 22−28°; pH 7.0; dCH 2°; dGH 10°; add 1−2 teaspoons sodium chloride or sea salt for every 10 litres of water. It seems that the species has not yet been bred in captivity.

Keep only a small number of fish in the tank for they are aggressive towards others of their own kind. In the daytime they burrow in the bottom or conceal themselves in other hiding places.

The genus *Mastacembelus* numbers more than 30 species that live in fresh and perhaps brackish waters in Asia and Africa. Asian species include *M. argus* Günther, 1961 (25 cm), *M. circumcinctus* Hora, 1924 (16 cm), and *M. taeniagaster* Fowler, 1934 (?). In 1923 Hora divided the species *M. armatus* into two subspecies: *M. armatus armatus* and *M. armatus favus* Hora, 1923.

Mastacembelidae

Family Tetraodontidae

The members of this family are mostly species that live in tropical and subtropical seas; only a very few dwell in fresh water, e.g. in African and Asian rivers. The body does not have an outer protective coat of scales but is covered only with a smooth skin. The intestines are equipped with sacs which may be filled with water or air until the fish are puffed up to a globular form. Some species when distended like this are also able to erect spines on the skin that serve as an effective weapon of defence. The water or air they have drawn up may be released again all at once.

The fish are aided in feeding on the live foods that are the mainstay of their diet, e.g. molluscs, crustaceans, by the strong jaw muscles and specially adapted teeth which are used to crush the shells of these animals.

1 Somphong's Puffer
Carinotetraodon somphongsi (KLAUZEWITZ, 1957)
Syn. *Tetraodon somphongsi, Carinotetraodon chlupatyi*   Tetraodontidae

Distribution: Thailand (only in fresh water). Full length: 6.5 cm. Diet: live foods (gastropods, earthworms, tubifex worms). Monospecies keeping tank. Breeding tank: with capacity of 50–100 litres, sufficient hiding possibilities and plant thickets. Sexual dimorphism: the dorsal fin rays of the male are rust-red, the caudal fin is white edged with a darker colour, and the body colouring is greyish. The female is a paler hue, with more distinct markings on the upper half of the body. Sex ratio: 1:1. Breeding water: 26–28 °C; pH 6.5–7.0; dCH max. 2°. Eggs: $\emptyset$ c. 0.5 mm, whitish transparent, very sticky; incubation period 60–72 hours. Feeding of fry: *Cyclops* nauplii.

2 Figure-8 Puffer
Tetraodon palembangensis BLEEKER, 1852
Syn. *Crayracion palembangensis, Tetrodon palenbangensis*   Tetraodontidae

Distribution: southeast Asia – fresh and brackish waters. Full length: 20 cm. Diet: robust live foods – larvae of aquatic insects, earthworms, gastropods, muscle tissue of bivalves, beef and liver, artificial foods in granules. Monospecies keeping tank with capacity of *c.* 500 litres, stony-sandy bottom, and sufficient hiding places. Breeding tank: same as keeping tank. Sexual dimorphism: monomorphic fish. Sex ratio: 1:1. Water: 24–28 °C; pH 7.0–8.0; add 1 tablespoon NaCl for every 10 litres of water. So far it is not known if this species has been bred in captivity.

Green Puffer
3 *Tetraodon fluviatilis* (HAMILTON-BUCHANAN, 1822)
Syn. *Arothron dorsovittatus, A. simulans, Crayracion fluviatilis, Dichotomycter fluviatilis, Tetraodon potamophilus, Tetrodon fluviatilis, T. nigroviridis, T. simulans*   Tetraodontidae

Distribution: southeast Asia from India to the Philippines – fresh and brackish waters. Full length: 17 cm. Diet: same as for *T. palembangensis.* Monospecies keeping tank. Breeding tank: with capacity of 200 litres per pair, stony bottom, sufficient hiding possibilities. Sexual dimorphism: not known. Sex ratio: 1:1. Breeding water: brackish, 26–28 °C; pH 7.0–8.0; Eggs: incubation period 4–5 days? Feeding of fry: brine shrimp nauplii.

Tetraodontidae

A guide to some standards (norms) for some of the cultivated forms shown at international exhibitions

The endeavour of breeders is to obtain by selective breeding genetically fixed strains of fish with special pronounced characteristics such as coloration, finnage shape, body profile and body size. It is a lengthy and time-consuming process based on the rules of genetics, i.e. the theory of heredity. Years of such efforts on the part of breeders throughout the world have produced a great many cultivated strains. Because it has long since become a tradition in the world of aquaristics to hold international exhibitions of cultivated forms, it was necessary to establish a set of standards for judging exhibition entries and serving as a basis for making awards.

Fish of the Poeciliidae family are very popular, above all the Guppy – *Poecilia reticulata.* Body measurements are the same for all male standards of this species, namely: basic body length (without tail fin) – 28 mm, body height – a quarter of the body length.

Standards (norms) for finnage of guppies – *Poecilia reticulata*

Common Roundtail – male: The caudal fin circular, equal in diameter to half the length of the body and to at least the maximum height of the body. The dorsal fin may be rounded or pointed, the point must extend to a third the length of the caudal fin.

Spadetail – male: The caudal fin shaped like a tear drop, the profile becoming circular at a third of its length. In breadth it should be equal to half the length of the body. It narrows into a point at the end. The caudal fin comprises four-fifths of the body length. The dorsal fin is drawn-out into a point and turns up in an arc at the end. The point extends to a third the length of the caudal fin. Other dorsal fin shapes are also permitted in competitions but with a loss of points.

Bannertail – male: The caudal fin angular and terminated by a point; it resembles a hexagon. The ratio of length to breadth is 5 : 4; its minimum breadth is generally equal to the height of the body. The dorsal fin is pointed and extends to the base of the caudal fin. Other shapes are also permitted in competitions but with a loss of points.

Lyretail – male: The caudal fin oval with a top spike and a bottom spike (extended tail rays). It comprises four-fifths of the body length; in breadth it should be equal to half the length of the body. The dorsal fin is drawn-out into a point and turns up in an arc at the end; it extends to a third the length of the caudal fin. Other shapes are also permitted in competitions but with a loss of points.

Upper Swordtail – male: The caudal fin oval with a single spike (extended tail ray) growing out of the top rays, its top edge parallel to the body axis. The length of the caudal fin with spike is equal to one and a fifth, but at the least four-fifths the length of the body. The dorsal fin is parallel to the body axis and pointed at the end, with the point extending to a third the length of the

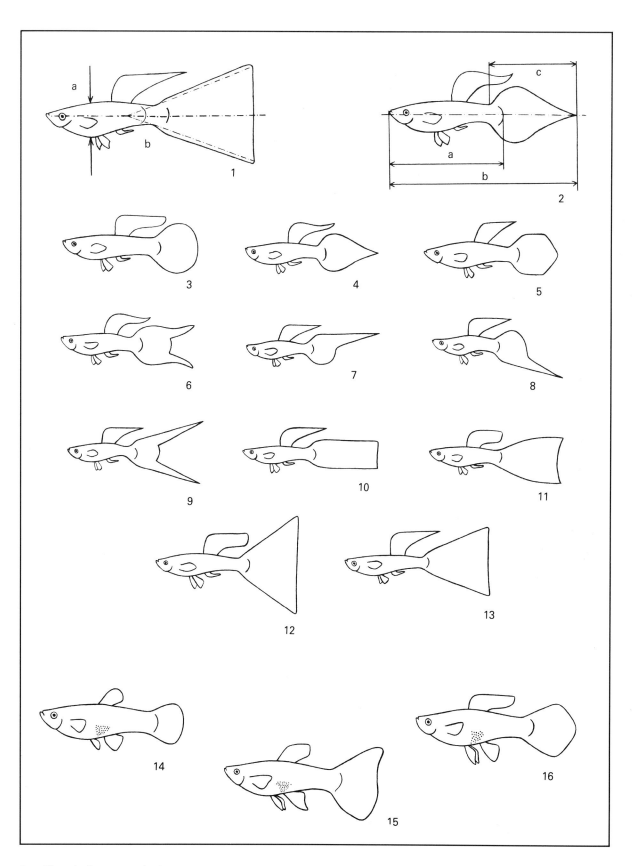

Poecilia reticulata – standards

1 – exterior a – body height, b – angle of caudal fin sides to body axis, 2 – evaluation of exterior a – body length, b – full length, c – length of caudal fin 3 – Common Roundtail, 4 – Spadetail, 5 – Bannertail, 6 – Lyretail, 7 – Upper Swordtail, 8 – Lower Swordtail, 9 – Double Swordtail, 10 – Square Flagtail, 11 – Sash Flagtail, 12 – Fantail, 13 – Delta Flagtail, 14 – short-finned female, 15 – sword-finned female, 16 – big-finned female

caudal fin. Other shapes are also permitted in competitions but with a loss of points.

Lower Swordtail — male: The caudal fin oval with a single spike (extended tail ray) growing out of the bottom rays. It includes an angle of 15°, but at the least an angle of 10° with the body axis. The length of the caudal fin with spike is equal to one and a fifth, but at least four-fifths the length of the body. The dorsal fin is parallel to the body axis, pointed at the end, and extends to a third the length of the caudal fin. Other shapes are permitted but with a loss of points.

Double Swordtail — male: The caudal fin oval with a top spike and a bottom spike (extended tail rays); the two spikes include an angle of 60°, but at the least an angle of 20°. The length of the caudal fin with spikes is equal to one and a fifth, but at the least four-fifths the length of the body. The dorsal fin is parallel to the body axis, pointed at the end, and extends to a third the length of the caudal fin. Other shapes are permitted in competitions but with a loss of points.

Square Flagtail — male: The caudal fin shaped like a parallelogram with two opposite sides parallel to the body axis. It curves in an arc where it joins the base of the tail. The top edge, bottom edge, and hind edge are straight. The length of the caudal fin is equal to one and a fifth the body length, but at the least four-fifths the length of the body. In breadth it is equal to two-fifths the height of the body, at the most the full height of the body. The dorsal fin is parallel to the caudal fin and pointed at the posterior end. The point extends to at least a third the length of the caudal fin. Other shapes are also permitted in competitions but with a loss of points.

Sash Flagtail — male: The caudal fin curved outward (convex). It is broadest at three quarters of its length; at this point its breadth is equal to three-fifths, but at least two-fifths the length of the body. The length of the caudal fin is equal to four-fifths, but at least half the length of the body. The end of the caudal fin is concave. The dorsal fin is rounded, drawn-out, and extends to the base of the caudal fin. Other shapes are also permitted in competitions but with a loss of points.

Delta Flagtail — male: The caudal fin has the shape of an equilateral triangle, with sides forming an angle of 70°, but at the least an angle of 55°, with the body axis. The length of the caudal fin is equal to four-fifths, but at the least three-fifths the length of the body. Its edges are straight. The dorsal fin is prolonged into a point that extends to a third the length of the caudal fin. Other shapes are also permitted in competitions but with a loss of points.

Fantail — male: The caudal fin has the shape of an equilateral triangle with sides forming an angle of 35°, but at the least an angle of 20°, with the body axis. The length of the caudal fin is equal to three-fifths, but at least half the length of the body. Its edges are straight. The dorsal fin is broad, rounded, and extends to the base of the caudal fin. Other shapes are also permitted in competitions but with a loss of points.

For the finnage of female guppies there are three standards: short-finned, sword-finned, and big-finned.

Standards for finnage of swordtails – *Xiphophorus helleri*

Body measurements are the same for all standards. Total length of males – 60–80 mm, total length of females – 80–100 mm. The sword tilted 15° to 20° from the body axis. Ideal ratio of sword length to body length – 1:1.

Common Swordtail – male, female: The fins are the same as those of the original wild type. The fin rays are fully developed. The stripe edging the dorsal fin is entire, continuous. The forward part of the dorsal fin must be at least 1 cm high; in males it is pointed at the posterior end, in females the end is rounded. There is a stripe on both the lower and upper edge of the sword or the sword is without stripes.

Simpson Swordtail – male, female: The dorsal fin is narrow at the base (8–12 mm) and drawn-out upwards. The upper edge is the same width as the base. The dorsal fin must be straight and well carried. Its height must be equal to at least half the length of the body. The gonopodium is short. There is a stripe on both the lower and upper edge of the sword or the sword is without stripes.

Veiltail Swordtail – male, female: The dorsal fin is approximately triangular. The longest side is at least twice as long as the base. The upper edge of the fin is straight, entire, or conversely finely wavy. The hind edge reaches to midway the length of the caudal fin. The gonopodium is short. There is a stripe on both the lower and upper edge of the sword or the sword is without stripes.

Lyretail Swordtail – male, female: The dorsal fin is pointed. The first two to three rays extend far above the others, which continue in a slanting line towards the rear, each slightly lower than the one preceding. The hind end is straight, somewhat higher than that of the Common Swordtail, and terminates in a point. When pressed to the body the hind edge (point) of the dorsal fin must not extend beyond the base of the caudal fin. The caudal fin of both the male and female has the top and bottom rays extended. Males are divided according to the shape of the lyre into two equivalent subtypes: a) lyre with a sword, and b) lyre without a sword. The sword must be tilted from the body axis by an angle of at least 15°. The gonopodium should be as short as possible, straight, and with an undeformed end.

Delta Lyretail Swordtail – male, female: This is a combination of the veiltail and lyretail types. The dorsal fin is approximately triangular. The front side must be at least twice as long as the base. The upper edge is straight, entire. The hind edge must not extend beyond the end of the caudal fin. The caudal fin of both the male and female is lyre-shaped; the sword must be tilted from the body axis by an angle of at least 15°. The gonopodium should be as short as possible, straight, and with an undeformed end.

Other types are considered to be nonstandard.

Xiphophorus helleri – standard

17 – exterior a – full length, b – body length, c – sword, d – length of sword, 18 – Common Swordtail, 19 – Simpson Swordtail, 20 – Veiltail Swordtail, 21 – Lyretail Swordtail, 22 – Delta Lyretail Swordtail

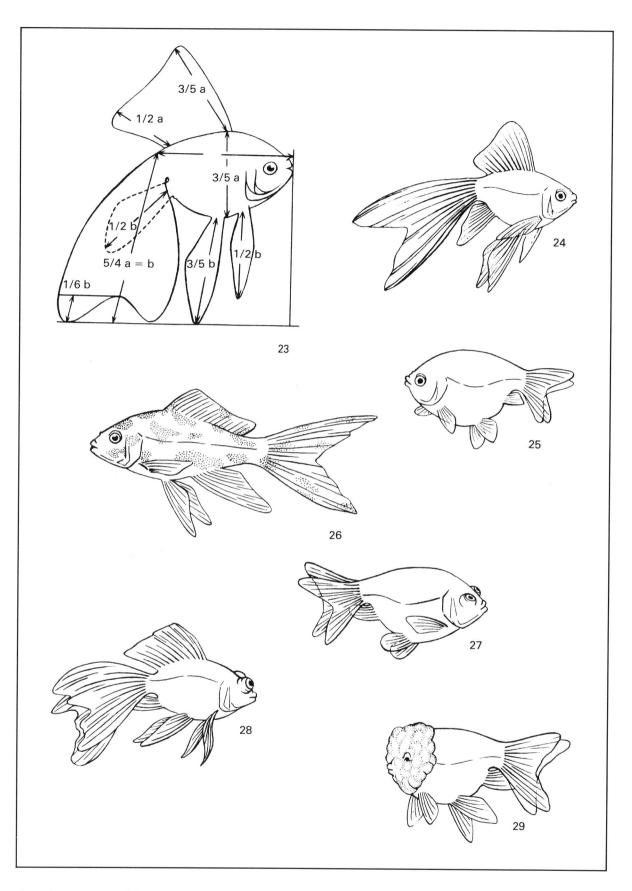

23 — exterior of classic veiltail

3/5 a
1/2 a
3/5 a
1/2 b
5/4 a = b
3/5 b
1/2 b
1/6 b

23

24

25

26

27

28

29

Carassius auratus var. *bicaudatus* — standards
23 — exterior of classic veiltail a — body length, b — length of   Shubunkin, 27 — Skygazer, 28 — Telescope Veiltail, 29
caudal fin 24 — Comet, 25 — Eggfish, 26 — Calico or   — Lionhead

Standards for Veiltails — *Carassius auratus* var. *bicaudatus*

The norms for the body structure and fins of the classic veiltails were established in 1908 in Berlin. Norms for other strains have not been established as yet.

Body compact and rounded, its height equal to three-fifths of its length. Head short and broad, the dorsal contour curved in line with the contour of the caudal fin. Pads of fat on the head or a compressed or pointed head decrease the value of the fish. Caudal fin divided to the base into two equal sections. Ends of the fins faintly rounded. The divided anal fin must be completely covered by the caudal fin. The base of the tail where it joins the fin should be covered with scales. The dorsal fin is carried held high and is superbly shaped (see illustration). The pectoral fins extend sidewards. For other dimensions see the illustration.

Examples of some strains of *Carassius auratus* var. *bicaudatus*

Comet: Body egg-shaped, scaly, variable in coloration. Dorsal fin markedly extended. Anal fin simple or double. Caudal fin simple, long, with sickle-shaped ends. Length of body — 50—60 mm, length of caudal fin — 60—70 mm or more.

Eggfish: Body extremely short with forked, short, quadripartite caudal fin. Dorsal fin absent. Head without any protuberances. Most highly valued colour forms are white fish spotted with red on the head and fins. Length of body — 180 to 200 mm.

Shubunkin: Body elongate, scaleless. Caudal fin forked or simple, veil-like. The fish are irregularly spotted in a combination of colours: red, yellow, black, most highly prized being grey and blue. Shubunkins may be a single colour, or a combination of two to three colours. Length of body is not given.

Skygazer: Body egg-shaped, scaly. Dorsal fin absent. Caudal fin forked, quadripartite, short. Other fins normal. Eyes greatly protruding and pointing symmetrically upward, their axis forming a right angle with the axis of the body. Eyes that are at a slant or irregularly positioned are considered a grave fault. Body colour gold or bright red, may be combined with white. Length of body — 100—120 mm, length of caudal fin — 50—60 mm.

Telescope: Body egg-shaped, scaleless. All fins well developed, the caudal and anal fins double. Diameter of eyes 12—15 mm. The eyes must point symmetrically forward and terminate in line with the tip of the mouth. In some forms the eyes are a vivid red. Colouring: from pale creamy hues to pure black. Length of body — 100 mm, length of caudal fin — 120 mm.

Lionhead: Body egg-shaped, scaly. Dorsal fin absent. Caudal fin forked, quadripartite, short. Other fins normal. Head broad, an intense red, covered with semi-transparent, sponge-like skin excrescences on top and on the sides. Eyes of normal size. Body colour gold or bright red. Length of body — 60—70 mm, length of caudal fin 50—60 mm.
Oranda, or so-called Dutch Lionhead, is another strain that has a well developed dorsal fin.

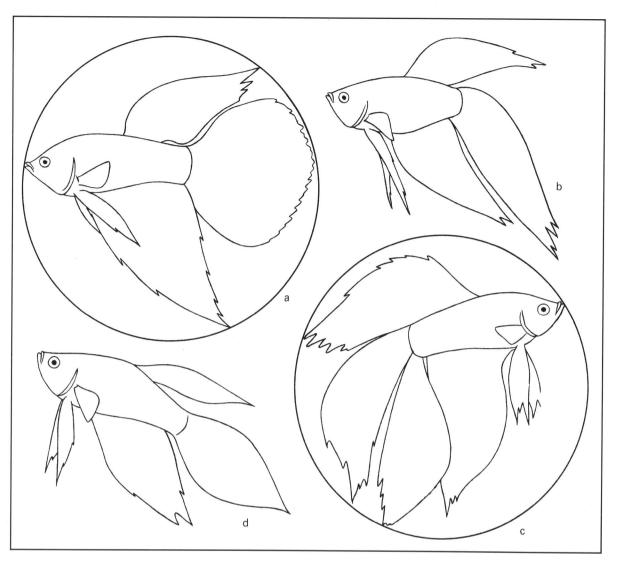

Betta splendens: a — classic exterior, b — old form, c — Libby Betta, d — pointed caudal fin

Classic dimensions and shapes
of the Siamese Fighting Fish — *Betta splendens*

Though there are no internationally established standards there exists among breeders an established concept of what the classic male *Betta splendens* should be like — the line connecting the tip of the snout, tip of the dorsal fin, periphery of the caudal fin, and tip of the anal fin should describe a circle. A similar type is the so-called 'Libby Betta', a large fish with divided caudal fin bred in the USA but not in Europe. Despite all efforts on the part of breeders, however, the prevailing type is the old form with drooping caudal fin, which detracts from the general appearance of the fish. Some populations include males with a tear-shaped or pointed caudal fin which must be considered undesirable for further breeding. Besides finnage, it is also necessary to evaluate the purity and intensity of the colours, or their combination, as well as the size of the fish, and whether these characteristics are genetically fixed. The length of the body should be no less than 5 cm. Females should be well developed and with the same colouring as the males.

Index of Common Names

Index of Families, Genera
and Species